LOOKING FOR
ANNE

Looking *for*
ANNE

How Lucy Maud Montgomery
Dreamed Up A Literary Classic

IRENE GAMMEL

KEY PORTER BOOKS

Library and Archives Canada Cataloguing in Publication

Gammel, Irene,
     Looking for Anne : how Lucy Maud Montgomery dreamed up a literary classic / Irene Gammel.

ISBN 978-1-55263-985-6

1. Montgomery, L. M. (Lucy Maud), 1874–1942. 2. Canada—Civilization—20th century. 3. United States—Civilization—20th century. 4. Montgomery, L. M. (Lucy Maud), 1874–1942. Anne of Green Gables. 5. Novelists, Canadian (English)—20th century—Biography. I. Title.

PS8526.O55Z687 2008   C813'.52   C2007-905453-6

The publisher gratefully acknowledges the support of the Canada Council for the Arts and the Ontario Arts Council for its publishing program. We acknowledge the support of the Government of Ontario through the Ontario Media Development Corporation's Ontario Book Initiative.

We acknowledge the financial support of the Government of Canada through the Book Publishing Industry Development Program (BPIDP) for our publishing activities.

Material written by L. M. Montgomery is excerpted with the permission of Ruth Macdonald and David Macdonald, trustee, who are the heirs of L. M. Montgomery.

Quotations from the unpublished journals of L.M. Montgomery © 2008 University of Guelph, are reproduced courtesy of the L. M. Montgomery Collection, Archival and Special Collections, University of Guelph Library.

Quotations from The Selected Journals of L.M. Montgomery, Volumes 1–5, edited by Mary Rubio and Elizabeth Waterston and published by Oxford University Press, © 1985–2004 University of Guelph, are reproduced with the permission of Mary Rubio, Elizabeth Waterston and the University of Guelph, courtesy of the L. M. Montgomery Collection Archival and Special Collections, University of Guelph Library.

L. M. Montgomery is a trademark of Heirs of L. M. Montgomery Inc.

Anne of Green Gables and other indicia of "Anne" are trademarks and Canadian official marks of the Anne of Green Gables Licensing Authority Inc.

Key Porter Books Limited
Six Adelaide Street East, Tenth Floor
Toronto, Ontario
Canada M5C 1H6

www.keyporter.com

Text design: Marijke Friesen
Electronic formatting: Jean Lightfoot Peters

Printed and bound in Canada

08 09 10 11 12 5 4 3 2 1

*To all those who have
been taken to new
heights by fiery Anne*

CONTENTS

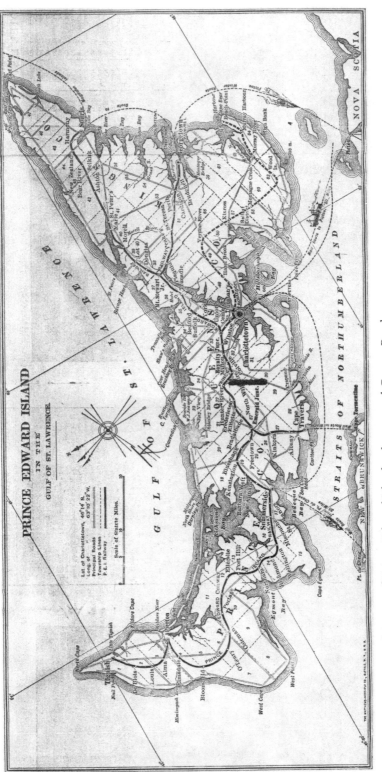

L. M. Montgomery sent this map of Prince Edward Island to her pen pal George Boyd Macmillan in Scotland on June 5, 1905, just around the time she began to write *Anne*.

Peace! ... You never know what peace is until you walk on the shores or in the fields or along the winding red roads of Prince Edward Island in a summer twilight when the dew is falling and the old old stars are peeping out and the sea keeps its mighty tryst with the little land it loves. You find your soul then. You realize that youth is not a vanished thing but something that dwells forever in the heart.
—L. M. Montgomery

Looking *for*
ANNE

The Mystery of
Anne of Green Gables

"Avonlea is a lovely name. It just sounds like music. How far is it to White Sands?"

"It's five miles; and as you're evidently bent on talking you might as well talk to some purpose by telling me what you know about yourself."

"Oh, what I know about myself isn't really worth telling," said Anne eagerly. "If you'll only let me tell you what I imagine about myself you'll think it ever so much more interesting."

"No, I don't want any of your imaginings. Just you stick to bald facts. Begin at the beginning. Where were you born and how old are you?"

—Anne and Marilla, from an early chapter entitled
"Anne's History" of Anne of Green Gables[1]

*L*ooking for Anne: How Lucy Maud Montgomery Dreamed Up A Literary Classic was sparked by a paradox and a mystery. With over fifty million copies of the novel sold, a multi-million-dollar tourist industry, and countless adaptations of the novel and its sequels in musicals, movies, cartoons, dolls, and figurines, millions of fans know Anne Shirley intimately, but they know surprisingly little about how she came about. How can a work be so famous and yet its history so little known? We know more about other literary texts whose creation is shrouded in mystery, such as Cervantes' *Don Quixote*, Mary Shelley's *Frankenstein*, or Charlotte Brontë's *Jane Eyre*, than we know about *Anne of Green Gables*. In her journal, Maud's quick pen would froth up the tiniest details of her life into dramatic events, but that same nimble pen never revealed a single word about *Anne* while Maud was writing the novel. As a result, the mystery of Anne has remained unsolved for over a century. Maud did leave her readers with a few sparse clues in her private writing, some planted years and decades after *Anne* was published. Why was Maud so secretive, never mentioning the novel while she was writing it, later forgetting and confusing crucial details including the year and month in which she began writing the novel? How do truth and fiction blend together in the legend she told about how Anne came about? And what does the story of *Anne's* creation tell us about *Anne of Green Gables* as a piece of literature with an enduring power to move readers?

Maud was thirty years old when she wrote *Anne of Green Gables* in 1905, and thirty-three when it was published. Already there was some gray in her hair, and the conflict between youth and age was raging inside. She had been working like a Trojan to combat her feeling that she had failed in life. We know that Maud was an addictive diarist who nostalgically dwelled on the past, letting it shape the present. But she was also ruthless in burning and discarding old letters, documents, diaries, and notebooks. The documents we have available today—journals, scrapbooks, photographs, and letters—do not contain the original notebooks that Maud used for her fiction writing. Only the distilled version that she wanted us to see was allowed to survive.[2] And yet she also left a few clues behind, as if she wanted to be found out, teasing us with little snippets of revelations.

Her journal was the stage on which Maud performed her artful version of the truth. She had a life-long habit of keeping secrets and masking her feelings and, moreover, after the publication of *Anne of Green Gables*, Maud, now a celebrity author, was preoccupied with her reputation and legacy. We know that she carefully edited, illustrated, and recopied her journals with the intention of having them published, and so these are calculated literary journals rather than spontaneous impressions of day-to-day events. Isabel Anderson, an Ontario schoolteacher who had a crush on Maud when Maud was in her fifties, wrote the author a romantic, yet illuminating letter: "You are a will-o'-the-wisp, elusive, exclusive, impulsively flitting here and there, leaving a trail of exotic sweetness that haunts one with a mad desire." Isabel pointed out that Maud had a way of creating intimacy in her writing, of seducing her reader, and of giving each fan the feeling that answers awaited those who had been disappointed in life. "It is because of something for which you stand, which they long for and have not," Isabel wrote of Maud's powerful hold over her fans.[3] Isabel was a passionate fan, and for all her frustrated and frustrating love for Maud, she was on to something. Isabel recognized that the strong emotional pull of Maud's fiction was not unlike the pull of Maud's personality.

One of the reasons Maud was so persuasive in convincing us of her version of events was that she was, indeed, *self*-deceived. An emotional and forceful advocate of her own legend, she rarely stopped to question her motives. Like the unreliable narrator in a modernist novel, Maud was able to draw readers into the maze of her splendid isolation, taking us into 'the palace of art,' to cite the title of one of her favorite poems by Alfred Lord Tennyson. To unravel the original pictures and sources behind *Anne of Green Gables* we will travel through the maze of her palace and unlock the rooms she kept closed. For the first time, readers will be able to see into the secretive world she constructed. Maud had an ingenious way of making her readers loyal kindred spirits and of creating a fiercely protective bond. But her fans will be intrigued and surprised by some of the things Maud did not tell them about the making of *Anne*.

Looking for Anne is the story of a literary mystery about the life of a beloved fictional character who mirrored, according to L. M. Montgomery's account, her own dreams and fantasies, her memories and emotions. Thus the book is also a biography of the enigmatic Maud at the time of writing and publishing *Anne*. We shall investigate the years in which Anne was taking shape, focusing on the crucial period from 1903 to 1908.

Telling the life of Anne is like peeling an onion. This book takes readers inside Maud's guarded life not only by reading between the lines of her unpublished journal entries for the period, but also by looking beyond the conventional sources that Maud wanted us to see. *Looking for Anne* highlights the sources that are not found among L. M. Montgomery's papers but that were crucially relevant to the creation of her story: the sources and pieces of writing she discarded or simply forgot. This investigation uncovers the surprising inspiration related to the creation of Anne; material that Maud carefully omitted, which forms a remarkable story, ripe for the telling. This book takes readers inside Maud's intensely private life to reveal Maud's sideways manner of telling the truth and the depth of her evasions. For the first time, we will be able to appreciate the stunning complexity of *Anne of Green Gables*.

What does the journal refuse to tell? What did Maud not want to say? How can we determine how Anne was "brung up"? These were some of the questions that guided my search. By delving into the story of Anne, we are uncovering the story of Maud. By digging behind the silences, the gaps, and the personae of the journals, photographs, scrapbooks, and letters, my goal was to recapture the original pictures and texts—including the ones that Maud had discarded or otherwise eliminated—to piece together the fragments that inspired the making of *Anne of Green Gables*. In the legend Maud told about the birth of Anne she noted that Anne simply "flashed into my fancy already christened, even to the all important 'e.'"[4] This book reveals a very different story.

The story of *Anne* has its origins, not merely in the turbulent nature of Prince Edward Island's north shore and the timeless romance of apple blossoms, but also in the popular cosmopolitan magazines of New York, Boston, and Philadelphia. This book is the untold story of a literary classic and its writer, who quietly quarried her material from the popular images of the era—beauty icons, fashion plates, and advertisements—and from American mass market periodicals. For the first time, Anne fans will hear the story of how the American model Evelyn Nesbit became the model for Anne's face. While her name has been identified, the story of how she came to figure in *Anne of Green Gables* has never been told. We know that Maud imitated the formula fiction of juvenile periodicals, religious newspapers, and glamorous women's magazines, but we are now also able to track how, in a perfect storm of inspiration in the spring of 1905, Maud ultimately transcended these influences to create a twentieth-century literary classic that would conquer the world.

PART 1

The Perfect Storm
Fall 1903–Spring 1905

ONE

Old Memories and New Ambitions

Of late I have been reading over this foolish old journal from the first and see-
ing the effect all my various experiences have had on me much more clearly than
when I lived them.

I was fourteen when I began it. Before that time I had kept a little childish
diary in various "notebooks" since I was nine. When I grew older I burned them.
I shall always regret having done so for they would have been interesting to me
now. But I remember my childhood with great vividness.

— *L. M. Montgomery, May 3, 1908, journal entry*[1]

In later years, Maud would often repeat that her earliest memory was
of her mother's coffined body displayed in the parlor of her maternal grandparents, the Macneills. The mental picture was a flashback
to September 1876. The toddler in her father's arms was too young to
mourn, but she remembered touching Clara Montgomery's white face,
and would never forget its chill. The fatal illness, consumption, had rav-
aged Clara's body but had apparently spared her beauty. Over time, Maud
would embellish the memory of her mother resting in her coffin, beautiful with long silken lashes and golden-brown hair. She had inherited both.
Many times, Maud would sit in the old rocking chair in the Macneill parlor, replaying this defining moment of her life. It was the moment her
family fell apart; the moment her future was determined. And she was
too young to realize the portentousness of the scene.

After Clara's death, Maud's father traveled first across the Island, and then to Boston and across Canada in search of a job, leaving the toddler for her grandmother to raise. Maud's status as an unloved "charity child" was a deep wound on her sensitive psyche, but also became part of a mythology she actively shaped in her journal, as in the unpublished entry of May 3, 1908, just one month before the publication of *Anne of Green Gables*.

> I was a dreamy, delicate child, very impulsive, heedless, shrinking from an unkind or sarcastic word as from a blow—and I received many such for Uncle John never lost an opportunity of saying something unkind to me and grandfather was also very hard on me. The latter did not mean to be, I think—but he was extremely irritable and had no consideration for the feelings of anyone.[2]

The hardships of a child forced inward for stimulus and consolation was the story Maud would tell and retell. It was a central theme in the story of her life as a writer—a rationale for self-involvement and self-centeredness. She sketched the compelling portrait of a little companionless girl locked in a strict Presbyterian household and stifled in her emotional life; imprisoned within the mausoleum of reluctant old-age parenting; ultimately pulled in different directions by her rebelling youthful spirit and her desire to fit in with the people who provided her a home. It was the story of adversity and mental exile as she grew up in a large family clan that would implant not only feelings of loyalty and pride, but also loneliness and resentment. For the rest of her life she would be torn between the demands of duty and desire, conformity and rebellion, adult stricture and youthful yearning, without ever being able to resolve them.

Childhood Memories

She was raised in Cavendish, Prince Edward Island, by aging grandparents: her literary yet irritable grandfather Alexander Marquis Macneill, and her reserved yet loyal grandmother Lucy Ann Woolner Macneill.

There were many uncles and aunts and cousins, including the children of her maternal grandparents, such as Uncle John and his family, who were the next-door neighbors farming the fields; Uncle Leander, a minister who came visiting each year during the summer; and Aunt Emily, who took care of Maud when she was a little child. The clan members all felt the need to help raise and correct the perceived foibles of Clara's dreamy little daughter. They were constantly "nagging" her, as the adult Maud described these collective efforts to mold her personality. As she would later assert, "big family connections are by no means a wholly good thing. They produce too much heart-burning and jealousy."[3] In recounting her childhood, the adult Maud would emphasize her isolation from the Cavendish townspeople. Her cranky grandparents quarreled with the community, they passed on as truths what she later recognized as prejudices, and they kept her isolated at home. Nor did Maud recall enjoying her first experiences of school life at age six: "I was an extremely sensitive child and such, I think, have always a hard time in a public school."[4]

"Looking back now," she added, "I see clearly how unwholesome it was and how easily it might have ruined forever the disposition of so sensitive, 'highly strung' a child." So detrimental was the influence, her later journal account implies, that she was marred and scarred by the experience: "I received an impression of which to this day I have never been able quite to rid myself—that everybody disliked me and that I was a very hateful person." She concluded that a "more unfortunate impression could hardly be made on a child's mind."[5] And yet these very circumstances also endowed her with a sense of pride and a sense of her own difference. Just as imaginative Anne is a little odd, and Emily Byrd Starr is "queer," so Maud was a little odd and wrapped up in herself.

And thus she was perhaps meant to become a writer. For she took refuge from her loneliness in books, retreating into a world of the imagination: she found companions in the trees surrounding the homestead, who became lifelong friends and whose demise would later fill her with more anguish than the deaths of some family members; she created imaginary friends who had names and personalities and who talked back to her in the oval glass of the bookcase in her grandmother's sitting room, a scene she would replay in *Anne of Green Gables*. Her imagined world seemed more lively and real than the world of prosaic farm chores involving cows and pigs and chickens, or the even more mundane house-hold chores of washing dishes and cleaning the floor.

When Aunt Emily married, the Macneill parlor became the setting for an emotional scene when little Maud cried bitter tears. The marriage meant the loss of a close contact and the increased loneliness of staying alone with the Macneill grandparents. Presumably Maud would have slept with Aunt Emily, as was the custom during the era. Yet Emily's absence was soon filled by the fortunate arrival of two orphan boys, Wellington (Well) and David (Dave) Nelson of Rustico, who boarded with the Macneills from around 1882 to 1885. They were a godsend to the lonely, friendless Maud, and the seven-year-old was particularly attracted to the handsome Well, who was her own age and whose birthday was just a week after hers in December. Together they would go to the spruce woods and pick blobs of yellow chewing gum from the lichened boughs, an exquisite pleasure; she would always remember its sweet nutty flavor and its change of color from clear sunlight yellow to creamy pink when chewed.[6]

Some winter Well and Maud "took to 'writing stories out of our own heads,'" such as Well's "The Battle of the Partridge-Eggs" in which the characters are cast into dungeons full of snakes and die predictably tragic deaths.[7] The story-writing experience would fuel an entire chapter ("The Story Club Is Formed") in *Anne of Green Gables* two decades later. The Nelson orphans, "although brought up in a nominally Christian family, were veritable little heathens, knowing almost nothing about God or a future state"[8] (just like Anne, who has little conception of religion). Instead they had a firm and rooted belief in ghosts: they named the spruce grove below the orchard "The Haunted Wood" and came to believe that it really was haunted; victims of a self-induced terror, they imagined falling into the clutches of a "white thing." (Here was the original plot for "A Good Imagination Gone Wrong": "Oh, Marilla, I wouldn't go through the Haunted Wood after dark now for anything, I'd be sure that white things would reach out from behind the trees and grab me." "Fiddlesticks!," said Marilla and commanded the terrified Anne to march through the forest.)[9]

"They were the nicest playmates I ever had," Maud later noted in her journal. "Well and Dave were as brothers to me. We used to have glorious fun together."[10] Yet after three years the fun came to an abrupt end. When she was eleven the Nelson boys disappeared suddenly and unexpectedly without even saying good-bye. Perhaps Grandmother Macneill had arranged it so, trying to avoid another tearful departure scene with Maud. And thus the closest people in Maud's young life seemed to have a way of disappearing without warning. The permanence of friendship could not be relied on and separation always seemed to leave a sense of unexplained mystery. The many goodbyes of her childhood, though, also prompted her writing and the resurrecting of the nostalgic childhood memory.

In fact, in Maud's childhood, it was the relationship with her absent father Hugh John Montgomery, nicknamed Monty, that created the deepest sense of loss and the most powerful dream of togetherness. The unpublished journal passage of May 3, 1908, in which the adult Maud discusses her childhood love for her father is worth quoting at length:

> Father came occasionally to see me and his visits were bright spots for me. I loved him so deeply and felt myself beloved in return. I think now that grandfather and grandmother resented this very love of mine for him. They saw that I did not turn to them with the outgush of affection I gave him. And it was true— I did not. But it was their own fault. I know now that they loved me after a fashion. But they never expressed or showed that love in word or action. I never thought they loved me. I felt that the only person in the world who loved me was father. Nobody else ever kissed me and caressed me and called me pet names. So I gave all my love to him in those years. And my grandparents did not like it. They thought that, as they were giving me a home and food and clothes and care that I ought to have loved them best.[11]

It would become a central conflict for Maud: on the one hand, the imagined ideal of family and love, longed for but seemingly never within her reach as a stable foundation; and on the other, the real, tangible family life with her grandparents and extended clan so profoundly imperfect as to be painful, making her reluctant to attach the word love to it. The impact of her mother's death and her unrequited dream about reconnecting with her father left a cavernous void. With pen in hand she took charge of her destiny, dreaming up a better existence in her head and making it "real" by putting pen to paper and chalk to slate.

Putting Together the Fragments: The Birth of the Writer

Indeed, it seemed that she was always busy putting the fragments of her life together in writing. As she would later assert in her memoir *The Alpine Path*, there never was a time when she did not remember writing. No doubt there was something to Prince Edward Island, the unyielding and addictive grip of the winds, the pungent scent of the firs, the glorious colors of the old orchards, even the blowing hurricanes and spitting snow. There was something about the people, salt-of-the-earth, tell-it-like-it-is, with a quick eye for singling out those "from away." And, finally, there was something about herself, perhaps her dreamy loneliness, that destined her to become a writer. Like Emily, little Maud wrote biographies of her cats, she wrote letters to her father, and she would write effusive love poetry to her girlfriends. Repressed and conflicted Maud found her most honest and enduring emotional outlet in her creative writing.

At the same time, Maud's desire to be a writer was never purely idealistic. A kernel of L. M. Montgomery's often-told legend is the romantic story of clipping a little poem, *The Fringed Gentian*, in her portfolio as inspiration on her journey to become a writer. The poem is about a woman's dream to "climb the alpine path" and become a famous poet. She named her memoir after it and would cite it in her autobiographical novel *Emily of New Moon*. Drawn from *Godey's Lady's Book*, a Philadelphia fashion magazine, to which her grandmother subscribed, the poem appears in Ella Rodman Church and Augusta De Bubna's "Tam! The Story of a Woman."

In March 1884, at age nine, Maud would have been turning the crisp pages, whose smell blended with the smell of Grandmother Macneill's good bread, when her breath caught in her throat, as her fingers ran across the lines: "Do you think I have any right to expect—when I have had more practice I mean—to receive pay for my verses? Actual *money*, as for a marketable merchandise?"[12] The question is asked by Tam Powell, a fictional country girl living in the backwoods of Pennsylvania, who writes poetry in secret. That one could write for *money* was a stunning revelation. This pragmatic attitude toward literature would fuel Maud's transformation into an ambitious and self-promoting author capable of launching herself from rural Cavendish onto the world stage. As much as the pleasure of writing, the idea of fame and self-sufficiency would become the drive that would give her writing distinct motivation and direction. Nothing less than rivaling the Brontës, as she later admitted, was the dream of her girlhood.

In her approach to publishing, Maud was driven by a pragmatism that we will see reflected in the practical Marilla Cuthbert or the hands-on Mrs. Rachel Lynde. She realized early on that dreamy poetry needed shrewd packaging to succeed in the world. To be successful as a professional writer, she required a stimulus from the wider world, which arrived at the Macneill kitchen in Mr. Crewe's mailbag. The mailbag always contained a magazine or two, which Maud read before it was picked up by its owner. As a girl, she read *Wide Awake*, a children's magazine with wonderful stories that inspired her to name her cats after the characters (Topsy, Pussywillow, and Catkin). She even read *Little Lord Fauntleroy* in the *Montreal Witness*.

According to her own journal account, at the tender age of twelve or thirteen, she secretly sent a poem to *The Household* magazine of Boston to which her grandmother had a subscription.[13] When it came back, she was crushed, but not deterred. As a teenager she shared her dream of becoming a writer with Nate Lockhart, her high-school sweetheart, a gifted writer, a kindred spirit, and the first boy, at age fifteen, to declare his love. The two were constantly writing epistles to each other that Maud would read underneath the school maples. But like the writerly heroines in *Godey's Lady's Book*, Maud would forego marriage to claim her independence as a woman and a writer; in lieu of an engagement ring, she secured her first published poem in the Charlottetown *Patriot*. Over the years she suffered dramatic setbacks, but the determination in her gray eyes was as steely as the North Atlantic just before it whirls into a gale. At age eighteen, she was thrilled when *The Ladies World* of New York offered to publish her poem "The Violet's Spell." She would never forget the moment when she received the envelope with the acceptance letter during her college year in Charlottetown. Over the following years, her name flashed in modest print through the pages of *Munsey's*, *The Delineator*, *Ainslee's*, *McClure's*, *Lippincott's*, and *Ladies Journal*, and each time she felt that strange excitement tingling through her nerves. These New York, Philadelphia, Boston, and Toronto magazines were the rungs of the ladder she climbed to success.

The old Cavendish post office was central to her writing and was her connection with the wider world. Grandmother Macneill was the post-mistress and Maud was her assistant. Today you can see the old desk with the pigeon-hole slots, the delicate scales used to gauge the weight of let-ters and parcels, and the stamp, bearing the round legend "Cavendish, PEI," displayed at the old homestead bookstore. Many writers, like Jane Austen, with whom Maud is often compared, began by writing for family and friends, testing their literature within an intimate circle before offer-ing it to a publisher. In Jane Austen's case, her father was not only one of the first readers and critics of her work, but also the person who first approached a publisher. In Maud's case, her great-aunt Mary Lawson, the sister of her much-maligned maternal grandfather Alexander Marquis Macneill, seems to have provided some support for her writing, and she credits the Macneill family with their literary prowess. Maud loved listen-ing to Aunt Mary tell the tales of the early years of the province colored by the sayings and doings and recollections of youth. Prince Edward Island also has an old and rich tradition of oral storytelling, and stories of the sea, of people and places, as well as ghost stories were popular. In 1901, Maud worked for half a year as a "newspaper woman" for the *Halifax Echo*, writing a column under her pen name Cynthia. Maud's ambitious drive was evident at an early age when she began testing her fiction and poetry on the world stage. To protect herself from the sneers of disap-proving family members such as Grandmother Macneill or Uncle John, proud Maud erected a wall of silence concerning her failures and strategi-cally revealed only her successes.

"New York is the metropolis of Canada as well as of this country," a book reviewer wrote in *Godey's Lady's Book* during the mid-eighteen-nineties. "There has never been a literary separation."[14] During the last decade of the nineteenth century, New York became a magnet for a num-ber of important Canadian writers who could not find appropriate publishing outlets in Canada. Maud was familiar with the work of "the Canadian Tennyson" Bliss Carman, and "the Longfellow of Canada" Charles G. D. Roberts, both Maritime poets who had moved to Manhattan and become popular icons in the metropolis. New Brunswick writer May Agnes Fleming had similarly gone to Brooklyn and become a sensational bestseller. So had many others.[15] In *Emily Climbs*, the Canadian-born New

York editor Janet Royal offers Emily, Maud's alter ego, the chance to work in New York: "You must have the stimulus of association with great minds—the training that only a great city can give. Come with me. If you do, I promise you that in ten years' time Emily Byrd Starr will be a name to conjure with among the magazines of America."[16] Emily is tempted, but resists, and Janet Royal's prediction is dire: "...the big editors won't look farther than the address of P.E. Island on your manuscript. Emily, you're committing literary suicide."[17]

Climbing Literary Heights: The Years Before Anne

In 1903, twenty-eight-year-old Maud was far removed from New York, the epicenter of literary power. Would she be able to climb literary heights from the obscurity of Cavendish? Or would she remain on the sidelines, never getting to play the game? Around this time, she began to recruit kindred spirits in a kind of virtual writer's space, casting a net of professional pen friends that would include Gerald Carlton, a writer of dime novels in New York, Lucy Lincoln Montgomery, an elderly poet and short story writer in Boston, and two younger novice writers, Ephraim Weber in Alberta and George Boyd MacMillan in Scotland, who would become lifelong friends. To the last, the twenty-nine-year-old Maud introduced herself with a fib: "I am 26 years old and like yourself have been scribbling all my life." Writing on December 29, 1903, a month after her 29th birthday, she elegantly rejuvenated herself.[18] She proudly asserted to be Canadian born and bred with ancestry from Scotland. She was "in literature" to make her living out of it, she confided. A *"good workman,"* with a knack for lucrative juvenile fiction, she had become an expert at formula stories.

We can glean from their correspondence that by this time Maud had seventy periodicals on her list of potential publishers. These she shared with MacMillan, noting the kind of stories the editors would be interested in. Like a New York stockbroker, she studied the market and recorded the rise of her income. That year she had made $500 from her writing, as she noted in her journal in December, the equivalent of a male stenographer's yearly income in New York. She was being listed by several magazines as one of "'the well known and popular' contributors for the coming year." The Presbyterian Board of Publications in Philadelphia was asking her for an autographed photo. And she had finally triumphed over those family and community members who had disparaged her writing. "The *dollars* have silenced them. But I have not forgotten their sneers. My own perseverance has won the fight for me in the face of all discouragements," she concluded with a trace of vindictiveness in her journal.[19] And yet a note of self-doubt rings clear as a bell in her December 29, 1903, letter to MacMillan: "I know that I can never be a really great writer."[20]

Still, strong-willed Maud had more on her mind than little Sunday School stories. Frustrated and restless, she was hard at work honing her literary skills, secretly pushing forward with her ambition—her dream of a novel. Around the turn of the century, Maud had made her first attempt at writing a full-length book. She called it *A Golden Carol*. Set in Halifax Ladies' College, a residential school in Halifax, Nova Scotia, which Maud had attended from 1895 to 1896, its conventional heroine was modeled after the popular Christian stories for children, the Pansy books of her childhood. Punned from the character's name Carol Golden, its ill-starred title seemed to betray that the writing was caught in the golden cage of formula fiction. The novel was uninspired. It preached. Its ending was predictable. The book failed to find a publisher, not because it wasn't a good story, as Maud later realized, but because the heroine, a goody-goody type, lacked life and spunk. Maud shuddered to think that even the Sunday school publishers had passed on the manuscript. But she never regretted burning the flawed book. As she would much later realize, "It was the re-action drove me to 'Anne' and probably kept me from making a dummy of her."[21]

Maud was ready to write about a different kind of heroine: not the goody-goody formula fiction girl of *A Golden Carol*, but one with depth and humanity—one more like Maud herself, and the heroine needed a face, as Maud revealed in a stunning disclosure almost three decades after writing *Anne*, on the day before her sixtieth birthday, a day when Lucy Maud Montgomery enjoyed the new Hollywood movie adaptation of *Anne of Green Gables* in Toronto's Uptown Theatre on bustling Yonge Street. Maud thought that the actress Dawn O'Day looked like she imagined Anne.[22] Her journal reminiscences that same night included a truly fascinating revelation and clue as to how *Anne of Green Gables* came about.

The "Original" Anne

On the evening of November 29, 1934, writing in her home in Norval, Ontario, Maud put the clipping of a young girl in her journal. The dreamy beauty, Maud said in a remarkably belated revelation, was the model for Anne's face when she was writing the novel decades earlier. "I wonder," she mused, "if she ever read of *Anne*, never dreaming that, physically, she was the original!"[23]

The memorable photograph shows a richly textured face in which the play of light and shadow tells a story. The girl's big, dark eyes are rapt with just a tinge of melancholy. Light floods her face. A satiny band accentuates her forehead. The girl wears two large chrysanthemums in her hair. When I examined the original clipping in L. M. Montgomery's personal papers at the University of Guelph Archives in Ontario, I could see the care with which she had put the clipping in her journal, using old-fashioned photographic corners to frame the picture. I also traveled to the Smithsonian Institute in Washington D.C. where, after even more intense security checks than in Guelph, I was able to examine the still-unprocessed papers of photographer Rudolf Eickemeyer, Jr. Along with the original photograph, I found a gorgeous color poster of the early-twentieth-century model and beauty icon.

Who was the mystery girl? "I have no idea who she was or where she lived," Maud claimed, but insisted that she was a "real girl somewhere in the U.S."[24] And since Maud had a way of forgetting and confusing names and dates, often cutting and pasting little snippets from magazines and sticking them pell-mell into her portfolio and notebooks, it is difficult to determine if she knew her identity or not.

In fact, the face belonged to Evelyn Nesbit, at the time a teenage model in New York who was one of the era's leading beauty icons and was also one of the famous Gibson Girls. While Evelyn's name was first identified by co-editor Wendy E. Barry in *The Annotated Anne of Green Gables* in 1997, we know very little about this picture's role in the creation of Maud's novel. Maud tells us that the American beauty arrived at the Macneill homestead between the covers of a magazine, but she does not say which magazine. Neither does she tell us when she first saw her. These mysteries pose the question of when Anne first entered Maud's mind. Knowing the date of the arrival of that picture allows us an important entry point into the enigma of Anne's birth. To explore the history of the photograph that inspired Anne's face, one must look back at the early years of the century in New York City, a world very different from the world of Green Gables.

TWO

The Model for Anne's Face

...an extraordinary observer might have seen that the chin was very pointed and pronounced; that the big eyes were full of spirit and vivacity; that the mouth was sweet-lipped and expressive; that the forehead was broad and full; in short, our discerning extraordinary observer might have concluded that no commonplace soul inhabited the body of this stray woman-child of whom shy Matthew Cuthbert was so ludicrously afraid.

—*Anne Shirley's first appearance in* Anne of Green Gables[1]

For decades, the taste and style of Queen Victoria had dominated an era known for its top hats, bangs, and bustles. Its ludicrously voluminous dresses, trains, and crinolines constrained generations of women. Growing up during this period, Maud had imbibed its images and values, its codified behavior, its rigid class structure, and its expectations of women's desire for marriage, children, and domesticity—all of which penetrated and structured the world of Cavendish and the fictional world of Avonlea. The Queen's death in January 1901 was an important threshold for societal changes that had begun during the 1890s, with women entering professions and universities, and even riding bicycles in public. In cosmopolitan New York the old Victorian icons had been crumbling for some time, and by the time the Queen died, the idealized domestic woman known as the "Victorian Angel in the House" was gone. Gone was the woman perfectly pure: her good image had become stale. The New Woman was in. She had entered the media in photos of the mischievous, fun-loving gamine, and, through the magazines, her image and the altered

31

expectations concerning her role filtered down into the quiet world of Cavendish, as the rains filtered through the soft clay soils in spring.

At the newly opened Campbell Art Studio on Fifth Avenue in Lower Manhattan,[2] fashionable women, actresses, and models flocked to have their pictures taken by one of the era's great portrait photographers— Rudolf Eickemeyer Jr.[3] His iconic photographs appealed to readers of *The Delineator, Colliers, Scribner's*, and *Century Magazine*, the very magazines Maud was trying to reach with her fiction. His knack for natural lines and perfect light effects gave the illusion of spontaneity and romance. He understood that "portraits, like Tableaux Vivants, were images designed to please."[4] He also had a way of bringing the New Woman into the commercial press by reassuring readers that she had not strayed too far from the old conventions. His modern girl heralded the change of time, but also accommodated the nostalgic and sensuous beauty in which Lucy Maud Montgomery found an inspirational spark.

Evelyn Nesbit

The photo that would inspire Anne was taken in the late summer of 1901, just around the time when twenty-six-year-old Maud was preparing to leave Cavendish to become a "newspaper woman" in Halifax, Nova Scotia. That summer, sixteen-year-old Evelyn Nesbit flitted to the half-timbered house at 564–568 Fifth Avenue. She had an appointment with Rudolf Eickemeyer.

Evelyn Florence Nesbit was born on December 25, 1884, in Tarentum, twenty-four miles from Pittsburgh. Her father, Winfield Scott Nesbit, a successful lawyer, had died when she was eight and Evelyn helped supplement the family income through cleaning jobs, sales clerking, and modeling for painters. In Philadelphia, she had posed as an angel, "barefoot, in long white robes, my hair hanging in uncoiled profusion down my back," as she recalled in her memoir.[5] She talked her mother and brother into trying their luck in New York. After months of hardship and toiling, Evelyn's fortune changed virtually overnight, from struggling model to celebrity, when she began posing for fashion photographers in early 1901. In the whirlwind of New York, her sudden celebrity was dizzying, as was her new friendship with the famous New York architect Stanford White. It was he who had sent Evelyn to Eickemeyer's studio that late summer of 1901, for he collected pictures of pretty teenage girls.

Eickemeyer, looking debonair, greeted Evelyn like someone used to catering to clients in the studio. He was efficient and courteous behind the hangdog expression of his shaggy moustache.[6] Her long lustrous copper curls cascaded over her shoulder and coiled up in a question mark at the end. "My eyes were hazel and very brilliant," she recalled years later in her memoir; "my nose was straight and almost Irish in its slight upward tilt, my mouth a very red—a bit full, the lips pouting."[7] At the Smithsonian, in Eickemeyer's personal papers, there is a postcard featuring one of Evelyn's more famous pictures. Scribbled on the back, in what looks like Eickemeyer's hand, is a curious note: "...she was not really as beautiful. She was very photogenic."[8] Evelyn, in turn, wrote in her memoir: "Eickemeyer, a genuine artist, had spared neither himself nor me in his attempts to get the right effect in his photographs of me."[9] Often he would work for an hour on just one plate, while Evelyn patiently followed his orders. They were both professionals in their craft.

There must have been a vase with chrysanthemums in the studio that day—white or yellow—brilliant with their simple beauty. Evelyn pinned five big mums in her hair and struck a pose. Kachunk-click went the shutter. The picture, an amazing blend of vixen and virgin, appeared in July 1902 in the *Theatre Journal*.[10] The model's stare was unblinking and willful. This was the look of a young girl become a modern woman. But this was not the photo that would inspire the face of Anne—this pose was missing the soft veil of nostalgia.

The changing of the plates always took a few minutes as the assistant scurried to the darkroom with plates in hand. Evelyn must have rushed into the next pose, for her hair was disheveled where she had removed the mums. Only a single flower remained on each side of her face. Eickemeyer arranged the lights. The pose was uncomfortable but the light immediately gave the rapt face a brilliant radiance. The flash, held in position by the assistant, exploded and filled her eyes with blinding stars.

This time, Evelyn's pose was sultry and mysterious, like an offering to a pagan god. When the photo took shape in Eickemeyer's chemical bath, the play of light and shadow was dramatic. There was something angelic and innocent in her expression. There was also something natural and honest about her. Nostalgic girlhood was captured in the fleeting snap of time before the shutter clicked and stole the image. The oversized flowers had come to life like sea-roses in water, and Evelyn looked like a wood nymph, a dryad who might roam in Lover's Lane. It was a backward glance to the Victorian age, where this kind of representation of innocent flower girls had been wildly popular. Still, the model's palpable eroticism also hailed the modern era. But could Eickemeyer and Evelyn have guessed that this very photograph would attract the attention of a solitary writer in Canada? Could anyone have imagined that the face of a beloved literary icon—the exuberant Anne—had just been conceived in a photographer's studio on Fifth Avenue through the artistic collaboration of a willing model and accomplished photographer for the benefit of an aging American millionaire?

In her memoir, Evelyn recalled that at age fourteen she posed for George Gibbs, the Philadelphia writer and illustrator, who coincidentally would illustrate several of the covers of L. M. Montgomery's novels. At age eighteen she posed for Charles Dana Gibson's pen-and-ink sketch *The Eternal Question*, which became iconic, appearing on posters, cushions, and advertisements as a new version of the free-spirited yet innocent Gibson Girl. Maud would have been familiar with this idealized snapshot of the modern girl. She would have been horrified to know, however, that Stanford White, who had commissioned her beloved photograph of Anne's face, aggressively took advantage of sixteen-year-old Evelyn probably just weeks following the photo shoot that inspired Anne's face. After her life became the fodder for tabloids, the world would remember Evelyn only as the mistress of the married New York architect Stanford White, who was murdered by Evelyn's husband Harry Thaw in 1906. That her face also decorated scores of churches and children's books has been obscured by scandal. Like Maud, history has a way of compartmentalizing truth.

Glossy Girl

When did Maud first see Evelyn's picture? There was nothing in Maud's extensive scrapbooks to answer this question. There was nothing in the more than two thousand published pages of *The Selected Journals of L.M. Montgomery* or in the many unpublished journal pages. The evidence had disappeared or been destroyed. There was nothing in Eickemeyer's personal papers indicating where and when he had sold this photograph to a magazine. We do know, however, that Maud was a voracious reader who consumed cover to cover whatever she could get her hands on, even a cooking book, as she once joked. We also know that she carefully read all of the magazines in which she published stories. "Among others, the *Delineator, Smart Set* and *Ainslee's* have opened their fold to this poor wandering sheepkin of thorny literary ways," she had jubilated in November 1901.[11] Knowing Maud's penchant for magazines, I combed through these century-old magazines of fashion and culture looking most carefully at those in which Maud had published her work and in which Eickemeyer also routinely placed his photographs. After three summers of searching, there was little progress in finding the source for the face of Anne. Maud's picture of Evelyn was mysteriously elusive.

Elusive, that is, until a visit to Donna J. Campbell, a private collector of L.M. Montgomery's work. In her farmhouse were a number of magazines in which Maud had published her early stories and one Sunday afternoon, I discovered the missing link that led me to the source. The copy of an American food magazine, *What to Eat,* in which Maud had published a story in September 1903, revealed that it was here, in her own complimentary copy, that she would have stumbled over a tiny reproduction of Evelyn's photo advertising the September issue of the *Metropolitan Magazine,* a glamorous literary periodical published in New York. Scanning the splashy full-page ad, Maud would have seen the teaser picture of the girl and the text:

Sixteen pages will as heretofore be devoted to portraits of beautiful women, and these full page pictures in the September Number will be printed in tint and will surpass all previous efforts made to enhance this distinctive feature of *The Metropolitan Magazine.*[12]

M-E-T-R-O-P-O-L-I-T-A-N. Would Maud, in September 1903, have capitalized the title in her mind, as she liked to do when she was excited?

The advertised magazine was urban, modern, and exotic. Hailing the world of the automobile, the stage, photography, fashion, and money, it represented the opposite of Maud's Cavendish life, which consisted of the post office, baking, cleaning, cooking, dusting, and shoveling snow in the winter. The highlights of Cavendish social life were the Church and the Literary Society, house parties, dances and, as one of her girlfriends had quipped, funerals. Maud's curiosity was piqued. A savvy businesswoman who earned her own living, an avid photographer with her own dark-room for photo development, a fashion lover who "put on bright hues and pretty garments, just as the flowers do,"[13] she dreamed about a world that was different from her rural existence. She loved Cavendish dearly, but hungered for a richer social life, better financial conditions, an appropri-ate standing in the community, a passionate companionship, her own house, and success in the world. Maud's delight in the American maga-zines resonated with these more worldly desires.

There in the ad was the *Metropolitan* address, 3 West 29th Street, New York, inviting her to request her own copy. If she couldn't go to Manhattan, perhaps she could bring Manhattan to Cavendish. Presumably it was old "Santa-Clausy Mr. Crewe," the mailman with his long gray beard, slouch, and limp who delivered the New York beauty on his rum-bling buggy, traveling down the old lane and around the bend to the red kitchen door. The world came to the homestead each day with the mail-bag. Coincidentally, just a month earlier, in August, Maud had placed the mailman's photograph prominently in her journal, along with a detailed description of this "incongruous messenger."[14] Perhaps, though, Maud procured her copy from Geo. Carter & Company, the Queen Street book-seller in downtown Charlottetown, who ironically was also the dealer in seeds for flowers, fields, and garden and whose ad she had glued in her scrapbook years earlier.[15] Inhaling the smell of the new magazines in his store, Maud often surrendered her Macneill thriftiness and snapped up a glossy periodical. Although there is no reference to *The Metropolitan* in her papers, the size and tinting of the clipping in her journal prove that it was in this magazine that she found the inspiration for Anne.[16]

According to her own account, but without acknowledging the source, she cut out the photograph from the magazine, framed it, and hung the pic-ture on the wall of her den. To use prefabricated, so-called "passepartout" cardboard sheets to frame magazine clippings was the fashion of the day. Portraits of beauty worked like advertisements that helped sell magazines such as *Cosmopolitan* and *The Metropolitan*. When Eickemeyer sold the photograph of the dark-eyed maiden to *The Metropolitan Magazine* in 1903, he paired it with another portrait of Evelyn. Robed in a white Greek gown, a laurel wreath tucked in her hair, she staged the popular pose of a Sapphic disciple. No doubt Maud would have seen the model's name, "Miss Evelyn Nesbitt" [sic],[17] but since no model was named for the chrysanthemum photograph, and since the two portraits of Evelyn look remarkably different, we cannot be certain that Maud realized that the model was the same. Nonetheless, she invited Evelyn into her inner sanctum, her den, where Evelyn's romantic eyes could seep into her life and imagination.

Taking residence in Maud's upstairs room, where Maud also housed her books and did most of her writing, the American girl with her nostalgic expression was a companion close by on the wall. As Maud sat at her desk in the waning light of dusk, overlooking the lane and the fields outside, Evelyn's enraptured face shared the afterglow of evening sunset, the stark light of a new moon, and the murmur of the sea in summertime. But their relationship was not all sweetly romantic. As Maud read the seasons, so she would have read the girl's visage, consuming the rich texture of her features. Just as Evelyn's girlhood pose was created in front of cameras, so Anne was created in front of Maud's imaginary lens. In fact, Maud was later consistent in emphasizing that all her characters "grew" over a long gestation period, contradicting her own memoir account of Anne as flashing into her imagination.

Evelyn Nesbit's pose heralded Anne's rapt and intense personality. Maud, who possessed a strong visual memory, liked to organize her compositions like an architect or painter, using vibrant colors and distinctive shapes such as arches, circles, frames, and curves.[18] But a picture is not a fully fleshed character, nor can it supply the narrative arc for a novel. Many other elements needed to blend with the picture in Maud's imagination. If we follow Maud's account, by now she had undergone a lengthy apprenticeship as a writer. Given how quickly Maud would write *Anne of Green Gables* in 1905, and how her Waverly pen would race over the pages less than two years later, it is safe to assume that a great deal of emotional and mental preparation had preceded the writing—making the twenty months following the arrival of Evelyn Nesbit's portrait crucial in our search for

Anne. Maud would later say that her own life, her dreams and desires were contained in *Anne of Green Gables*. And something of the yearning, melancholy expression of Evelyn's face also seemed to hail Maud's nostalgic picture of her own youth that she sketched in her journal.

A Picture of Youth

In the year Evelyn Nesbit's photograph arrived in Cavendish, Maud missed her childhood friends who had left the town one by one. Her cousin and friend Clara Campbell in the neighboring town of Park Corner had become a stranger since she had gone to Boston as a domestic worker. Embarrassed by Clara's choice of profession, Maud found they had little to talk about when Clara returned for a visit. Her Cavendish cousin and friend Lucy Macneill had married and gone to live in Lynn, Massachusetts. Such was the exodus that was part of Island life and that took many Islanders to the Canadian west or south of the border in search of jobs. The young female teachers who arrived to take the Cavendish school supplied a ready pool of friends but they inevitably left to get married or take better positions elsewhere.

Maud missed the intellectual and social stimulus that a writer needs to craft great fiction. As a Victorian citizen, she was also highly discriminating about the company she liked to keep, reflecting the class and cultural prejudices of her time. There was a solitary, self-involved, and occasionally misanthropic streak to her personality that made her feel comfortable only in the presence of a small group of congenial friends, whom she would later call kindred spirits. In her journal Maud often claimed that there where two Mauds—the jolly, public Maud, who could be seen laughing and dancing her feet off at her cousin Alec Macneill's, and the private, morbidly self-scrutinizing Maud. The public Maud would never let it be known that she felt lonely in the company of uncongenial family.

Maud had ways of traveling into the past and reviving memory pictures of youth, some tinted with the same melancholy brush that had perfected Evelyn's picture. When grayness and dampness heralded the lonely days of winter, Maud liked to take refuge in the attic, where she would rummage through her old trunk and reconnect with her own past.

On the night of November 20, a Friday, 1903, she found an old familiar text from her schooldays—the *Third Royal Reader*. Here, she discovered the pieces that had once moved her to tears when she was a child, among them, "The Child's First Grief," and "The Dog at His Master's Grave"— the very same verse that Anne offers to recite in Sunday School in chapter eleven of *Anne of Green Gables* because she finds it sad and melancholy.[19] But what solitary Maud found in the recesses of the old house were not only the little nuggets she would squirrel away and use in her fiction, but also ways to transport herself to a realm of adolescence, the age represented by Evelyn Nesbit's picture. It was in these moments of *reliving* the past that Maud found the originality and authenticity of her voice as a writer of juvenile fiction. Because she read her journal before writing she received not only an important spark of inspiration, but also a method for blending fact and fiction, past and present, adulthood and childhood.

Adolescence is the age when the mind is racked with intense emotions.[20] Although she was a disciplined, mature writer, Maud's genius was in her ability to call up those passionate emotions and temperaments. The key to that skill was Maud's adolescent journal, which began on September 21, 1889, just before her fifteenth birthday, the same day she destroyed her childhood journal. By actively remembering and reading through her journals, scrapbooks, and notebooks—often moved to laughter and tears, joy and sadness—Maud shaped her adolescent musings into art that would appeal to both young and old. But what she read also shaped Maud's adult self—cementing the emotional obsessions and preoccupations of the past in the present. Addicted to her journal throughout her life, she would find the truth of her emotions on the pages of the diary she wrote years and decades ago.

As Maud found her remedy for loneliness and isolation in dreaming and writing, the months that followed the arrival of Evelyn's picture were like an incubation period during which she whirled up deeply embedded emotions. The photo inspiring Anne's face would bring together diverse feelings that Maud had felt over the years: youth slipping away, friends leaving, and family threatened. It was these unsettling realities that prompted Maud to create what she called "castles in Spain," daydreams in which she had everything she was missing in real life. Nourished by her reading of romance, this dreamland of fiction would help Maud become an agent in transforming her own fate. She dreamed up Anne.

THREE

Building Castles in Spain

Glittering castles in Spain were shaping themselves out of the mists and rain-bows of [Anne's] lively fancy; adventures wonderful and enthralling were happening to her in cloudland—adventures that always turned out tri-umphantly and never involved her in scrapes like those of actual life.

—Anne Shirley daydreaming in front of the
stove in the Green Gables kitchen[1]

Maud believed that literature should engage with the real world by transforming negative realities. Never should her reader's pleasure be spoiled by the fact that some of the cheeriest episodes in *Anne* were sparked by the darker side of life. Indeed, Maud's losses and disappointments fueled her imagination into high gear, transforming bleakness into hope. This transformation, or the elevation of existence to a higher level, was part of what drove her writing. Daydreams were a central part of her creative life, even though she made a clear distinction between her daydreams (in which she was the star) and her stories (in which she was an outside observer). Whenever Maud felt listless and dull, she would escape into her world of dreams, staring into space and building castles upon clouds, a habit readers of *Anne* will recognize as familiar, as when Anne sits daydreaming at the kitchen table, or in front of the kitchen stove in the epigraph. "Oh, if it were not for my dreams I would go crazy!" Maud noted in her journal on Saturday, February 20, 1904, when the very mercury was freezing in the thermome-ter. "In them I can be as adventurous and...triumphant as I wish, while the world around me is a prison to the body."[2] By making Anne a day-dreamer, Maud was drawing on her own daydreaming habits and alluding to the creative method that would fuel the novel.

Great writers from Leo Tolstoy and Anthony Trollope to Virginia Woolf have tapped their daydreams to create literary masterpieces. In his classic essay "Creative Writers and Daydreams," Sigmund Freud writes that even mundane daydreams can powerfully affect the daydreamer, and when these daydreams blend with other forces, they can offer a poetic art that produces great pleasure in the reader. Daydreams spark "the less pretentious authors of novels, romances, and short stories, who nevertheless have the widest and most eager circle of readers of both sexes."[3] Notwithstanding Freud's bias against popular literature, we know that daydreaming, far from being a purely passive indulgence, can be an exercise in creating a sustained narra-tive, an imagined story with a beginning, middle, and a satisfying end. Daydreaming, as Maud's obscured journal entries suggest, was an important training ground that helped shape her first novel, even as her dreams also had a way of facilitating forgetfulness and blindness.

Storms and Stresses

The year 1904 began with emotional storms and stresses in which Maud's emotions gathered strength like the nor'easter blowing up the coast. In January Maud was called to Uncle John Macneill's home. His second daughter Katie was seriously ill with pneumonia. As a single woman, a spinster, Maud was expected to help her relatives, especially when a fam-ily member was sick. Maud did not like Uncle John, whom she considered overbearing and domineering and uneducated. But she did like nineteen-year-old Katie, who was a bright girl. Each day that January, Maud crossed over the snow drifts to go to the farm next door and sit by Katie's bedside. The vigil stretched over three long weeks, leaving Maud distraught and worn out, all the more as she was unable to save her patient. Katie died during the icy cold days of that winter.[4]

In *Anne of Green Gables*, Maud would transform the depressing ordeal into its opposite by giving the dark episode a happy ending. When Diana calls for Anne's help, also in January, the two friends race hand in hand across the snow-crusted fields to prepare for the late-night rescue mission. In chapter eighteen, "Anne to the Rescue," three-year-old Minnie May is saved from a bad attack of croup by Anne's deft dispensation of ipecac and hot compresses. No doubt the personal memory of Maud's vigil also blended with *Godey's Lady's Book's* February 1892 health column, a How To manual teaching the mother how to be a heroic savior at a sick child's bedside: "Among the most frightful diseases, and one which attacks young children without a moment's notice, is croup." The *Godey's* column continued: "Then it is that a mother, while waiting for a physician, may be able to save the life even of her little one." When Anne saves the life of Diana's little sister by administering ipecac she appears to be following the *Godey's* instructions step by step: "Give syrup of ipecac in small doses, every five minutes, until vomiting is induced." *Godey's* also instructs that "[c]loths wrung out in hot water and applied to the chest will give great relief,"[5] and so Diana heats up hot water, while Anne administers the treatment. In the morning Anne returns home by crossing the long white field. The "fairy arch" of Lover's Lane is a signpost that signals an alternate reality, one that sprang from the transformed memory of the same field that Maud had crossed in returning home after her nightly vigils at Katie's bed. No doubt Katie's death would have necessitated such transformative work, given that the long hours of bedside vigil would have conjured up memories of other deaths—her mother had died of consumption, and, more recently, her beloved father had died of pneumonia, the very same illness as Katie, also in January, four years earlier.

Just a few months after Katie's death, the dream of reassembling her family, which would become a central theme of *Anne of Green Gables*, gripped Maud's imagination. It was connected with the fantasy of her father, one of her earliest dreams, and perhaps also a mildly delusional one that she would carry well into adulthood. On May 5, 1904, exactly a year before *Anne* would leap fully formed into her consciousness, Maud made a find during spring cleaning that she recorded in the unpublished journal entry that day. It was a box of yellowed letters her father had written to her grandfather when she was a small child, and that she must have destroyed for they are no longer extant. In these letters, he referred to "dear little Maud."[6] To the twenty-nine-year-old writer, here was welcome evidence of her father's love and pride, although she interestingly did not quote the letters, nor reveal their contents. Unfortunately, the lovable romantic and king in the castle of Maud's dreams was also the Victorian incarnation of a deadbeat dad—a truth Maud was unwilling to admit.

Monty's Airy Castle

A man largely absent in her life, Maud's father Monty was a man with big dreams. In a photo, his eyes stare into space, vacant and sad.[7] Born in 1841 on the farm in Park Corner at the north shore, Hugh John Montgomery came from a prominent Island family of farmers and politicians; his father was the Canadian Senator Donald Montgomery. In contrast, Monty was an unsuccessful storekeeper, a shipwrecked captain, a popular auctioneer, and a politician who failed to win a majority. But the lack of worldly success only increased his potential for Maud to turn him into a romantic hero. Intriguingly, the last job of his career was as a prison warden, working alongside his wife who helped supplement the family income. A man of dreams, he called his modest little house on the prairie "Eglintoune Villa" because of a tenuous family connection between the Montgomerys and the Earls of Eglinton in Scotland. Maud promptly repeated this genealogy when she introduced herself to G. B. MacMillan of Scotland in 1903.[8] She even used "Maud Eglinton" as one of her early pseudonyms, clearly identifying herself as her father's daughter. Like Monty, she had no qualms about laying it on thick behind Grandmother Macneill's back, who would have shaken her head and pinched her lips, irritated at so much highfalutin' pretension. Separated by 3,500 kilometers, a six-day train ride at the time, Maud asserted that she and her father always "remained near and dear in spirit." Yet there was ample evidence of neglect and abandonment that Maud chose to ignore.

In 1890, fifteen-year-old Maudie, as her father called her, had traveled to Prince Albert with a wide-eyed dream of reassembling her family in her father's house. Reading between the lines of the journal entries of that year, we sense that she expected to be welcomed as the long-lost daughter and to become the center of attention, basking in familial pride and comfort, and to be given the longed-for education that would launch her life. Was she already formulating what she would later articulate as her fondest dream—to have a real university education, a "full-fledged B.A.," as Anne would receive in the 1915 sequel *Anne of the Island*?

Yet when Maud arrived in the western frontier town, her dream of a happy family and education quickly collapsed. The center of family attention was not the first-born daughter, who had been waiting her turn patiently, but her half-brother Bruce, the first-born male, "son and heir" to the "house of Montgomery," born while she was in Prince Albert.[9] Just as she always felt on the outside of the Macneill clan, she was once again on the outside, looking in. Her position was awkward. The sixteen-year-old was expected to help in the household, and was scandalized that there was no servant. A proud Macneill to the bone, she assumed her role resentfully, complaining in a letter to her cousin Penzie Macneill: "I don't like the job a bit for I hate minding babies."[10] The disappointment and injury of her pride sparked by her rereading of her Prince Albert journal in January 1904 would fuel some of the social satire in *Anne of Green Gables*. For example, Anne's foster parent Mrs. Hammond, who like Maud's own stepmother, "lived up river," puts Anne in charge of a brood of eight children and neglects to send her to school. Shrewish Mrs. Blewett, a "terrible worker and driver," offers to take Anne on as a full-time baby minder: "The baby's awful fractious, and I'm clean worn out attending to him. If you like I can take her right home now."[11]

Maud's pain was great, but she managed to keep her dream of the perfect father intact, even in the face of contravening evidence. Meanwhile, her rage oozed into her cruel private remarks concerning Monty's second wife, Mary Ann MacRae, "a woman whose evil temper and hateful disposition made his life miserable."[12] Her sting unalleviated by her usual wit, Maud never said a good word about Mary Ann. Maud had found a way of channeling her great disappointment. We do know that the second Mrs. Montgomery, who did express her disappointment in Monty, was an accomplished singer who involved her stepdaughter in the social activities of St. Paul's Presbyterian Church.[13] The tension at "Eglintoune Villa" was palpable, and Maud, lonely and homesick, returned to Cavendish in the fall of 1891. When Monty died unexpectedly of pneumonia in January 1900, he left her two hundred dollars in his will.

In the winter of 1904, Maud was busy rereading the journal entries of her Prince Albert year, reliving the time when she visited her father in Saskatchewan. A few months later, on May 5, stimulated by her reading of her father's letters, Maud spun an elaborate daydream in her journal, reassembling her lost family and creating for herself a brother in the image of her father:

> All my life I have longed for a brother—a big brother just a year or two older than myself.…a brother—to love me and stand up for me and be proud of me! I *know* my brother would have been a dear for he would probably have been like father. I like to dream about this imaginary brother…looking a little bit like me, perhaps with dark hair and dark blue eyes and a merry tender smile. I like to dream of walking in the twilight with him and talking of our futures and our plans for them. Oh, such dreams are pleasant! But to waken from them and realize that there is nobody—neither father nor mother nor sister nor brother—oh, how it hurts![14]

There is nothing unusual or spectacular about this everyday scene depicting an adult daydreaming about her desire for restoring her lost family—except perhaps that it is a fantasy more common to childhood or adolescence. There is nothing outstanding about its use of language. It is an ordinary daydream. And yet this obscure, never before cited scene is crucial evidence that, exactly one year before *Anne of Green Gables* would take shape, Maud Montgomery's consciousness was at work—rebuilding, once again, her lost family, as she had unsuccessfully tried to do as an adolescent in Prince Albert. The adolescent fantasy was still prominently alive. Father and phantom older brother are at the core of this dream family, and, as we shall see in the next chapter of this volume, her mother would join the fantasy in early 1905. Already her journal fantasy narrative anticipates the theme of her novel—the power of family—which would become the heartbeat of *Anne of Green Gables*. Distilled from Maud's yearnings throughout her life, her desire to restore a lost family was so strong it would eventually compel millions of readers with its power. In fiction, ironically, she was able to merge what she had so clearly compartmentalized in her real life: love based on a fantasy and love that had a practical foundation. In reality, she was sadly unappreciative of the imperfect but enduring attention provided by her own grandparents.

During that winter of 1904, with her restored family at the forefront of her daydreams, Maud was also coming to terms with her personal understanding of friendship and kindred spirits, themes that, along with the ties of family, would become central in *Anne of Green Gables*. In her mind, these emotional effects were all entangled, born out of the sense of loneliness and longing for fellowship. Anne fans, who recognize each other as "kindred spirits" (there is a *Kindred Spirits* newsletter and a *Kindred Spirits* electronic mailing list for fans), may be surprised to learn that it was during a most painful and hysterical night of crying and suicidal despair that Maud made important headway in bringing the "kindred spirits" concept to light.

The Summoning of Kindred Spirits

On the night of Wednesday, March 16, 1904, Maud could not sleep. Perhaps prompted by her earlier rereading of the Prince Albert journal, she decided to reread the letters of Will Pritchard, her closest male friend in Prince Albert. A redhead with green eyes and a funny, crooked smile, Will had been in love with her and declared his love in letters. He had worn her little golden ring at the time. They had flirted and Will had listened to Maud's woes about the Prince Albert teacher Mr. Mustard, who was unsuccessfully courting Maud and was most jealous of Will's attentions. During a picnic, Maud and Will had carved their names together on an old poplar at Maiden Lake. When she left Prince Albert, their friendship settled into a solid pen-friendship that Maud enjoyed and cultivated. When Will died of influenza a few years later in 1897, the year when Maud was teaching school in Belmont, Prince Edward Island, she was heartbroken.

Even though Maud had grieved Will's death at the time, her rereading of his letters on the night of March 16 brought about a belated and stormy mourning. In her journal she reports that she sobbed madly. She was inconsolable. She felt like a sick, frightened baby. In the small hours of the night, she detailed her feelings in a lengthy, melodramatic journal entry. What explains this excess of emotion? We know that menstrual symptoms wrought havoc on her efforts to control her emotions and caused many a "white night," as Maud called these sleepless nights. We know she was restless from being lonely, and felt caged during the long winter. And yet, it was a productive night. Sitting in her bed with her journal and pen, trying to control her hysteria, she began to examine her feelings for Will. It was her hunger for "sympathy" that had whirled up her nighttime emotional storm, she explained. It was not love, nor a sexual attraction that she had felt for Will. Rather, she desired to tell Will when something nice happened, when something nasty happened, and when nothing happened at all. As we read her account, it becomes clear that Maud was consolidating emotionally and mentally the meaning of a "kindred spirit," the intimate friendship that would become central for *Anne of Green Gables*.

In fact, the very first time Maud referred to "kindred spirits" in her journal, it was to describe her bond with Will and his sister Laura in 1891, and she was plumbing the depth of her psyche for inspiration by reliving the concept in the night of 1904. Will was a "brother" or a "jolly good comrade,"[15] just as she and Laura were "twin spirits in every way." She could share "the thoughts of [her] inmost soul" with Laura.[16] The ideal of the kindred spirit was all the more important to Maud because she lacked the security of a family. Despite her family pride, she felt often on the outside of the Macneill clan. Despite her love for her father, she knew she could not rely on him when she needed him. There was safety in a kindred spirit. It was the fellow feeling, the sharing of sentiments, and the agreement of minds that she missed most profoundly in her daily life. That stormy night in May, Maud charged the concept of the kindred spirits with powerful emotion that she would call up a year later in *Anne*.

Perhaps Maud may have seen, in her perusal of her magazines, American painter Asher B. Durand's painting *Kindred Spirits* (1849). Nowhere is Maud's concept of the kindred spirit better visualized than in this dramatic work, which celebrates the intimate friendship of two American artists—nature poet William Cullen Bryant and landscape painter Thomas Cole. In this romantic landscape painting, the two friends are enveloped by the wildness of the Catskills. The branch of an old, old tree provides the prominent arch that shelters the pair, who stand in intimate conversation high on a rock plateau; the lofty height evokes the friendship ideal, while the decomposing tree stumps in the foreground speak of death. It was Cole's untimely death in 1848 that had prompted New York art collector Jonathan Sturges to commission this painting along with the request that the two artists be painted as "kindred spirits" in the spirit of John Keats's poem "To Solitude" ("...it sure must be / Almost the highest bliss of human kind, / When to thy haunts two kindred spirits flee").[17]

The painting illustrates that the bond between kindred spirits continues to grow after death, just as Maud's relationship with Will intensified after his passing, elevating their bond into a timeless ideal. This adolescent friendship and Will's early passing provided the template for other idealized friendships in her life and fiction. Out of Maud's own loss grew the ideal of spiritual twosome-ness that outlives death and has permanence when nothing else does. In the sea of life's mutability she was seeking immutable ideals. These ideas and feelings all came together for Maud to create a friendship ideal of kindred spirits, a concept that would eventually draw legions of readers to *Anne*.

The Passing of Time

A few months after consolidating her emotions about loss, loneliness, and sympathetic fellowship, the long-unpublished journal entry of July 5, 1904, reveals Maud's preoccupation with the passing of time and the slipping away of youth. "I have changed very much," she wrote. "Ten years ago I was a schoolgirl," she explained, evoking a time when she was, like Anne, "too wildly elated" over joys, and "too much cast-down" over sorrows. She no longer suffered as intensely over trivial, inconsequential things. "I have learned to be tolerant of other people's whimsies, failings."[18] And yet we are not entirely persuaded by her emphatic assertion. The year 1904 marked Maud's thirtieth birthday. Yet her journal, so loquacious on other issues, makes no mention of this watershed birthday on November 30. It was a gap with a vengeance—evidence of Maud's self-censorship.

Anne of Green Gables and its apotheosis of girlhood sprang, in part, from Maud's own fear of aging, a fear she never openly confronted in her journal (as we shall also see later), but that was very much on her mind. At the cusp of thirty, she reread her old journal, reliving the summer of 1894, tasting the youth when she was nineteen-going-on-twenty and returning home from studying for her teacher's license at Prince of Wales College in Charlottetown—just as Anne Shirley would study at Queen's Academy in Charlottetown in the novel. Here, then, was the world that would make up many of the incidents of the last third of *Anne of Green Gables*, with its cramming for Latin, Geometry, and English exams; a world of youth and friendships and laughter in Charlottetown; as well as a world of healthy competition—although not nearly as fierce as the rivalry between Anne and Gilbert in the novel. It was a world when her relationship with school chum and bosom friend Amanda Macneill (nicknamed Mollie) was pleasant and uncomplicated on the occasions she returned to Cavendish, staying all night with Mollie talking and laughing.

Why could "carefree" childhood not last forever? Why could pleasures not last forever? As she relived her girlhood in her upstairs room through the pages of her journal, the laughter from long ago would have echoed within Evelyn Nesbit's photographic presence. The veil of longing covering these entries would have blended with Evelyn's wistful pose. Evelyn's reflective reverie and picture of nostalgia—looking, longing, missing, wanting—would have invested Maud's memory with romance and pleasure, but also with the aching feeling of loss and the melancholy that we see in Evelyn's eyes.

That time in Maud's life was rife with nostalgic memories: the old Cavendish school was being torn down; the old familiar world was disappearing. Maud was leaving home to teach in Bideford, Prince Edward Island, against her grandfather's will. Like pearls on the necklace of life, her journal records of yesteryear were an assembly of happy memories: picking apples in the old Macneill orchard, the rustling trees around the house where she slept, the old paths and lanes, and the murmuring sea— they all seemed "radiant with 'the glory and the dream.'"[19] Drawn from Wordsworth's "Ode: Intimations of Immortality from Recollections of Early Childhood," "The Glory and the Dream" would become the title of chapter thirty-six in *Anne of Green Gables*.[20] Unchanged where everything else had changed, her beloved trees always appeared to Maud the perfect symbol of permanence. The almost thirty-year-old author yearned for her early girlhood, when her life was full of dreams. Here, then, was the emotional basis for writing a novel, a sustained work of literature, about romanticized girlhood—a central subject in *Anne of Green Gables*.

The Architecture of Blue Castles: Ephraim Weber

At the same time that nostalgic Maud was reliving her own youth, crafty Maud was busy pushing herself beyond Sunday School mantras of truthfulness and simplicity. She enjoyed making things up, twisting, shaping, dramatizing, and transforming the real—even in her personal life, the borders between life and fiction had a way of becoming blurred. During the months that preceded the writing of *Anne of Green Gables*, she cultivated her building of airy fantasy castles in her correspondence with pen pal Ephraim Weber. Born in 1870 in Ontario, but living in Didsbury, Alberta, Ephraim was the ideal correspondent, and his role as a catalyst and muse in the birth of Anne has never been considered. A handsome man, he was also a dreamer who must have reminded her a little of her father. Plagued by asthma, he was single and restless and tried his hand at numerous jobs including farming, writing, studying, and teaching. A superb letter writer, he was intellectual and poetic. Most important, he listened to Maud. He admired her. Having grown up in a German-Mennonite community, he had spoken his first English sentence at age twelve, but loved Tennyson and Shakespeare. With his own writing career stalling, he was an ideal creative Muse for Maud, who generally felt most comfortable with men who were stimulating but less brilliant than she was. She could let herself go and share intimate details with this stranger that she would never tell the people of Cavendish. With the faraway Mennonite farmer and writer, who had never learned to dance because it was sinful, she felt free and safe to be daring and adventurous. Seduced by her dreamy personality and vivacious style, Ephraim encouraged her to share her dreams and fancies. In turn, Maud enjoyed writing flirtatious letters and offering glimpses of her rich personality to the admiring prairie bachelor to whom she transformed her mundane reality.

Maud's short story "A Correspondence and a Climax" (*Sunday Magazine*), published a year later, in August, gives insight into her relationship with Ephraim during this time. It is, in fact, a fascinating story about truth bending. Twenty-year-old romantic orphan Sidney Richmond escapes her dreary existence on a farm by corresponding with John Lincoln, who entertains her with breezy accounts of ranch life and his adventures on the far western plains. So alien and remote seems his world from snug Plainfield life that Sidney always has "the sensation of crossing a gulf" when reading his letters. Sidney is not interested in ever meeting him, but the letters she sends him, and his responses, are a lifeline in her lonely and dull existence. In her letters she makes up a wildly fantastic life of dances and pretty clothes and social activity. She indulges in a glamorous, though shamelessly fabricated life. When they finally meet, she has to confess the truth. Life was empty and ugly, she says: "So I wrote instead of the life I wanted to live—the life I did live in imagination."[21] Here was also the motto for Maud's life.

Though not nearly as fanciful as Sidney's letters, Maud's prose to Ephraim is rather whimsical. And while her correspondence from 1904 no longer exists, Ephraim's responses and the letters of 1905 give insight into their relationship. For instance, her journal details her desperate loneliness for the years preceding the writing of *Anne of Green Gables*, but if we were to read Maud's letters to Ephraim, we would be convinced that she was a social butterfly with no shortage of opportunities for literary and romantic stimulation. She liberally sprinkled her letters with allusions to other men in her life. In one letter she referred to two ministers with whom she had conversed about George Du Maurier's scandalous book *Trilby*, and "a friend in Scotland" who had just sent her a delightful gift, a mountain tansy. She had to end another letter because "some friends have called." Coquettish, she closed her letter with a romantic word picture of herself, a little pink rose nodding over her shoulder, the scent of a mayflower wafting from Cavendish to the Prairies.[22] She also promised to send him her short story "The Schoolmaster's Love Letters," ostensibly because it shows her stylistic experimentation. The story contains the erotic daydreams of a repressed schoolmaster, and even though hopelessly clichéd, the topic immediately caught Ephraim's attention. The flirtation was all on Maud's own terms, however. As soon as Ephraim tried to get closer, the door closed with an audible click. When he playfully invited her to go skating, presumably indulging a little fantasy of his own, she cut off the thread of the conversation: "Sorry, but I can't skate."[23] Years later, in 1926, when she published *The Blue Castle*, she dedicated the novel to "MR. EPHRAIM WEBER, M. A. WHO UNDERSTANDS THE ARCHITECTURE OF BLUE CASTLES."[24] The dedication says more about her than Ephraim: he was the man who allowed her to escape the mundane world by weaving her little fancies.

Given Maud's habit of shutting out prosaic reality and building airy castles, it comes as no surprise that she was becoming increasingly fascinated by split personalities and double consciousness as found in popular Gothic fiction, such as *Trilby* or *Dr. Jekyll and Mr. Hyde*. Her "dreamy self" was at home in the woods, she told Ephraim, while her "city self" came alive with people. But her personality had more than two or three sides, she averred: "there's a hundred of me.... It's better than being just two or three, I think—more exciting, more interesting." People who are only one must find life a bore, she added.[25] What is fascinating is that in chapter twenty of *Anne*, "A Good Imagination Gone Wrong," Anne Shirley would repeat Maud's sentence, describing her personality as compositing many different Annes. Of course, trouble comes from these many personalities but adds to the excitement, as Anne says.[26]

Maud's sketch of her own character for the eyes of Ephraim cannot be overestimated in creating the bridge to shaping Anne. In several letters she described herself as flirting with a more complex side of life that transcended Sunday school tradition. Simplicity and sunshine and truth telling were the heartbeat of Sunday school writing. Maud's imaginative side, the side that liked to dream and invent, was particularly fascinating to her. It was a side that went counter to Sunday school teaching and preaching but that she could explore in her letters to Ephraim. She was becoming bored with stories that inevitably culminated in a simple moral at the end. She was yearning for a heroine with richer blood—a more provocative personality.

First Glimpses of Anne

In fact, one such provocative heroine would anchor herself in Maud's mind just months before writing *Anne of Green Gables*. Maud would round out the year 1904 by rereading George du Maurier's novel *Trilby* in December, a novel she loved (and would reread and comment on many times in later years).[27] In it, androgynous seventeen-year-old model Trilby O'Ferrall undergoes transformations and displays multiple identities, providing a trajectory to Anne. A sensationally popular and iconic Gothic novel, *Trilby* was first serialized in *Harper's Monthly* in 1894 (presumably the year when Maud first read it). Creating a craze in North America, it gave its name to the Trilby hat, as well as to a town in Florida that was named Trilby in 1896. It also inspired spin-off novels, such as *The Phantom of the Opera*. *Trilby* is the story of "the three Musketeers of the Brush," the Laird, Little Billee, and Taffy, three painters working in the Latin Quarter in bohemian Paris. There, they meet the Scottish model Trilby, who poses in the nude (she calls it "for the altogether," a phrase that would become iconic with her character). Yet so good-hearted and sweet was Trilby that all of America, including Maud, fell in love with her.

Trilby's high-spirited personality anticipates Anne's exuberant temperament. They are kindred even in their appearance. Trilby's face "could scarcely be called quite beautiful at first sight, since the eyes were too wide apart, the mouth too large, the chin too massive, her complexion a mass of freckles."[28] But like Anne, she undergoes a transformation and becomes beautiful, losing her freckles, growing her hair, and revealing the sweetness of her mouth. Unlike *Anne of Green Gables*, *Trilby* is a mesmerizing tale in which the conniving hypnotist Svengali holds the heroine under his spell. In the end, Trilby dies, much to the chagrin of millions of readers who mourned her passing. The rereading of *Trilby* rounded out Maud's mood of that painfully introspective and lonesome year of 1904, in which glimpses of Anne were darting through her consciousness—yet without the fullness of her character or the clearly defined narrative arc.

Trilby was not the only imaginative influence on Anne. *Peter Pan*, by Scottish author J. M. Barrie, was first performed on the stage in December 1904, and Maud may well have read about its success in her magazines. In fact, Maud knew and admired Barrie's work, having not only read his novel *Tommy and Grizel* when it first appeared in 1902, but also having just recently reread it during the cold spell. "*Tommy* lives and is lovable in spite of—or is it because of—his faults," she commented in an unpublished journal entry of April 20, 1904. "I hate people, in books or out of them, who haven't any faults!!"[29] Here is an arc that leads to Anne. Endowed with plenty of faults, Anne breaks the template of the perfectly good and virtuous, but uninteresting, Sunday school heroine.

Maud's reading of adult literature would exert a substantial literary influence on *Anne of Green Gables*.[30] Hawthorne's melancholy adult romance *The House of the Seven Gables* (which we will hear more about in the Green Gables chapter of this volume) loosed a flood of tears in April 1903. She also read George Eliot's fiction, and the *Rubaiyat*, the ancient Persian verses famous for their sensuous celebration of wine and love. (The inscription in her personal library indicates that she had purchased the volume in 1903.) She mused about its epicurean philosophy that encouraged readers to enjoy the moment and not to worry about tomorrow.

But the most important literary text that filled her with undiluted pleasure during her reading marathon was Washington Irving's sensuous 1832 travelogue, *Tales of the Alhambra*. This was also the book that would have sparked Maud's favorite expression about building "castles in Spain." For Maud, Irving's book was a "gateway of an enchanted world," a book that allowed her to shut out "the real prosaic world," as she remembered years later in a letter to her long-time pen friend Mr. MacMillan.[31] The Alhambra, which means literally red in Arabic, referring to the rich color of the sun-baked stone, is a palace and fortress in Granada in Southern Spain. Surrounded by gorgeous woodlands and gardens, and enveloped in the spice of flowers and foods, the Alhambra was an important tourist destination during Maud's era. The residence of Moorish monarchs had an exotic appeal. With Irving as the guide through the palace, Maud was able to see, feel, and smell the dreamlike space in which there were recesses and alcoves for ottomans and couches on which "the voluptuous lords of the Alhambra indulged in that dreamy repose so dear to the Orientalists."[32] The water supply brought through the mountains by old Moorish aqueducts circulated throughout the palace, supplying the baths and fishpools. Just as Irving's delicious gardens and murmuring aqueducts invited Maud into a world of reveries and thralldom, so she would bewitch her readers with the murmuring brooks, the sensuous gardens, and the spicy fragrances of old orchards and woodlands in remote and solitary Avonlea. This world of enchantment would become Anne's natural habitat in *Anne of Green Gables*. Anne, too, has a guide, pragmatic

Marilla, who ensures that she does not get lost in the labyrinths of the romantic palaces and turrets. In the tradition of the Romantics, Maud projected the enchanted architecture onto the Cavendish landscape, configuring it through the lens of Romantic travel literature.

Anne is a voracious consumer of romantic poetry and plots, and so was Maud. A lover of Alfred, Lord Tennyson, Lord Byron, Elizabeth Browning, Walter Scott, and Henry W. Longfellow, Maud felt at home in the company of Romantics and Victorians. She roamed freely in the world of Hans Christian Andersen's fairy tales, and the fiction of Charles Dickens, George Eliot, the Brontës, and Jane Austen. Today many of these authors' books are found in her personal library in the University of Guelph Archives with inscriptions that reveal they were in her possession or read before she wrote *Anne*. Careful to acquire only those books that she considered masterpieces, she made sure she had read each book *before* buying it. She disliked modern fiction, such as Henry James. "I read 'What Maisie Knew' but couldn't discover what grisly knowledge Maisie *did* possess," she had quipped on February 15, 1902, when she had read the novel in Halifax.[33] Maud's protest was disingenuous. Of course, she liked to crawl into a book as one crawls underneath a warm blanket, seeking emotional pleasure and satisfaction. In fact, she loved reading in bed with a bag of butterscotch candy. And yet, she demanded her book be good literature, stimulating her with its language, its images, its ideas—and most important, its lively characters. Like Anne, Maud feasted on literature like a famished soul, entering the literary universe as if she were one of the characters.

Only on the surface did Maud seem unwilling to enter Henry James's modernist narrative maze, which involved the reader's intellect more than her emotions. In fact, she would create a dazzling narrative maze in her journal and fiction that would reveal profoundly modern sensibilities. She would poke fun at Anne Shirley's wild mimicking of conventional literature and cliché, thereby poking fun at herself and her own mimicking of formula fiction. She created a text with a playfully modern irony underneath its quaint and old-fashioned vocabulary and nostalgic yearning.

On October 31, 1904, the sea called to Maud. Crossing the fields and coming home down the hill, Maud noted that there was one star out, just as there would be one shining star when Anne first arrives at Green Gables (although Maud will transfer the season to spring, the season of youth). The unpublished journal entry is a rhapsody to her beloved brook: "Brooks are always in good spirits. They are always laughing."[34] This is the same familiar brook whose chatter, murmur, and laughter echoes through numerous journal pages—and, a few months later, would sound through the pages of *Anne of Green Gables*. Anne readers know well the "intricate, headlong brook" of the opening scene, which becomes a subdued and quiet little brook as it passes Mrs. Lynde's house; they come to know this brook intimately as it meanders from chapter to chapter, linking the episodes with its chattering sound.[35] Maud had first encountered this babbling brook in Tennyson's "Song of the Brook," which had appeared in the *Pansy Sunday Book* of her childhood: "I chatter, chatter, as I flow/ To join the brimming river;/ For men may come and men may go,/ But I go on forever."[36]

For something new to be born, something old has to die. The old adage applies to a year marked by Maud's most intensely lonely and introspective period, but also her most creative efforts. By December, she had published approximately thirty-seven short stories, a tremendous increase from the year before when she had published sixteen; she had made nearly $600 income from her pen, as she proudly tallied her productivity in her year-end report to Ephraim Weber.[37] Among these publications are numerous adoption stories, including "Freda's Adopted Grave" (*Zion's Herald*) and "The Softening of Miss Cynthia" (*Living Church*). In the latter, the adoptive single parent has to be cajoled into adopting. But, as Anne readers can see, in these stories Maud was busy writing bits and pieces of what would become *Anne of Green Gables*, although the author would presumably not have been aware that she was, in a way, pre-writing her novel, one that was also a rewriting of her earlier novel *A Golden Carol*.

Despite the glimpses of *Anne*, however, there is no evidence of Maud's planning, organizing, or structuring a novel during this year. There didn't appear to be any pushing for achieving an overall *gestalt*. There seems to be no awareness of a novel in the making. Why the mysterious silence and delay, when elements of Anne were so obviously present during this period? Despite Maud's increased productivity, there was something amiss. In reading her journal and correspondence, we cannot help but sense that, despite her prolific output, she had reached a stalemate in her creative life; that she had become caught in the rut of writing formula stories for money. Moreover, writing a sustained work of fiction, such as a novel, requires just the right balance of solitude and social stimulus, and the balance was not right that year, given the disruptions caused by uncongenial houseguests such as her Uncle Leander, a regular summer guest along with his family. At the same time, here in this very restlessness of the year 1904 is also the evidence of Maud submerging herself into her innermost and shadowed crevices, reaching for a new level of literary writing. The restlessness we sense behind her pen is the necessary whirl of emotion that precedes the writing of a truly inspired piece of literature.

FOUR

The Orphan Girl and the Snow Queen

I was so scrawny and tiny and nothing but eyes, but...mother thought I was perfectly beautiful....I'm glad she was satisfied with me anyhow; I would feel so sad if I thought I was a disappointment to her—because she didn't live very long after that, you see. She died of fever when I was just three months old. I do wish she'd lived long enough for me to remember calling her mother.
—*Anne Shirley to Marilla Cuthbert about the death of her mother*[1]

The start into the New Year of 1905 was as rocky as a crossing of the Straits during high winds. But Maud had nobody but herself to blame. She, and only she, was responsible for brewing up the emotional storm that let loose just a few months before writing *Anne of Green Gables*. As the old year turned into the new, heralding the months that would give birth to Anne, the mental and emotional conditions that would give shape to our exuberant redhead were intensifying. The time has come for us to enter the homestead and get close to elusive Maud.

Set back from the wild north shore, the legendary ship graveyard of the North Atlantic, the Macneill homestead was nestled in the woodlands. Yielding to decades of fiercely gusting northern winds, the large apple tree in front of the kitchen window had become a wind-swept statue, creating a gate-like entrance to the house. In the kitchen, a low-ceilinged and white washed room, the curtains were drawn. A fire was flickering in the old cast-iron woodstove. Next to it stood Maud's bathtub, neatly tucked away, as everything had to be. The old homestead had no bathroom, and Maud was accustomed to creating her makeshift bath every fortnight. A proud, introspective woman with her mother's thick mass of hair, Maud stood disrobed, her skin smooth and white. Her figure was petite, with delicate curves that would not be lost on her many suitors. She carefully stepped into the tub and eased herself into the water, letting the heat envelop her body. Some petals, harvested from the summer's bounty, released their fragrance, blending with the smell of the wood and the fire. She closed her eyes and sighed with comfort. Consumed by the pleasurable warmth, Maud smiled and her thoughts began to drift.

Crackling and sputtering, the woodstove radiated its heat throughout the quiet kitchen. Grandmother Macneill's bedroom, off the kitchen, was still. She had gone to sleep at nine o'clock. As usual, the ritual of going to sleep had been fraught with tension, as Grandmother's fidgeting around the kitchen always started like clockwork and signaled it was time for both her and Maud to go to bed. At age eighty, Grandmother was set in her ways. She looked upon bathing with suspicion, as if it was some kind of weird, pagan ritual. She was truculent and resentful when Maud insisted on staying up to take a bath.

Born in April 1824, in Dunwich, England, Lucy Ann Woolner Macneill had arrived in Prince Edward Island at age twelve, had married at age twenty, and had had her first child at age twenty-one. A farmer's wife, postmistress, and mother of six, Grandmother Macneill was practical and reserved. She found herself baffled and irritated by Maud's dreamy, odd, and stubborn ways. One imagines the two women sitting at the dinner table with Maud occasionally staring into space, as Anne does in the novel. Grandmother Macneill was not easy to live with, but she was the only mother Maud had ever known.

Canadian writer Margaret Atwood sees the growing relationship between Anne and Marilla as the novel's emotional core.[2] Yet Maud's journal account of her relationship with Grandmother Macneill would suggest that the imagined love bond between Marilla and Anne was written on the wall of silence that was part of the homestead's architecture. The love that unites Marilla and Anne in fiction was sparked by Grandmother Macneill and Maud's awkward rubbing against each other during the long and cold winter months when the winds were howling outside and irritation was mounting inside. Grandmother's reserve could be like the icy wind that blew across the Atlantic during that long winter of 1905. But Maud's emotional storm was also connected with the memory of her mother.

Frozen in the Past: Clara

On Monday night, January 2, 1905, Maud had reread an old letter that a girlfriend had sent to her mother, Clara Macneill, long before her marriage. Maud would let her imagination travel through the girlish prose, following the little allusions and the jokes, ferreting out their intimate meaning and mysteries as she liked to ferret out the secrets of the brook in the woodlands behind the house. And by delving so deeply into the past, she brought herself into a state of upset. That night her brooding induced such stinging grief about her young mother as she had never experienced it before. Coming just months before writing *Anne*, a novel whose plot is prompted by the heroine's loss of mother and father, this self-inflicted storm of mourning cannot be overestimated in the shaping of her book.

We know very little about Maud's mother, for nobody ever spoke about Clara in the Macneill home. Grandmother Macneill had sealed her pain inside. Maud's great-aunt, Mary Lawson, Grandfather Macneill's sister, prepared biographies of the other family members but left a mysterious blank on Clara. It is as if her life and death were shrouded in silence. There was a formal portrait of Clara that overlooked the parlor from above the colonial mantelpiece. Her face was eternally young and pretty, but the over-accessorized pose betrayed a lack of stylistic maturity, one that Maud would never have been guilty of. The upswept hairstyle was unflattering and contrived. Clara may well have been the life of a party (a suitor was said to have killed himself over her beauty),[3] yet neither of the two photos available suggests that she would have possessed that wit or the intelligence that Maud valued in spiritual kin such as her great-aunt Mary, who was a brilliant conversationalist and literary mind. Would Clara have understood her daughter's odd dreams? Or would she have been like her sister Annie, jolly and lovable but no kin to Maud's poetic soul? Even worse, would she have been like Emily, who nagged and found fault and sneered at Maud's literary efforts? Frozen in time, Clara's portrait gave no answers. Had Clara left a letter to her daughter, Maud would have been able to bring her to life. But without words, she was a ghost. Still, there was a glimmer of hope: Just recently her aunt Eliza Macneill, a girlhood friend of her mother's, had reassured her that Clara was a poetical girl, not a bit like her two sisters.[4]

These and other thoughts built up in Maud's mind in early January 1905 and culminated in an anguished cry for her mother: "*She* would have understood—*she* would have sympathized."[5] Maud's cry for sympathy echoes a popular mother's column of the era. "Again it is sympathy; sympathy first, last and always sympathy," Mrs. Birney had written in the April 1904 *Delineator*, urging mothers to show kindness and understanding toward their little ones, especially toward sensitive and temperamental children. Maud had evidently absorbed the message advocated by Mrs. Theodore W. Birney, the Honorary President of the American National Congress of Mothers. A mother embodies "the sympathy which *comprehends*, which inspires and encourages to fresh effort."[6] That elusive "sympathy" was missing from Maud's grandparents' parenting, causing the lonely adult to despair of ever filling so cavernous a hole. In Mrs. Birney's column, Maud found the ammunition to critique the child-rearing skills of her grandparents.

In fact, Maud's lengthy journal entry of January 2 reads like an evidentiary brief to a grand jury. Putting pen to paper that night, Maud spoke in the voice of prosecutor. The accused: her grandparents; the victim: herself as the orphaned child. Missing is the redeeming note of humor that is the hallmark of her fiction. Her tone was dead serious: "The older I grow the more I realize what a starved childhood mine was *emotionally*," she lamented. In just one such example, Grandmother Macneill refused to console her as a nine-year-old when her kitten died. Instead, the farmwoman had turned the event into a teaching moment, just as Marilla would apply a practical and not always sensitive moral to each and every situation.[7] "It is a great misfortune for a child to be brought up by old people," Maud concluded to her grand jury that Monday night. The gap of youth and old age cannot be bridged, she noted, except by "exceptional natures that do not grow old in heart."[8]

Here lay the core of her loneliness, the shadow that had always followed her. Here in her own entrapment and rebellion against parental authorities lay also a powerful emotional spark for *Anne of Green Gables*. Only in fiction could she dream her way out of her prison; only in fiction could she bridge the insurmountable gulf between youth and old age that was at the root of her loneliness since early childhood.

The realization that she was a charity child with no rights and no inheritance was equally painful. In March 1898, when Grandfather Macneill died in the middle of a Saturday afternoon, struck down by a heart attack, Maud had rushed home by sleigh and train from Lower Bedeque on the South shore where she had been boarding as a teacher and romancing Herman Leard. Cold and solitary, Alexander Macneill lay in the darkening parlor, just as her mother had lain there two decades earlier. He had willed the farm to his eldest son John. All property and monies went to Grandma Lucy. Annie and Emily were left one hundred dollars each. Maud was not mentioned in his will, which he had made a year earlier when Maud was teaching and boarding in Belmont.[9] His last wishes spelled out Maud's status: no amount of dreaming could remove the bald fact that she was a charity case. In the wake of his death she would be expected to care for her grandmother in order to earn her stay in the home. Her pride was hurt. She was angry. She did not really resolve this cold anger but used it to fuel her dream of Matthew, the kindred spirit who fulfills Anne's desires. Eleven-year-old Anne finds in sixty-year-old Matthew a spontaneous and immediate kindred spirit. Shy, gentle Matthew is the opposite of cranky Grandfather Macneill, who had been a stern father until Maud left the homestead. That Marilla opens her heart to love Anne at the very same time that Maud's own grandmother, with increasing age, was becoming more recalcitrant further underscores the novel's role as a wish fulfillment dream. In a fairy tale the constraints of real life can smoothly be turned into their opposite. Just how much Maud was operating within fiction and fairy tales is seen in a singular event that would also have revived and amplified the entwining of birth and death that was such a key element of her own personal narrative.

Birth and Death Entwined

In early February 1905, Maud's cousin George Campbell's baby boy Jack died of pneumonia. Maud traveled to Park Corner to stay with the family for two weeks. Relieved to be away from Cavendish, Maud's mentioning of the boy's death is almost perfunctory, as she describes this visit largely in terms of the distraction it provides to her; there is no mention of the family's grieving, no mention of the baby's name, and no mention of the funeral in her journal entry of March 3. In her March 7 letter to Ephraim she mentions it only as a social visit. She was fond of her cousins at Park Corner, so how could Maud be so callous? The situation provides a window into her psyche. Maud, who would soon write with great compassion about Anne, had a way of subtly closing off her feelings toward real-life suffering. With the center of her universe fueled by dreams and emotional storms, the rest of the world sometimes had a way of becoming peripheral, perhaps shielding the production of her art from the deep core of her imagination. This aloofness in real life, which she was able to mask in society, contrasts with the finely feathered sensitivity with which Maud explores her own feelings—past and present. As an artist, she had a way of distilling, filtering, and channeling emotions into her literature.

In fact, it seems that she worked the images she saw into her novel. Driving the twenty-one kilometers of hill and wood, river and shore from Cavendish to Park Corner and back that February, Maud would have twice passed her birth place located in the lovely little town of Clifton (today New London). The "small, yellowish-brown house" near the harbor held a fascination for her, as her journal entries from a few years earlier show. Clara and Monty and Maud had lived in Clifton only a year, where Monty ran the general store.[10] It was a time when the family was complete and happy. It was the Eden of Maud's life, and, sadly, she did not remember it. But she could imagine it. Today the restored Lucy Maud Montgomery Birthplace is a tourist destination during the summer, with displays of her scrapbooks and wedding dress. As a girl, Maud was saddened to see that each year left her birth house looking a little shabbier than before. In the early chapters of *Anne of Green Gables*, the house makes a cameo appearance. Maud lovingly restored the house to its brilliant yellow, scrubbing off the layers of brown dirt and sealing the magic of her birthplace in "a weeny-teeny little yellow house...[with] honeysuckle over the parlor window."[11] It became the idealized house in which Anne was born, though Anne *imagines* it as such; Anne never sees it until the 1915 sequel *Anne of the Island*. Perhaps, in 1905, that was the contentedness Maud was dreaming of instead of dwelling on the baby that had just died.

Inside the Ice Palace

An undeniable northern and Canadian element contributed to the shaping of *Anne of Green Gables*: the seemingly eternal winter of 1905, one of the fiercest in Island history. Large ice drifts and hummocks were hemming in the north shore of Prince Edward Island. Ice, sleet, snow drifts, and storms changed the pastoral isle into a frosty prison, keeping farmers and families cooped up. Mountainous ice shards transformed the white shore into a surreal landscape. The icebreakers, *The Minto* and *The Stanley*, provided winter passenger and mail-service runs, but found themselves routinely blocked by ice in the straits. Unable to move, they prevented the hay from being delivered for livestock and the mail from being delivered to the post office. The Island was cut off from the world. When the icebreakers finally succeeded in making their way, the railway lines were blocked, and the mail could not be delivered.

The Macneill homestead was crowded on all sides by mountains of snow. On February 25, the *Examiner* reported that a Prince Edward Island farmer dug a twenty-meter tunnel through the snowdrifts to reach the livestock in the barns.[12] By early March, the snow drifts in front of Maud's homestead were six meters high. What was a single woman to do during the worst winter in Island history? She shoveled snow in the morning, wrote for a couple of hours, typewrote in the afternoon, and kept her hands otherwise busy with lace work and dishes and correspondence. On good days, Maud was prowling in the snow, sensitive to the beauty of winter and taking pictures of the historic snow drifts, pictures that she would insert into her journal years later. She appreciated the brooding stillness of the winter landscape, but the romance of her glittering ice palace was short lived.

"Another storm! No mail! Abominably dismal!" was Maud's scream in an unpublished journal entry.[13] She was suffering from an acute state of cabin fever that thrust her thinking and feeling inward, into her world of dreams. This intensified period of introspection was all the more excruciating as the lonely and restless months from the year before accumulated into a long period of turmoil and isolation. But perhaps this intense period of contemplative solitude was necessary for the seeds from her life to blossom into her novel. Flowers in all shapes and colors dominated the landscape of her dreams. To her beleaguered mind, the snow drifts were a mausoleum under which her flowers and her hope were buried.

At night she dreamed of daffodils and tulips. While sleet pellets drummed against the western kitchen window in February, Maud sat by the wood stove with the flower seed catalogue on her knees. She was day-dreaming, her mind arranging her spring garden: a bed of dahlias, a clump of lilies, and a patch of asters. The old-fashioned spring and summer gardens would run riot in *Anne*, long catalogues of flowers without end. "There were rosy bleeding-hearts and great splendid crimson peonies; white, fragrant narcissi and thorny, sweet Scotch roses; pink and blue and white columbines"; there were also "clumps of southernwood and ribbon grass and mint; purple Adam-and-Eve, daffodils, and masses of sweet clover."[14] This fictional flower garden grew from Maud's pent-up wintertime dreams and frustrations. Maud's vivid word paintings make us see, smell, feel, and hear the gardens and orchards of her dreams through a filter of aching pleasure and longing. The intensity of life and imagery seemed to be in proportion to her anguish and imprisonment. The flower garden was also one of the few passions that Maud shared with Grandmother Macneill, who, unlike Marilla, loved flowers and encouraged Maud to decorate the house with them.

The winter imprisonment lasted into April, when slush and mud forbade even a little walk at sundown. Bitter and sick at heart, Maud released her feelings in her journal. She took refuge in daydreams. "I'm always glad when the end of the day comes—these days at least—and I can get to bed," she confided in an unpublished journal entry. "I like to curl up by myself and dream gorgeous waking dreams—brilliant affairs where I have everything I haven't got in the real world. They help me a lot, those blessed dreams."[15] Maud does not tell us what her dreams are about, but they were presumably the fuel that would soon drive *Anne of Green Gables* with a deeply personal charge that would finally crack the polished façade of the formula orphan story.

She was "pegging" at her writing, she told Ephraim in March.[16] Nothing in her correspondence or journal indicates anything but the regular run-of-the-mill toil of churning out formula stories. And yet, for those of us looking for Anne, the calm concealed the storm underneath. Amazingly, as we look for Anne in Maud's short fiction during this period, we discover a number of prequels to *Anne of Green Gables*. Always disciplined and organized, Maud numbered her stories in the chronological order of her writing, allowing us to see that the world of Anne was already vibrant and alive.

A Prequel and a Timely Invitation

Rippling with personal emotion, "The Understanding of Sister Sara" is Maud's story of how Anne Shirley's parents met. The story was published in the Michigan magazine *The Pilgrim* in August. In fact, Beatrice (a short leap to the more prosaic name of Anne's mother, Bertha) is an orphan and dreamer, matched with a pragmatic sister, Sara. "Oh, I wish I had a mother! She could understand," says Beatrice in the story, using Maud's very own words from her journal that winter. Beatrice meets Walter Shirley, the name of Anne Shirley's father in the novel. He is handsome and distinguished with dark and inscrutable eyes. Beatrice falls head-over-heels in love with him. They keep their engagement secret. "I want to dream my dreams first," Beatrice says. Clinging to romance, the fanciful Beatrice wants nothing more than to shut out the real world for fear it might interfere with her dream. In the story, the Shirley couple is described as "a pair of romantic children," a metaphoric arc that leads to Anne Shirley's parents in *Green Gables*, who were "a pair of babies and as poor as church mice."[17] Here in this little-known short story is the prequel to Anne; all it took was a few minor changes. Other stories contained similar glimpses of Anne, such as Maud's formula story "The Running Away of Chester" that she had published in *Boys' World* in late 1903, in which several sentences, including freckle-faced orphan Chester's desperate determination for a home ("I'll try to do everything you want me to do") anticipates orphan Anne's ("I'll try to do and be anything you want me, if you'll only keep me.").[18]

Meanwhile the *Sunday School Advocate* in New York, to which Maud would contribute stories that year, was running a serial entitled *The Major's Sunshine*. "An Adopted Daughter" was the title of the first chapter, featuring a little orphan girl with a glorious head of golden hair who charms the aging Major into adopting her.[19] Sunshine girls and sunshine stories, with mottos such as "When things go wrong, smile and find a better way," were popular in Sunday school magazines, offering the proverbial chicken soup for the soul during the cold months of winter.[20] These were the formula stories that offered a blueprint for *Anne*. They reflected the self-help impulse embedded in American culture and presented a popularized transcendentalism with their belief in the innate goodness of humanity.

Add to these influences from New York a timely invitation from Toronto, and the stage was set for a sequence of events that would lead to the creation of *Anne*. In her March 7 letter to Ephraim Maud described receiving a letter with the return address of 20 Richmond Street East, Toronto, the headquarters for the Canadian Sunday School Publications and the Presbyterian Sabbath School Publications.[21] They were asking her to submit some of her stories. Keen on featuring Canadian contributions, the editors were recruiting promising and established writers from across Canada. Publishing three papers for juveniles of varying ages, they were looking for good stories, as well as essays and sketches that would appeal to young people.[22] Maud was selling her stories to the flourishing American Associated Sunday School Publications but was intrigued to hear that the Canadian rates were competitive. Flattered by the attention and never one to sit on her hands when it came to publishing, Maud had promptly mailed a girls' story of 2,500 words to Toronto. Entitled "Lavender's Room," the story contained the character of Mrs. Lynde, and was published in *East and West: A Paper for Young Canadians* in early February. Already, Mrs. Lynde, anticipating the character in the novel, was "one of those people who pride themselves on saying just what they think, and who always seem to be thinking unpleasant things."[23] Maud received five dollars. This kind of speed and professionalism was refreshing to a writer who desired a decent income for her literary activities. In fact, the new contact provided a new source of regular, if modest, income and she would publish numerous stories in *East and West* and in *King's Own* (the Sabbath School Publication of the Presbyterian Church in Toronto). Exuberant Maud was pleased with her new "discovery." Here was a "really truly Canadian affair that opens its eyes and says 'papa' and 'mamma,'" she enthused in her March 7, 1905, letter to aspiring writer Ephraim Weber.[24] She warmly recommended the Toronto syndicate to the writer in Didsbury, Alberta, reassuring him that the periodicals were of the same quality as their American counterparts.

That year, Canada was pushing westward; Alberta and Saskatchewan would become provinces in the year Maud was to write *Anne of Green Gables*. There was obviously a market for stories with Canadian content— even in the United States. Other writers were also being tapped for content. "What we are in need of are good Canadian stories," wrote Miss Elizabeth Ansley, the associate editor of *Boys' World*, to the Mohawk-Canadian poet Pauline Johnson in November. "We have experienced considerable difficulty in procuring Canadian stories with the real patriotic ring—stories where the loyalty does not seem forced."[25] It was a magazine to which Maud had also been contributing since at least 1903. They paid six dollars per one thousand words. As even the famous Pauline Johnson discovered, stories were lucrative enough to make a living.

For Maud, the invitation was timely and tangible encouragement to set future Sunday school stories in Canada—a fact she delighted in. One wonders to what extent it was this Toronto invitation that prompted her to set her new Sunday school serial *Anne of Green Gables* in Prince Edward Island, Canada. It is very plausible that she first intended her *Anne* serial, with its distinct Prince Edward Island setting, for Toronto's Sunday school magazine *East and West*. Unfortunately, she never named the "ephemeral" religious paper she had in mind for the *Anne* serial, but her description most certainly echoed her opinion of *East and West*.[26]

According to a brief journal entry of August 16, 1907, her first account of how *Anne* came about, it was during the spring of 1905 that she turned to her notebook in search of inspiration for the new serial she wanted to write for a Sunday school paper. She found an old, faded entry written years earlier: "Elderly couple apply to orphan asylum for a boy. By mistake a girl is sent them."[27] Here in this stunningly simple entry was the kernel for the novel. There was nothing here yet about a fiery redhead, a passionate bosom friendship, kindred spirits, or Avonlea—there was nothing yet about any of the classic topics and characters and settings that would make Anne so beloved and memorable.

An Orphan Girl from Nova Scotia and a Fateful Mistake

The girl in the entry was Maud's adopted cousin Ellen Macneill, but there was a story behind the entry. Born in 1889, the little orphan girl with soft hair and hazel eyes had come from Halifax accompanied by her five-year-old brother Ray. On September 22, 1892, two prosperous Cavendish farmers, Pierce Macneill and John C. Clark, had arrived in their buggies at the Hunter River train station only to discover that there had been a mistake: instead of two orphan boys, a little girl and her brother disembarked from the train. Despite the mistake, Pierce and his wife Rachael, who were childless, adopted the three-year old girl and named her Ellen. Ellen's birth date and year had never been officially recorded, and, for the rest of her life, Ellen would celebrate her birthday on September 22, the day she arrived in Cavendish and found a home with the Macneills. Seventeen-year old Maud promptly recorded the event in her notebook.[28]

According to information provided by Ellen's daughter Ruth Gallant in Hamilton, Ontario, and corroborated by a turn-of-the-century census report, Ellen was born in Nova Scotia and her ethnic background was English.[29] A Canadian-born orphan, she was not a Barnardo child, as claimed in the biographical book dedicated to her and simply titled *Ellen*.[30] During Maud's era, under the farm immigration programme, Barnardo children were sent to Canada by the Barnardo organization, a British society named after Dr. Thomas Barnardo. In fact, *Anne of Green Gables* was one of the first novels to refer to the Barnardo boys, albeit in pejorative terms, when Matthew suggests that they adopt a Barnardo boy to help with the farm work and Marilla declares that she wants "a born Canadian" boy, not "London street Arabs."[31] She was referring to children of no fixed residence who wandered the streets of London. The Canadian agency for the Barnardo Organization placed advertisements in the Canadian newspapers. Prospective parents filled out applications so that the children could be directly transferred to their new homes on the day they arrived in Canada. The idea was to ship them quickly to the designated farms, minimizing cost to the government.

Unfortunately, mistakes were frequent, and since many adoptive parents preferred boys to help with the farm work, there was always a shortage of boys.[32] Perhaps it was the error—the orphan girl sent in lieu of the boy—that made this ordinary adoption more memorable. As for Maud, she was attracted to the fateful mistake in this Cavendish adoption story. And the fact that it took place so close to home, within her own family, would also have encouraged her to use Cavendish as a setting.

Pierce Macneill's farm was on the road to Stanley Bridge in what was known as Pierce's Hollow, not far from the Macneill homestead and across from the place now known as Green Gables.[33] When *Anne of Green Gables* was published, people immediately recognized Pierce's Hollow as one of the novel's landmarks, only with a different name—Lynde's Hollow. The year the orphaned Ellen arrived in Cavendish, seventeen-year-old Maud would have encountered the little girl, for Maud was no stranger to Pierce Macneill's home. In fact, it was here that Maud regularly picked up Selena Robinson, the Cavendish teacher who was boarding with Pierce and Rachael; it was also from Pierce that she occasionally borrowed a buggy. Moreover, Maud would have talked with Ellen at the Macneill post office, for Ellen picked up the family's mail. Maud may even have taught Ellen in the Cavendish school, when she occasionally replaced the regular teacher in 1903. Yet Maud never mentioned any of these encounters and her later judgment of Ellen was rather insensitive and defensive: "There is no resemblance of any kind between *Anne* and Ellen Macneill who is one of the most hopelessly commonplace and uninteresting girls imaginable."[34] Ellen was a quiet and modest little girl, without the mettle to become the silver-tongued heroine of our story. Sadly, Maud felt the need to denigrate Ellen, to whom she owed, after all, an important spark for her book. It was a spark, however, that she was loathe to acknowledge: "Ellen Macneill never crossed my mind while I was writing the book."[35] Maud was furious that people did not sufficiently recognize the power of her imagination.

The Flash of Anne

It would, in fact, take a unique blend of weather, memories, and influences for Maud's inspired imagination to give birth to Anne that spring. We know that Maud always carefully mapped out her stories and serials before writing them. She would first "brood up" a character, as she called it, and then over weeks and months "block out" chapters and incidents and map the architecture of her writing in a meticulous process she called "spade work." To Maud, writing was like planning and planting her beloved garden. In late March, the spring rains brought a thaw and Maud's troubled mind soared. The thought of being in her garden and exploring the orchard infused her with life. After a long and exhausting winter, spring was a resurrection. In early April, she went into the garden amid slush and mud and took the spruce boughs off her tulip and daffodil beds. At the sight of the new spikes of life, she felt a flash of pleasure.

April finally brought the turning point. A spark was needed to bring together all of the different influences, images and memories; to galvanize the feelings and dreams; and channel them into the creation of a serial. Did the inspired book require a fairy-tale intervention of sorts? Perhaps it was a happy coincidence that the world-renowned author of fairy tales, Hans Christian Andersen, born in Odense in Denmark on April 2, 1805, celebrated his centenary in April 1905. Maud had most certainly read the April issue of the *Delineator*, which featured a biographical appreciation, "Hans Christian Andersen: The Friend of the Children" (along with a piece on Tennyson's "Elaine," which Anne enacts in chapter twenty-eight, "An Unfortunate Lily Maid"). The brilliant Danish author was quoted as saying, "I am the Ugly Duckling." Not only was he poor and homely, with his huge feet and hands, but his feminine and bookish and dreamy nature always seemed to make him the odd person out. (Rumors about his alleged homosexuality had been surfacing even in the early twentieth century, although the *Delineator* made no mention of these.) His critics reviled his lack of education and, as the *Delineator* article pointed out, "Andersen's sensitive soul suffered no little from this petty persecution."[36] Yet with his fancy he had conquered the world. He always remembered his father, a shoemaker with a poetical mind, who would often sit gazing before him as if in a dream. When his father died, the young Hans

Christian simply believed that it was the ice-maiden that had come to get him. This childhood experience later led him to write the fairy tale "The Snow Queen," the story of the orphan boy Kay who is abducted by the Snow Queen and becomes cruel as a result of a splinter from an ice mirror stuck in his heart. Embedded in the story of "The Snow Queen" was the fear of the eternal winter, and the emotional chill that can freeze the human heart. This was the story that Maud would have read in the *Delineator* in April.

One of the early chapters, "Morning at Green Gables," pays tribute to Hans Christian Andersen, whose work Maud had first read with Well Nelson, the little orphan who had boarded with the Macneills along with his brother, releasing her from her excruciating loneliness. Outside Anne Shirley's window in the east gable room is a cherry tree, its blossoms so heavy you can't see the leaves. She names the tree "Snow Queen." We delight in Anne's creativity and imaginative flights of fancy, but the name is also a tribute to the Danish fairy-tale author whom Maud loved. Not only she delighted in "The Ugly Duckling" and "The Snow Queen;" these tales were popular with millions of readers then and now. *Anne of Green Gables* is in essence the story of the ugly duckling.[37] Anne is the odd outsider, seemingly ugly and unloved, who turns out to be the beautiful swan in the end. It is the story of the Snow Queen, in which old, emotionally frozen characters are awakened by the exuberance of youth and spring.

Not only were flowers stirring that spring, but also the ghosts of the past were rustling their chains. On May 21, Maud once again reread her journal of the Prince Albert period, traveling in spirit through the old friendships and revivifying the kindred spirits of Will Pritchard and Laura Pritchard. She cried and mourned, her father's memory was so vivid: "Oh, my dear father. How far away your grave is! You should be lying by my young mother's side near yonder in the churchyard."[38] With her lost mother's unquiet spirit stirring in the parlor, it was time to summon up the familiar waking dream of reassembling her family. In real life she had been failed, but in fiction, in her own fairy tale, she could realize the dream. *Anne* was a wish fulfillment dream, one of "those blessed dreams" that never failed her.

In the theatre of Maud's mind, the stage was set, the curtain rising. Anne was suddenly flashing in Maud's fancy, adorned with fiery red braids and fully christened down to the *e*, as Maud would later describe in her memoir. Just as the garden burst into life, so all of the different influences, fuelled by the release of pent-up creative energy after a long hibernation, were finally coming together. Anne was a girl with infectious optimism, with enough charm to soften even the most hardened inhabitants of the village of Avonlea. Romantic Anne was a pagan wood nymph gazing up at the stars and dreaming, like Evelyn Nesbit. She was the orphan girl who was supposed to have been a boy, like Ellen Macneill. There were also some traces of Trilby in the freckled high-spirited witch who conquered the world with her magnetic personality. Intelligent and verbally dexterous, Anne was a dreamer and appealed to the author with her vivid imagination. "Somehow or other she seemed very real to me and took possession of me to an unusual extent. Her personality appealed to me," Maud later recalled in her journal.[39]

Like her readers, Maud was enthralled by her character. Presumably what Maud would have noticed first about Anne was that she was more alive than other girls. Her exuberance glowed from inside. She seemed to embody life. Her eyes were luminous and bright. Spunky, red-haired Anne was already running away from Maud and breaking the formulaic orphan mold. By injecting her own feelings and dreams into this lively and gangly figure, Maud was giving birth to a "real-life" character, throwing Sunday school morals to the wind, as she would later remember it. She had meant to write a serial but the heroine took such possession of her that she would soon decide to turn the serial into a novel. Not only was Maud flying high, but also millions of readers would fly with her soon.

As Anne skipped through Maud's imagination, fleet of foot and fleet of mind, somehow she was liberated. Here was a new character who surprised Maud and excited her. A character who shared her own dreams and passions, and some of her complex contradictions. She was now ready to begin writing—as yet unconscious that she was embarking on a story that would change her life and make literary history.

PART 2

Writing Anne
Spring 1905 — Winter 1907

FIVE

Romantic Orchards, Kindred Spirits, and a Spring Flirtation

"... What did that tree, leaning out from the bank, all white and lacy, make you think of?" she asked.

"Well now, I dunno," said Matthew.

"Why, a bride, of course — a bride all in white with a lovely misty veil. I've never seen one, but I can imagine what she would look like...."

—Anne during her first ride with Matthew[1]

The spring of 1905 was sweeping into Cavendish like a late lover, swaying through the arms of the trees in the Macneill orchard, teasing the apple blossoms and mayflowers, and frolicking in the sweet-scented purple clover. Catching the last, dying rays of light at the end of a warm and rainy day, Maud was perched on the end of the kitchen table at the western window, her feet on the high old-fashioned sofa, her portfolio on her knees.[2] This was one of her favorite roosts.

With an ease borne from years of writing, she penned a title in the top center of the page—*Anne of Green Gables*. The ink rippled across the page as easily and swiftly as a rejuvenated brook in spring:

> Mrs. Rachel Lynde lived just where the Avonlea road dipped
> down into a little hollow traversed by a brook that had its source
> away back in the woods of the old Cuthbert place; ....[3]

And she was off! Here was the "wild headlong" brook she had so often communed with since childhood. It was the streamlet in the Cavendish woods that ran below the Webbs' farm and through Pierce's Hollow. "I go there nearly every day and love the spot," she had written to her Scottish pen friend George MacMillan on November 9, 1904, referring to the little bridge spanning the brook.[4] In Maud's universe, the brook, Lover's Lane, and the orchard were timeless. "Dear old brook!" she had written in an unpublished December 1892 journal entry. "Many a fair dream have I spun over your dancing silver in days gone by, when the mosses and ferns grew on your banks and blue summer skies mirrored themselves in your pebbly shallows."[5] By evoking the brook like a Muse, she was entering a world where the real blended with the fictional, the past with the present—a world where time stood still.

With her busy pen in hand, Maud was soon absorbed in choreographing the actions of her characters—the town's busybody Mrs. Rachel Lynde making her way to Green Gables, Marilla Cuthbert sitting in the kitchen, suspicious of the sunshine, and gentle Matthew driving up the hill, wearing a white collar on a regular working day. "What was Matthew up to?" Maud was engrossed in the goings-on of Avonlea when the red kitchen door opened and a visitor entered. No more of Anne was written that night.

It was the minister, the man who had taken the Cavendish Presbyterian Church and the church of the nearby village of Stanley two years earlier. The Reverend Macdonald had only just recently moved from Stanley to Cavendish, and was now boarding at John Laird's pretty homestead. He had come to pick up his mail from the post office. This was his first call at the homestead and he lingered to talk with Maud. With black eyes and thick black hair, the thirty-four-year-old was a handsome man with an elegant, chiseled face and endearing dimples when he smiled. His posture was dignified and priestly. There is a remarkable intensity in the few photographs taken of him from the era. In his 1903 graduation photo, for instance, his hand is clenched to a half-fist, every pore of his body exuding the upright citizen. He seems not entirely comfortable with posing for an audience. His first name was Ewen but Maud would consistently misspell his name as Ewan, a habit that has been adopted by scholars.

Ewan was born at Bellevue in the eastern part of Prince Edward Island. The offspring of Christy Cameron and Alexander Macdonald, Ewan was raised in a family of ten children. The Scottish farming family was not rich but valued education. The eldest son Angus was already making a brilliant career as a doctor in Warsaw, Indiana. While his siblings settled in Indiana and Montana, Ewan attended Prince of Wales College in Charlottetown and taught school in Orwell. He graduated with his B.A. from Dalhousie University in Halifax, Nova Scotia, where he also attended the Presbyterian College. In June 1903, he came to Cavendish and was inducted into the Presbyterian Church of Cavendish and neighboring Stanley on September 1.[6]

Maud's retrospective 1907 journal account suggests that his arrival in Cavendish had the flair and drama of a Jane Austen comedy. Like the unmarried Mr. Bingley, upon leasing the Netherfield estate, the unmarried Mr. Macdonald attracted the attention of eligible women. The Reverend Macdonald had no great fortune, but he had stature and would confer the role of mistress of the manse onto his chosen wife. That fact was not lost on several of the women in his new community, and Ewan became the subject of much idle talk and gossip. Even Maud had mockingly swooned in a June 21, 1903, entry in the diary she co-wrote with her friend Nora Lefurgey: "My heart pitty-patted so that I could hardly play the hymns."[7]

Smoothing her dress, Maud sprang up, quickly putting aside all thought of gentle Matthew Cuthbert driving to the train station to fetch the little orphan. The handsome bachelor with the dimpled cheeks was not a brilliant conversationalist, but his Scottish burr, inherited from his parents, was appealing, and the encounter contributed to her buoyancy. Meanwhile, Ewan thought the petite, slender woman with gentle curves would make an excellent minister's wife, as she would note in her journal many months later. He had seen her decorate the church with musky fern and listened to her nimble playing of the organ. He had noticed her deftness with children in her teaching of Sunday school. He most definitely liked the way she looked at him with her mischievous, gray eyes underneath long, sensuous lashes. In fact, when he had first seen her, he had resolved to pursue his cause as a suitor if she was not yet "bespoke" to another man—but that confession would not be made until many months later.[8] Rumor linked Maud to Edwin Simpson, and despite her flirtatiousness and vivaciousness, when Ewan tried to get closer she would become ever so slightly remote. When Ewan left that first evening, however, he had initiated what would soon become a pleasant ritual of chatting with the lively Maud Montgomery.

And so it came that the writing of *Anne of Green Gables* would overlap with Ewan Macdonald's courtship. Two threads that would change Maud's life forever had crossed that evening in the homestead kitchen. It is entirely possible that she wrote down her impressions of Ewan that evening or later that year, but if she did, she later destroyed the evidence. No trace of Ewan is left in her writing for this period. The mystery of Ewan has forever become entangled with the mystery of *Anne of Green Gables*.

Romantic Gardens and Orchards

Spring was glorious that year, and the opening scenes of *Anne of Green Gables* were written under its happy banner. They were also written under the felicitous influence of a popular work that Maud had picked up in the Cavendish Literary Society Library. Elizabeth von Arnim's 1898 *Elizabeth and her German Garden* was a thinly veiled autobiographical account of one year, from spring to spring, depicting her reveling in her secluded garden in Pomerania. Today the Australian-born author is better known for *The Enchanted April*, her 1922 novel which was adapted into a popular movie in 1992. In spring, the season of resurrection, Elizabeth's garden sang, drenched with heady scent and purple glory. The garden also looked "like a wedding" to her, with trees wreathed with white blossoms. Every tree was a lover, every flower a friend, every visit to the orchard an adventure. Maud was enthralled when she read this book, written in the diary form she cherished. "My 'twin soul' must live in *Elizabeth*," she noted in her journal on May 20. Elizabeth's enthusiasm and language seemed to penetrate Maud's imagination: "I know exactly what I shall feel like on the resurrection morning," she noted in the unpublished part of the entry, echoing Elizabeth's sentiments. "My dear garden!" Maud exclaimed. "Oh, the joy of it! The way I felt was a prayer."[9]

Every year Maud was ecstatic about spring and the birth of new life, but that spring she felt especially inspired by Elizabeth's German garden. She promptly wrote "The Old South Orchard" about the Macneill homestead orchard, and sent it to the New York *Sunday Christian Advocate*. After many delays, it was published in January 1908 by the New York outdoor and recreational periodical *Outing*. The first-person fictionalized essay is about Grandfather Abraham King, who planted two bridal trees when he married grandmother Elizabeth: "Those two trees were yet living when we of the third generation were born."[10] For each child, grandfather planted a birth tree, just as Maud's grandfather Macneill did. Elizabeth von Arnim's orchard was a space of escape, but Maud's orchard was a symbol of family loyalty and permanence. Springing from the wall of her memory's picture gallery, this nostalgic essay was an idealized and fictionalized tribute to her grandparents' long and happy marriage. It is also a long-lost companion piece to *Anne of Green Gables* and its nature haunts are scattered throughout the pages of *Anne*. There is the red soil that Anne so delights in; "King Bubble," which would become Dryad's Bubble in the novel, the spring of pure water and fountain of youth that gurgled up in the southwest corner at the foot of a gentle slope; "Uncle Stephen's Avenue," a double row of apple trees, a bowery arcade running down the western side of grandfather King's orchard, is the same as "the Avenue" that Anne Shirley will soon call "The White Way of Delight" during the first ride home to Green Gables. The ancient orchard's bridal romance was about to spill into the writing of the inspired early chapters of *Anne of Green Gables* (and would later also be worked into *The Story Girl*, including the surname King).

By now, Maud had returned to the writing of her novel during the evening. Guided by her deft pen, Matthew Cuthbert arrives at the Bright River Station and discovers Anne Shirley waiting on the pile of shingles, already planning to spend the night in the white-blossomed cherry tree. The pair rides in the buggy along the country roads that lead from Bright River Station to Avonlea, the locale Maud would later identify as corresponding to the ride from Hunter River railway station to Cavendish.

Accompanied by her carpet bag containing all her worldly belongings, Anne Shirley loses no time in taking charge of the conversation, expressing her exuberance about the landscape. What does the white-blossomed cherry tree make you think of? She provides her own answer, "Why, a bride, of course—a bride all in white with a lovely misty veil," and continues: "I don't ever expect to be a bride myself."[11] Only a missionary might be willing to marry her with her red hair and freckles, she says, referring to the cliché about a foreign missionary not being too particular in his choice of brides. A white dress would be earthly bliss, says Anne. Maud's writing was flowing as smoothly as Anne's ingenuous clichés. Already the roles were set for the rest of the novel: Anne talks and Matthew listens. Which would he rather be, if he had the choice, "divinely beautiful or dazzlingly clever or angelically good?" "Well now, I—I don't know exactly,"[12] replies shy Matthew.

Her little white face animated, her spirit rapturous, her eyes luminous, Anne Shirley is recruiting disciples—or kindred spirits.

For Elizabeth von Arnim, the garden presented an escape from her husband and children and visitors: "I long more and more for a kindred spirit," she exclaimed in the book Maud was reading. "It seems so greedy to have so much loveliness to oneself—but kindred spirits are so very, very rare; I might almost as well cry for the moon."[13] Maud's opening chapters seem to respond directly to Elizabeth's complaint. So powerful is Anne's imagination that she casts even crabby and socially awkward people in the role of kindred spirits and molds them to her vision. Her ability to harness the most ordinary of people to her fiery chariot is nothing short of extraordinary. And yet, all of her recruits are also a little "queer," like Anne herself. Shy Matthew Cuthbert, who was old even in his youth, is rejuvenated after gobbling up the lofty fabrications of her imagination. He is bewitched, as Marilla will say. Already Anne has transformed the landscape and has baptized the prosaic Avenue "the White Way of Delight." When they pass a pond, long and winding almost like a river just below the crest of a hill, Anne is thrilled by the effects of its scintillating light reflected from the sunset. The name Barry's Pond just will not do for such a poetic vision, and Anne calls it the Lake of Shining Waters. Two Lakes of Shining Water exist today as tourist attractions on Prince Edward Island. One is in Cavendish and the other in Park Corner close to the home of Maud's Campbell cousins. It was the latter that Maud later said was her model, but it may well have merged with the light effects on the Cavendish pond.[14]

Enter Diana

"Has Mr. Barry any little girls?" Anne asks after the matter of the naming of Barry's Pond has been settled. "He's got one about eleven. Her name is Laura," Matthew replies.[15] Anne fans may gasp at this line, written in Maud's original manuscript. She was presumably thinking about her Prince Albert friend Laura Pritchard about whom she was longingly writing at this time in an unpublished journal entry of May 21: "Laura, too, is now an 'old married woman' with *three* boys," she had recorded, noting that a sad gulf had opened up between them. "Could we again meet on common grounds? I fear not. The years and our different experiences must have pushed in between us."[16] Who would have thought that a few intriguing strokes, visible only in the original manuscript at the Confederation Centre of the Arts in Charlottetown, would help unseal the mystery of Maud's thoughts on the day she first introduced Anne's bosom friend?

No sooner had Maud penned Laura's name in her Anne story than she paused; somehow Laura's name did not seem right for Anne's bosom friend. Perhaps the name, which conjured up intense emotions for Maud, was too intimate and distracting. Tears easily welled up and she couldn't exactly cry her way through her story. With a quick and steady stroke of the pen, Maud crossed out the name Laura and wrote above it, "Gertrude." Again she paused, crossed out Gertrude, and wrote "Diana."

Diana. Yes, that was it! She closed the quotation mark of Matthew's speech. Anne's bosom friend had been born and christened with an evocative name already familiar to Maud who had used it in a story titled "Diana's Wedding Dress" published in March 1902 in *Farm and Fireside*.[17] Meanwhile, Matthew explains just how unconventional this name is for Avonlea. When the little Barry girl was born, the local schoolmaster had been given the task of choosing the name and he called her Diana. A heathenish name, says Matthew. A lovely name, counters Anne. Diana, the Roman mythological goddess of the moon and the hunt blended with the pagan world of the Druids. Paganism was being discussed widely at the turn of the century, and 1905 marked the beginning of Druidic rituals at Stonehenge, the prehistoric monument of large rocks, or *menhirs*, in southern England. Earlier in February, Maud's copy of *East and West* magazine (the one that contained the story with her character Mrs. Lynde) had reported on "The Strange Temples of the Druids." In contrast to her Sunday school periodical, which linked these rituals to a dead and vanished race, Maud resurrected the rituals in *Anne of Green Gables*. In the tradition of the Druids, she deified nature; venerated groves, lakes, hills, and ponds; and worshipped the beauty of the sun and the moon. Anne was endowed with an extraordinary spiritual gift: her imagination and her understanding of nature's beauty never failed to inspire the emotions of others. Anne's religion is an earthly spirituality that belonged to the White Way of Delight and Lover's Lane. She is herself a creature that belongs to the irreverent world of wood nymphs and dryads. This pagan world poked fun at solemn Sunday school decorum.

Anne Is Adopted

In a burst of energy and exuberance that coincided with the arrival of spring, Maud wrote the first six episodes of *Anne* during the spring and early summer. The writing was delightful and profoundly satisfying, culminating in the happy adoption of a fiery redhead and the emotional awakening of Matthew and Marilla. "Marilla Cuthbert," Marilla says to herself while straining the milk into the creamers at the end of chapter six. "Did you ever suppose you'd see the day when you'd be adopting an orphan girl?"[18] Or that Matthew, who was always afraid of little girls, was at the bottom of it. The aging brother and sister couple had begun their transformation. Marilla's decision to send Anne to Sunday school in chapter seven, would have ended the story, had Maud written the serial she intended to write.[19] But if she had ended here, we would probably not even know today that Anne Shirley ever existed. Our heroine would have been forgotten within a few months of the story's publication, as many good short stories are.

But already Anne had a mind of her own. Maud was hitched to her chariot of imagination, having fallen in love with her heroine. She was hooked by the story's emotional depth—Marilla's awakening love and belated maternity, Anne's ability to cultivate kindred spirits across generational and gender boundaries, and Anne's uncanny ability to transform the world of Green Gables. Perhaps Maud was getting a little dizzy listening to Anne, just like Matthew, who felt as he had once in his youth when he let himself be enticed to go on a merry-go-round. As Maud recalled decades later, "Anne, spelled with an e, red-haired, dreamy-eyed and elfin-faced," somehow seemed very real to her.[20] It was as if Anne was walking beside her like a lively little companion.

When the verbosely romantic redhead demanded more scope than a serial, Maud was willing to indulge her, keen on seeing where this intense and dramatic heroine was headed next. The novel she had started was in episodes, like *Don Quixote* or *Adventures of Huckleberry Finn*, with no complex structure or subplot. One episode simply followed the next with subsequent stories amplifying earlier motifs and developments like musical variations on the same refrain. She had a leading character who was fiery and charismatic enough to carry a novel, a setting that, like Elizabeth von Arnim's German garden, was rich with beauty and spirituality, and a topic, the heroine's quest for love, that had universal appeal. All Maud needed to do was write up the episodes that she had been dreaming about for years. No sooner was this task conceived than it was translated into action.

While Maud wrote, Evelyn Nesbit's picture of idealized girlhood was nearby on the wall, her eyes angled upward like a radiant Madonna. Her face was a constant visual reminder of Anne's youthful idealism and spirituality. In chapter eight, "Anne's Bringing up Is Begun," Anne, "her face uplifted, and her eyes astar with dreams," is viewing a chromolithograph of the religious legend "Christ Blessing Little Children." Just as Evelyn's exquisite face is flooded with light, so the white and green light strained through apple trees and "fell over the rapt little figure with a half-unearthly radiance."[21] At the same time, Maud peppered her novel with wicked irony and satire, and has Anne confront parochial Avonlea, as we shall see. Her new heroine was full of mischief and ready to leap into inspired misadventures that would endear the novel to readers the world over.

Meanwhile, the author was so immersed in writing and reveling in the garden that she neglected her journal. Perhaps this is because, in the wake of her painful failure with *A Golden Carol*, she did not want to jinx this piece of writing and stayed mum concerning the progress of her new novel. Nor did she drop a word in her journal or in letters to her literary pen friends, wrapping the novel in such secrecy that in later years she herself was confused about the exact date on which she had started writing.[22]

On June 28, a cold day when the orchard was too wet to go outside, she sat downstairs by the kitchen fire, writing a letter to Ephraim Weber. She told him she had devoted May to spring cleaning and had neglected her literary work, but had been busy writing all June. She said nothing about Ewan Macdonald or her novel, but continued to titillate Ephraim with sensuous flower talk. The pink carnation was her favorite flower, she said. But she also loved the pink rose in her garden, "deep pink at heart, shading to almost white on the outer petals like a blush dying away."[23] Maud could not resist the opportunity to chastise Ephraim for his old-fashioned preference for bouquets by reciting the rules of good taste. "I never mix flowers and very seldom colours," she wrote, shamelessly echoing the latest fad.[24] In January 1904, the New York *Delineator* had advised its readers of the rules for flower arrangements: "One point is generally conceded: that flowers of one kind are more effective than several kinds in one combination, and that a single color in a vase or other receptacle is far more beautiful than mixed colors."[25] When she poked fun at perfectionist housekeepers Mrs. Lynde and Marilla Cuthbert, she knew firsthand what she was talking about. Maud herself was a bit of a snob when it came to the rules of taste and fashion.

Romantic Affinities

Over the next weeks and months, Maud continued to write *Anne*—in secret—during the evenings. And during the afternoons, Ewan Macdonald continued to use the routine mail run as a pretext for lingering and talking with Maud. There was an affinity in how they both approached this new friendship, both drawn to the reciprocal teasing tension of the courtship dance.

One imagines that Maud would have been flaunting her attributes and fanning her feathers for the minister, as she did for Ephraim. Although she thought the word "flirtation" silly, she admitted in her journal that she loved the "thrill of power" she was able to exert over men. Flirting was a game at which she had become an expert. With come-hither moves of the eyes and the ankles she turned up the heat only to cool it when the man followed. It allowed her to have her fun and not become too involved or too distracted by the courtship. This choreographed dance was sure to bring the suitor back and string him along. Maud was a mistress of flirtation, but that did not translate into comfortable erotic explorations. Although she boasted many beaus, the tentative physical dimension of these relationships had been awkward and uncomfortable. Kissing, as she would comment in later years, was "a very boring and silly performance...at best and at worst very nauseating."[26] The one exception had been her intensive on-and-off affair with the young farmer Herman Leard when she was a twenty-four-year-old teacher in Lower Bedeque. The clandestine affair had stopped short of being consummated, while conveniently allowing her to break off her nine-month engagement with Ed Simpson, of whom we will hear more later. Since age twenty-four, she had had no other erotic encounters with men, seemingly contenting herself with a few sporadic sexual dreams about boyish Herman, who by then was dead and thus a safe indulgence. "Last night I dreamed of Herman Leard," she had written in an unpublished February 28, 1904, journal entry. "I was in his arms—his lips were on mine—and the old rapturous thrill coursed through my veins as of yore."[27]

She liked Ewan's gentle friendliness. The fact that he was not making any demands on her as a lover may have been a boon, for there was nothing in this blossoming friendship that suffocated her as she had felt with others. She was free and immersed in her writing. In fact, so neutral and unassertive seemed Ewan in establishing himself as a lover that Maud claims she did not even view his visits that year as a serious courtship. At this point, she considered their relationship a friendship—flirtatious yes, but comradely like her relationship with Ephraim. Consequently, her romantic liaison with the handsome minister was deep enough to be exhilarating, and distant enough not to keep her from what was quickly becoming her main task and pleasure that summer—her novel.

Of course, one wonders about reticent Ewan's point of view. The rules of courtship and engagement were much stricter during that era. For instance, a jilted woman was exposed to much gossip and humiliation and was even entitled to legally pursue the man responsible for damages. In his student days, during one of his visits back to the Island, Ewan had let himself be enticed into an engagement with a Prince Edward Island woman who was older than he was.[28] He realized his mistake as soon as he returned to Halifax. Ewan counted himself lucky to have been able to extricate himself quietly from his predicament, and perhaps he was more cautious about forming a second attachment. He probably enjoyed lingering with Maud, whose seductive charms were balanced by a certain detachment and distance that was refreshing for a man who had just escaped the more overt favors and pressures of Mabel Woolner of Rustico. Despite his position and university degree, there was a certain shyness and lack of self-confidence about him. The more assertive women may have scared him into the arms of the soft-spoken Maud who seemed to be in no rush to get married.

When Ewan came courting he had little knowledge of the secretive world of love and romantic ritual that was enveloping Maud. For now, we will leave Ewan in John Laird's pretty homestead and we will look for Anne in the female world, a separate sphere. In contrast to the cagey mental games Maud played with her male suitors, the more intimate and earthy relationships in her life were those shared with her girlfriends and would become an important part in *Anne of Green Gables*.

SIX

Maud's Bosom Friends

"Marilla," she demanded presently, "do you think I shall ever have a bosom friend in Avonlea?"

"A—a what kind of a friend?"

"A bosom friend—an intimate friend, you know—a really kindred spirit to whom I can confide my inmost soul. I've dreamed of meeting her all my life...."

Anne Shirley to Marilla Cuthbert[1]

When we first read *Anne of Green Gables*, we are struck by Anne Shirley's intense romantic attachment to girls. It is a world of girls holding hands, writing love poetry to each other, and swearing everlasting devotion. To understand what the bosom friendship meant to Anne, one needs to consider her intimate friends in the context of the time. It is important for today's readers to rediscover and understand the rituals and loves that are embedded in *Anne of Green Gables* and that many of Maud's readers looked back to nostalgically for the very rituals that had been lost.

When Maud was growing up during the 1880s and 1890s, romantic female friendships, often largely platonic effusions and crushes among girls and women, were tolerated by nineteenth-century society precisely because they were believed to be "innocent." "The bosom girl friend will go nicely in a love-story, for I notice that is where bosom girl friends *do* go, in real life," wrote M. J. Shepperson in *The Ladies' World* in October 1902.[2] The nineteenth century had a rich history of girls longing to hold each other in their arms, swearing everlasting devotion to each other, and mourning their physical isolation and separation. These romantic female friendships were characterized by emotional intensity as well as sensual and physical explicitness. Such bonds often lasted a lifetime and were frequently integrated into women's marriages.[3] *Anne of Green Gables* captures these rituals of love and longing that were a central part of Maud's romantic life.

Sapphic Values

"Romantic friends courted each other, flirted, were anxious about the beloved's responses and about reciprocity," writes Lillian Faderman in *Surpassing the Love of Men: Romantic Friendship and Love Between Women from the Renaissance to the Present*. Faderman admits that the term "friendship" does not appear entirely appropriate given the passion and obvious love binding women together, often over several decades. The women believed their relationship to be eternal, and in fact the faithfulness of one often extended beyond the death of the other. "The fondest dream of many romantic friends, which was not often realized, was to establish a home with the beloved."[4] The reason for the ubiquity of this erotically charged female network is found in the rigid gender segregation of the era. Biological and social realities bound girls and women together in physical and emotional intimacy, while severe restrictions were placed on intimacy between men and women. The extent to which these relationships were platonic or physical is debated by scholars. Today many of the same behaviors would be classified under the rubric of "lesbian," yet eighteenth- or nineteenth-century society would not have classified them as such, for the category did not exist; in fact, such relationships were frequent enough to constitute a norm and society generally tolerated them, although there is also evidence of hostility.[5]

A tolerance for "Sapphic" values was ironically also promoted by Grandmother Macneill's *Godey's Lady's Book*, the magazine avidly read by young Maud. Illustrations of the Grecian poet Sappho appeared in *Godey's*, along with stories and poetry with tributes to Lesbia or Sappho.[6]

Millington Miller's 1895 essay "Sappho—The Woman and the Time" celebrated the female poet as a woman of art and intellect. Although Sappho
was not unusually beautiful, she was brilliant. A "joint foster-child of
Venus, Cupid, and the Graces," writes Miller, Sappho combined in her
person "the twin characters of Muse and Venus." She may not have felt
any great love for her husband, who was generally known only as "the
husband of Sappho," but "it does not follow that we should regard such a
woman as at all immoral."[7] The article was illustrated with artwork by
German painter Wilhelm Amberg featuring Sappho posing like a dis-
tressed mermaid against the rock high above the sea, as if before the final
leap. Such regular tributes to Sappho in a magazine dubbed the "Victorian
Bible of the Parlor" may seem strange or out of place today. Yet the values *Godey's* associated with Sappho—high-quality women's poetry,
steeped in sensuous beauty—went hand in hand with the magazine's
attempts to serve as a mentor for aspiring female authors, by providing
instruction and soliciting submissions of creative writing. Sappho was
part of the culture Maud imbibed during the 1890s and beyond.
Translated by Maud's favorite poet Bliss Carman, Sappho's poetry was
published, in 1903, under the title *Sappho: One Hundred Lyrics*, by L.C.
Page, the Boston publisher of *Anne of Green Gables*. A new novel entitled
Sappho in Boston was advertised, in 1908, in the same periodical as *Anne*.[8]

Romantic Codes and Rituals: Mollie and Pollie

The affectionate names of Maud's closest girlfriends thread through her
journal like the pearls on a rich necklace: Lu (Lucy Macneill), Pen (Penzie
Macneill), Frede (Fredericka Campbell), Mary C. (Mary Campbell), Laura
(Pritchard), Bert (Beatrice McIntyre), Nora (Lefurgey), and so on. Little
attention has been paid to this rich company of women, neither in biographies nor in Maud's own legend of how Anne came about.[9] The
powerful pull these bosom friends exerted on Maud is reflected in her celebration of the friendship between Anne and Diana. Maud's unpublished
journals unfold a tale of passion and intimacy, but also reveal that her
bosom friendships coexisted with flirtations and romances with men.

Lovable Anne is destined to find Diana, although she has to soldier on alone until chapter twelve when she finally meets her soulmate and instantly bonds with her for life. Maud had a similar genius for recruiting girlfriends and also shares Anne's pervasive fear and panic of losing her friends. Maud's earliest friends were imaginary companions, Katie Maurice and Lucy Gray, as she recalls in her journal on March 26, 1905, just a few months before she began writing *Anne.* "I called her Katie Maurice, and we were very intimate," says Anne about her imaginary friends, using the same name as Maud's imagined companion. Even imaginary friends feel the harsh shock of separation; as Anne says, "I know she did, for she was crying when she kissed me good-bye through the book-case door."[10]

Passionate Maud loved her chums and hated her enemies. Pretty Amanda Macneill had been Maud's friend since they were tots. The two were so inseparable that the boys referred to them as Mollie (Amanda) and Pollie (Maud). She had bartered with the older school girls—for there was a tradition of the older girls claiming newcomers as desk partners—and "won" Amanda in exchange for four sweet apples from the Macneill orchard. "They bought me Mollie," as Maud recalled.[11] They shared a desk for the duration of their school years and, like their fictional counterparts, Anne and Diana, were separated only once.

A picture of Amanda around age twelve shows an appealing girl with a silver pendant, thick wavy hair, and a naughty pout. Like Anne and Diana on their daily walk to school through Lover's Lane, Willowmere, Violet Vale, and the Birch Path, so Mollie and Pollie walked to school together, crossing through the fields and Lover's Lane in "short dresses, stiffly starched white aprons, and long-braided 'tails' of hair."[12] They sealed their bond by means of written "Notes of Promise," in which they vowed everlasting faith to each other. The contract was witnessed by two school friends and finished with a red seal. What is perhaps most note-worthy is how seriously Maud took the ritual: "I think I was true to *my* vow,"[13] the thirty-six-year-old writer noted in 1911, revealing her lingering resentment over Amanda's inconstancy. There was also an undertone of guilt, for it was Maud who had changed more dramatically than Amanda, and who felt attracted to more intellectually stimulating companions. Frustrated by the adult Amanda, whose naughty pout had become petulant, she was unable to break her friendship and even continued some of the old rituals, such as walking Amanda back to her home when she came to pick up the mail. The ritual had lost its pleasure, however. She resurrected the ideal in Anne and Diana, turning the shadow of loss and frustration into a sunny relationship in fiction.

In March 1888, thirteen-year-old Maud had sworn eternal friendship with an orphan girl named Maggie Abbott, whom she had met on a visit to her Aunt Emily and Uncle John Montgomery in Malpeque. The swearing took place in the big barn, the pair standing on a high loft beam to heighten the solemnity of the act. As a tantalizingly brief journal passage makes clear, Maggie, though her parents were from a "low and immoral class,"[14] was sensitive and sweet. At age eighteen she was significantly older than Maud. Given their ages, the ritual should be regarded, not as pre-puberty childhood play, but as evidence of a more mature, adolescent relationship. Maggie gave Maud a little geranium that she named "Bonny," and it too makes a cameo in the novel. "I shall call it Bonny," says Anne about Marilla's geranium, commemorating Maggie's little gift of yore.[15] The mementoes of Maud's "eternal" friendship are thus preserved forever in fiction.

Modern readers will be intrigued by the romantic rituals Maud shared with her girlfriends, rituals that may be all the more compelling today for the reason that they no longer exist. In the summer of 1894, when the old school was being torn down, nineteen-year-old Maud indulged nostalgic memories. She discovered an old box of papers and souvenirs that she had stashed away and forgotten. Among the papers were some of her love poems to other girls. Maud's lengthy, unpublished journal entry dated July 1, 1894, provides a rare glimpse into a well-guarded world of girlish intimacy with its own codes, rituals, and language that anticipate the world of *Anne of Green Gables*. We learn that it was at around age twelve that Maud first began to write gushing "po'try" to girls. Addressed to her school chum Alena Macneill, Maud's poem enthused over Alena's beauty, her golden hair, blue eyes, pink cheeks, and dimples. Alena "painted the lily very freely in my case also—in especial did she rave over my 'wondrous braids of nut-brown hair.' Well I always had plenty of hair!"[16] Instead of sharpening their intellects with arithmetic, the two mischievous girls would sit together on the old side bench lampooning the Cavendish boys with satirical poetry and mooning about each other. They were constantly in disgrace with their teachers.

Here in the old box of intimate treasures was Maud's "A Moonlight Walk," an effusive poem she had written for Mollie when they were fourteen. Mollie and Pollie had planned a special sleepover night that was to include a secret moonlight walk along the lane and into Maud's favorite woods. Anticipating this romantic event, Maud already imagined her pleasure in a poem. Alas, she forgot the draft poem in her school desk, where it was found and read by her two school beaus Nate Lockhart and Jack Laird. Assuming that Maud was detailing her love affair with one of the Cavendish males, Nate and Jack made copies of the poem and distributed it among the boys, creating a jealous firestorm. The box also contained a piece of fur, a memento of a special moment shared with her cousin Frede Campbell. When seventeen-year-old Maud spent a winter with her cousins at Park Corner, the two girls baptized Frede's pet cat, a spotted gray and yellow critter, with the elaborate name "Mignonnette Carissima Montgomery Campbell."[17] *Mignonnette* means "little darling" in French, and *Carissima* is the Italian equivalent, Maud explains. The romantic memory was preserved with the cat's yellow fur wrapped in a piece of paper labeled "Carissima."

After discovering the love poetry and Carissima's fur in 1894, Maud burned the entire box of secret treasures. Life was too short to "moon over rubbish," she explained in the unpublished journal entry.[18] Yet it is likely that she was also fearful that these unguarded intimate mementoes might be found by others. By recording and shaping these memories in her journal, she controlled how they would be received and read. As Maud grew older, she tried to distance herself from these romantic friendships, using the same tone of irony to describe her box of letters and souvenirs that she would use in *Anne of Green Gables* to describe the girls' rituals of love and bonding. In fact, since she had reread this July 1894 journal entry in 1904 (see chapter two of this volume), these personal friendships and effusions of beauty and love would have been a vibrant memory when she was writing *Anne of Green Gables*.[19]

Darling Penzie

Far from being idyllic, her romantic friendships with girls also filled her with pain and anguish. Maud shared a close friendship with her cousin Penzie Macneill, a blue-eyed, auburn-haired beauty, who was two years older, and would become a teacher like so many of Maud's friends. Penzie was one of the few girls Maud was allowed to visit as a child. The girls enjoyed going to the woods to pick the nutty, bitter chewing gums from the spruce trees; they collected mussels at the shore; they watched Penzie's brother Russel pick up seaweeds with the horse; they brought the cows home at night for milking in the shadowy lane under the willows and poplars. Most of all Maud enjoyed visiting and staying the night at Penzie's home, and she would always remember the old orchard enveloping the house with the scent of blossoms wafting up into the bedroom on a summer night. When fifteen-year-old Maud left Cavendish for Prince Albert, the friend she missed most was Penzie. She wrote effusive love letters to her that were preserved by Penzie's son.[20] Since Maud destroyed all of her early effusions and letters, these rare letters grant unfiltered insight into her state of mind at the time.

These uncensored letters inevitably begin with "My dear old darling"[21] and "My own dearest love."[22] They also end like lovers' letters with "Piles of love and kisses to your own dear self from your ever loving old chum."[23] Maud enthused about the redhead in a love poem, calling her "My own sweet wildwood rose."[24] She swore Penzie to secrecy. Her love for Penzie was as deep as it was painful, and she was less reserved in expressing her emotions than she would become in later years. "Oh don't I wish that instead of writing to you I could go to you and get my arms around you and kiss you," the fifteen-year-old wrote in September 1890. "I am waiting with the greatest impatience for a letter from you."[25] These unedited words contradict her later defensive assertion in her March 1928 journal entry: "To me, it has always been positively abhorrent to kiss or caress one of my own sex."[26] The desperate neediness of her letters to Penzie ring more of truth than the journal, which by 1928 was being consciously written and revised for an audience.

But the relationship became strained. In contrast to bosom friend Mollie, who filled her letters to Maud with Cavendish gossip, Penzie was neither a frequent correspondent nor a satisfying one. Maud's letters to Penzie indicate that she felt abandoned and lonely. Emotionally needy Maud overwhelmed Penzie with a barrage of letters, and was not above sarcasm:

> Whatever has come over you in the wide wide world. Have you got married and left Cavendish? Have you gone to Boston. Or have you as seems more likely forgotten all about me and your promises of writing.[27]

Maud's panic at what she clearly regarded as Penzie's emotional desertion is evident in her courtship, her tearful complaints, and her iron-clad demands of loyalty. When Penzie answered in a more light-hearted tone, teasing Maud about her own boyfriend Nate Lockhart, of whom we shall hear more later, Maud responded rudely. She dismissed him as "that detestable pig" and forbade Penzie to speak of him again, as if to speak of boyfriends was tantamount to severing their own love bond.[28] Years later, in October 1936, when Penzie's son showed Maud her own letters, which he had preserved, Maud dismissed her romantic effusions to Penzie, saying it was "harmless exaggeration." She did admit that she would have preferred it if the letters had been burned.[29] These surviving letters, though, provide a rare glimpse of the tone and content of writings Maud later preferred to censor from the public.

Even while flirting with boys, girls were passionate as well as physically affectionate. They slept together, dressed together, and shared their innermost thoughts. It was a rich homosocial and erotically charged network. What exactly went on in the bedrooms we will probably never know, but one wonders if the "spooning" Maud refers to in later years may also have been a part of the relationships. "As for 'petting' . . . well, it isn't an entirely new institution, is it? We called it 'spooning,'" Maud wrote in a personal essay for girls in 1931, in which she talks about girl's "normal" desires for boys, but also emphasizes that girls should be allowed to have secrets. "She has a right to her own secrets, her own inner, unshared life." But as always, it is difficult to determine where Maud really stands, as she seems to advocate all positions, advising mothers to teach their daughters to be an "aristocrat of the body."[30] What is remarkable is

VOL. LXV   JANUARY, 1905   No. 1

THE DELINEATOR

PUBLISHED MONTHLY BY   THE BUTTERICK PUBLISHING CO. (LTD.)   PARIS—LONDON—NEW YORK—TORONTO

$1.00 A YEAR   ENTERED AT THE POST OFFICE, NEW YORK, AS SECOND CLASS MAIL MATTER   15 CENTS A COPY

The Delineator (January 1905) cover girl drawn by George Gibbs would become the official cover image for *Anne of Green Gables* in 1908.

The Metropolitan Magazine (September 1908), cover. In the year *Anne* was launched, red hair seemed omnipresent in *The Metropolitan Magazine.* This auburn beauty, with a crystal ball in an underworld forest, was just one example.

General Research Division, The New York Public Library, Astor, Lenox and Tilden Foundations

The Delineator of January 1904, an issue Maud owned, celebrated the Victorian styles of the 1830s. *Anne* similarly evoked earlier times and fashions at the cusp of the modern era.

General Research Division, The New York Public Library, Astor, Lenox and Tilden Foundations

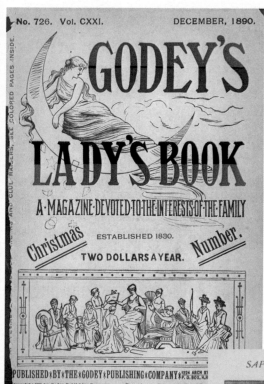

Godey's Lady's Book (December 1890), cover. Grandmother Macneill had a subscription to this Philadelphia fashion and family magazine which Maud devoured as a girl and young woman. It was a major literary influence, but Maud later disparaged it.

"Sappho—The Woman and the Time," Godey's Lady's Book (February 1895). Known for her sensuous poetry, the Greek poet Sappho was often seen and celebrated in the magazines Maud read.

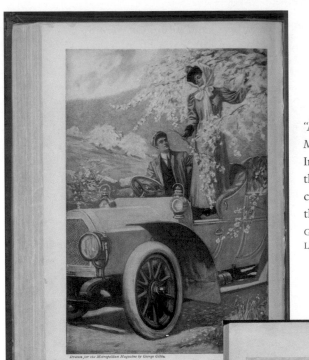

"A Detail of Spring Motoring," *The Metropolitan Magazine* (June 1908). In 1908, when *Anne* was published, the symbols of modernity such as cars and motorboats coexisted with the symbols of romantic nostalgia.

General Research Division, The New York Public Library, Astor, Lenox and Tilden Foundations

In "Motor-Boating," *The Metropolitan Magazine* (February 1908), modern speed and technology are in harmony with the pastoral landscape. Both drawings on this page are by George Gibbs, the artist whose Gibson Girl was featured on the cover of *Anne*.

General Research Division, The New York Public Library, Astor, Lenox and Tilden Foundations

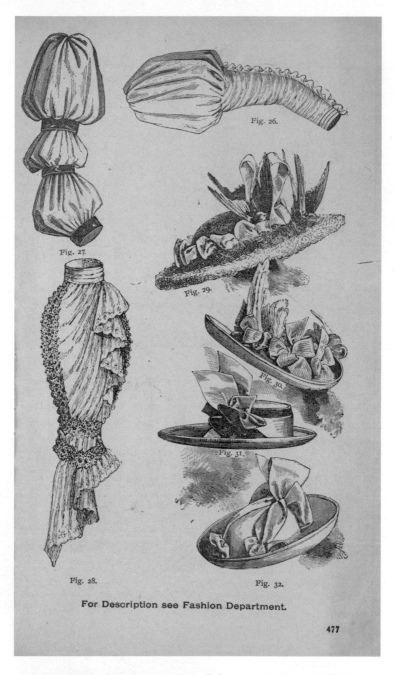

Fig. 26.

Fig. 27.

Fig. 29.

Fig. 30.

Fig. 31.

Fig. 28.

Fig. 32.

For Description see Fashion Department.

Godey's Lady's Book (May 1892). Detailed sewing instructions for the glorious puffed sleeves cherished by Anne were provided on the pages of *Godey's Lady's Book*.

"Queen of Hair Tonics," *Modern Women* (June 1905). Ads for Sicilian hair dye with promises to color gray hair brown and black appeared in *Modern Women* alongside warnings of the dangers of hair coloring. The stage was set for Anne's dyeing her hair green.

General Research Division, The New York Public Library, Astor, Lenox and Tilden Foundations

George du Maurier's iconic novel *Trilby* (1894) helped Maud break the habit of creating sweet but uninteresting Sunday school heroines.

Archives and Special Collections, Modern Literature and Culture Research Centre, Ryerson University, Toronto

" WISTFUL AND SWEET "

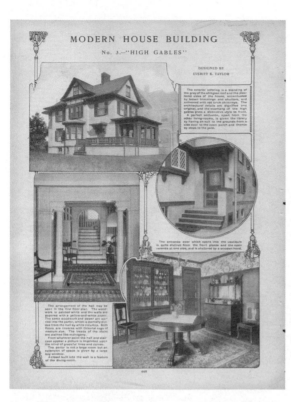

LEFT: "Modern House Building, No. 3—High Gables," *The Delineator* (March 1905), appeared just weeks before Maud wrote *Anne of Green Gables.* Maud knew this New York magazine well.

General Research Division, The New York Public Library, Astor, Lenox and Tilden Foundations

BELOW: Gray Gables, President Grover Cleveland's White House idyllic summer cottage, was described in *Godey's* in 1892.

General Research Division, The New York Public Library, Astor, Lenox and Tilden Foundations
Bourne Historical Society, Bourne, Massachusetts

GRAY GABLES.

The Pansy books of Maud's childhood influenced her writing, though *Anne* is more complex. Pansy publisher Lothrop, Lee and Shepard of Boston turned down *Anne of Green Gables* in 1906.

"Now I Lay Me"

Now I lay me down to sleep—
Don't want to sleep; I want to think.
I didn't mean to spill that ink;

I only meant to softly creep
Under the desk an' be a bear—
'Taint 'bout the spanking that I care.

'F she'd only let me 'splain an' tell
Just how it was an accident,
An' that I never truly meant.
An' never saw it till it fell.
I feel a whole lot worse'n her;
I'm sorry, an' I said I were.

I s'pose if I'd just cried a lot
An' choked all up like sister does,
An' acted sadder than I wuz,
An' sobbed about the "naughty spot,"
She'd said, "She shan't be whipped, she shan't,"
An' kissed me—but, somehow, I can't.

But I don't think it's fair a bit
That when she talks an' talks at you,
An' you wait patient till she's through,
An' start to tell your side of it,
She says, "Now that'll do, Hon', Hon';
I've heard enough," 'fore you've begun.

'F I should die before I wake—
Maybe I aint yet quite whole;
Maybe there's only just a hole
Where't ought to be—there's such an ache
Down there somewhere! She seemed to think
That I just loved to spill that ink!
—*The Century.*

To find recreation in amusements is not happiness; for this joy springs from alien and extrinsic sources, and is therefore dependent upon and subject to interruption by a thousand accidents, which may minister inevitable affliction.—*Pascal.*

the campers I don't w…nt
my bare feet, you know!'
brown toes were tucked q…
faded skirt.

Bob, flinging himself ov…
ach, wriggled along, snak…
the hopple bushes and peer…
of white-stemmed birches.

"It *is* some o' the camp…
a loud whisper. "One of …
headed young lady staying…
The other one is the fat …
prying around our house …
her camera, you remember…
wanted to 'get a perspect…
'they were scarce this ye…
ered—'and she looked …
thought I was a lunatic o…

Nan, who had crawled al…
brother lay, scowled fierce…
her—the stuck up old thi…

"Sh! if you don't want …
hear you!" Bob whispe…
"What are they doing, a…
cornel berries and calli…
greens, I declare!" and B…
…a high-pitched voice drov…

"Yes, my dear Miss An…
saying, the natives around…
iar—very peculiar. I sup…
idea of life is to eat—to …
hunt. Now those people …

ABOVE: "Now I Lay Me," *The Sunday School Advocate* (June 10, 1905). The popular children's prayer was inadequate for Anne.

General Research Division, The New York Public Library, Astor, Lenox and Tilden Foundations

BELOW: "Charity Ann," *Godey's Lady's Book* (January 1892). The "Ann" character in this ephemeral story by Canadian writer Mary Ann Maitland provided the blueprint for Anne's history and adoption.

General Research Division, The New York Public Library, Astor, Lenox and Tilden Foundations

Charity Ann.

FOUNDED ON FACTS.

BY M. A. MAITLAND.

THE little clock in Christy McKay's kitchen (an ancient "waf at the wa'") had just struck eleven, and yet the old couple lingered at the fireside. It was not often that this late hour found them out of bed; for to them, as to all old people who "in the sweat of their faces have eaten bread," the early morning hours brought only wakefulness. It may have been that the rheumatism had made Christy's joints a little stiffer than usual, and so she was unwilling to stir, or it may have been that they waited by the fireside, bright and cheery, to see the old year out and the new year in, or it

"Weel, wha are ye, and what do ye want at this time o' nicht?" he said, bending down and looking into the little face.

"Do you want a servant," inquired the mite, in a trembling voice.

"A servant! What to dae, my bairn?"

"To work."

"And whaur's the servant, pray?"

"I'm her."

"You, you a servant! How auld are ye?"

"I'm eight."

"And what can ye dae?"

"Oh, lots o' things. I can wash dishes, and scrape pots, and peel tawties, and mind the babies, and everything."

By this time Christy had hobbled to the door, lamp in hand, and interrupted the conversation by saying to her guid man, "Why dinna ye tak the bairn inside?" Sure enough; but in his won derment Donald had not thought of such

LUCY ANN

J. L. HARBOUR.

A VERY prim-looking maiden lady, wearing a severely plain black hat and an equally plain gray serge gown, drove away from a country railroad station with a little girl by her side on the seat of an old and somewhat rickety buggy. The little girl was an alert-looking child of about twelve years. She wore a cheap straw hat with a faded blue ribbon band and a limp little blue feather. Her blue and white cotton dress was faded but clean, and she made unnecessary use of a large fan with Japanese figures on it. She regarded the fan as a very elegant addition to her toilet. It had been given to her by a kindly-disposed visitor to the "Home" in which the little girl lived in the city she had left behind her a few hours before.

"What did you say your name was?" asked Miss Calista, as they drove away from the station. "The cars made so much noise I did not understand you clearly when I asked you before."

"My name is Lucy Ann Joyce, ma'am."

"Lucy Ann," *Zion's Herald* (July 29, 1903). This newly discovered formula story by American writer J. L. Harbour was another important yet never acknowledged influence for *Anne of Green Gables*.

By the Grace of Sarah Maud ❦ By L. M. Montgomery

Drawings by Maud Tousey

"Betty said 'good-evening' very icily and completely ignored the fact of Sarah Maud"

NESBITT panted into the station — too late. The train, with its load of picnickers, was gone and there was no other train going west until late in the afternoon.

"Confound it," he said blackly. "And confound Murchison," he added, thinking of the acquaintance who had delayed him on the street to discuss a slight matter of business.

He was left — there was no blinking that fact. The selected picnic ground was fifty miles away, so that the wild notion that had crossed his brain of getting a team and driving thereto had to be dismissed. No, there was no picnic for him, and, as things had fallen out, much depended on that picnic.

Nesbitt left the station in a mood of sickening depression. All the hope and exhilaration of the morning had vanished. Betty would think he did not care — and Clark was on the train. For a whole day Clark could wander with Betty through romantic haunts, while he, Nesbitt, sulked in town. Only a fool could fail to make use of such a golden opportunity, and Clark was no fool.

"That is *my* role," Nesbitt thought miserably.

He was in love with Betty Stewart. But Betty was independent. They had some tiffs with a resulting half coolness. Nesbitt had not been sure enough of his welcome to call for a fortnight. Then, with her usual caprice, Betty unbent. She had sent him a note the previous day inviting him to join a private picnic party to Maiden Lake.

"We will leave on the 10:15 train," she wrote, "so be a good boy, stop sulking and come with us. If you come I shall know how to be very nice to you, but if you don't I shall know you are still sulking and I shall be nice — to other people."

Nesbitt had not been sulking, take his word for it, he was merely on his dignity. That, of course, went to the winds at Betty's beck. And this was the result —

he was wandering homeward alone through the People's Square behind the station and Betty and Clark were on their way to Maiden Lake.

Nesbitt sat down on a bench in the square and was about to give himself over to sulking in right good earnest, when he heard somebody crying. Some twisting of neck discovered a small girl of about eight or nine curled up on a bench across the walk behind him, with her face buried in her head shaking in the emphasis of her woe. She was sniffling in an unrestrained luxury of grief, evidently thinking herself alone.

"Hello," said Nesbitt, who hated to see children or animals suffering, "it seems there is somebody besides myself in the world who is miserable after all. This must be seen to."

He went over and sat down on the other bench.

"What is the matter, sissy?" he asked gently.

Sissy squirmed around with a start, revealing a freckled, tear-spotted face, and a very red little nose. She was not shy and she did not at all resent his intrusion into her private troubles.

"I — can't — get to the — pickernic," she said between sobs.

"Did you miss your train, too?" asked Nesbitt with a smile. He could still smile

In June 1905, L. M. Montgomery's short story "By the Grace of Sarah Maud" appeared in the Boston magazine *Modern Women*. Maud's first prototype for Anne was Irish.

The photograph of Evelyn Nesbit by Rudolf Eickemeyer that eventually became the face of Anne. Maud cut out the picture from *The Metropolitan Magazine* (September 1903) and hung the sensuous and nostalgic flower girl on the wall of her room.

LEFT: *Dawn* posed by Evelyn Nesbit in a tinted postcard by Eickemeyer's A. S. Campbell Art Co.—just as Anne poses in tableaux in the novel.

Archives and Special Collections, Modern Literature and Culture Research Centre, Ryerson University, Toronto

BELOW: In *The Metropolitan Magazine* (September 1903) where Maud discovered the chrysanthemum picture of Evelyn was a second picture identifying the model as "Miss Evelyn Nesbitt" [sic].

General Research Division, The New York Public Library, Astor, Lenox and Tilden Foundations

Photo by Rudolf Eickemeyer, Jr.

Evelyn Nesbit, one of the era's most
famous models, also posed as a Gypsy
girl in a semi-transparent dress (*The
Theatre Magazine*, December 1903), and
as a willfully modern flower girl boldly
staring at the camera (*The Theatre
Magazine*, July 1902).

Toronto Reference Library

The Birch Path for Diana and Anne's romantic rambles was based on D. Davidson's photo "As the Trail Nears the Summit" clipped from *The Booklovers Magazine* (October 1904).

Archives and Special Collections, Modern Literature and Culture Research Centre, Ryerson University, Toronto

On the Road, North Shore to Hunter River, Prince Edward Island

This postcard in L. M. Montgomery's papers featuring a ride along the north shore to Hunter River evokes Matthew Cuthbert's ride to Bright River to pick up the little orphan.

University of Guelph Library Archival and Special Collections

SIMPLICITY
(Miss Millie James)

REV. THOS. SINGLETON
(Mr. Ernest Hastings)

ACT IV. "LOVERS' LANE" AT THE MANHATTAN

SIMPLICITY: *"Pops, how would you like to have your church back again?"*

"Lovers' Lane" at the Manhattan (*The Theatre Magazine*, May 1901) was a popular play on Broadway. "Diana and I are reading a perfectly magnificent book and there's a Lover's Lane in it," says Anne about her magic woodland lane.

Asher B. Durand, *Kindred Spirits* (1849), oil on canvas, 46 x 36 in. Maud's ideal of the kindred spirits is best visualized in this popular American oil painting in which two intimate friends commune in nature. The painting depicts poet William Cullen Bryant and painter Thomas Cole in the Catskill Mountains.

Crystal Bridges Museum of American Art, Bentonville, Arkansas that even though she grew up in a strict Presbyterian household, Maud did not show any signs of feeling guilty about these romantic infatuations—at least not at the time.

Secrets

The two friends closest to Maud while she was writing *Anne of Green Gables* were two school teachers, Nora Lefurgey, who was five years younger, and Fredericka Campbell, who was seven years Maud's junior. The first relationship was receding, while the second was intensifying. In 1903, Maud had shared her room and bed with Nora, and had co-written a diary for fun featuring two interlocking hearts on the cover. Independent and mischievous Nora had dark flashing eyes, and Maud would later remember her "elfin" smile. Maud's later inscription in Nora's copy of *Anne of Green Gables* recalled their rambles in Lover's Lane: "To dear Nora, with the author's love, in memory of many happy hours spent together in 'Lover's Lane' and elsewhere with a 'kindred spirit.'"[31] Their rambles also inspired a poem published in the *Delineator* in July 1903. Entitled "In Lovers Lane," it describes the ideal of a romantic love that does not need any words:

> And there my love and I may walk
> And harken to the lapsing fall
> Of unseen brooks, and tender winds,
> And wooing birds that sweetly call....[32]

By the summer of 1903, Nora had given up the Cavendish school and returned to North St. Eleanor, a train's journey away from Cavendish. Maud missed her terribly, but was also relieved that peace had returned to the homestead, for Grandmother Macneill objected to Nora's presence. The next summer, when Nora returned for a visit, she and Maud picnicked on the shore and took wild dips in the stormy waves. Discarding their Victorian skirts, they explored each other with the camera: Maud in the nude save for her makeshift bathing suit, posing against the dark rock above the sea like some mythological nymph mating with the land, her face turned away from the camera toward the sea. Maud hid the photos lest they scandalize Cavendish but inserted one of the photos three decades later in her journal during an era when the modern fashion of undress, as she reasoned, had made their scanty bathing suits almost up-to-date.[33]

Just months before writing *Anne of Green Gables*, twenty-nine-year-old Maud visited twenty-four-year old Nora in North St. Eleanor. "I enjoyed every minute of the time and just *lived* to my fullest capacity," she confided in an unpublished journal entry of October 24, 1904. "It makes me feel blue now to think of those delightful companionable days."[34] Two photos accompany this text. The first is a photo of Nora's room, the setting for their overnights. The second is a staged portrait of the couple entitled *Secrets*. In it, they are standing in front of the house. Maud looks relaxed, facing the camera and laughing with her mouth open, while Nora snuggles up, her cheek touching Maud's. Their playful intimacy provides us with a visible emblem of Maud's effusive treatment of "bosom friends" and "kindred spirits" in *Anne of Green Gables*. Intimate girlfriendship, far from being a passing phase that ended when she grew up, was at the core of Maud's emotional and mental makeup—a lifeline essential to her well-being. There is an earthiness and comfort in these photos that we do not see in the photos with her later husband, Ewan Macdonald.

At the same time that lonely Maud was relying on her romantic friendships with women for both companionship and creative inspiration, the pendulum in the popular press seemed to swing backward. The modern periodicals were increasingly negative about passionate female friendships. *The Ladies' Home Journal*, for instance, encouraged girls to uphold their ideals and dreams in the tradition of Emerson and Dickens, but came down hard on girl crushes, which were targeted as "unwholesome." A January 1904 column entitled "Crushes Among Girls" warned of the dire consequences of girls' "mushroom affection" and "'flashlight' friendships." The author Emma E. Walker, M. D., cautioned that "healthy feelings will soon become spent and the capacity for them stunted." She advised her girl readers as follows: "When you go to a concert, even though you have your 'best friend' next to you, don't sit and hold her hand during the performance. That does you no good and when you think of it in sober earnest it is pretty silly, isn't it?" Such affection, which can some-times be directed to a teacher noted for her "so-called personal magnetism," is always "a sham."[35]

The implication that holding on to girl love would thwart a woman's healthy development may explain Maud's increased caution. She put a great deal of trust in advice columns, in some cases, blindly accepting the experts' arbitrary rules. Her love for her cousin Frede (pronounced Fred) began to intensify in 1902, yet she expressed it with understatement, sign-ing her 1907 letter to her, "truly and lovingly and good-comradely."[36] Many of Maud's relationships with females were intense and long-lasting. Her bond with Frede, likely the most meaningful connection of Maud's life, covered seventeen years and the one with Nora more than four decades, albeit with a lengthy disruption.

In *Anne of Green Gables*, Anne and Diana allowed Maud to celebrate romantic friendship with abandon, but Maud also signals its convention-ality within the era's social norms. "It's so nice to have a lot of little girls to play with," Anne says after her first day in school. "But of course I like Diana best and always will. I *adore* Diana."[37] The cliché reveals the bosom friend jargon that Anne has learned in school. She is mimicking the lan-guage of romantic friends. There is nothing secretive about the relationship, and when Anne becomes too romantically involved, the nar-rator views her histrionics ironically, suggesting that her behavior is overly dramatic. And yet, by setting the story of Anne during the late nineteenth century, when romantic friendships were still acceptable and expected, Maud could celebrate these rituals with abandon—and she could also cel-ebrate the time and space that allowed them to flourish. Most importantly, she was able to repair in fiction the friendships that had crumbled in life. Maud's own idealization was colored by nostalgia, by an understanding that these rituals were passing away and yet were an important part of her life and well-being. Her perspective was subversive even as her irony echoed the era's increasingly critical approach to the topic. Maud's girlfriends were the amalgam that went into her writing of the ideal bosom friendship that joined Anne with Diana.

SEVEN

Pagan Love and Sacred Promises: Anne and Diana

The two little girls walked with their arms about each other. At the brook they parted with many promises to spend the next afternoon together.
—Anne Shirley accompanied by Diana Barry on her way home from Barry's farm[1]

As spring turned into summer in 1905, the Macneill rose bushes budded and then bloomed as they never had before. In the twilight of the evening, sitting in her upstairs den at her little window overlooking the fields, Maud wrote chapter twelve, "A Solemn Vow and Promise," drawing from a deep and personal well. In it, Anne Shirley, hungry for a "bosom friend," has come to the Barry home to meet Diana and finds her on the sofa reading a book. Anne compels Diana to put down her book and step outdoors into the world of action, demanding: "Will you swear to be my friend for ever and ever?" Diana titters, "You're a queer girl, Anne," but she complies with her new girlfriend's wishes.[2]

Like an epicurean philosopher, Maud evokes a world of discriminate pleasure. The oath swearing takes place in a bower of wildflowers, as if Eros and his mother Aphrodite had set the stage. The summer garden wilderness unfolds its sensuality as a backdrop for the couple's joining. Crimson peonies, white narcissi, purple Adam and Eve, pink and blue and white columbines arouse the mind's eye. Musk flowers, sweet clover, sweet roses, fragrant sprays, and mint pleasure the nose. Humming bees and purring wind titillate the ears. Maud's love of the flower catalogue provided the seeds for this orchard, while the rhythmic poetry of her prose provided the rain and the sun that made it blossom into perfection.

In fact, the old orchard's unrestrained sensuous beauty was also fuelled by Maud's nostalgic memory. To "go and stay all night" with Penzie was bliss when they were children. She vividly remembered spending the nights with her chum in that "little old house under the huge willows, with the most delightful, unworldly old garden behind it, ablow with roses and musk." These same old willows and the same old orchard and musk scent now made their appearance in *Anne of Green Gables* as the site in which Anne and Diana's friendship is blessed. The sunshine message of the original religious magazine story is turned on its head in this unrestrained reveling of pagan joy. "What chums Penzie and I were in those long ago days! And what fun we did have!" she had exclaimed in her journal in April 1902, after dreaming of Penzie and the old garden, and admitting that, sadly, their friendship had fallen apart.[3] In her fiction, Maud could repair the broken friendship.

Red-haired Anne and black-haired Diana are physical and temperamental complements. Thin and finicky Anne feeds on romance and ethereal dreams and intoxicating words. Plump and earthy Diana Barry loves food and drink. Mistakenly gulping down several tumblers of wine in one episode, Diana embodies aspects of Maud, who fondly remembered the late-night Park Corner chicken bones and hams, the caramels and chocolates. Maud took obvious pleasure in joining the felicitous twosome under happy stars. A firm believer in astrology and graphology, in dreams and premonitions, she presumably drew the girls' birth months from the June 1905 issue of *Modern Women* (which also contained Maud's own story "By the Grace of Sarah Maud"). "February—Humane and affectionate as wife and tender as mother; March—A chatterbox, fickle, stormy and given to quarrels." In chapter twelve, the two bosom friends' temperaments are intriguingly matched to these "astrological" birth months in the magazine column "What Month Were You Born." As Anne Shirley informs Marilla, "Diana's birthday is in February and mine is in March. Don't you think that is a very strange coincidence?"[4]

The loyal pair represents a dream friendship without quarrels, disappointments, or betrayals. Theirs is an ideal friendship that belongs to the realm of fantasy. Sharing an idyllic love, the couple differs from the sisterly community that surrounds Jo March in Louisa May Alcott's *Little Women* (1868), a work twenty-two-year-old Maud had purchased, read, and annotated in 1896. "Their friendship never falters," writes scholar Temma F. Berg about Anne and Diana, "the two girls remain true to one another even while kept apart."[5] They seem welded to each other, like two opposite sides of the same personality.

Recognizing the pair's romantic closeness, fans, journalists, and scholars have debated the nature of the relationship with great passion.[6] Is it the embodiment of the perfect friendship? Is it a platonic love between girls and women? Is there evidence of lesbian (read: physical) desire? The latter suggestion created a media quake in Canada. "'Outrageously sexual' Anne Was a Lesbian, Scholar Insists," read the headline in the *Ottawa Citizen* on May 25, 2000, after an academic had combed the Anne books for evidence of "lesbian desire." Asked in a *Globe and Mail* interview if Maud had lesbian tendencies in later life, her biographer Mary Rubio answered with a categorical "absolutely not."[7] It was an echo of Maud's own assertion "I am not a Lesbian" in a February 1932 journal entry.[8] The fifty-seven-year old author felt she had to defend herself in her journal when she was being courted passionately by thirty-six-year-old teacher Isabel Anderson, who had accused her of being incapable of love. And yet Maud's genius in fiction consisted precisely in evoking a world and era in which such complexities and clear-cut categories did not exist.

The Playhouse in Idlewild

Immersed in her writing and the beauty of summer, Maud's fast pen raced across the pages as she poured out her vivid imaginings. Soon, it was time to send Anne and Diana to school after summer vacation. We can sense the ease and speed with which she wrote the novel. On a "crisp September morning" the girls enjoy their romantic walk to school in chapter fifteen.[9] Maud was in her element. The girls and their love belonged to the pagan geography she herself reveled in. Each day the two girls walked through Lover's Lane, through Mr. Barry's back field, and past Willowmere—beyond which came Violet Vale and the Birch Path, named so by Diana. Maud admitted that this landmark was drawn from a photograph she said she found in *Outing Magazine*. This photograph, originally found in *The Booklovers Magazine* in October 1904, was taken by D. Davidson in 1901, and was part of a series of images poetically titled *Twin Sentinels of the Trail, The Path Through the Birches, As the Trail Nears the Summit, A Dim Forest Aisle*.[10] It was the inspiration for the "narrow, twisting path, winding down over a long hill straight through Mr. Bell's woods,"[11] the evocative path traveled by Anne and Diana each day on their way to school. Maud had become excellent at describing scenes she had seen in photographs. In fact, as she told her friend Ephraim, *East and West* often sent her pictures and told her to create a story to match the illustration.[12] While she did not enjoy being thus constrained, she had become an expert at whipping up a story based on a visual image.

Anne and Diana set up their "playhouse" in a spot Anne names Idlewild. As the name suggests, they are seeking to set themselves off from the larger society of rural Avonlea, which values neither the "idle" nor the "wild." As if to contain their pleasure within the boundaries of childhood innocence, Anne and Diana are forced to give up Idlewild before they turn thirteen, that is, prior to puberty. When Mr. Bell cuts down the trees, Diana declares that they are too old for the game anyway. Maud imposed boundaries, signaling that crushes, sensuous as they are, are meant to be read platonically. The year 1905 was when *Huckleberry Finn* and *Tom Sawyer* were banned from the children's section of the Brooklyn Public Library for setting bad examples of behavior, and Maud's limits are clear. And yet Maud left possibilities open particularly for the adult literary reader who was invited to decode rich literary and mythological allusions.

According to Maud's journal account, the Idlewild scene was modeled on episodes with Maud's little playmates the Nelson boys, the two orphans who boarded with the Macneills when Maud was aged seven to ten. "Every summer we devoted our playtime to our 'house' and gardened and swung and picnicked and had no end of fun," Maud recalled in her unpublished journal entry of 1892, reviving her memory of their little playhouse in the spruce wood, north of the front orchard.

In the purple dusk of a fragrant summer evening we would go
out into the front orchard, and, lying at ease in the delightful tangle of musk and caraway and 'dandies' we would pull the yellow
stars to make the 'curls' and 'chairs' that were so plump and brave
while fresh and so withered and unsightly when they dried.[13]

In describing this nostalgic childhood scene, Maud also recalled an old
green boat named Daisy Dean, turned upside down. On and under this
boat she played housekeeping with Well, a game that involved a fascinating class and gender bend: "Well was my 'mistress' and I was his
'servant'"; this meant that Maud "did all the work" while "he looked on,
gave orders." One day Maud, craving some little compliment in compensation for her labor, asked Well to pretend they had a visitor, to whom he
was to say, in a line supplied by Maud herself, "I have such a good servant." Well, quick on the intake, agreed to the imaginary visitor, but
revised Maud's script, to say, "I have such a bad servant. She can't do anything right and she won't obey my orders." Maud recalled in her journal
that "I had a fortunate sense of humor, even then, so I sat down, with my
hands full of 'chickenweeds' and laughed until I cried."[14]

Pagan Diana

In Roman mythology, Diana was the huntress who was at home in the
woods. Maud would have been familiar with the Diana verses by Canadian
poet Gertrude Bartlett, who published in the same magazines as Maud.
Her 1902 "A Pagan's Prayer" in *Ainslee's* fetes "Dian's beauty" poetically:

Lithe-limbed dryades my will is
    To encounter, where the lines
Of tall, yellow, woodland lilies
    Burn like torches 'neath the pines.

In the forest is a portal
    I would find and wander through

> To the hidden source immortal
>   Of the joy the pagan knew.[15]

Diana belongs to the world of the woodlands and woodland nymphs, the world of fauns and placid streams and scented orchards—the world of *Anne of Green Gables*. Linked to the moon, Diana was also the goddess of fertility and childbirth. In both mythology and the era's popular culture, Diana's name was associated with paganism, and we recall that Matthew finds the name "dreadful heathenish."[16] Literary readers would also have associated the name with the unconventional female figures of Romantic female friendship, such as *Diana of the Crossways* (1885) by British author George Meredith. In *Godey's Lady's Book*, Maud would have read about Margaret Oliphant's 1892 novel *Diana*. "Diana is a charming woman and the author has sprung a rare surprise upon us by not letting her marry."[17] Neither does the title character ever form an attachment with a man in Florence Converse's 1897 American novel *Diana Victrix*, a novel focusing on female friendship.

A Part of One Another

Fredericka Elmanstine Campbell was Maud's closest confidante while she was writing *Anne*, yet there is suspiciously little about her in the journal entries of that time. Called by the androgynous name Frede, Maud's friend was the youngest of her beloved Aunt Annie's children, the Campbell cousins Clara, Stella, George, and Fredericka. Their house in the little village of Park Corner, opposite her Grandfather Montgomery's house, was a place that resounded with laughter. In her 1933 novel *Pat of Silver Bush*, Maud immortalized the Campbell home, using it as a model for her character Pat's beloved home. Since then the Campbell house has been known under the name Silver Bush, and the Campbell descendants operate the *Anne of Green Gables* Museum. Behind the house is the pond that Maud later claimed was the Lake of Shining Waters.

In many ways, Frede remains a mystery. Only after Frede's death in January 1919 did Maud provide a detailed and idealized portrait. Colored by the pain of loss, the lengthy journal entry is a chronology of their companionship, which, according to Maud's account, began in earnest in August 1902 when Maud overnighted at the Campbell's home. "I recall the night distinctly," Maud wrote in 1919:

> It was a hot night. For some forgotten reason we all three occupied Stella's room. Stell herself slept on the floor. Frede and I were in the bed. We began to talk confidentially each finding that we could confide in the other. Stell was furious because our chatter kept her from sleeping, so we buried our heads under the blankets that sweltering night and whispered to each other all our troubles—I, the woman of 28, Frede the girl of 19. We discovered that our souls were the same age![18]

From that hour on, the two women were, as Maud paraphrases years later, "part of one another."[19]

As if she meant to weld Frede to the bosom friendship of Anne and Diana, Maud's retrospective journal portrait of her cousin mirrors the figure of Anne Shirley physically, spiritually, and emotionally. Like Anne, Frede was vivid, dramatic, and intense. Like Anne, she was also homely, freckled, and sallow, and her "enemies called her ugly" because there was "too much spirit and character in her face." Maud gave Anne Frede's gray-green eyes and quality to dilate into black orbs. In the right light, Frede's mocking eyes looked fascinating and attractive to Maud. Like Anne, Frede was lonely, odd, and queer; in Frede's own words, she was "the cat that walks by herself."[20] An excellent letter writer with a knack for recalling memories Maud cherished, Frede recalled in a 1917 letter drinking Grandmother Macneill's currant wine,[21] and we are reminded of Diana's enjoyment of Marilla's currant wine in the famous raspberry cordial episode in chapter sixteen. Maud's relationships with her girlfriends had a freedom that she would not have shared with the men in the same measure; dealings with the opposite sex were much more curtailed, especially when living with Grandmother Macneill.

Intelligent and witty Frede finished Prince of Wales College at age fourteen with a first-class teaching license. Regrettably, girls were given just enough education "to 'earn their own living,'" writes Maud in her

1919 journal entry, paraphrasing Marilla's more positive words for Anne ("I believe in a girl being fitted to earn her own living whether she ever has to do or not"[22]). In the fall of 1904, Frede took the school in Stanley, ten kilometers from Cavendish. Perhaps because Frede was a relative, and perhaps because she put up a smiling front where Nora may have been more critical, Frede was accepted as a regular visitor by the crabby Grandmother Macneill and later by Ewan Macdonald. In fact, Maud liked to involve a girlfriend in her relationships with men, often feeling perfectly at ease with a man only when one of her girlfriends was present. Frede was Maud's confidante with a privileged window into Maud's private life. Frede was a rare emotional and intellectual match—they were true kindred spirits, belonging to "the race that knows Joseph," a concept Frede had coined to describe their special bond and to suggest that they were different from commonplace people; they had affinities with the biblical Joseph, an exiled figure famous for his special gifts including his coat of many colors and his ability to interpret dreams. Just as Anne is the dominating character in her friendship with Diana, so Frede had always looked up to her older cousin with admiration. Yet it was only many years later, when she thought Frede was dying in 1915, that Maud first acknowledged her as "my more than sister, the woman who was nearest and dearest to me in the world!"[23]

A Boston Marriage

At age thirty, when Maud was writing *Anne*, she was at a crossroads in her life. The good people of Cavendish expected her to marry. "The court of last resort" was what the women's magazines she read called marriage at her age. In May, *The Ladies' Home Journal* had featured a table showing the "percentage of chances a woman has to marry at different ages." The statistics were dismal: 20–25 years, 52 chances; 25–30 years, 18 chances; 30–35 years, 15½ chances; 35–40 years, 3¾ chances.[24] Yet Maud also yearned for freedom. In a story she had recently published in New York's *The Delineator* magazine, she had explored the "Boston marriage," two women living together as a couple. Truth be told, she was conflicted and confused as far as her personal life was concerned. And this confusion was a secret she most definitely did not share with Ewan Macdonald.

In February 1904, just a year before she began work on *Anne of Green Gables*, Maud published in *The Delineator* a short story entitled "The Promise of Lucy Ellen." Although the story was reprinted in Catherine McLay's collection of rediscovered short stories by L. M. Montgomery, *The Doctor's Sweetheart and Other Stories* in 1979, its remarkable content has never been considered in relation to *Anne of Green Gables* or Maud's own life. In this story, Maud described "a Boston marriage," two women cohabiting as a couple. Wearing bonnets like two married women, sharing breakfast and dinner at the table, Cecily and Lucy Ellen Foster, two cousins, share a gabled, old-fashioned house ("hers and Lucy Ellen's"[25]) in a place called Oriental. Together, the pair have made a "sacred" vow to each other:

> It was Lucy Ellen that had first proposed their mutual promise, but Cecily had grasped at it eagerly. The two women, verging on decisive old maidenhood, solemnly promised each other that they would never marry, and would always live together. From that time Cecily's mind had been at ease. In her eyes a promise was a sacred thing.[26]

The story opens on a scene of domestic happiness, as Cecily and Lucy Ellen have cohabited for a considerable although unspecified length of time. Yet what follows is the sad story of the breakdown of the women's bond when former suitor Cromwell Biron returns with a belated marriage proposal. Shocked by their impending divorce, Cecily tries to hold Lucy Ellen to her vow: "'But he sha'n't get her,' Cecily whispered into her hymnbook.... 'She promised.'"[27] The promise is like a sacred contract, an indissoluble marriage bond. Anger, pain, and resentment mount. "This was her reward for all the love she had lavished on Lucy Ellen." Eventually she releases Lucy Ellen from the vow. "I hope he'll be good to her," she says.[28] The heterosexual marriage supersedes the Boston marriage, yet the new couple is depicted in unflattering terms. Lucy Ellen is simpering, nervous, and trembling. Cromwell Biron is weak, bald, and fat. In contrast, Cecily is saved by her sense of humor. Still, it was perhaps prescient that Maud wrote the Boston marriage as a divorce story. Was she exploring her own future?

In *Anne of Green Gables*, these deep-seated fears provide the material for comic relief, as Anne expresses her rage against Diana's imagined future husband: "I hate her husband—I just hate him furiously," cries Anne, while a bemused Marilla listens. "I've been imagining it all out—the wedding and everything—Diana dressed in snowy garments, with a veil, and looking as beautiful and regal as a queen; and me the bridesmaid, with a lovely dress, too, and puffed sleeves, but with a breaking heart hid beneath my smiling face."[29] Poking fun at the girl's fear of losing her girlfriend, Maud also introduces the possibility of a Boston marriage. "Diana and I are thinking seriously of promising each other that we will never marry but be nice old maids and live together for ever," says Anne, yet Diana hesitates to commit herself to this plan.[30] Maud, who at the time she wrote her novel was considering what future she wanted for herself, played with these literary associations by creating, in contrast to the more free-thinking Anne, a Diana character who assumes without question that she will become a wife and mother. It is puckish and pagan Anne who has absorbed all of the Dianic qualities.

By this point, the girls' bond has twice survived the test of cruel separation: first when Anne refused to go to school, after her altercation with Gilbert, and second, when Mrs. Barry insisted that the two must part after Diana became drunk after having tea with Anne. The dramatic farewells allow further reiterations of eternal love drawn from girls' keepsake albums. The former episode was modeled on Maud's own life, when her grandfather took her out of school in 1888 for several months after a disagreement with the teacher, Miss Izzie Robinson. Thirteen-year-old Maud would never forget the monotony and loneliness and separation from Mollie.[31]

Veiled by the comedy is Maud's own separation anxiety and panic and her lifelong desire to bind her female friends to her by means of contracts, vows, and promises. When Penzie married Will Bulman and moved to New Glasgow in July 1898, she did not say a word about her marriage to Maud, who recorded the "shabby treatment" in her journal, noting, "I suppose she has dropped out of my life forever."[32] That Penzie should feel unable even to mention her upcoming marriage speaks volumes.

Similarly, when Frede suddenly married in 1917, Maud was "dumfoundered, flabbergasted, knocked out and rendered speechless,"[33] even though, in practical terms, their relationship was essentially unchanged. Frede's husband, Cameron MacFarlane, was a soldier and Frede continued to live alone. Maud and Frede, too, had made a promise—a "compact" as Maud calls it—that when either of them died, the deceased woman's spirit would "come back" to appear to the survivor. The ritual was a variant of the *Liebestod* (death-in-love) that, in romantic literature, unites heterosexual lovers, such as Romeo and Juliet, in death. Years later, in January 1919, when Frede was dying of the Spanish flu in a Montreal hospital, Maud, hysterical with grief, reminded her of their mutual promise: "Frede," Maud said earnestly, "you won't forget your promise to come and see me, will you?" "No," Frede answered.[34] Frede's death unleashed a stormy and excessive grieving that would last until the end of Maud's own life and that leads us to conclude that Frede was the central love of her life. Even before her death, Maud had cast her in a remarkably physical and sensuous description. Her cheeks were flushed, she writes about her favorite memory, her eyes brilliant, a pendant glistening on her breast, and earrings caressing her cheeks.[35] In her grief she fantasized about having a child from Frede which she would have loved to bring up. "I shall always feel as if I belonged 'back there'—back there with Frede and laughter and years of peace."[36]

While involved in her slow and unhurried courtship dance with Ewan, her look into her own future of possible marriage and motherhood also fueled her nostalgia. In *Anne of Green Gables*, she was able to explore the bosom friendship with unrestrained enthusiasm and passion. The writing of this passion ironically followed right on the heels of her afternoon visits and flirts with Ewan Macdonald. Through clever wit and irony, Maud had a gift of bringing her readers tantalizingly close to unspoken feelings of sensuality and sexuality, while ingeniously portraying these feelings as universal and innocent.

EIGHT

Good Enemies and Old Love Letters

She flashed one indignant glance at Gilbert from eyes whose angry sparkle was swiftly quenched in equally angry tears.

"You mean, hateful boy!" she exclaimed passionately. "How dare you!"

And then—Thwack! Anne had brought her slate down on Gilbert's head and cracked it—slate, not head—clear across.

—Anne's first encounter with Gilbert Blythe[1]

Reading *Anne of Green Gables*, we are struck by the explosiveness of emotions as Anne lobs hostile insults against school heartthrob Gilbert Blythe or local authority Mrs. Lynde. Turning from bosom friends and kindred spirits, we now consider the enemies in Anne's life, which include not only annoying boyfriends but also authority figures and an entire family clan (such as the much-maligned Pye family). Anticipating popular twentieth-century developmental theories (such as Jean Piaget's), Maud believed that rivalries, jealousies, and conflicts were not necessarily negative but could expedite cognitive development in children.[2] Maud's 1902 poem "To My Enemy" sums up her philosophy regarding the positive power of a good enemy:

Thine anger struck from me a flame
That purged all dull content away.

111

Our mortal strife to me hath been
Unflagging spur from day to day.[3]

In February 1938, bitter about her son Chester, whose self-indulgence and lack of responsibility were a great source of distress, she recited this poem at a tea and injected so much "venom" that the audience was taken aback. By that time, her feelings toward the girl who had inspired the poem were long gone, but the venom in the poem has remained as if it had been bottled in a vial. Readers of *Anne* will remember hateful Josie Pye.

Maud was profoundly influenced by her Scottish culture's rich tradition of verbal sparring, debating, and orating; she also had an ear and gift for elocution, which was popular during the Victorian era. But it was the tangled web of clan bonds, also an important part of growing up in a proud Scottish-Presbyterian family, that provided a rich source for life-long tensions and feud, as did several old, unresolved love affairs. The good enemy, as Maud proposed, is often a kindred spirit in disguise. And for Anne, that "good enemy" is Gilbert Blythe.

The Simpsons

There was one family that Maud loved to hate. "By the way have you Simpsons in Alloa? Cavendish is full of them," Maud told her friend George B. MacMillan in 1905, adding that her great-great grandmother was a Scottish-born Simpson.[4] Known for their pride and vainglory, the Simpsons, along with the equally vainglorious Macneills and Clarks, were among those who founded Cavendish in 1790. They were the educated and outspoken authority figures of the little hamlets of Cavendish and Belmont. They were also related to the Macneills through intermarriage. (In fact, there was a great deal of intermarriage in Cavendish, which was perhaps the reason Maud's grandfather Macneill was dead set against first cousins marrying each other.) Despite (or perhaps because of) these intense clan bonds, Maud loved to poke fun at her relatives in her journals, with frequent jibes at what she called "Simpsonism" or "Simpsony." She was no doubt echoing the jabs she had heard around the Macneill kitchen table as she grew up, for Grandfather and Grandmother Macneill had always had a distinct dislike of the Simpsons.[5]

But what was the other side of the story? "The Simpsons were community people and they were always at the forefront. They were the pillars of the community, they were the pillars of the church, and if the roads needed to be broken for the mail person in the winter, they would be out doing it."[6] Descendants are still farming the Simpson land, and the homestead where Maud boarded when she was a school teacher in 1897 is still standing. "I'm glad Maud Montgomery is not alive today because I would wring her neck for the things she said about my father and his family," said ninety-three-year-old Ruth Johnson, offended by Maud's uncharitable journal comments about the Simpson family, including her disparaging remarks about Johnson's own father, who was living in the house when Maud was a boarder.[7] The old wounds are still sore, and family pride still rules as it did more than a century ago.

As Maud recounts in her journal, the schism between Macneills and Simpsons had opened with a children's prank. The Cavendish youth had been playacting "the resurrection of Lazarus," with Ernest Macneill in the role of Lazarus. The performers dug a shallow grave, buried the dead Lazarus under clay sand, and performed the resurrection miracle. The entire performance was witnessed by a group of wide-eyed school children. When they took the story home to their parents, simmering family animosity exploded into outrage over the desecration of sacred subjects. The Simpsons accused the Macneills of desecrating religious subject matter and founded a church of their own, the Baptist Church. This was when the old Baptist Church was built in the beautiful maple grove close to the Cavendish Hall.[8] The family acrimonies were now entrenched in a religious divide separating the Presbyterian Macneills and Baptist Simpsons.

Close to the Baptist Church was the Cavendish Hall, which would figure prominently as the Avonlea Hall in the novel. The whitewashed building with a raised platform and library shelves to one side came alive during the winter months when the Literary Society convened for discussions, debates, and musical entertainment. Perhaps because of the family enmity, her grandparents were at first opposed to Maud's visiting the Baptist Church and the Hall, but the Literary, as it was dubbed, would play an important role in Maud's development as a writer. When the Cavendish Hall was razed early in 1960, the Literary Society minute book was recovered and a typescript was prepared by the Prince Edward Island Public Archives in Charlottetown. Yielding fascinating insight into the political, social, and cultural concerns of Maud's era, it also illuminates the local power play and animosities. As we sift through the minutiae of the minute book, from the February 1886 founding of the Literary Society to its 1924 ending, important pieces in the puzzle of *Anne of Green Gables* are revealed.[9] Discussion topics of the annual winter program varied from Walter Scott to Lord Tennyson, from Confederation to Prohibition, from dairying to pork packing. Opinions were duly noted in the minute book along with some exquisite howlers, such as a recitation of Tennyson's "Crossing the Bar" recorded as "Crossing the *Barley.*"[10] Here the young fry of Cavendish practiced public speaking and musical performance before an audience.

During the time Maud was writing *Anne of Green Gables*, the President of the Literary was Arthur Simpson. The conservative town elder with a distinct dislike for strong women had been a dominant presence over the years, and the minute book is peppered with his incendiary opinions. "Arthur Simpson considered the paper good and George Elliott [sic] bad."[11] This entry of March 27, 1890, followed Miss C. J. Clark's presentation on the daring female British writer Mary Ann Evans, aka George Eliot, who had taken a lover and given herself the male pseudonym. It was heavy stuff for some of the elders. "Arthur Simpson...thought there was little to admire in the Character of Elizabeth," we read for February 5, 1891, about the red-haired Queen Elizabeth I whom Maud admired.[12] In fact, her personal library in the University of Guelph Archives contains the full set of James Anthony Froude's five-volume *Reign of Elizabeth*. It must have irked Maud, too, that Arthur Simpson misspelled her name as "Maude" when he was the minute taker.[13] In fact, it was Arthur "Pa" Simpson whom Maud detested "with an undiluted hatred." In turn, she said, he hated her and her music recitals.[14]

Another formidable presence at the Literary was the Honorable George W. Simpson, a farmer and, from 1903, a Liberal member of the Legislative Council. In the photo Maud glued into her scrapbook, a drooping moustache dominates George's slim face. His eyes are piercing.

Judging from the comments in the minute book, he spoke with flair and panache. In 1906, at age 48, he died of blood poisoning, leaving a cavernous gap in the Literary as "our ablest debater."[15] It was George W. Simpson who presided at the Literary when Maud came out on Friday, November 22, 1889, just days before her fifteenth birthday. It was her first public recitation on the platform of the old Cavendish Hall—a personal milestone that she never forgot.

Taking the Stage

The Hall was full. For weeks, standing in front of the mirror of her den, she had practiced "The Child Martyr," May Anderson's poem of sacrifice and pathos. Mollie went first, then Nate Lockhart. Finally George Simpson called up "Miss Maud Montgomery." Trembling, she stepped onto the platform and felt herself drowning in the sea of faces. Looking up at her paralyzed figure were Arthur Simpson, George Simpson, the other town elders, her teacher Hattie Gordon, her treasured school friends, and her odious foes. Maud collected her wits and began to recite.[16] In chapter thirty-three, "The Hotel Concert," Maud replayed in fiction her overwhelming attack of stage fright. Anne's knees tremble, her heart flutters, and she feels as if she is going to faint; that is, until she sees in the audience her archenemy Gilbert. "She drew a long breath and flung her head up proudly, courage and determination tingling over her like an electric shock. She *would not* fail before Gilbert Blythe—he should never be able to laugh at her, never, never!"[17]

When the choir concluded the evening of Maud's first recital by singing "God Be With You Till We Meet Again," she was hooked. The platform would always hold a special magic for her, and she returned year after year to recite poetry by Tennyson, Scott, and Longfellow. Though she had no professional training, Maud had a natural talent for elocution. For women of her generation, it was an important form of cultural entertainment and public expression. In November 1890, Canadian elocutionist and Boston College instructor Agnes Knox had performed in Prince Albert to great acclaim. Maud admired the performer who looked like a queen swathed in a black velvet dress; she, too, would make a cameo as Mrs. Evans, when Anne Shirley recites at the American concert. In August 1900, Pauline Johnson stopped in Charlottetown during her Maritime tour. By the early twentieth century, however, elocution was also coming under attack and was considered increasingly old-fashioned. Its critics charged it to be overly dramatic, encouraging conventionalized and exaggerated emotions, rather than natural expressions. *Anne of Green Gables* was a nostalgic return to Maud's thrilling performances of the past when she had first won public acclaim. Maud savored the "puffs" she received in the local papers in Cavendish and Prince Albert. With glee she glued the newspaper raves into her scrapbook. "Miss Montgomery deserves special mention. She was encored again and again."[18] Since her first recital, she had also read critical papers on literary subjects, and none other than George W. Simpson had praised her on February 3, 1899: "Miss Montgomery then took the platform and in an excellently written critical paper took up most of the present day novelists of front rank giving a brief anyalis [analysis] of some of their work in a concise and forcible manner."[19] In fact, George W.'s generous praise of Maud's work each time he recorded the minutes forces us to qualify Maud's sweeping criticism of the Simpsons as self-involved. Maud's hunger for public praise is evident, and that hunger would be mirrored in her red-haired heroine. These accolades flooded her with warmth and pride; they also whetted her appetite for more.

Despite her elocutionary talent and George W.'s praise, Maud felt inadequate in comparison to the brilliant Simpson men. They were outstanding debaters, clever at verbal sparring, and eager to engage on any subject. The Literary was the epicenter for debate, just as the Avonlea Hall is the meeting place for the Debating Club in *Anne of Green Gables*. Maud, however, was fearful of adversarial situations. After attending the Literary Society in French River, Maud recorded "another big fight" in an unpublished May 1892 journal entry: "It was simply disgraceful the way they went on and I never was so sick of anything in my life."[20] She does not say what the topic was. A wordsmith with her pen, she was by no means a dazzling conversationalist and remained mute during debates. Quiet and introspective, her wit sparkled only in a group of kindred spirits. Whenever she had anything delicate or uncomfortable to communicate she would rely on a go-between—even later in life and even with people she considered close friends.

Anne Confronts Gilbert Blythe

During the happy summer of 1905, Maud was not only delighting in roses and rambles, but also quickly reaching chapter fifteen, "A Tempest in the School Teapot," with its first meeting and clash between Anne and Gilbert. Maud had adopted the character of Gilbert from her earlier February story "Aunt Susanna's Birthday Celebration," where she had first introduced Gilbert Martin and Anne Douglas as a "fine-looking couple." They did have their shortcomings, as the narrator Aunt Susanna explains: "Anne's nose was a mite too long, and Gil had a crooked mouth. Besides, they was both pretty proud and sperrited and high-strung."[21] The "crooked mouth" was imported from Maud's kindred spirit Will Pritchard of Prince Albert fame. It was a lovable but distinctive flaw. Perhaps it was too distinctive—too much of a reminder of Will.

With a few strokes of the pen, Maud repackaged and refashioned Gilbert Martin. She softened his angles, neutralized his features, and feathered the edges as the photographer airbrushes a picture. And voilà! A happier and less prickly boy was born in Gilbert Blythe. "He was a tall boy, with curly brown hair, roguish hazel eyes, and a mouth twisted into a teasing smile."[22] After quarreling with Anne, bright and nice-mannered Gilbert Martin had gone out west to Manitoba. In *Anne of Green Gables*, Maud brings him back to the Island from the prairies, for fourteen-year-old Gilbert Blythe is catching up in school after a three-year stint in Alberta where he accompanied his sick father on his convalescence. The makeover complete, Maud spells out the name of the village Romeo on the school porch wall along with Julia Bell's. "He's *aw'fly* handsome, Anne," Diana moons. "And he teases the girls something terrible. He just torments our lives out."[23]

With her cast of characters crowding into the whitewashed Avonlea school, Maud relived the atmosphere in the old one-room school behind the dusky fir woods near the brook. This was the old world of Nellie and

Clemmie, Mollie and Pollie, Snip and Snap, Alma Macneill, Penzie
Macneill, Alena Macneill, and so many others. She remembered the hiero-
glyphics and initials of generations of students carved in the old brown
benches. Teaching was a rich arena for satire. Teachers' salaries were
unfortunately a pittance, attracting teenage women and men who were
not always the most competent or accomplished educators. The women
would marry and the men would move on to become doctors or ministers, more lucrative professions. At least three of Maud's suitors, Prince
Albert teacher Mr. Mustard, the model for the incompetent Mr. Phillips in
Anne of Green Gables, Belmont teacher Ed Simpson, and Ewan Macdonald
followed this path. The school lent itself easily to social satire, even
though Prince Edward Island was also one of the first communities to
introduce free education in the British Dominion, doing so in 1852. The
bench where Maud so often sat daydreaming and looking out of the window is the bench where Anne Shirley sits on her first day at school, her
eyes fixed on the Lake of Shining Waters.

The stage was set for one of the novel's most popular scenes. Trying
to capture Anne's attention, Gilbert Blythe picks up the end of her braid
and whispers, "Carrots! Carrots!" Anne fans the world over know in a flash
what will happen next and probably know some of the wording by heart.
Millions of readers have delighted in the explosive scene, when Anne leaps
from her seat and brings down the slate, "Thwack!" cracking it on Gilbert's
head, much to the horrified delight of the Avonlea school. Diana gasps.
The teacher Mr. Phillips stalks down the aisle to assign unequal punish-
ment. The explosive act described in the epigraph fuels the plotline for the
rest of the novel. What caused the blazing emotions behind the drama?
There was a simple honesty and spontaneity about this act. There was
great pleasure and release in this blunt, rude, unforgettable breaking of
Victorian etiquette and decorum. What could inspire such a passionate
outburst in thin-lipped and retiring Maud writing in her spinsterish den in
the twilight of the day? It is a particularly rich episode in which a number
of adventures and influences came together in one powerful scene. They
all had to do with Maud's own unique set of conflicts with boys.

The most obvious influence for the scene takes us to February 1893,
when eighteen-year-old Maud was back in the Cavendish school to prepare for her teacher's college entrance examination, as Anne would in the

novel. "Cavendish Carrots," the boy she had nicknamed for his flaming red hair had made her scream in class by poking and startling her. Embarrassed, she took revenge by writing the ditty "The Boy With the Auburn Hair." It sparked a feud that continued for months, as she reports in her journal. Yet much suggests that Gilbert was also an amalgam of many characters, including several foes who were worthy of her steel and stirred up complex feelings of both friendship and hostility. Maud engaged their memories just around the time she would have written the scene.

Love Letters from the Past: Nate Lockhart

An unpublished journal entry reveals that in the evening of Sunday, August 6, around the time she would probably have prepared to write the Anne and Gilbert "Tempest in the Teapot" episode, Maud had pulled out an old packet of letters from her trunk. They were from her first boyfriend, Nate Lockhart Spurr (the same boy she had called "that detestable pig" in her letter to Penzie). "I wonder what Nate is doing tonight?" she asked in the unpublished journal entry.[24] She untied the red ribbon that held together the letters and began reading, delving into the old Cavendish school days.

Witty, brainy Nate Lockhart was thin and pale with a freckled face and expressive eyes. He was unlike any other boy in the Cavendish school. The half-orphan, whose father had drowned at sea during a storm, had arrived from Nova Scotia in 1885, the year that brought electricity and the telephone to Prince Edward Island. He was a breath of fresh air for Maud. Equipped with a poet uncle, Arthur John Lockhart (better known in Nova Scotia as Pastor Felix), Nate had impeccable pedigree. To this kindred spirit Maud first confessed her most secret desire to become a writer. At the same time, a rivalry developed between the two that anticipated the Gilbert and Anne rivalry. At school, Nate vied with Maud to be the head of the class. He bested Maud in the Prince Edward Island essay competition in May 1890,[25] and although Maud was Nate's senior by two months, the minute book indicates his forceful presence in the august Cavendish Literary Society almost two years before Maud made her first appearance.[26] Behind the bland entries of the minute book, it is startling to learn that the future Saskatchewan crown prosecutor in fact outshone the future author of *Anne* in literary matters. This must have irked the ambitious girl who had devoted her life to writing and whose determination was unswerving. She did admit, in her journal, that Nate often "vexed" her.

Encroaching on her literary turf, this competitive male was the model for Anne's rivalry with Gilbert, the "foeman worthy of [Anne's] steel."[27] The rivalry propels Anne to scholastic excellence far beyond the Avonlea school. Maud may have gotten even with Nate by teasing "his life half out,"[28] but the fierceness of Anne's competitiveness with Gilbert, which stretches over two thirds of the novel, may also suggest the author's underlying and unspoken resentment. Only in fiction could she give full vent to her feelings. Was the new boy from away perhaps given preference in the Literary because *he was a boy*?[29]

She thrilled over their romantic moonlight walks, and their talks, talks, talks. Nate was the first boyfriend to propose to her, when she was just fifteen. In his love letter, he wrote on February 18, 1890, two days after his fifteenth birthday, "Of all my feminine friends the one whom I most admire—no, I'm growing reckless—the one whom I *love*…is L.M. Montgomery, the girl I shook hands with, the girl after my own heart."[30] The letter was written in red ink.

Yet, as Maud writes in her journal, when the friendship became physical—just around the time following this love declaration—the romance sadly collapsed. She loved the kindred spirit but his kisses left her strangely cold. She desired a brother more than a lover, a pattern that would repeat itself with other suitors. She simply could not stand the feeling of somebody taking possession of her, moving into her space, her body, shifting things around. There never was a clear resolution, however. Had she been able to communicate with frankness and sensitivity, she might have saved her friendship. But frankness was never Maud's style. Elusiveness was. The awkward affair fizzled out after she went to Prince Albert and he went to study law at Acadia College (today Acadia University) in Nova Scotia. The affair remained unresolved and there was resentment on both sides. His graduation photo captures a cerebral yet lovable schoolboy with curly hair, striking eyes, and a serious look. Nate became a lawyer, married a Nova Scotia woman (which Maud duly recorded in her scrapbook and journal), and settled in Estevan, Saskatchewan, where he later became a crown prosecutor.[31]

Rereading Nate's letters that night of August 6, Maud thrilled once more over "his boyish compliments." She had no interest in seeing "the Nate of today," however. In fact, the old memories had given her a heartache, having stirred up "sleeping dogs."[32] Yet the memories of unresolved love and resentment helped fuel the powerful mixture of hostility and attraction in *Anne of Green Gables*. In fiction, she was also able to transform the experience for Anne. While her relationship with Nate had ended, she had managed to keep the embers of another love-hate affair smoldering, as revealed in journal entries for the crucial *Anne* years, 1903 to 1908.

The Embers of Love and Hate: Ed Simpson

The man who had aroused Maud's deepest and most complex emotions was Edwin (Ed) Simpson. Handsome and brilliant, he plays a prominent role in her journal, never failing to arouse instant agitation and antagonism. Maud first flirted with Ed in 1892, at age seventeen, when she visited in Park Corner. Five years later, in August 1896, when she had no teaching offers from any of the local schools, Ed, who was moving on to another school, called to tell Maud that she would be offered his position in Belmont. Presumably he had put in a good word for her. Maud would transform the event in her novel by having Gilbert give up the Avonlea school for Anne. In June 1897 she became secretly engaged to Ed when he was a student of theology, the details of which are well known through her lengthy journal account.

Unlike the photo in her published journal, the unpublished later portrait that hangs in the Baptist Church at Belmont speaks volumes about Simpson's refreshing unconventionality. Like a Wildean bachelor, the Reverend Ed Simpson lounges on a chair with book in hand, a lock of hair brushing his forehead, the faintest hint of a smirk playing around his mouth. He looks cheerful, confident, artistic, and sophisticated. Maud thought that Ed, with his thick curly hair and fine eyes, had absorbed the good looks of the family. She dismissed his brothers Fulton, Alf, and Burton as unattractive (thereby incurring the wrath of Fulton's daughter). Yet Ed also struck her as "awfully conceited—and worse still, *Simpsony*."[33] Clever and intellectual, he talked incessantly about himself, she said, forcing her to be the audience. Two strong egos clashed, and Maud was, no doubt, intimidated by his strong personality. But there was also an unconventionality in Ed that must have fascinated her.

Ed's grandnephew Arnold Barrett at Belmont remembers Ed's yearly visits, for he would stay at their home. "I was only a kid when Edwin would come home from Wisconsin," Arnold remembers. "I would have a cap on and he would say, 'Here's the boy with the cap that won't come off!' and nearly tear the hair off my head, holding the cap and my hair and pulling me off the seat." The prankish behavior is reminiscent of Gilbert Blythe, who teases Anne about her red braids and pins Ruby Gillis's yellow braid to her chair. "Edwin was a tease," admits Ed's niece Ruth Johnson, and it appears he never outgrew his love of pranks. A bit of a showman, Ed was also competitive, even later in life. He would check his watch in Belmont, then drive his car as fast as he could to Summerside and check his watch again upon arrival. "It's the funny things you remember," says Arnold, who hastens to add that Edwin was a great preacher.[34] Ed visited once a year, usually in the fall, and would preach in the church.

Gilbert was, in part, a combination of Nate and Ed. The same physical repulsion Maud had felt with Nate had sabotaged her engagement with Ed. She recoiled from his kisses with what she melodramatically called an "icy horror."[35] What is remarkable, however, is that like a Spartan soldier, she fought for nine long months to overcome her emotional and sexual aversion. When she finally broke her engagement with Ed, she avoided explaining her reason. Like her romance with Nate, the relationship with Ed remained unresolved, filling Maud with the same lifelong feelings of shame, confusion, anger, and, ultimately, regret.

Something of Maud's unresolved feelings of love and hate for both Nate and Ed lived inside the story of Anne and Gilbert. But she molded the character of Gilbert to make it possible for Anne to achieve her fairy-tale ending. Maud's retouching and airbrushing technique rendered Gilbert curiously neutral and non-threatening—very much unlike the real-life models. In this fairy-tale novel, he is the very idea of a perfect lover. As Canadian author Alice Munro has put it bluntly, "Her Gilberts and Teddys are curly-haired magazine cut-outs, useless except for obligatory marriages and pasted-on happiness."[36] In literary terms, the Avonlea beau is a "flat" character, the foil to the "rounded", more complex, and lively, though flawed, character of Anne. But the combination of vivid emotion and airbrushed silhouette, of bad-boy prankster and patiently waiting chivalric hero, appealed to a wide range of readers who could project their romantic desires on this paragon of masculinity. As a romantic figure, Gilbert is popular.

Maud was careful to avoid forays into sexuality. It was a zone in which she felt uncomfortable. Even in the 1936 sequel *Anne of Windy Poplars*, when Anne writes love letters to Gilbert Blythe, the love talk is cut out by an imaginary editor (making the suppression of sexuality all the more overt). As a result of this clear delineation of boundaries, the action remains focused on Anne and her independent life, even when she becomes friends with, and then engaged to, Gilbert. Gilbert's appearance creates a romantic tension but never detracts from the heroine.

Maud's comfort, and the spark for her creativity, was the female arena. The world of *Anne of Green Gables* is matriarchal, presided over by Mrs. Rachel Lynde, Marilla Cuthbert, Mrs. Barry, Aunt Josephine Barry, Miss Muriel Stacy, and Mrs. Allan. In contrast, the male characters tend either to be overshadowed, in their personal lives, by the females (Matthew Cuthbert, Mr. Thomas Lynde, Rev. Mr. Allan), or to be embarrassed by their flawed professional lives (Mr. Phillips, Old Mr. Bentley).[37] Gilbert is assigned a clearly defined space; Anne is allowed to carve out her own individual space and identity. "She made brave sounds, this independent, semi-feminist Maud," as her biographer Mollie Gillen has written.[38] Her insistence on independence, for both Anne and herself, was loud and clear, even as she tried to uphold the traditional Victorian ideals of the woman's place in the home as wife and mother.

NINE

Wicked Satire in Small-Town Avonlea

"...Mrs. Lynde says Canada is going to the dogs the way things are being run at Ottawa, and that it's an awful warning to the electors. She says if women were allowed to vote we would soon see a blessed change. What way do you vote, Matthew?"

"Conservative," said Matthew promptly. To vote Conservative was part of Matthew's religion.

"Then I'm Conservative too," said Anne decidedly.
—Anne Shirley and Matthew Cuthbert talking politics[1]

Like Mark Twain, Maud was a consummate social satirist who denounced the self-important authorities and self-righteous adults who dominated the small-town rural community of her childhood and youth. She was brilliant at ferreting out the pride-and-prejudice side of her Scotch-Presbyterian community and at painting an authentic and witty portrait of small-town life. The world of Anne was not all sunny; it was also a bit of a minefield. And so was the world of Maud. After having considered some of Maud's enmities, animosities, and feuds, we shall now look at the cultural animosities and prejudices of her era. When it came to the domains of temperance, prohibition, Sunday school, politics, suffrage, culture, and race, emotions ran high, and sometimes Maud, a creature of her own upbringing, was guilty of the same prejudices that she would mock in her fiction.

124

But how did polite and soft-spoken Maud learn to sharpen and wield verbal daggers? What was at the bottom of her pleasure and expertise in stabbing and wounding the enemy with words? "Humor, for Montgomery, was a way of managing anger," writes one scholar in her study of the role of gossip in Maud's fiction.[2] "To read her as a rosy-hued optimist who only wrote romances with happy endings is to misread her profoundly," warns another.[3] The novel's happy ending has misled some readers into ignoring the shafts of prickly satire. Yet Maud was a brilliant satirist, having honed her skills from childhood.

Anne Confronts Mrs. Lynde

While Maud hated open clashes, she sought them out with her pen. Adept at writing dialogue based on vigorous verbal clashes, she also developed an ear for the expletives and speech mannerisms that convey a personality. Think of Marilla's "Fiddlesticks," Matthew's "Well now," or Mrs. Lynde's "That's what!" Indeed, Maud's satire is particularly pointed when Anne clashes with her enemies, and the novel is punctuated by a number of dramatic confrontations, a pattern that is also continued in the sequels.

One of the most dramatic showdowns occurs early on in chapter nine, "Mrs. Rachel Lynde Is Properly Horrified," when skinny, homely Anne clashes with Mrs. Lynde, who, at two hundred or more pounds, is literally the most weighty authority figure in Cavendish.

> Mrs. Rachel was one of those delightful and popular people who pride themselves on speaking their mind without fear or favor. "She's terrible skinny and homely, Marilla. Come here, child, and let me have a look at you. Lawful heart, did any one ever see such freckles? And hair as red as carrots! Come here, child, I say."

> Anne "came there," but not exactly as Mrs. Rachel expected....

> "I hate you," she cried in a choked voice, stamping her foot on the floor. "I hate you—I hate you—I hate you—" a louder stamp with

each assertion of hatred. "How dare you call me skinny and ugly? How dare you say I'm freckled and redheaded? You are a rude, impolite, unfeeling woman!"[4]

The scene may well have been inspired by the fictional Anne Winter, a slender Annapolis maid with flashing eyes who defends her empire loyalist father against the patriots during the American revolutionary war in 1774.[5] Echoing the wording of Sophie Gates Kerr's 1902 fiction story in the *The Ladies World* (Anne Winter also stamps her foot, slams the door, and flings herself sobbing on her bed before outwitting an army of patriots), Maud's story involves nothing nearly as extraordinary as a revolutionary war, but that is precisely the point. Maud's genius consisted in revealing the power of ordinary, everyday rebellion. Our sense of social justice loves to see Mrs. Lynde dumbfounded, and we can rely on Anne to get the job done.

"She is the rebel, the nonconformist, the independent spirit who appeals to the child reader who chafes at adult strictures or to the adult who sometimes feels restricted by society's expectations," writes one scholar.[6] Anne's rebellious spirit has made legions of readers clamor for more adventures. It was the edgy and tempestuous Anne they had fallen in love with, an Anne that they did not want to grow up and become a polite society lady. Intriguingly, chapters nine and ten, "Mrs. Rachel Lynde is Properly Horrified" and "Anne's Apology," were used in Japanese language textbooks for junior high school students.[7] The formal, ritualistic politeness, the cult of humbleness, and repression of anger associated with the ideals of traditional Japanese femininity reverberate in the novel; Anne's outburst may well help alleviate readers frustrated with repression and silence.

In scenes such as these, Maud deftly advocates the viewpoint of the child, rather than that of the adult. Maud, who first began reading contemporary advice columnists in order to challenge her grandmother's faulty child-raising practices, derived many of the themes developed in her fiction from these experts. "Grown people are often remiss in the matter of speaking to children," said Mrs. Theodore Birney, President of The National Congress of Mothers, who, in the *Delineator* of January 1904, used wording that clearly anticipates Mrs. Lynde's overbearing commands. Impolite and ungracious, they utter commands, "Johnnie, come here this minute." The adult must employ graciousness, Mrs. Birney advised, in particular when talking with the "shy, timid child or the dreamy, absent-minded one, whose thoughts may be far away even while she looks at you."[8]

By describing how to adopt, so to speak, a problem child and educate her properly, the novel also reveals the maternal feminism of its author.[9] Marilla, though not a biological mother, soon demonstrates that she is a "natural" at child rearing, although even she requires some correction from gentle Matthew. "The child of nervous or sanguine temperament who has what is termed 'tantrums,' should be left alone," says Mrs. Birney.[10] This is the very treatment that Marilla applies to punish Anne for her tantrum: Anne must stay in her room and cool down until she is ready to apologize. The "apology" episode that follows is one of the most ironic and original scenes in girls' literature. Wrapped up in her own theatre, overly dramatic Anne is unconscious of the force of her rebellion and unaware that she is playing her role too well. She drops on her knees with mournful penitence on her face, imploring Mrs. Lynde's forgiveness: "Oh, Mrs. Lynde, I am so extremely sorry."[11] Marilla, who recognizes that Mrs. Lynde is being duped by Anne's theatrical behavior, becomes an involuntary accomplice by smiling, while the narrator and reader, equipped with the highest level of perception, observe the initial stages of Marilla's transformation. It is this fine layering of subtle dramatic irony that moves the narrative beyond the formulaic into sophisticated literary satire.

Giving Them Bars

Maud, who was as hypersensitive as Anne when it came to being criticized or shamed, had personal experience in the fine art of the mock apology. One morning at the Halifax Ladies College, Maud stepped into the parlor and greeted the two young teachers present by remarking, "Isn't this a lovely morning, girls?" When maidenish Miss Claxton promptly poked her head up from behind the sofa to admonish Maud for calling them "girls," Maud apologized, explaining that she had not seen the teacher. "Of course," she added wickedly, "I would never refer to *you* as a girl."[12] She knew that "Clack," as she had nicknamed her nemesis, would be sensitive to the implied barb. Maud could not have delighted more in her mischeivous sense of revenge.

Maud recalled that her Uncle John Montgomery, Aunt Emily's husband, was "the most comical soul alive," and remembered Herman Leard's teasing and jesting with great pleasure.[13] Great-uncle William Macneill had had a knack for satire, but it was her Grandfather Alexander Macneill who was probably the greatest influence, for she was a witness of his barbs on a daily basis. He loved to tease people; "giving them bars," he called it, presumably for "barbs," which could be mordant and aggressive.[14] In fact, so insulting was his humor—peppered with jibes and jeers—that he offended the prickly teacher Miss Izzie Robinson, who was equally sarcastic and whose classroom sneers cut like lashes. "Poor grandfather and grandmother had set the whole community against them by their behavior," Maud noted about the tiff with the teacher years later in an unpublished May 3, 1908, journal entry. "It was very wrong of them to fill a child's life with their own spite—and bitterness."[15] And yet, Maud would also show a similar lifelong propensity for drawn-out quarrels, feuds, and stored-up resentments that, more positively, would fuel the satire of her fiction.

At the same time, Maud's talent for the genre was also honed through her friendships with girls. Maud recalled her satiric verses of her school years in a lengthy unpublished July 1, 1894, journal entry written just a day before the old Cavendish school was being torn down: "...of all his mischievous pupils Alena and I were most constantly in disgrace." This was during teacher Jim MacLeod's reign, when the two girls would write immortal ditties such as the following composed by pretty Alena Macneill:

Have you ever heard of young Charlie McKenzie?
If you have not just inquire of Pensie
You will find him going to see May McLure
Or driving old Jack o'er a pile of manure.[16]

During class, they filled their slates with verses lampooning their teacher (a scene that would later be dramatized in *Emily of New Moon*).

The girls bonded by dressing down and burlesquing the boys, or, as Maud says, "at least those whom we did not like." "Lu and I have invented a lot of nicknames for our friends and foes," she had noted in the unpublished journal entry of February 17, 1893. "Jack is 'Mamma's pet,' Austin is 'Cavendish Carrots,' Neil is 'The Swamp Angel,' Ches is 'Chow-Chow' and Don is 'Rats.'"[17] "Cavendish Carrots" was a capital spark for the novel. As readers know well, "Carrots" was the cue for Anne's dramatic outbursts. They also had a nickname for the handsome Ed Simpson: "Ed is 'The Dancing Master'—because nothing else could be so little like him."[18]

One might think the girls would outgrow these burlesquing games, but this was not so with Maud. As young adults in their twenties, and in fact, as gray-haired matrons in their fifties, Maud and Nora Lefurgey "ragged"—that is, mocked, insulted, reviled, maligned, and scandalized— their foes and each other. Jokes about undergarments, Nora's hollow tooth, and Maud's sick stomach and vomiting ("to give up all for her country") are the stuff of the 1903 diary they co-wrote for fun.[19] The girls would recite literature to each other, bandying words like a ping-pong ball. They delighted in parodying literature, misspelling words, punning, and dialect humor. Frede had a similar gift for teasing and gave as well as she got. Hidden behind the jokes was also a little mean streak in Maud, a window into the resentment fermenting in her mind during those seemingly quiet, introspective moments. Frede and Maud, too, would tease each other and "hate" each other before they became close friends, although Maud's later idealization quickly brushes over this early phase.

When she sketched out her characters, Maud decided that Matthew must be silent so that Anne could be a talker. "But am I talking too much?" Anne asks, and of course she is, but Matthew doesn't mind.[20] Anne forces her conversational partners to listen, talking compulsively as if to fill up a void. The satire of the person too much in love with her own tongue to listen to anybody else was a subtle way of getting even with the Simpsons. Maud had endowed Anne with the *Simpsony* gift of the gab that she herself found so irritating in others. But this was also a fantasy and fairy-tale reversal. When quiet and introspective Maud gave rhetorical superpowers to Anne, she must have been indulging in the private fantasy of bursting forth from her own silence, triumphing over her inability to debate at the Literary, to hold her own with Ed Simpson, and to defend her position to Grandma and Grandpa Macneill, Uncle Leander, and Uncle John.

Maud's primary tool of communication was her pen. In the Literary, she worked quietly as the newspaper editor, librarian, treasurer, and secretary. She listened and took the minutes.[21] As the minute book indicates, a great many unacknowledged *Simpsonisms* found their way into *Anne of*

Green Gables. On several occasions Anne Shirley probes the rights of women—a hot topic in the Literary from its inception in 1886. George W. Simpson was an outspoken advocate. "The question of womens [sic] rights and suffrages was then brought up by Geo. Simpson who spoke strongly in favor of woman rights and suffrage," the minute book recorded in December 1894.[22] But the majority of Cavendish elders were opposed to women's voting rights. Arthur Simpson stated categorically that since women were not required to bear arms, they should not have the right to vote.[23] Even though Maud would become Prince Edward Island's most famous writer, the highest position she ever held in the Literary was that of Secretary-Treasurer; the positions of President and Vice-President were always filled by males.

Cultural Stereotypes

Some of the Literary Society's discussion topics throw a bright light into the dark prejudices of Maud's era. The minute book recorded the cultural biases of the time concerning various groups. "Do savage nations have a full right to the soil" was announced as a topic of debate on November 2, 1899.[24] A paper concerning "a defense of the Acadian exile" was read on March 1, 1901.[25] "Resolved that the extension of American influence in the Pacific and Central and South America would be for the best influence of mankind" was the topic on November 15, 1901.[26] Asians were discussed in terms of "The Yellow Peril" in a debate opened by Arthur Simpson on November 15, 1907.[27] *Anne of Green Gables* satirizes the parochial xenophobia of Mrs. Lynde, who assumes an orphan will bring mayhem and destruction to Green Gables. According to Mrs. Lynde, the foreign orphan may suck eggs, or poison the well with strychnine. Yet the novel's humor also relies on some of its own cultural stereotyping, for example, concerning the Italians (Marilla: "how often have I told you never to let one of those Italians in the house!"), the Jewish people (Anne, speaking of the peddler who sold her the dye: "he wasn't an Italian—he was a German Jew"), and the Irish (Mrs. Lynde: "A body can get used to anything, even to being hanged, as the Irishman said").[28]

Yet the worst treatment was reserved for the Acadians, Maud's closest neighbors on the north shore. Even today North Rustico remains a vibrant Acadian settlement. Yet the Acadians are represented as being uneducated (the farmhand Jerry Buote), disloyal (the Acadian farmhands who leave after having been trained), and stupid (the buxomy Mary Joe, an adult, appears to have less knowledge than Anne in treating little Minnie May Barry for croup). Marilla refers too "those stupid, half-grown little French boys."[29] The Acadians, the first settlers on Prince Edward Island, had suffered expulsion and expropriation, and were reclaiming their cultural rights during Maud's era. Buote was a respected Acadian name. For instance, Gilbert Buote, well known novelist, educator, and founder of the first French-Acadian newspaper on Prince Edward Island, had died a year earlier in 1904. For decades English-language accounts had denigrated the Acadians of Prince Edward Island, accusing them of inciting the Indians to acts of barbarity against the English-speaking settlers. Possibly these accusations and attitudes originated "in an unconscious desire to justify the harsh treatment to which the Acadians were in some cases subjected," as the Rev. Murray wrote in 1899, in the *Easternmost Ridge of the Continent*.[30] Maud's biases were those held by many English-speaking Canadians at the time, and, in fairness, Maud also made her own cultural group a target for satire (Marilla: prim and rigid; Mrs. Lynde: short-sighted and parochial). This satire, though, is qualified and balanced. When it comes to the Acadians and the Québécois, Maud's bias was clear. In January 1910, Maud would complain that there were only a dozen pupils left in the Cavendish school and "half of those are French."[31] Snobbish Maud could be as parochial in her prejudices as Mrs. Lynde. At the same time, *Anne of Green Gables* is brilliant at making light of other controversial social topics.

Satirizing Sunday School Morals

During Maud's era, temperance was the perennial hot topic in the Literary and in Sunday school periodicals. The *Ram's Horn* Sunday school periodical of Chicago, for instance, featured flaming editorials like "Suppress the Saloon," along with articles on the progress of saloon suppression in

Ontario: "The temperance people of the banner Canadian province were never so hopeful and aggressive as today."[32] In the Cavendish Literary Society, the Prohibition side was represented assertively by the Simpsons. The Hon. Geo. W. Simpson argued vigorously that Cavendish schools should be teaching temperance and should adopt textbooks on temperance.[33] Arthur Simpson concurred. Later in life, Ed Simpson was also involved as a spokesman for the temperance cause.

"Big" George R. Macneill, in contrast, favored a moderate license fee for businesses to sell liquor, arguing that "liquor was very benifical [sic] to human body and inspiring to its immortal soul."[34] Grandmother Macneill was famous for her currant wine, which she served Maud's friend Frede. These fierce oppositions provide the context for the clash in the seemingly innocent chapter sixteen, "Diana Is Invited to Tea with Tragic Results," when Anne mistakenly serves Diana currant wine instead of raspberry cordial. As a result, Diana's pro-temperance mother, Mrs. Barry, forbids her daughter to socialize with Anne. Readers recall the "tragedy" of the bosom friends' separation. This misadventure reveals that Marilla Cuthbert makes her own currant wine, ostensibly for medicinal purposes. In 1901, Prince Edward Island was the first Canadian province to enact Prohibition legislation. The provincial temperance act varied throughout Canada. Although it criminalized the sale of liquor and entailed the closing of drinking establishments, private possession and consumption was legal in some areas. One way of obtaining liquor was to have it prescribed by a doctor, with the result that there were long lineups at the drugstores at Christmas time and other holidays during the Prohibition era in Canada.[35] The raspberry cordial episode, in which Diana inadvertently consumes several tumblers of Marilla's homemade wine, is Maud's satiric response to the didactic preaching of the temperance movement. Yet in having a child become drunk, Maud also provided some ammunition for the Prohibitionists. In any case, during her visit to Boston in 1910, she enjoyed her publisher's Chateau Yquem so much she had difficulty walking straight.[36] Once she presided over her own household in Ontario, she also decanted her own wine.

From 1900 to 1911, Maud was the organist and choir director in the Cavendish Presbyterian Church. She also taught Sunday school and wrote stories for Sunday School magazines. Does it follow that the broth of *Anne of Green Gables* was thickened with Sunday school teaching and preaching? "There is a lot of Sunday School—and 'Pansy'—about Anne, not only in the original seven chapters, but throughout the book," writes the editor of a scholarly edition of *Anne of Green Gables*. "Anne's story is...directed toward an exemplary and 'moral' conclusion."[37]

True, and yet the novel would not have had its enduring success in a secular twentieth-century society if it were one-dimensionally didactic or moralistic. In fact, the popular Christian books written by Isabella Alden, under the pseudonym Pansy, were often referred to and parodied by Maud and her girlfriends. Like Huck Finn, Anne is an irreverent little heathen who pokes fun at sanctimonious church practices. She criticizes the old minister Mr. Bentley as a poor orator whose sermons are long-winded and boring. "Even at a church entertainment, audiences do not take kindly to a dreary harangue," the *Delineator* had reminded its readers in March 1905. "Ministers and preachers today are striving for brief, bright, local effects."[38] In her journal, Maud dissected bad sermons as severely as a drama critic might excoriate a boring theatrical performance: "He is a good speaker but it was a missionary sermon and I'm tired of them—I've heard so many lately," the nineteen-year old noted about the Reverend McKenzie of Brookfield Church in March 1894.[39] "We went to preaching at O'Leary and heard that miserable McLeod again—he seems to be ubiquitous," she noted in August.[40] There is a great deal of irreverence that veers toward unorthodoxy and fun. "I actually fell sound asleep while the Rev. John. M. was praying," she recalled about a visit to Long River Church after a long-night's partying.[41]

But there is also more subtly subversive criticism. Marilla contemplates teaching Anne "Now I lay me down to sleep," before realizing how inadequate the popular children's prayer actually is for Anne. To understand the satiric meaning of this scene we must know that the little prayer was virtually omnipresent in the popular religious magazines and newspapers of the era. Typically it was illustrated by a picture of a little girl in her nightshirt kneeling by her bed to pray, as, for example, in *The Sunday School Advocate* in January and June 1905.[42] The *Ram's Horn* of January 1903 featured a double illustration entitled "Two Mothers." The first mother, dressed in a fur coat, hands over her child to the nanny as she leaves for an evening out with her husband. The second mother sits teaching her child a prayer, identified in the caption as "Now I lay me down to sleep."[43] Maud rejected the simplicity of such Sunday school teaching. She suggested that genuine spirituality was far more complex and could also be subversive. In fact, during this time, Maud would have discussed these religious topics with Ewan Macdonald, for she later tells us that they talked "theology and philosophy."[44]

A Young Unmarried Minister "On Trial"

On the first Sunday in August, early in the morning, Maud went to gather some ferns to decorate the Presbyterian Church in Cavendish, as her unpublished journal entry of that evening reveals.[45] She always felt that walking through Lover's Lane brought her nearer to a spiritual experience than any service in church. It was a scene she would later, during the revision of the book, insert into chapter eleven, "Anne's Impressions of Sunday-School." Anne feels bored to stone in church, but moving among the white birches discovers something akin to spirituality. Her soul's expansion requires no institutional blessing. Maud's parody had bite, for she loved to flirt with the idea of a pagan spirituality in which religion and nature blended.

That Sunday morning, Maud took her pagan fare into the Presbyterian Church, where the tangy fern she had collected in the moist forest undergrowth provided the ambiance for Ewan Macdonald's sermons. Just as Maud showered Ephraim with flowers, so she showered the Presbyterian Church with musky fern whose spicy scent and pagan beauty was not lost on Ewan. Maud did not mention Ewan Macdonald in her journal that evening, but we know that the minister visited and contributed to her good cheer during the summer months while she was also making rapid progress on her novel.

In January 1904, Reverend Macdonald had given a paper on the "Evolution of Religious Thought," and in March 1905, on "Socialism" at the Literary.[46] Presumably they would have continued discussing these topics during Ewan's visits. Unfortunately, three of Maud's 1905 letters to Ephraim are lost, but his responses indicate that they too were discussing theology. Would Maud have been as irreverent in her opinions with Ewan as she was with Ephraim? Or did she repress her doubts with Ewan to release them all the more with Ephraim? With her Alberta pen friend, Maud shared her pagan spiritualism, her belief that heaven was a rather boring place, and that Christ might have been a willful imposter. Writing about heaven in April 1906, she remarks that even the "people who call themselves devout Christians" (read: Ewan Macdonald) do not seem to find the prospect of heaven "especially inviting either."[47] Maud spiced up the Church with pagan ferns, bringing the natural world into the church, just as Anne Shirley does on her first church visit in the novel by wearing a wreath of wildflowers. Yet Maud's courtship with the minister was a very cautious dance around academic subjects, allowing them to consort and become friends but also keep a safe distance. Meanwhile, behind the veil of fiction, the imagined courtship was moving at much faster speed.

In her journal Maud writes that she was not seriously interested in Ewan until 1906. The inside jokes in her novel tell a different story. In chapter twenty-one, "A New Departure in Flavorings," the minister, old Mr. Bentley, leaves the congregation and new candidates arrive to preach "on trial" in the Avonlea church. Mrs. Lynde and Anne take a keen interest in the marital status of each candidate, just as Maud and Nora did and recorded in their diary during the year Ewan Macdonald arrived in Cavendish. Concerning one handsome young candidate, Anne remarks:

> "...Mrs. Lynde says he isn't married, or even engaged, because she made special inquiries about him, and she says it would never do to have a young unmarried minister in Avonlea, because he might marry in the congregation and that would make trouble. Mrs. Lynde is a very farseeing woman, isn't she, Matthew?"[48]

Anne is, as usual, calling humorous attention to Mrs. Lynde's parochial short-sightedness. Her creator was lambasting the whirlwind of marital politicking that swept through Cavendish when handsome Ewan Macdonald arrived. Gossip immediately linked the new minister to three marriageable candidates, herself included: "This morning we had a Highlander to preach for us and he was 'chust lofely' and all the girls got struck on him," she herself had written on June 21, 1903, in the diary she coauthored with Nora.[49] Moreover, in the novel, Mrs. Lynde decrees that "sound doctrine in the man and good housekeeping in the woman make an ideal combination for a minister's family"—the very combination Ewan and Maud were to represent. In fact, she was quoting Mrs. Dr. Macneill in Cavendish who said about Ewan Macdonald that he was "a young man who is very sound in doctrine," using the same phrase from her earlier Sunday, June 7, 1903, diary entry.[50]

Although their engagement was still a full year away, in the novel Maud and Ewan already make a cameo appearance as the happy couple, Mr. and Mrs. Allan, who are still on their honeymoon. What is perhaps most intriguing is the positive yet bland portrayal of Mr. Allan (Ewan), who is constantly upstaged by the gentle, lively, and attractive Mrs. Allan (Maud), though Mr. Allan continues to worship the ground she walks on. Maud even made use of Ewan's dimples when she conceived these characters—but attributed them to Mrs. rather than Mr. Allan. When the young couple visits Green Gables, "[a]ll went merry as a marriage bell" until, of course, Anne's ill-flavored cake is passed around the table—a prophetic sign, perhaps, of what was to come for Maud and Ewan.[51] Anne had accidentally flavored the cake with anodyne liniment instead of vanilla, an episode based on an event she witnessed during her year as a teacher in Bideford when she boarded at the Methodist parsonage. The minister's wife flavored her layered cake with liniment and served it to a guest who ate every crumb of the cake.[52] In a final tongue-in-cheek comment—"we couldn't expect a perfect minister for seven hundred and fifty dollars a year"[53]—Maud criticized the low salary paid by the Avonlea (read: Cavendish) parish, which was certainly a consideration as she was weighing the options of what it meant to be a minister's wife. Here in her fiction, she could play through the ideal scenario. Underneath the novel's inconsequential remarks, she was plotting her future in idealized terms.

"My forte is in writing humor," Maud said. She thought that only children and elderly people could be treated humorously in fiction. "Young women in the bloom of youth and romance should be sacred from humor. It is the time of sentiment and I am not good at depicting sentiment—I can't do it well."[54] But she was the mistress of humor and satire, of childhood and old age—and had such a knack for her art that in *Anne of Green Gables*, even her foes laughed along with her.

TEN

This Old Place Has a Soul, Green Gables

I wrote it in the evenings after my regular day's work was done, wrote most of it at the window of the little gable room which had been mine for years.
            —*Maud about writing* Anne of Green Gables *in the*
                        upstairs den of the old homestead[1]

I n the summer of 1905, Maud made rapid progress on her chapters. During the evening hours, she would sit at the window of the little upstairs gable room that had been hers since childhood, her black Waverly pen racing over her writing portfolio at the speed of her own voice. At her desk in the twilight of the day, Maud's southern view overlooked the green fields of Cavendish. That year the Cavendish summer throbbed with lazy rhythm, and nasturtiums and roses were blooming around the homestead.

Landscape was central to Maud's Romantic aesthetic and she structured the world of her novel from her little window. In her journal and memoir, Maud would later link many of the landmarks of the fictional village of Avonlea to local sites, but like the character of Anne herself, the design and landscape of Green Gables, Lover's Lane, the Birch Path, and the Lake of Shining Waters were a blend of the personal and the borrowed, the literary and the popular, the local and the global.

The fictitious Green Gables was based not only on a neighboring farm, but on the old homestead that Maud loved intensely. The atmosphere of the homestead, the comings and goings, the vistas and surroundings, and the unique stresses concerning the homestead that year shaped Green Gables. Even more important, Green Gables was built on national, literary, and aesthetic ideals of home that would resonate with readers who felt uprooted in a modern world of flux. That tension could be felt underneath the peaceful surroundings of Green Gables.

The Old Homestead

"This is the fag end of a very doggy dog-day and was never meant for writing letters at all," Maud began in a letter to George MacMillan on August 23, when she was almost midway through her writing of *Anne of Green Gables*. What exactly caused her bad day, she does not reveal. Touring Ireland, her Scottish pen pal had sent her a fragment of a stone from the famous Blarney Castle. It had arrived that very day and prompted an immediate, exuberant response. A superstitious believer, Maud immediately kissed the fragment, for the Blarney Stone was said to bestow the gift of the gab to those who kissed it. "Even although it isn't the Blarney Stone itself surely some virtue must have *leaked into it* during the years. I shall expect an added smoothness of tongue henceforth—or perhaps it will show itself in my pen, which the gods permit!"[2]

Perhaps the Blarney stone helped build the soulful walls of Green Gables, for Green Gables, like Lover's Lane, was almost a character in her novel. A house, Maud believed, had its own unique personality. Her prose convinces us that rooms can soak up tears and laughter, sorrow and happiness. We *feel* that the walls of Green Gables, New Moon, and Silver Bush are filled with memories and emotions—Maud's own emotions. We know she loved the old homestead, where she had spent virtually her entire life, from 1876 until 1911—a total of thirty-five years. Yet we know little about how the homestead shaped the world of Green Gables.

The homes of famous writers are fascinating because they are the spaces that mold the interior lives of their inhabitants. Writers frequently rely on the rooms they live in to sharpen one or more of the traditional five senses, and to tap their emotional inner spaces. Emily Dickinson rarely left her homestead in Amherst, Massachusetts, and drew mostly on sight to create her poetry. In Easton, Connecticut, the blind and deaf Helen Keller relied on touch. Sigmund Freud, in his specially arranged Vienna consulting room, perceived the world through hearing. Marcel Proust, who battled asthma and was confined to his bedroom in Paris, drew upon taste and smell. "The sensory experience of dwelling animates the work of all four writers, in ways both intensely physical and deeply philosophical," writes literary scholar Diana Fuss in her book *The Sense of an Interior: Four Writers and the Rooms that Shaped Them.*[3] The house, its layout, its literary interior, and the writer's physical movements as they live and move through it, as Fuss documents, become an agent in shaping the literature.

All that remains of Maud's old homestead today is a large hole with old cellar walls, surrounded by birches, poplars, spruces, and the old apple trees. The ruins invite the imagination of literary tourists and fans who have traveled here from as far away as Japan, Sweden, and Florida, trying to recapture their own childhood memories of reading and loving the novel. What were the visual landmarks and social relations within the house and how did they sharpen Maud's visual perception and imagination? This is the story of how the imaginative world of Green Gables was born out of the shell of an old and dying homestead. We will look for Anne by tracking Maud's physical movements through the old rooms and corridors before we solve the mystery of what shadowed Maud's beautiful August, halfway through the writing of *Anne of Green Gables.*

Set back from the main road and nestled among tree groves, the homestead was built in the early nineteenth century. The one-and-a-half storey house on the forty-acre farm had been home to several generations of Macneills. To the north, a copse of trees sheltered the house from the ferocious and unrelenting north shore storms. Facing west, the homestead overlooked the front orchard, which great-grandfather William Macneill had planted many years earlier. Maud's grandfather, Alexander Macneill, had planted the back orchard, naming the trees after the children: John's tree, Emily's tree, Clara's tree, and so on. In the novel, Maud similarly delivers the "big, rambling, orchard-embowered house" called Green Gables, which, like her homestead, is accessed via a long deep-rutted, grassy land bordered with wild roses.[4]

In a March 1917 letter, Frede Campbell recalls the ambiance of the backyard, which faced east toward the sea. Here, she writes, painting a nostalgic picture of a summer's day, you could see Grandmother feed the chickens, or watch the bucket go down in the ferns by the well. Frede fondly recalled visiting and sitting at the kitchen table, eating Grandmother's good bread with ham and pickles and drinking her homemade currant wine.[5]

The kitchen reflected Grandmother Macneill's realm and rule, just as the painfully clean Green Gables kitchen (tidy as an "unused parlor") reflects Marilla's controlling personality.[6] During the day Grandmother might be busy sorting the mail in the post office in the eastern corner of the spacious kitchen wing. Her mouth was pinched, and she was hard of hearing and not easy to talk to. Posing for a rare family photograph taken in the orchard in 1900, Grandmother Macneill held little Edith Macneill on her lap, wildflowers at her feet; her face produced a reluctant smile that reminds one of Marilla's "rusty" smile in the novel.[7] From the kitchen, Marilla made pilgrimages into the cellar to pick up apples and potatoes. It is the same ruined cellar found at the site of Lucy Maud Montgomery's Cavendish Home today.

In the winter, the world of the large homestead contracted like an old drafty castle in which only a few rooms are livable. The women virtually lived in the kitchen: cooking, entertaining, sorting mail, reading, writing, bathing, and occasionally sleeping in the warm room. The large woodstove, centered against the coldest northern wall, radiated its heat throughout the room.[8] From November to April, there was little privacy. There were three small bedrooms downstairs—Grandma's, Maud's winter bedroom, and the spare bedroom—all facing east, with kitchen, parlor, and sitting room facing west. "I hate that room venomously," Maud wrote about her downstairs bedroom. "It's dark and dull and I can't even fix it up as I want to because it was 'newly papered' *ten* years ago and poor grandmother would have a convulsion if so much as a tack were driven into that 'new' paper. So I have no pictures and feel as if I had no eyes."[9]

In winter, at Grandmother's command, the lights went out at 9:00 p.m. Maud's gaze, already focused on herself, was forced to delve even further inward to her world of dreams. It seems appropriate that toward the end of the novel, Marilla should be threatened with losing her eyesight, as nothing could be more incapacitating and cruel from the writer's own perspective. Maud's own eyes had weakened early in life and she used an elegant pair of pince-nez for reading and writing. The specter of blindness must have been a horror for a young woman who perceived the world through her eyes and had sharpened her sense of visual perception through her camera work, scrapbooking, needlework, and fashion style. Winters were long and dark, and her journal reveals that her bottled-up feelings collapsed into depression in seasonal patterns. As we have seen earlier, they also sought release in vivid imaginative dreams.

Maud's creative life took place upstairs. As a child and teen she would lie awake in the old Cavendish farmhouse by the eastern sea and compose stories in her mind, thinking out plots and stashing them away in her "mental storehouse."[10] During the summer, Maud lived in her beloved den, the gable room that was hers since age twelve. She spent time here when she was not reveling in the garden outside. "I love this room—but it's the Mecca of my heart," she had gushed the year before on April 30, 1904. "Here I am a woman not a child, and order my ways as suits me."[11] Here was her bed, where she would fling herself and cry, or lie and daydream. Here she escaped Grandma's sharp eyes. She was queen of the entire upstairs, with views in almost all directions. The trunk room faced north. The boudoir west. The den south. Missing only was the eastern view, a vista Maud will give Anne by locating her room in the east gable, thus completing the 360-degree panorama.

From her upstairs window, Maud could peer down the lane and see visitors approaching without being seen. She would watch Mr. Crewe drive up the lane in the buggy to deliver the mail, or observe friends approach the house. Her position was not unlike the panoptic Mrs. Lynde's who keeps watch over Avonlea's main road, registering all the comings and goings. Maud referred to the boudoir dormer as her lookout, and like her boudoir, Maud's den was a tiny hideaway, a refuge giving her privacy, peace, and intimacy. She loved the pretty white wallpaper with its delicate flowers, and papered Anne's room in the same pattern in the second half of the novel.

At Green Gables, life has a similar texture and structure. The upstairs contains the east-gable room and Marilla's room; the downstairs contains the kitchen and Matthew's room. Anne's introspective life takes place upstairs, where Matthew sets foot only once in the novel, when he walks up the stairs to persuade Anne to apologize to Mrs. Lynde. Similarly, because Grandmother Macneill rarely climbed the stairs, the gable room became Maud's space of freedom where she could be both worldly (earning an income with her pen) and romantic (daydreaming and indulging her emotions).

Maud's den was a modest room with sloping eastern and western walls, crowded with the double bed underneath the slope. Double beds were customary in rural houses, allowing families to sleep "double" when guests arrived. The miniature chair at the foot of the bed added a child-like element, while cushions, lace work, and doilies dressed the room with a maidenish and old-fashioned femininity. The room housed the author's tools of her craft, such as her books. "I like to look up from my work occasionally and gloat my eyes on them," she had written of her book collection in a June 17, 1900, journal entry. "They are all my pets."[12] The modern typewriter she procured in 1903 is absent from the many photographs she took of the room. Maud's red scrapbook rests on the floor in the left front of one of the photos, as if inviting the viewer to reach out and open it.[13] Three vases of ferns brought the garden and surrounding woodlands into the room, connecting the inside with the outside and providing the musky fragrance with which she spiced her novel. A clock shows that the photo was taken at ten minutes to ten in the morning, yet the photo is timeless with its old-fashioned flair. Holding the pictures and letters of yore, the den was a museum in which Maud archived her memories. It was a place where time seemed to stand still.

While Maud wrote the first sentence of her first Anne book in the kitchen, she wrote most of the novel in her little upstairs room, sitting at the wooden table in the evening, near the gable window with its beautiful vista. From here she watched the emerald light over the hills and trees. She saw the fields—green and dewy and placid. "Oh, how I love summer twilights!"[14] We can almost hear her voice. She named the view of the fields from her window "haunts of ancient peace" adopting the Tennyson quotation in the unpublished entry of July 3, 1904.[15] The southern vista, framed by the window casement, was like a painting or a moving picture that changed depending on the angle of light, the weather, or the curtain stirring in the wind. In fact, this little window, with its muslin shroud, was the threshold connecting the inside with the outside. In the summer the old casement window would be open, and she would hear the "subtly sweet 'voices of the night'": the rustle of poplars, the voice of a frog, and the singing of birds.[16] In the twilight she could see the pasture dotted with sheep. The description of this view seems timeless, and journal entries decades apart echo the same descriptions.

"It opened on a world of wonder," she had written about this very window in a rhapsodic poem published in the *Ladies' Journal* in May 1897. Evocatively titled "The Gable Window," the poem anticipates the title of *Anne of Green Gables*.

> 'Twas there I passed my hours of dreaming,
> 'Twas there I knelt at night to pray;

Just as in the novel, Anne Shirley kneels and prays by the open window under the evening stars. The windowsill is a bridge between the inside and outside:

> The airy dreams of child and maiden
>   Hang round that gable window still,
> As cling the vines, green and leaf-laden,
>   About the sill....[17]

Windows were central to Maud's aesthetics. The sights, scents, and sounds that entered through the window animated her writing, sparking memory and emotion and daydreams: "The view from here is such a pretty one and it is also dear to me for all the sweet old memories associated with almost every feature—brooks, woods, and fields," she noted in an unpublished May 10, 1893, journal entry.[18] From her upstairs rooms she surveyed her territory—the spaces that she explored in her daily rambles, never straying too far from the homestead. Consider that the Green Gables kitchen has two windows, a western one (its view corresponding to the western view from the homestead kitchen) and "the east one, whence you got a glimpse of the bloom[ing] white cherry trees in the left orchard and nodding, slender birches down in the hollow by the brook... greened over by a tangle of vines."[19] This view was drawn directly from the southern gable window of Maud's upstairs den. Looking down the lane as she wrote, she could see the cherry trees in bloom, the birches along the lane, and the green tangle of vines around the windowsill.

Maud's landscape poetry was embedded in the Romantic sensibility. In fact, eighteenth-century Romantic aesthetics had strongly influenced English-Canadian poetry, in particular the landscape poetry of Thomas Cary, Charles G. D. Roberts, Bliss Carman, Isabella Valancy Crawford, and others.[20] The pastoral and peaceful nature environment described by these Canadian poets, like that of *Anne of Green Gables*, belies the image of hostile nature that Northrop Frye and Margaret Atwood recognized as being at the heart of Canadian literature. Indeed, the twentieth-century Canadian literary establishment disparaged Romantic nature writing of this sort for decades. Having read and reread the British and Scottish Romantic poets during childhood, Maud was profoundly influenced by Robert Burns; William Wordsworth; Sir Walter Scott; Lord Byron; Alfred, Lord Tennyson; and Robert and Elizabeth Browning.[21] She was also influenced by American Romantic poets William Cullen Bryant, R. W. Emerson, H. W. Longfellow, and John Greenleaf Whittier. In depicting landscape, she was even influenced by the travel literature of the Romantic era, as seen in her fondness for Washington Irving's *The Alhambra*. Her depiction of Prince Edward Island is similar in tone and imagery to the tourist literature in print during the era. Enveloped in lush greenery against the sparkling blue of the gulf, Maud's garden isle evokes the tranquility and beauty of the vacation spot.[22]

From the vantage point of her den, sitting beside the window, Maud's Romantic eye structured and organized the landscape like a work of visual art, as did photographer Rudolf Eickemeyer with images and captions that were both pastoral and poetic, or the artwork of the Hudson River School painters. Influenced by European philosophies, this Romantic sensibility endowed nature and childhood with purity and innocence. It celebrated strong emotions, both love and hatred, as well as wild mood swings. It also endowed the child with a special vision and spirituality.

Who can forget the visual and emotional power of Anne's buggy ride with Matthew from Bright River Station to Avonlea? The formulaic scene, common to much popular fiction, in which the urban girl first awakens to the beauty of nature, became, in Maud's hands, a holy experience, beginning with Anne's first vision of the sun setting over the White Way of Delight:

By 1910, Maud had perfected her role as a celebrity author and posed for this publicity photograph in Boston.

University of Guelph Library Archival and Special Collections

Dreamy eyed Maud faced the camera with serious intensity.
University of Guelph Library Archival and Special Collections

Mischievous Maud at age seventeen. A consummate model, she dressed up for and flirted with the camera.
University of Guelph Library Archival and Special Collections

ABOVE: "Secrets." Posing with Nora Lefurgey circa 1903, Maud channelled her own "bosom friendships" into writing *Anne*.

RIGHT: Maud posed on the rocky beach of Cavendish with Nora taking the picture.

University of Guelph Library Archival and Special Collections

ABOVE: Bridesmaid Maud in a puffy organdy dress at Bertha MacKenzie's wedding in Cavendish, Christmas 1905.

John and Jennie Macneill, Cavendish, Prince Edward Island

LEFT: The Reverend Ewan Macdonald, Maud's future husband, officiated at the wedding.

University of Guelph Library Archival and Special Collections

RIGHT: The newlyweds kept a formal distance in the honeymoon picture taken in Scotland, 1911.

BELOW: The happy family in Leaskdale, Ontario, in 1912: Maud, Frede Campbell, Ewan, and baby Chester.

University of Guelph Library Archival and Special Collections

ABOVE: Amanda Macneill, Maud's earliest "bosom friend." "Mollie" and "Pollie" inspired the friendship rituals of Anne and Diana.

University of Guelph Library Archival and Special Collections

RIGHT: Maud's "sweet wildwood rose." Penzie Macneill (1872–1906) was dying when Maud completed *Anne*.

Heather Toombs and Ronald Toombs, North Rustico, Prince Edward Island

Fredericka "Frede" Campbell shared aspects of Anne.

RIGHT: Unresolved love affairs colored the portrait of Gilbert Blythe: Maud's school friend and rival Nate Lockhart.

Esther Clark Wright Archives, Vaughan Memorial Library, Acadia University, Nova Scotia

BELOW: The brilliant Edwin Simpson, Maud's former fiancé.

Belmont Baptist Church, Miscouche, Prince Edward Island

ABOVE: Hattie Gordon, circa 1890s, Maud's idealized school teacher and model for Miss Muriel Stacey, the teacher loved by Anne.

University of Guelph Library Archival and Special Collections

RIGHT: Ellen Macneill—Maud's adopted little cousin provided a spark for the plot of *Anne of Green Gables*.

Ruth Gallant, Hamilton, Ontario

Clara Woolner Macneill—Maud's mother died when she was just twenty-one months old, leaving Maud an orphan.

Hugh John "Monty" Montgomery lived in "Eglinton Villa" (below) in Prince Albert, Saskatchewan. Maud's lifelong dream to restore her lost family fuelled her fiction.

" . . . the only mother I ever knew. . . ." Grandmother Lucy Ann Woolner Macneill
was reserved and undemonstrative.

ABOVE: Maud staged this Macneill family photo among wildflowers. Uncle Leander, his son Murray, and Grandmother Macneill with baby Edith—and with a rare smile.
University of Guelph Library Archival and Special Collections

RIGHT: John Franklin Macneill— Maud's pragmatic uncle. Portrait by Pach Brothers, NY.

John and Jennie Macneill, Cavendish, Prince Edward Island

With Alberta pen pal Ephraim Weber, Maud could indulge her fantasies about herself that would find their way into her portrait of Anne.

TOP: Maud's photograph of Alma Macneill's Cavendish home circa 1900 anticipates the tableau of Anne and Marilla sitting together at the door of Green Gables.

BOTTOM: The old mailman, Mr. Crewe, delivered glossy magazines to the Macneill post office. Photo by L. M. Montgomery.

Thomas Moore the Poet's House, St. Anne de Bellevue, P.Q.

"I dwell in Macdonald Halls, but the sweetest thing is that you love me still the same." Fredericka Campbell to L. M. Montgomery, postcard, November 1910.

"The Avenue," so called by the Newbridge people, was a stretch of road four or five hundred yards long, completely arched over with huge, wide-spreading apple-trees, planted years ago by an eccentric old farmer. Overhead was one long canopy of snowy fragrant bloom. Below the boughs the air was full of a purple twilight and far ahead a glimpse of painted sunset sky shone like a great rose window at the end of a cathedral aisle.

Its beauty seemed to strike the child dumb.[23]

Like visual art, the landscape (blooming apple trees and sunset sky) is composed of colors (purple, painted, rose), architectural forms (arch, window, cathedral), and light (twilight, sunset, shone). Maud used her lyrical prose to transform the landscape into artwork and to cultivate an aesthetic perception of nature.

Anne's uplifted and dumbstruck gaze at the colorful cathedral-like picture is evocative of Jean-François Millet's illustrious painting *The Angelus*, which depicts two field workers praying at the ring of the vesper bell in the day's twilight with the church spire in the background. Drawn to the glorious waning of day in a moment of spiritual devotion, Anne's expression also mirrors Evelyn Nesbit's enraptured pose. In *Emily of New Moon*, this unearthly experience of the "flash" is likened to this moment at the windowsill, when the movement of the thin curtain blown by the wind provides "a glimpse of the enchanting realm beyond."[24] The magical moment at the windowsill, like the sudden flash of a camera in the dark, is the threshold where light and dark, nature and art, inside and outside, past and present converge to create magic.

Anne's nature reverie is a reflection of Maud's own. Laird's Hill in Cavendish was her favorite spot for sunsets; here she had stood many times viewing the Cavendish pond and the sea beyond.[25] It must have been gratifying to relive these moments in the quiet of her den, as she wrote the eleven extended scenes of sunsets or sunset afterglow scenes that appear in the novel.[26] But from the vantage point of her little window, Maud also imposed her interior order on the world of Avonlea by rigorously cropping unwanted edges, silencing and censoring perceptions that would have marred her picture and pleasure.

Avalon

In March 1905 the New York *Delineator* published Zona Gale's story "The Things That Are Real," which would have deeply resonated with Maud, for it seemed to echo her own loneliness and dreamy imagination. Its heroine was another Anne. Dreamy and bookish Anne Davenport lives with her pragmatic aunt, who would like her niece to be more in touch with the real world. Anne is profoundly lonely and misunderstood. Then Anne Davenport meets Jared Dixon, a writer and teacher who appears at a town reception with a book in his pocket. It's love at first sight. He reads a verse of romantic poetry, and Anne catches her breath and spontaneously supplies the stanza's final line:

"In Avalon he groweth old!"[27]

In fact, the verse is drawn from William Morris's "Golden Wings," and the romantic line alludes to the legendary King Arthur and the misty isle of Avalon where his fabled sword Excalibur was forged. Since Avalon is also the Celtic island of apples, the evocative name would have been a short imaginative leap to Prince Edward Island with its famous apple blossoms. Certainly the timing of this reference here in the familiar *Delineator* magazine in March 1905, just months before she would write the first page of *Anne*, is noteworthy. Was it here that Maud struck on the idea of baptizing Cavendish with the romantic name of Avonlea?

The word was rich in associations and would be recognized by millions of readers. Everybody knew Shakespeare's birth place Stratford-upon-Avon. Maud also knew "Avon," the beautiful pastoral river in Nova Scotia described in the romantic poetry by Arthur John Lockhart (the uncle of her school sweetheart, Nate Lockhart). Maud would have made these associations in a flash probably without even thinking about them or being necessarily conscious of them.

Winter

Writing *Anne of Green Gables* from the vantage point of her den allowed Maud to erase the parts of nature she did not like. As she grew older, she hated winter. It was the season in which she was deprived of sunlight and became a prisoner of the house. Maud could have chosen to romanticize the Prince Edward Island winter, as American author Marian C.L. Reeves had done in *Godey's Lady's Book* in February 1892. Reeves's short story "On Her Sixth Birthday" describes a rough crossing from Nova Scotia to Prince Edward Island, onboard the icebreaker Northern Lights, as a winter sublime. "It was an awesome thing, to stand looking down on that wild frozen ocean," she noted about the iced-in Strait in February. "The wildness of it! The beauty of it! No storm-tossed seas could have so heaved and billowed in white crests, as those great drifts and hummocks of ice, swaying hither and thither with the tides, and hemming us in, resistlessly."[28] Maud lived close to the sea, just a short walk away, but there are no descriptions or photos of the dramatic ice shards that pile up each winter and transform the landscape with a truly surreal beauty. Their total absence suggests that in the winter she did not venture out as far as the shore. The only winter photographs of the homestead were taken just meters from the kitchen door, although her journal reveals that she did venture into Lover's Lane.

Anne of Green Gables covers five years in the life of Anne, from age eleven to sixteen, but almost half of the plot is set in June, Maud's favorite month on Prince Edward Island and the season of young girlhood. For Maud it was the month of pagan resurrection, when she could feast on sensuous vegetation, dancing sunshine, and lovely blue skies. The novel does contain equally glowing references to autumn with its crisp and fine September mornings and its glorious October. Three chapters evoke the shorn harvest fields and the beautiful and myriad fall colors. Maud's own birth month November, however, is omitted altogether from the account of Anne's first two years in Avonlea, to be dismissed in the third year merely as "dull November." Maud hated November with a passion.

The harsh Prince Edward Island winter months are rarely described even though February and March are Diana and Anne's birth months. Suffering from seasonal depression, Maud relegated these dark months to her "grumble book," her private journal. When winter is mentioned at all in *Green Gables*, it is to remember the nostalgic winter rituals of child-hood. It is remembered for Christmas (when Matthew gives Anne her brown dress with puffed sleeves), and for the romantic sleigh ride shared by Diana and Anne. Maud's complaints in her journal concerning the masses of snow covering the roads in February, which frequently kept her snow-bound in Cavendish, or the large ice shards that blocked the passage of the legendary ice-breakers, thus severing the Island from the mainland, are absent from this novel dedicated to spring pleasure.

The June 1905 newspaper weather columns reported numerous showers, and it was so cold that year that even by the end of June Maud still had to sit in the kitchen, writing by the fire. Yet a rigorous censorship all but eliminates precipitation from Avonlea. Prince Edward Island's lushly green pastures and rich fields depend on generous rainfall (130 to 160 wet days per year with an average of 1,100 millimeters of precipitation, according to Environment Canada), and, as Islanders know, spring and summer rainfalls are so constant that outdoor events are routinely announced with alternate indoor locations. Rain turns the soft red clay roads into muddy quagmires; rain spoils picnics and hairdos. Yet, like other unmentionables such as sex, divorce, and the outhouse, precipitation in form of rain, sleet, hail, and snow is for the most part banished from the novel. By contrast, in Maud's 1917 sequel *Anne's House of Dreams*, which was written during the war and explores a woman's entrapment in a hellish marriage, as well as Anne's marriage and childbirth, the atmosphere is drenched in humidity, from the fog that hangs over Four Winds Harbor to the storms battering the ships in Captain Jim's stories.

If the pattern in which she wrote the sequel to *Anne* is any indication, Maud would have spent three hours of concentrated literary work each day: one hour of magazine work in the morning, her bread-and-butter job, one hour at the typewriter in the afternoon, and one hour in the evening on her new novel. "Yes," she confirmed to her friend Ephraim Weber on April 5, 1908, "I only do three hours' literary work a day—two hours' writing and one typewriting. I write fast, having 'thought out' plot and dialogue while I go about my household work."[29] Besides writing, each day was filled with housework, post office work, and caring for her grandmother. She also had her correspondence and magazine work, publishing at least forty-four stories in 1905.

As Maud sat in her den by the window overlooking the fields and hills of Cavendish in the twilight of the day, her writing was compressed in space and time. The daily rhythm of her writing influenced the novel's episodic structure: there is no intricate plot, just one interconnected story following the next, each with its own emotional peak. And something else: her novel was meant to provide daily moments of pleasure for both the writer and reader.[30]

Writing the novel was like writing the journal, with no immediate commercial return. And so the novel was also a gamble, and the episodic structure her safety net. If her gamble didn't pay off, she could dismantle the book into a serial—just as she mined her journal for fiction. She might be able to get $40. Not all would be lost. In the meantime she enjoyed the adventure. Such pleasure she had in writing! Would this be the novel to bring her fame? It was like flirting with a suitor without the pressure of serious commitment.

With so much joy in writing her novel, what caused the mysterious downturn she first alluded to in her August 23 letter to George MacMillan? July had come and gone with apparent happiness, and she was still on a high on August 4, when she returned to her journal after a long hiatus. "This August day was a great golden dulcet dream of peace through which the heart of summer throbbed with lazy rhythm," she wrote in the unpublished entry. On this calm and golden August night, she had gone for a walk over the hill. "In its arch I *saw* a poem. Two spruces were clasping dark hands over an arc of silvery twilight sky; and right under the arch formed by their boughs was the new moon, like a sickle of red-gold." It was a picture-perfect day and yet there was already a faint scent of farewell. That day she had sung the requiem for the roses, picking the last bud. But summer wasn't done yet. The yellow poppies were out. "It has taken the sunshine of the summer to color them." The sweet peas were out. "My own soul seems filled with flowers."[31] Intoxicated by blossoms, she still seemed perfectly happy. What happened? What were the shadows that she was able to keep out of her novel, as she would cryptically note in later years? What was the mystery behind quiet, unmysterious Green Gables?

Family Quarrels

Probably within just one or two weeks of this happy August 4, 1905, entry, Uncle John and his son Prescott came visiting on important business. Grandmother Macneill's second son and his family lived on the seventy-five acre farm immediately adjacent to the old homestead, and he had gradually assumed the operation of his aging father's farm, as was the practice in farming families.[32] A rare private photograph taken in the studio of the Pach Brothers on Broadway in New York City shows that the younger John Franklin Macneill was strikingly handsome. Virile, with a heavy moustache, his strong features reflect a dashing Hemingway type of handsomeness. His expression is regal and proud. At the age of fifty-four, Uncle John still looked the same but his expression had mellowed. In a later photograph with his wife Annie he looks more established and more relaxed. Although Maud had been friends with his daughter Lucy and had nursed Katie, there was no love lost between uncle and niece.

He was a domineering man, said Maud, who had disliked and feared him since early childhood. He was uneducated, insulting, unjust, and bad-tempered, she charged. He was a miser and a bully. As she saw it, Uncle John destroyed the landscape for a few more bushels of potatoes. It was Uncle John who cut down the old trees for firewood but did not plant new ones, she said. In *Anne of Green Gables* she evokes the dryads (with her naming of Dryad's Bubble), the mythological wood nymphs who live in trees and die when the tree dies. Dryads are believed to punish those who destroy their beloved abodes. Uncle John obviously did not share Maud's ecological consciousness, her love of nature, or her poetic sensibility. But was Uncle John the monster Maud portrayed him as? Caring very little for the farmer's perspective, Maud's dreamy attitude clashed with her uncle's pragmatism. He was concerned with the business of farming; she was concerned with the charm of the landscape. Although she might be seen walking down Lover's Lane to help a friend get the cows for milking, she was more interested in the cats than the cows. Potatoes don't make for good poetry (although folk singer Stompin' Tom Connors of "Bud the Spud" fame might disagree) and are referred to only perfunctorily by Anne and Diana during the raspberry cordial episode. Making clichéd conversation, the bosom friends talk about the potato harvest but readers would never be able to tell that the two girls were talking about the main staple of the Prince Edward Island economy.

No doubt jealousy and mistrust also played a role in the soured family relations. The purpose of Uncle John's midsummer visit was serious. Twenty-five-year-old Prescott was hoping to get married and wanted the house. A few years earlier, in 1902, Prescott had been living with Grandma to enable Maud to go to Halifax and work as a proofreader. But Grandmother was not contented with Prescott and was happy when Maud returned several months later. So when Uncle John suggested that Prescott and his bride move into the old homestead, Grandmother Macneill did not encourage the proposed change. The commotion of a new family, and presumably children, would have been overwhelming for Grandma and Maud who both liked things just the way they were—quiet. In fact, the two women both hated change. As for Maud, she had little enough control in the house with just Grandmother Macneill giving orders. Moreover, Maud needed solitude to write. With half a novel written, a serious disruption such as a move or sharing of the home with uncongenial family would have put the book in jeopardy. Given Maud's sensitive radar for incompatible houseguests, the stress and upset she voiced in her journal are understandable.

Uncle John's proposal might have been as laughable as Mr. Collins's verbosely clumsy marriage proposal to intelligent Eliza Bennet in *Pride and Prejudice*, but for the tricky legal situation. Grandfather Macneill's "absurd will," as Maud called it, had transferred the homestead to Uncle John, and the personal property to Grandmother Macneill. It was practice at the time for Grandmother Macneill to be given lifetime occupancy, but these rights were not stated clearly in the will. Celebrating her eighty-first birthday that very month, on August 28, Grandmother Macneill was becoming old and "childish," as Maud described in a letter to George MacMillan. Maud's frank words suggest the usual failings of age, but may possibly also allude to a mild form of dementia. Never a very social person, Grandmother Macneill was sometimes rude to visitors, causing Maud to feel embarrassed and ashamed. As was her habit, Maud tried to cover up and maintain a façade of normalcy.

In fairness to Uncle John, as head of the family, he may well have tried to solve several problems with one stroke of his pragmatic, but not always sensitive, genius. No doubt what he had in mind was to equip his son with a house, enabling him to marry and settle down. Prescott would have taken care of the old homestead that, from lack of proper maintenance, was deteriorating from year to year. In exchange for the house, presumably Prescott's wife would have taken care of Grandmother Macneill. Or Uncle John may have offered his mother to move into his home. Maud refused to provide the details, but both alternatives would have freed up Maud instantly to get married to the minister who was spending a lot of time visiting at the homestead. From their neighboring home, John and his wife Annie would have been able to see the minister come and go, and they may have put two and two together. Besides, they must have figured, dreamy and head-in-the-clouds Maud was not getting any younger. They may even have commented on how stuck-up Maud had foolishly let Ed Simpson slip through her fingers when he visited and lingered in 1903. Perhaps they thought a little pressure would do the trick to get her finally settled. They probably sensed that Maud, regal and proud with her books and writing, with her education and ambition, thought she was better than the farmer's family who worked with their hands planting and harvesting hay and potatoes. It is safe to assume that Uncle John would have been content to see Maud go.

Uncle John's plan was all mapped out except for the fact that Grandmother Macneill, assisted by Maud, resisted it with more force than expected. Grandmother had lived and worked in the house for almost six decades. She had moved in as a young wife and mother. Here, in the old home, she had given birth to five more children. Here she had nursed Clara when she was sick with tuberculosis. Here she had been given a second chance at life when she herself became deadly sick after Clara's death. Here she had lived a happy marriage and had seen her husband die—all in the old homestead. In that turbulent summer of 1905, the prolonged family crisis might have been avoided had Uncle John kept his cool and simply stepped away and respected his mother's wishes. But the Macneill pride and stubbornness won out. Once Uncle John had started his campaign, it took on its own dynamic. Had Uncle Leander been visiting, he might have negotiated a peace settlement. But Maud's lack of communication and negotiation skills presumably did not help, nor did the fact that she was a woman. Like all feuds, this one involved accusations, recriminations, and the dredging up of past failings and insensitivities. Uncle John dug in his heels. He and Prescott persisted in their pressuring campaign throughout the summer. Sitting in her rocker at the kitchen table, Grandmother Macneill was upset and crying. Maud was outraged. That they were trying to "oust" Grandma from her home was how Maud eventually formulated the event after a two-month delay on October 1 in her journal.

Grandma won the battle. What exactly she said to her son we will probably never know. But we know from Maud's journal that Grandmother Macneill could be blunt and rude. There must have been words that caused the bitter chasm in the family. Uncle John ceased to visit. He ceased to speak with his mother. He ceased to provide help with the homestead. There were no winners in this war. Prescott never married; a year later, he became gravely ill with tuberculosis and died in 1910. In Maud's journal we look in vain for expressions of sympathy. "It is hard to feel sorry for him after the way he has acted," she noted on April 18, 1906.[33] Her heart had hardened, as the family acrimony had calcified. Humiliated about not even having a place for the visitors' horses, for the barns belonged to Uncle John, she could no longer encourage visitors to come to the house. One wonders if Maud would have discussed these unsavory family matters with Ewan Macdonald. Most likely she did not. Her impulse was always to maintain an image of propriety. The dark feud in her own backyard was too unsavory to confess in full even to her journal; as so often when upset, she kept the entries exceedingly short. The journal reveals that the only person she confessed these secrets to was Frede Campbell, her confidante and spiritual kin.

For Maud, the altercation with Uncle John made it clear that her own days in the homestead were numbered. "Uncle John and his brood detest me," she wrote in her October 1, 1905, journal entry. "It will, of course, hurt me deeply to leave this old home which I have always loved so passionately."[34] During the very same time that this family feud was unfolding from summer to fall, poisoning the relationship with her closest blood relations, Maud was ironically in the midst of writing her family romance with "quiet unmysterious" Green Gables at its center. The loss of the homestead was the threat that hung over her head as she composed the second half of the novel, in which Green Gables and its potential loss are being discussed. Marilla breaks down sobbing, as she discusses the selling of Green Gables after Matthew's death. It is at this point that Anne takes the decision in her hand. "'You mustn't sell Green Gables,' said Anne resolutely."[35] One wonders if the conversation might have gone in similar ways at the homestead that summer. "It is only on grandmother's account I am worried," Maud wrote.[36] Yet this sacrificial pose was perhaps a little disingenuous. She too had a stake in the homestead, having lived there for three decades of her life and hoping to finish her novel in the solitude of her home, but she avoided confrontation at all cost, whereas Anne *acts* by making a decision to stay. *She* saves the house.

Nostalgia

The old homestead went through steady decline while the women were living there alone. In winter, it was Maud, never physically strong, who shoveled the snow to open a path to the back door. Anyone who knows firsthand the masses of snow that cover the Maritimes will appreciate the hard physical labor required. The blustery winds and winter storms bombarded the house, and when the spring thaws set in, the old house sprang leaks, making the plaster and wall-paper blister and soften. Maud's makeshift repairs (she used cotton to patch up the breaks and leaks) could not prevent the house from slowly falling into disrepair. When she replaced the wallpaper in her upstairs den, in lieu of clean edges and smooth surfaces, there were bumps and bubbles visible in the photographs. In the winter of 1911, a big chunk of ceiling plaster came crashing down. Her beloved den was literally falling apart.[37] The house needed serious repair, even while Maud was writing the novel. It's intriguing that in the novel, Marilla comments that the Green Gables buildings are old and not worth very much. Similarly, the Macneill apple orchard had been neglected for years. Its trees were scraggly and ugly, giving a personal touch to Marilla's pragmatic comment about the Green Gables cherry tree: "…it blooms great, but the fruit don't amount to much never—small and wormy."[38] These were the emotional currents that fueled the second half of Maud's novel with a deeply personal charge that was also connected to her nostalgic vision of Prince Edward Island.

Since for Maud, the Island was an extension of the homestead, and the entire novel was a nostalgic ode to home and homeland all at once, it's worth remembering that nostalgia was originally identified as a medical condition. The roots of the word consist of *nostos*, "homeland," and *algos*, "pain" or "longing". Its German variant is *Heimweh*, literally "home-pain," a feeling generally accompanied by the suppression of negative memories related to home. Unable to prevent the loss of her home, Maud reconstructed in fiction the home of her dreams: Green Gables. In chapter twenty-six, Maud describes the love of home from Marilla's point of view as she returns home, her eyes dwelling affectionately on Green Gables, "peering through its network of trees and reflecting the sunlight back from its windows in several little coruscations of glory."[39] In another scene, Anne returns home to see the kitchen light burning—the very beacon of home that was Maud's own when she returned from her twilight walks.

The Webb Farm

In fact, Maud went to great lengths to ensure that readers would not mistake Green Gables for the homestead. She veiled her personal investment. The house she identified as the model for Green Gables belonged to her distant cousins David and Margaret Macneill, an aging brother and sister, who lived back in the woods across the street from Pierce Macneill's. "[T]he truth of my description of it is attested by the fact that everybody has recognized it," Maud wrote in her January 27, 1911, journal entry.[40] Built in 1831, the gabled, one-and-a half storey house with a kitchen addition was typical of Prince Edward Island architecture. There was a large barn, a woodshed, and a granary to the north. The farm was located west of the Macneill homestead, beyond the Cavendish school, the cemetery, and the Haunted Wood, but it was probably its romantic proximity to Lover's Lane that enabled its transformation into idyllic Green Gables. Of course, Maud conveniently overlooked the fact that the farm's unromantic outhouse was placed just at the opening to Lover's Lane.[41] In imagining Green Gables, Maud did not copy the architecture of the house but was inspired by the scenery and situation. The reality of the historical pictures and the untidy surroundings belie the romanticism of Maud's vision of Green Gables.

There was another secret. Maud was mum about the fact that midway through her writing of *Anne*, the house she had secretly named "Green Gables" hosted a grand event at which she was present: the wedding of Maud's distant cousin Myrtle Macneill to Ernest Webb. Myrtle was the woman who stood to inherit the "Green Gables" farm, named as such only in Maud's imagination. Born in 1883 in New Brunswick, Myrtle had been adopted at age eleven in 1894 by elderly brother and sister David and Margaret Macneill. No doubt something of Myrtle's history had blended with the myriad of other influences that went into imagining Anne. The wedding took place on Wednesday, September 20, 1905, at eleven o'clock in the morning. Maud had received a wedding invitation in neat, old-fashioned handwriting, which she tucked into the scrapbook, the only reference to the wedding. Maud would have worn her pretty organdy dress with the beautiful puffs and thrills, the same she would wear again in December when she was the bridesmaid at Bertha McKenzie's wedding. The Reverend Ewan Macdonald officiated at the happy event, presumably also quietly eyeing the woman he was hoping might become Mrs. Macdonald. It is strange that Maud should never mention the event at all in her journal, all the more as the house was playing such an important role in her creative life at that very time. The total silence amplifyes the aura of secrecy and mystery surrounding Ewan's courtship and her writing of *Anne of Green Gables*.

Still, the wedding at "Green Gables" may have shaped aspects of Anne's wedding in *Anne's House of Dreams*. In chapter four, "The First Bride of Green Gables," Anne, like Myrtle, is a September bride: "it was a happy and beautiful bride who came down the old, homespun-carpeted stairs that September noon—the first bride of Green Gables, slender and shining-eyed, in the midst of her maiden veil, with her arms full of roses."[42] They are married by Mr. Allan in the old orchard.

The name "Green Gables" was brilliant in its evocative simplicity. It was a name that appealed to the heart. "Everybody *likes* color; with me it is a passion. I revel in it," she told George MacMillan on August 23: "My emotions were exactly what you describe yours as being when listening to music. Everything you say of music I can say of color."[43] Maud could revel in the color of the fields in spring, the view from her window. Also, the green of the house created a flashing contrast with the red of her heroine's hair and the Prince Edward Island soil. Like a painter, Maud would visualize vibrant color contrasts and striking shapes. Gables, a distinctive feature of Maritime architecture, adorned all of the houses Maud loved, including her birthplace in Clifton (New London), the Campbell house in Park Corner, and her Grandfather Montgomery's house across the road from the Campbell home. The Green Gables title evoked childhood memories, but it did more. In choosing her title, Maud was building her house of dreams on a solid literary foundation.

Seven Gables and Gray Gables

On Tuesday, April 12, 1903, Maud had noted in her journal that reading Nathaniel Hawthorne's 1851 novel *The House of the Seven Gables* had made her cry.[44] It is the story of a house haunted by the ghost of Matthew Maule, a former inhabitant executed for witchcraft during the Salem trials. *The House of the Seven Gables* filled Maud with pleasure and pain, perhaps the same blend of feelings she had toward her own homestead. In the preface to the book, Hawthorne defined romance as a legend prolonging itself, a comment that must have intrigued Maud, given her preoccupation with the influence of the past on the present. Two of the main characters in Hawthorne's novel are elderly sister and brother Hepzibah and Clifford Pyncheon. Phoebe, the young heroine of Hawthorne's novel, has the same boundless optimism as Anne. She brings new life and energy into the House of Seven Gables, which is marked by decay and ancestral guilt (not unlike the Macneill homestead). Even the names of Hawthorne's characters are echoed in Maud's novel. Matthew is a common name, so perhaps we should not make too much of the fact that the shy Matthew Cuthbert shares his given name with the humble Matthew Maule of *Seven Gables*. Hepzibah, in contrast, is a most unusual name, yet Anne recalls, in the first chapter of *Green Gables*, that "There was a girl at the asylum whose name was Hepzibah Jenkins."[45] It was common practice, in the literature of the day, to embed subtle allusions of this type in titles and texts; the point was to underscore the work's literary value by tantalizing the educated reader with intertextual play. As the architect gives the house good bones, so she gave her novel strong literary antecedents that would resonate with well-versed readers of Maud's era.

Green Gables represented the dream of the simple and authentic life. Anne fans may be startled and delighted to discover that the *Green Gables* spark that inspired Maud likely was attributable to the President of the United States; the name "Green Gables" may have been inspired by the name of Grover Cleveland's summer White House at Cape Cod in Massachusetts named "Gray Gables." Grover Cleveland, the twenty-second and twenty-fourth president of the United States, loved to spend time at Gray Gables, particularly during the 1892 Presidential election campaign that pitted Democrat Cleveland against incumbent Republican President Benjamin Harrison. Mrs. Grover Cleveland was pictured at Gray Gables, a "quaint little cottage," in Maud's beloved *Godey's Lady's Book*.[46]

Gray Gables was a typical New England cottage, a two-storey, wooden Queen Anne with a wrap-around deck and many gables and dormers. There was also a Victorian Gray Gables railway station that serviced the president at his summer resort and that is still standing. Sadly, Gray Gables burned down in the 1970s, but the Bourne Historical Society has preserved its memory. One of its veteran volunteer staff members, Thelma Loring, who worked at the Gray Gables inn before it was destroyed, remembers Gray Gables. "It was nothing spectacular, definitely not luxurious," she said, "but I think that's why the president and his family liked it; they did not have to put on airs."[47] There is a kinship between the spirit of Gray Gables and Green Gables. One of the first houses Anne Shirley sees when she looks out of her gabled window has a "gray gable end."[48]

Maud would have seen Mattie Sheridan's article in *Godey's Lady's Book* in September 1892, coincidentally (or not?) the same year and month that the little orphan girl Ellen Macneill arrived in Cavendish to provide the kernel for Anne's story. It was the year Maud was squirreling away many other references in *Godey's* that would figure in her novel. Sheridan describes Mrs. Frances Folsom Cleveland, "the sweet girl-wife" (she was twenty-seven years younger than her husband) at her Gray Gables home. During Cleveland's first term she had become a much-photographed celebrity, yet Mr. Cleveland had a "violent objection" to any association of his wife with politics. She avoided overshadowing her husband's re-election campaign by withdrawing to Gray Gables. "Since her wedding-day, she has probably lived through no days so uneventful, so quiet, so secluded from public friction as those of the past summer." Meanwhile, for the president, Gray Gables was a place to escape from "the restless, resistless political atmosphere."[49] These subliminal associations of peace and escape with Gray Gables were certainly a factor in the novel's appeal to a mass reading public, including Americans.

Finally, Maud ensured that Green Gables was a tasteful work of art, like a simple but elegantly dressed woman. What better way to ensure that than to follow the experts. Unlike contemporary novels such as *Rebecca of Sunnybrook Farm* or Helen Winslow's *Peggy at Spinster Farm*, Maud's title avoided the reference to farm and opted for the more noble and poetic name of Green Gables. At around the very same time that she would have chosen her title *Anne of Green Gables*, an article entitled "High Gables" appeared in the March 1905 *Delineator* (the same issue that featured Zona Gale's orphan story, "The Things That Are Real").[50] This article devoted two full pages of illustrations and text to the "High Gables" architectural design, which entailed multiple gables, a gray shingled roof, and red chimneys. The interior design favored different shades of—what color? Green, green, and more green. Green burlap covers the library walls, green silk the window, and green velour curtains are hung over the door. The fireplace is made of red brick with a white wood mantel. It seems that all home decorator Maud had to do was to turn the interior décor outside and voilà: green gables, white siding, and red clay soil. She had given the old gray gables a lick of fresh paint and a modern punch, as well as a more exalted status.

Green Gables is evoked rather than described. More details are provided in the sequels. In the 1917 sequel *Anne's House of Dreams*, Green Gables appears as the "old gray-green" house.[51] A different picture of the Green Gables' exterior does not appear until the 1936 sequel *Anne of Windy Poplars*, when Anne describes her new Summerside home to Gilbert Blythe:

> I may describe it to you as a white frame house...very white... with green shutters...very green...with a 'tower' in the corner and a dormer-window on either side.... In short, it is a house with a delightfull personality and has something of the flavor of Green Gables about it.[52]

Evocative of the genteel New England family home of the nineteenth century, this belated description reflects the sprucing up of the Green Gables house by Ernest Webb, after the success of *Anne of Green Gables* had made the house famous. A popular postcard from the 1930s featuring the Green Gables house in Cavendish is found in Maud's 1936 journal. With the siding looking nice and white and clean, the polished Green Gables tourist site now served as a concrete image of what Green Gables looked like. By being vague and evocative in her first novel, Maud created in Green Gables an idealized home into which millions of readers from different backgrounds could project their own ideal of home.

Lover's Lane

The little cow path, which Maud had romantically named Lover's Lane, and that was at the heart of the Green Gables mythology, had its beginnings south of Margaret and David Macneill's farm from where it led down to a wooded trail to where two bridges crossed a cool streamlet— a capital place for trout fishing with the Nelson boys and, later, with Frede.[53] Maud had first discovered the path when she was twelve, close to Anne's age when she arrived at Green Gables. To Maud, the lane had magic. She spent pages describing it in her journal, tracing it through different seasons and colors. Lover's Lane was like a companion. Here, she said, she never felt depressed or sad; the lane always lifted her mood. Here she thought out many of the chapters for *Green Gables*. Prowling with her camera in the sunshine and snow she took possession of it imaginatively. She never tired of the fascinating tunnel effect achieved by focusing her camera down the lane toward the flood of light at its end. As she chased the tunnel of light with her camera she was composing a story about it. She never tired of registering the lane's different colors and moods in her journals, pasting in, years later, the different photos she had taken.

Walking through Lover's Lane was therapy for Maud, as was writing about it. She had first given the world a glimpse of her beloved Cavendish lane in her poem, "In Lovers Lane," which appeared in July 1903 in the

Delineator. A fragrant space where wild roses grow, where beeches provide shadow, and where the invisible brook can be heard, Lover's Lane causes hearts to commune with no need for words:

> And eyes will meet with seeking eyes
> And hands will clasp in Lovers' Lane.[54]

A few months later, in January 1904, Maud was jolted to see "Winter in Lovers' Lane" in the same magazine. Signed by Clinton Scollard, a prolific New York State poet whose name she had seen many times in *Godey's Lady's Book*, the poem read as if it were a sequel to hers: "In Lovers' Lane 'tis winter now/ (Will spring tide never come again?)" the poet asks and seems to speak to Maud directly:

> Will hearts no more be wooed and won
> In memory-haunted Lovers' Lane?[55]

Maud must have felt a curious combination of flattery and irritation in seeing her own "Lover's Lane" appropriated by the American poet. As she had done with the photo of Evelyn Nesbit, Maud took a pair of scissors, clipped out the poem and glued it in her scrapbook (without identifying its source). She did more. As if hoisting a flag underneath the poem, she glued a red maple leaf, big and prominent, taken from a tree growing in her own Lover's Lane. Even though the maple leaf would not become the national flag until 1965, during Maud's era it was featured on Canadian coins and in Alexander Muir's song *The Maple Leaf Forever*, written in the year of Canada's Confederation in 1867. Indeed, Maud's description of spring in chapter twenty is much more specifically Canadian than the Romantic effusions that appear in earlier chapters:

> Spring had come once more to Green Gables—the beautiful, capricious, reluctant Canadian spring, lingering along through April and May in a succession of sweet, fresh, chilly days, with pink sunsets and miracles of resurrection and growth. The maples in Lovers' Lane were red-budded...[56]

Whenever the lane is mentioned in *Anne of Green Gables*, the maples are close by. For example, when Anne and Diana walk up the lane to school, "under the leafy arch of maples," Anne remarks that "maples are such sociable trees…they're always rustling and whispering to you." With its glimmering beech and maple woods the land was a space of stillness and peace. "I like that lane because you can think out loud there without people calling you crazy," Anne explains to Marilla. Maud must have chuckled as she wrote that sentence, for she was the one talking out loud to herself in her lane, composing her novel.[57]

"*Lover's Lane* of course was *my* Lover's Lane," Maud would later write in her journal with a curious proprietary emphasis.[58] And yet Anne admits that she and Diana discovered the name in a book: "Diana and I were reading a perfectly magnificent book and there's a Lover's Lane in it. So we want to have one, too. And it's a very pretty name, don't you think? So romantic!"[59] Lover's Lane was found in many places, and that was part of its emotional power. Maud could tap into the emotions readers felt about their own romanticized lanes, the ones they had been walking along as children or lovers. Enabling romantic identification, the landscape and architecture of Avonlea and Green Gables were a unique blend of the personal and the borrowed, literary and popular, local and global, Canadian and American.

"How shall I ever be able to live without it?" Maud wailed in her journal about her Lover's Lane, less than a year before she would leave Prince Edward Island for good.[60] The question, like the answer, was rhetorical. By memorializing her home and the lane, she found a way of not only taking it with her, but also transporting Lover's Lane and Green Gables, across space and time and borders—between the covers of a book.

The Myth of Home

Just as the beloved homestead was dying a slow death, so Maud perceived Prince Edward Island's geography as marked by the passage of time. In her August 23 letter to George MacMillan, she describes rapid crumbling of the soft red rock of Prince Edward Island.[61] Similarly, its forests were disappearing at an alarming speed. The Reverend Robert Murray wrote in 1899,

"There was a time when the maple was so abundant that the people made from its sap most of the sugar they required, but that time has vanished like the golden age."[62] The youth of Cavendish—Maud's own generation—were also vanishing. Maud felt depressed by the outward migration that left her isolated in Cavendish beginning in the 1890s. Nate Lockhart, Jack Laird, Hattie Gordon, Ed Simpson, and many others who belonged to the Island's best and most educated had left to find careers and livelihoods in the Canadian west or in the United States (a trend that continues today). "All Maritime province ambition turns to Boston," Maud later commented in an interview. "The farmer's daughter is educated for a teacher or trained for a nurse and goes to Boston. The fisherman's daughter goes to Boston to get high pay in housework." She further emphasized that a large percentage of the professional men of Massachusetts were "natives of our Maritimes" and that when Maritime people went on a long trip, it was more likely to be to Boston than to Montreal or Toronto.[63] In *Anne of Green Gables* the Acadian farm boys go to the States to work in the lobster canneries. In Marian Reeves' story "On her Sixth Birthday: A Leap Year Story," two homesick Acadian maids return from service in Boston to Prince Edward Island, "homeward to a north-shore Acadian village."[64]

One of the old traditions on Prince Edward Island is Old Home Week, celebrated annually with exhibitions showcasing livestock and homemade arts and crafts. The year of 1905, in fact, marked the first Old Home Week. It was an attempt to lure back the many Island expatriates. Its preparation had been discussed for months and was front-page news in the Charlottetown newspapers during the year Maud was busy writing *Anne*. On the night of July 24, the railway was thronged with homecomers. The Olivette brought seventy-one passengers from Boston, the Princess over one hundred, and more were expected. They were welcomed with renderings of Home Sweet Home and God Save the Queen. There were horse races at the Charlottetown Driving Park and evening theatricals, exactly the type of events that Maud evokes in her novel.[65] Maud immediately incorporated Old Home Week into the novel, blending it with the Charlottetown Exhibition of September 1905, in the latter part of the novel, where rural meets urban.

In fact, readers of *Anne* may remember Anne's first trip to the provincial capital in chapter twenty-nine, "An Epoch in Anne's Life." "Charlottetown was thirty miles away," the narrator remarks about this pleasant ride along the harvest-shorn fields in September with Diana Barry. Anne exults in the long journey to town. Diana's aunt in Charlottetown, Miss Josephine Barry, takes the two girls to the Exhibition Grounds (still operating today in the Charlottetown Driving Park as a harness racing track and exhibition grounds). In the Market Place, horses, flowers, and fancy work are on display. Prizes are given for the most impressive apples, pigs, painting, and homemade cheese, and "there were thousands of people there."[66] There are horse races. A man going up in a balloon. And a concert at the Academy of Music. Anne enjoys the excitement and adventure, yet echoes Dorothy, in L. Frank Baum's *The Wonderful Wizard of Oz* (1900), when she says: "I've had a splendid time....But the best of it all was the coming home."[67] Just as Maud preferred to stay put in Cavendish, resisting the lure of New York, Boston, and Halifax, so Anne concludes that she was not born for city life. Later in the novel she reiterates that her identity is linked to her home: "I'm quite content to be Anne of Green Gables."[68]

The myth of the home associated with Prince Edward Island has "connotations of the rustic, the premodern, the traditional, the authentic, the quaint, the pastoral, and the picturesque,"[69] writes Shauna McCabe in her doctoral dissertation on the topic of "Representing Islandness." Although such values may seem contrary to modernism, in fact, they are an integral component of the changes that swept over the country and continent in the early twentieth century. Although there had been little in the way of a tourist industry when Maud was growing up, by the time she began writing her novel the Island was a favorite destination. In 1899, for example, there were an estimated seven thousand tourists, many of them American.[70] So many Americans purchased or built summer homes on the Island that its land and real estate was advertised in New York and Boston. In 1896, Cincinnati oil magnate Alexander McDonald built an enormous, Queen Anne–style summer home, with many gables and dormers, on the north shore of the Island. He named it "Dalvay" after his boyhood home— a gesture that reinforced the image of Prince Edward Island as a place where one might return to simpler, more innocent times. Today Dalvay-by-the-Sea is a summer resort hotel. It appears in the *Anne of Green Gables* and *Road to Avonlea* television series as the White Sands Hotel.

In the novel, the White Sands Hotel is the site for the concert for the benefit of the Charlottetown hospital for which Anne Shirley has been selected to recite in the last third of the novel.[71] The novel suddenly moves from the old-fashioned, mellow oil lamps of Green Gables to the blazing electric lights in the White Sands Hotel. The contrast could not be any more striking. The tourists are stock characters. For Anne and her girl-friends, the bejeweled and stout pink lady, wife of an American millionaire, represents the lure of a better life in Boston or New York. "I just wish I was a rich American and could spend my summer at a hotel and wear jewels and low-necked dresses," says Jane Andrews. "I'm sure it would be ever so much more fun than teaching school."[72] In fact, Maud's own cousins Clara and Stella Macneill settled in Boston and Los Angeles respectively, although by no means marrying millionaires, as the nice but talentless Jane Andrews eventually does when she marries a Winnipeg millionaire in *Anne of the Island*.

For Anne Shirley, it is but one of the temptations to be sampled and resisted, as she recognizes the value of home and youth and family. In a world experiencing rapid change, fiction accommodated modernization by emphasizing the need to restore mental and physical health, and by upholding the pastoral ideal. Maud's longing for home and community was emblematic of a nostalgic undercurrent rippling through an entire era of transition from the Victorian to the modern.

Canadian Icons and Landmarks

Maud's loyalty to home also extended to Canada. Specific, yet unobtru-sive, references to Prince Edward Island and Canada make it possible to claim *Anne of Green Gables* as a Canadian classic even though the novel was published in Boston, then the capital of Prince Edward Island's outward migration. Because the Charlottetown Conference of 1864 paved the way for Confederation in 1867, Prince Edward Island is often regarded as the birthplace of Canada. The "Confederation" label has been inscribed across the Island on major landmarks such as the Confederation Bridge (which links the Island with the mainland), the Confederation Trail, and the Confederation Centre of the Arts. Ironically, however, it was not until 1873, just one year before Maud's birth, that Prince Edward Island actually joined the Canadian Confederation. Confederation would prove a mixed blessing for Canada's smallest province, creating a culture of dependency. Political delegations from the United States had been courting the little province energetically. Should Prince Edward Island have favored a Maritime Union, an alliance of the Eastern provinces with the Eastern United States? The question continues to be asked on Prince Edward Island, even as the re-enactment of "The Fathers of Confederation" has become an important annual ritual performed in front of Province House for summer tourists.

By far the most iconic political presence in *Anne of Green Gables* is that of the first Canadian prime minister, Sir John A. Macdonald, who appears in chapter eighteen, "Anne to the Rescue." Although he is not named, Marilla provides a caricature of Macdonald after having attended his "monster mass" election rally in Charlottetown: "Such a nose as that man had! But he can speak. I was proud of being a Conservative."[73] Sir John A., as he was known, did have a prominent nose, as Canadians knew well, and by alluding to him in her novel, Maud commemorated her own meeting with the legendary prime minister. On August 11, 1890, the fifteen-year-old Maud had taken her first train ride ever, and what a ride it was. At the Kensington train station, she boarded the special train carrying the prime minister. Her grandfather, Senator Montgomery, who was hobnobbing with Sir John A., introduced her, and she accompanied the prime minister ("spry-looking") and his wife (dressed "dowdily," said fashionista Maud) to Summerside.[74] In the city's Market Place, Sir John A., a passionate advocate of the nationalist cause, gave an eloquent and memorable speech to a large crowd, an event Maud transformed into a "monster mass" rally in the novel (somewhat unrealistically, as it would have been unlikely for any prime minister to venture to Prince Edward Island in January). Sir John A.'s message was patriotic. The Dominion had made great progress since 1867, and the provinces were connected by the Canadian Pacific Railway. He was smart and witty in his remarks to the ladies, as *The Journal-Pioneer* reported, reminding them that he had introduced a clause in the franchise act that would have given women the right to vote, but had to drop the clause for fear of being defeated by the men. But if the ladies would stand by him, he said, the Island would do so too.[75] The speech was followed by a storm of applause, and Maud was impressed by the prime minister's eloquence. His appeal to the women later inspired the episode in which those two formidable ladies of Avonlea—Marilla and Mrs. Lynde—go off to the political meeting, while Matthew stays home and Thomas Lynde looks after the horse. Just a few months after the Summerside speech, on May 29, 1891, Canada's first prime minister suffered a massive stroke, passing away a week later. His cameo in *Anne of Green Gables* was the memorializing of an important Canadian figure, albeit in humorous form.

That Marilla should insist on adopting "a born Canadian" in the first chapter of *Anne of Green Gables* is a patriotic proclamation.[76] The novel includes numerous Canadianisms, referring to the Ottawa government and to learning Canadian history, but generally avoids loud expressions of patriotism.[77] Grits (Liberals) and Tories (Conservatives) are mentioned, but neither political party is given preference. Matthew votes Conservative, but Gilbert's father is a Liberal. The references would be easily recognized by Canadian readers, but would not alienate readers from elsewhere. "At the turn of the century, Canadian political and cultural commentators debated the question of Canada's national and political existence," writes Janice Fiamengo in her study of the novel's landscape, suggesting that *Anne of Green Gables* was part of a national literature that helped Canadians to possess their homeland imaginatively. As the Vancouver native confesses, as a child she was prompted by Anne's example to name herself "Janice of Emerald Firs."[78]

A Shrinking World

On the weekend of October 14, Frede Campbell visited, and her presence was "an unspeakable comfort" to Maud.[79] The tone of Maud's unpublished journal entry of Sunday evening, October 15, is elusive and fascinating. It is clear that Maud had shared delicate confidences with Frede, and her friend would have listened with sympathy as they shared confidences in bed until the early hours as they always liked to do. However, she did not give any details of their discussion in her journal, other than to confess that she was sadhearted and lonely. The quarrels with Uncle John and her own uncertain situation were weighing on her. A tongue-in-cheek reference to Dickens' novel *Martin Chuzzlewit*, with its greedy family members, makes it clear that she was referring to the quarrels with Uncle John. Even Dickens' eternally cheerful Mark Tapley, she writes, would not be able to keep up his spirits under the current circumstances.

Perhaps it was a walk with Frede in Lover's Lane that prompted the memory of her long ramble in the woods a week before. She had spent an entire afternoon in the woods. It was an exquisite experience but for the fact that her worries made for such "a dour companion." The trees, presumably the maples of Lover's Lane, were red. The winds rustled softly in the leaves. "I wished that I might lie down there among the bleached ferns and fall into a pleasant dream that might have no ending and no return to unrest and anxiety. Oh, those dear old woods and fields! I love them with all my heart and have found in them fullness of joy in all my years."[80] The fantasy of the ultimate escape, the wish to merge with the landscape, indicates both her despair during this period and her romantic, escapist way of dealing with problems.

"I bade them farewell very sadly for I do not expect ever to have a garden here again," Maud continued in a sad farewell to her flower garden. "I do not feel welcome even to so much soil as would suffice for a flower plot. It is very bitter to think of giving up my garden—my one sole pleasure apart from books and pen."[81] As she headed into the final stretch of writing *Anne*, her world was shrinking. She felt herself slowly starved and deprived of the oxygen of life—her beloved garden, which she was forced to give up. She was suffocating. Maud passionately loved the old house and garden but Uncle John must have claimed the land. Here was a loss that would be hard to digest for someone whose life was tied to the garden.

ELEVEN

Red Hair, Puffed Sleeves, and the Rituals of Growing Up

"...I cannot imagine that red hair away. I do my best. I think to myself, 'Now my hair is a glorious black, black as the raven's wing.' But all the time I know it is just plain red, and it breaks my heart. It will be my lifelong sorrow...."
—*Anne Shirley to Matthew Cuthbert*[1]

Even though the words "adolescent" and "teen-age" were not yet in common use during Maud's era, precocious Anne has the classical adolescent temperament. Like a modern-day teenager, she is constantly reinventing and testing herself—inhabiting countless roles that add to the reader's delight, suggesting both a fantasy of unfettered freedom and a coming to terms with a distinctive personal identity that is also carefully negotiated with respect to its social context. Like her author, Anne is able to play a myriad of roles, even contradictory ones. Thus she experiments with hairstyles (Anne's hair changes color and goes from long to short) and clothing (witness the dramatic changes from gray aprons to modern dresses). She also showcases her performance talents as an actress (Elaine), an amateur model (Dawn of Hope), and stage performer. Like Maud, who tried out a number of different pseudonyms (Maud Cavendish, Joyce Cavendish, Maud Eglinton, Belinda Bluegrass, Cynthia, J.C. Neville),[2] so Anne plays at renaming herself (Geraldine,

169

Cordelia, Elaine). As Anne of Green Gables, she also gives herself a noble connection to a place like the famous medieval redhead and free spirit, Eleanor of Aquitaine.

The self-defining female child is an adolescent myth, in addition to being a powerful myth in Canadian literature and culture: "For this story of the sensitive young woman who doesn't somehow 'belong' in the environment into which she has found herself situated, who must somehow refuse to be limited by her birth-identity, who creates for herself a new identity more appropriate to her 'finer' qualities, occurs again and again in Canadian writing after *Anne of Green Gables*."[3] We find an exuberant pattern of female reinvention in the work of Maud's literary daughters including Canadian icons such as Margaret Atwood, Alice Munro, and Margaret Laurence. In fact, there may be a trajectory from Anne Shirley to the Honorable Kim Campbell, who also renamed herself, rejecting her birthname Avril Phaedra (though her fame as the first woman prime minister of Canada was short lived, unlike the enduring popularity of the Island redhead). As for Anne Shirley's compelling journey into selfhood, she is equipped with tools she shared with her author including a highly developed sense of fashion, a talent in performance, and a dynamic personality. Her multiple roles suggest that the story of Anne is at heart a fable of identity.

The Art of Beauty

Beginning with Anne's focus on her red hair to her love of puffed sleeves and flowers in her hair, *Anne of Green Gables* is laced with the philosophy and principles found in the Victorian fashion bible *The Art of Beauty*. Based on British feminist author Eliza Haweis's popular column, her 1878 book formulates the era's fashion principles. Dress, Haweis theorizes, "bears the same relation to the body as speech does to the brain; therefore dress may be called the speech of the body."[4] As a philosophy of fashion, the book transcends the simple instructive morals of other advice columns. Haweis writes that "The Plain Girl" is in the very best category of girlhood. The "Stupid Girl" or "The Uneducated Girl" cannot be made witty, she argues, but the ugly flower, or the ugly building, or the ugly face all exhibit a certain "crooked beauty" of their own. "There is a 'beauté du diable,' stricken with imperfection, but with its own charm," Haweis writes, anticipating the exact same wording that Maud used to describe her friend Frede's unusual beauty. In fact, numerous cross-references can be found in Maud's journal and fiction and she must have been familiar with Haweis's fashion philosophy, although she never mentions this book.

Anne, Emily, Pat, and Jane—all of Maud's major heroines are painted with the charm of physical imperfection. With her serious expression and red, tousled hair, Anne Shirley is a perfect physical specimen of the Pre-Raphaelite ideal. This art movement favored natural, long-haired, disheveled, soulful, and untraditional beauties. William Morris, Edward Burne-Jones, and other Pre-Raphaelite painters had made redheads fashionable, as Haweis noted: "Red hair—once, to say a woman had red hair was social assassination—is the rage."[5] It is from this Victorian fashion adviser that the narrator in *Anne of Green Gables* derived the rule that Anne is "forever debarred" from wearing the pink rose in her red hair. "Pink," Haweis had stipulated, "is suitable for most young faces, especially the fair, except when the hair inclines to red."[6] Iconoclastic Haweis encouraged women to discard artificial flowers for headdresses and use real flowers in hair and hats. Thus she also anticipated the photograph of Evelyn Nesbit and Anne's pagan wildflower get-up for church.

With her love of wildflowers and celebration of beauty for beauty's sake, Anne is an aesthete. Could she possibly be a spiritual kin of Oscar Wilde, who famously carried a sunflower or lily on his walk down Piccadilly, or other beauty devotees who placed Madonnas in pagan and underworld settings in paintings and stained-glass church windows in London and Berlin? The cult of youth was very much part of this fin-de-siècle movement. In fact, Wilde, the Irish pope of aestheticism (the pursuit of beauty for its own sake), stopped in Charlottetown, Prince Edward Island, on his tour to America, on October 11, 1882. Dressed in a light traveling suit and wearing knee-breeches, he had come to deliver his gospel of beauty—a lecture on the Decorative Arts. In the Market Place, the so-called "Butcher Market," where the air was thick with the smell of cheese and butter and cabbage, Wilde had preached the gospel of beauty to an enthusiastic Prince Edward Island crowd. He said that, as summarized in the *Examiner*, "we could get along very well without philosophy if we surrounded ourselves with beautiful things." Wilde concluded that "Art is the perfect praise of God, being the exemplifications of his handiwork."[7] The self-cherishing parts of Anne's character are at home in this tradition. Maud, who was seven going on eight years old when Oscar Wilde visited Charlottetown, would probably not have been allowed to attend the lecture, and so we should perhaps not make too much of this connection, but she certainly flirted with ideas of aestheticism and placed her heroine in that tradition through the distinctive tint of her hair.

Fiery Red

When people asked Maud why she gave Anne red hair, she said, "I didn't. It was red."[8] Growing up among Scots and Irish folk, Maud took great pleasure in teasing and stereotyping redheads, but she was also fascinated by this vibrant hair color and its potential to evoke a distinctive personality. All she remembered about one of her early teachers, Mr. Lamont, was his red hair and red whiskers.[9] Even as an adult, she poked fun at Artie Moffat's red hair "dazzling up in the air off to one side" and distracting her during a church service.[10] But she admired the auburn-haired beauty of Penzie whose rich tint she likened to the wildwood rose. "Little freckled Maud McKenzie with her elfin head of short silky red curls and 'cute' face is a nice little thing," Maud noted about one of her Bideford students.[11] No doubt she was the model for the post-shingled, short-haired Anne Shirley (and may have been the model for another redhead, Sarah Maud, of whom we shall hear more later).

As a fable of identity, *Anne of Green Gables* is a journey toward coming to terms with her distinctive fiery red hair—a symbol of Anne's uniqueness and queerness that does not always fit into the social order smoothly. In the course of the novel, the depiction of her hair changes from "carroty" to "auburn" to "Titian red," each with increasingly positive connotations. In fact, in October 1905, just around the time that Maud would have been writing about Anne's "Titian" hair in the novel, *Modern Women* featured an article titled "The History and Hygiene of Hair," detailing that "Titian" hair had always been admired by painters. Just so, Anne's "splendid Titian hair" attracts the attention of an artist at the American concert who promptly expresses a desire to paint her face.[12] Presumably, it is not the actual hair color that changes, but rather, the perceptions of those who are judging Anne.

Though despised by Anne, her hair color links her with the red clay roads of Prince Edward Island. The iron contained in the island soil has turned the roads a distinctive red. In fact, red sandstone is everywhere in the novel, and the reader makes the connection before Anne does. Red hair causes its owner to stand out. Anne's red hair also marks her as the creative thinker and trendsetter among the conformists and followers who surround her. After the novel was published, Maud was inundated with fan mail from red-tinted girls, for Anne had also inherited all of the inflictions of redheads. "Her temper matches her hair," as Mrs. Lynde remarks.[13]

The red of Anne's hair is part of her ambivalence, part of the divided self that is pulling in different directions and providing glimpses of the many diverse facets that make up her dynamic character (a topic to which we shall return in chapter twelve of this volume). When *Anne of Green Gables* was translated into Japanese in 1952, the color was emphasized in the title *Akage no An*, Red-Haired Anne. The popular media during Maud's era were fascinated by red hair. "Red Hair and Genius" read the title of an article in New York's *The World* newspaper in March 1901. "Red hair is an indication of ardor, passion, intensity of feeling and purity of character and usually goes with a sanguine temperament," writes the author who cites Sappho, Cleopatra, Queen Elizabeth, Helen of Troy, Joan of Arc, and even Shakespeare and Caesar as redheads.[14] But western literature and culture also features a slew of red-haired villains, including Charles Dickens' Fagin in *Oliver Twist* and Judas Iscariot, who was represented with red hair in medieval paintings. Red-haired women such as the biblical Mary Magdalene or William Thackeray's Becky Sharp are often portrayed as lascivious or mischievous. Anne herself has absorbed the stereotype regarding redheads.

With her adolescent drive to transform and reinvent herself, Anne decides to dye her hair raven black, but succeeds only in coloring her red locks a ghastly green. "Dyed it! Dyed your hair! Anne Shirley, didn't you know it was a wicked thing to do?"[15] Marilla is horrified—again. In earlier literature girls cut and sold their hair to help others—think of Jo in *Little Women* or the heroine in O'Henry's story "The Gift of the Magi." Anne's dye job is the classical act of adolescent defiance, self-assertion, and reinvention. Modern readers, in particular, will empathize with Anne given the current popularity of hair coloring. The episode was purely imaginary, Maud said,[16] but readers will be intrigued to learn that she may also have had a personal stake in the dramatic matter of hair dyeing.

Proud of her thick hair, Maud wore it pinned up with a little curly bang that flattered her high forehead. Just a year or two before she wrote *Anne of Green Gables*, she had suffered her own hair tragedy. One morning, she had found the first gray hair. Looking closer, she found more. Devastated by the prospect of going gray before she was settled for life, before she had published her book, she cried all night. In the novel, as readers know well, the gray strands in Marilla's dark hair serve as a sober reminder of middle age. Marilla twists her hair up into a hard little knot; the two wire hairpins that she "aggressively" inserts are the bitter marks of old-maidenhood.[17] But help was on the way, or so it seemed. For earlier that year, in June, Mr. Crewe had delivered *Modern Women*, which besides containing Maud's other little redhead, "By the Grace of Sarah Maud," a precursor to Anne, as we shall see, also featured an attractively illustrated advertisement for "Hall's Vegetable Sicilian Hair Renewer. Always restores color to gray hair." The fine print advertised the dye for whiskers and moustaches: "It colors instantly a rich brown or a soft black."[18]

The illustration showed the "Queen of Hair Tonics" wearing a royal robe and a crown; her luxuriant and youthful dark hair ripples over her shoulders. Hair coloring ads were often written in fine print and bashfully hidden like the ads for underwear or "hygienic belts." They were taboo like the shameful act of coloring itself. Hall's "Sicilian Hair Renewer," in contrast, was prominently and attractively displayed and ran over several months. It's only a short imaginative leap from the Hair Renewer to the Italian peddler whom Marilla suspects sold Anne the wicked hair dye. Of course, any method of coloring long hair was an uncertain experiment that could lead to disaster, publicly exposing the woman who tried to cheat nature—and Maud interestingly had an uncanny eye for those who did. When she met her former teacher and friend Hattie Gordon Smith in

1927 in Toronto, not only was Hattie divorced, but Maud noticed disapprovingly that Hattie had bobbed her hair and perhaps tried to alter her natural color. The once attractive golden hair had "faded to a neutral brown—less beautiful than if it had become gray."[19] Maud was certainly in the know as far as the vanity and vexation of the spirit were concerned, and as always held strong opinions. No doubt she was captured by the fantasy of rejuvenation.

The matter of freckles was also one that preoccupied the beauty columns of women's magazines. Earlier in January, the *Delineator*'s "Good Looks" column had declared "freckles" as a "great mystery of the human skin." Freckles were discussed as a blemish, in the same category as moles, birthmarks, warts, liver spots, and "port-wine marks." The column suggested that freckles be treated with iodine. "Apply the iodine to each freckle with a camel's-hair brush or, better, by means of a swab made by wrapping a wisp of cotton around a toothpick."[20] Another way to make freckles fade was to apply lemon juice. As for Anne, she has her own, much easier way of making unwanted freckles disappear. "I can imagine them away," she confides to Matthew.[21] In *Anne of Avonlea*, however, she will in fact dye her nose scarlet when trying to remove the freckles with what she thought was a lotion advertised in a magazine.

Being Elaine

Like an actress, Anne can change roles and identities, and like Maud in the pages of her journal, she also occasionally veers toward melodrama. From the time we first meet her, Anne fantasizes about starring as the unlucky heroines Cordelia or Geraldine. When she dabbles in story writing, she is true to her motto, "It's so much more romantic to end a story up with a funeral than a wedding."[22] The pale, tear-stained face, the piercing shrieks, the clasped hands; these are the gestures of grand opera. Our red-haired heroine frequently bursts into tears, like her creator. There is also a surprising amount of violence and disaster—always embedded in stories, such as Anne's history of abuse and neglect, the death of Mr. Thomas, or Gilbert's recitation, in which he assumes the character of a soldier dying in Bingen on the Rhine. The ups and downs, the exuberant highs and tragic lows that characterize Anne Shirley's personality correspond to the mood swings that gave birth to the novel. "'The trouble with you, Anne, is that you're thinking too much about yourself,'" says pragmatic Marilla, "hitting for once in her life on a very sound and pithy piece of advice."[23] In passages such as these, the author—who could be as self-involved as her heroine in her own sorrows—serves up a stiff dose of self-irony and self-mockery, as Maud's own addiction to emotional drama is played out on the pages of her journal.

In chapter twenty-eight, "An Unfortunate Lily Maid," Anne is inspired, after studying Tennyson's poem "Lancelot and Elaine" in school, to dramatize Elaine, the fair and lovable lily maid of Astolat. It is a classic melodramatic plot that Anne would fall in love with. In the poem, when Elaine realizes that Lancelot can never love her, she resigns herself to die. Elaine arranges for her body to be taken down the river to Camelot, with a letter in her hand explaining her love and death. Anne throws herself into the role with gusto, while spurning Mrs. Lynde's dire warning about the wickedness of playacting. With her short and silky curls, an old piano scarf of yellow Japanese crêpe, and an iris in place of a lily, Anne lies down in the old flat and begins to float down the river. As readers of *Anne* know well, her journey comes to an abrupt end, however, when the flat begins to leak. Clutching to a bridge pile for dear life, Anne suffers the humiliation of being rescued by Gilbert Blythe. This scene parodies the popular Victorian tales of love and sacrifice that Anne has been reading and, as one scholar has written, "the boat (weighted down, perhaps, by too many romantic aspirations) is sinking."[24]

So far, so familiar. Yet there is an untold story behind the brilliant parody that also highlights Maud's fascination with role-playing and performance as metaphor for life and personal identity. Consider the intriguing and not so coincidental fact that just a few months earlier, in April, renowned music historian and critic Gustav Kobbé wrote in the *Delineator* about American actress Annie Russell and her popular role as Elaine. Simply called *Elaine*, the play was adapted from Tennyson's poem "Lancelot and Elaine" and performed in the Madison Square Theater in New York City. The scene required the actress to lie in the funeral barge simulating death for eighteen minutes.[25] So involved did Annie Russell become in her portrayal of the dead Elaine that on several occasions, she became unconscious on stage and had to be rescued. As an actress she had to remind herself of "the demarcation line" between the imaginary and the real: that she was not Elaine but Annie Russell.[26] The successful actor, explained Kobbé, has a "dual personality," constantly communicating by "wireless" with the character he projects on the stage. Kobbé described this ability to merge the self into another personality an "emotional technique."[27] Kobbé's remarks concerning Annie Russell's performance apply equally well to the way in which Anne Shirley blurs the demarcation line between real and imaginary.

What happens when real-life dangers arise during a performance— the situation Anne faces during her portrayal of the Lily Maid? The true actor "will try to save not himself, but the play," says Kobbé.[28] In professional lingo this is described as "swallowing the file." Anne, of course, prefers life and is rescued, albeit reluctantly, by her favorite foe, Gilbert Blythe. And yet, the entire episode is recounted with relish, giving Anne another opportunity to perform and dramatize the scene for the pleasure of Mrs. Allan. Maud, who no doubt read Kobbé's piece, endows her heroine with the talents of an actress, the "emotional technique." But she cannot and does not allow for the possibility that Anne might pursue a professional career on the stage. Even though Anne's face was inspired by that of a model and actress, it is out of the question that Anne might become a professional performer, for the simple reason that Maud herself was unable even to imagine such a possible future for herself.

The September 1903 *Metropolitan* containing the picture of Evelyn Nesbit also featured an autobiographical essay by American actress Corinne Parker. Parker discussed the hardships of a stage career for a woman with few means. Parker, who was sixteen years old when she took to the stage in New York, describes a life of self-denial and danger, exposed to predators and exploitative theatre managers.[29] In contrast, Maud, who was herself an avid amateur actress, restricted her heroine to the safety of the amateur stage. Maud's contract with her reader is clear. She may put Anne in a leaking boat, she may have Anne fall from a rooftop and break her ankle, but she will not expose Anne to the dangers of the professional stage. It was as unthinkable as it would have been for her to send her heroine to work as a domestic helper in Toronto or Boston. It is here that Maud's class boundaries are clad in stone. She has all the Macneill pride and prejudice. That Anne has the dramatic talent and temperament to pursue a career as an actress, or as a model, is made evident in the episode where Anne recites at the Hotel Concert and the American artist recognizes her potential as a painter's model. But Maud is firm. Anne is to live her life at home, in Avonlea, Prince Edward Island, not under the footlights or in an artist's studio in some faraway American city. Ultimately, for Maud, the performance of self takes place in everyday life, and she imported the metaphors of the stage into her shaping of Anne's identify. Just as she built her own identity in her journal on such performances of self, so Maud gave her heroine a nimble flexibility to operate within the constraints of society while also maintaining an important measure of freedom.

Puffed Sleeves

Anne's love of fashion is central, and the fashion symbol that may stand out the most in the reader's memory is the glorious puffed sleeved dress, which is invested with all of Maud's love and nostalgia but also with a good dose of humor. "Stuff me in," the Dalhousie college girls would say to each other in the mid-nineties when fashion dictated sleeves so ridiculously large that the girls had to assist each other when they put on their coats.[30] The fashion plates of the Victorian era tended to exaggerate the giant ballooning arms. This point is alluded to in *Anne of Avonlea*, where the blunt Mr. Harrison refers to an overdressed Charlottetown lady, "She looked like a head-on collision between a fashion plate and a nightmare."[31] Although Maud had carefully consulted her scrapbook earlier in July 1905, the puffed sleeves were more than inhabitants of those dusty pages; they were also the latest Edwardian style. Exhibited in the February 1905 issue of the *Delineator*, puffs had, ironically, appeared on the same page that featured the new sleek fashion for automobile outings. There were detailed sewing instructions for "full puffs," "deep puffs," and "double puffs" made by means of a line of shirrings near the elbow. "The popularity of automobiling is responsible for many innovations in women's dress," the *Delineator* fashion editor noted.[32]

While the streamlined motoring look avoided fancy decorations that might have interfered with the increased speed of the car, the puffed sleeves satisfied longings for old-fashioned ornament. This explains the amicable co-existence of the fashion symbols of modernity with the symbols of Victorianism. Fashion is the arena in which social contradictions are both encoded and negotiated, and Maud's comedy takes pleasure in exploiting fashion as a domain for both arbitrary rules and for breaking those rules and celebrating self-expression.

One of the novel's most humorous and brilliant episodes occurs when shy Matthew Cuthbert ventures on his quest to buy fabric for Anne's puffed sleeves dress. In the immensely satisfying chapter twenty-five, "Matthew Insists on Puffed Sleeves," the comedy relies on both Cuthberts inadvertently violating the strict gender boundaries of the Victorian period. As the narrator makes clear, pragmatic Marilla is blind to the feminine fashion faux pas she commits in dressing Anne in gray and dowdy aprons. "A happy medium may be found between silly extravagance and excessive economy in dress," the January 1905 *Delineator* had advised in a piece entitled "A Girl's Personal Appearance and Dress."[33]

It was Matthew who, after much smoking and "cogitation," recognized that something was amiss in the picture of Anne "so plainly and soberly gowned" among a group of girls "all gay in waists of red and blue and pink and white."[34] It was Matthew who understood Anne's hankering after puffed sleeves, thus becoming the unlikely instigator for the sartorial revolution at Green Gables. In August, two months after Maud had published a story in *Modern Women*, a piece appeared in the magazine entitled "Man's Humiliation," in which columnist Charles Battell Loomis dramatized, tongue-in-cheek, the sad spectacle that ensues when an otherwise competent male, sent on a shopping errand by his wife, is reduced to a sack of fright and incompetence as soon as he steps over the threshold and into the store:

> ...[he] shuffles into the store, meek-eyed and diffident and going up to the spool counter (after wandering all over the store looking for it) says 'Give me some of that,' and pointing at the paper shoves it at the young sales-woman. And she looks at him with

pitying eyes as a poor fool and reading the directions, hands out the goods.

He goes home with them and ten to one they are wrong but he is safe.[35]

The columnist's hapless male may have inspired the hilarious scene in which Maud sends Matthew shopping for Anne's puffed-sleeve dress. Who can forget the picture of Matthew, helpless and harassed, having to confront Samuel Lawson's young saleswoman in her pompadour and clacking bracelets, losing his composure and common sense, and returning home in the middle of December with no dress, but with brown sugar and a garden rake. The desired dress must then be secured with the help of a woman, Mrs. Rachel Lynde. And yet, Matthew's journey into the nether world of feminine fashion brings healthy excitement to his life. Where braver men have failed, he eventually triumphs, securing the puffed sleeves for Anne. Much of the pleasure of *Anne of Green Gables* relies on such subversive ironies.

Gloria, the evocative name of the fabric of Anne's lovely and glossy dress, is not very well known today. Curious readers can take a look at the Edwardian umbrellas in the Royal Ontario Museum in Toronto, for gloria was used chiefly for umbrellas and parasols during the era. "It's tightly woven so obviously waterproof enough to use as umbrella cloth, and not pure silk but silk mixed with worsted (which is a fine wool cloth) or cotton, which might possibly make it less expensive than pure silk," explains Alison Matthews David who teaches at the School of Fashion at Ryerson University in Toronto.[36] Like denim, gloria featured a diagonal twill weave but would have been a fine rather than a thick, heavy cloth. Today it is no longer obvious that Maud's color choice sprang from the era's fashionably earthy color palate. This same palate was also a reaction to the technological era. "The popular colors are brown in all its shadings, with cinnamon, perhaps, in favor," the January 1904 *Delineator* had proclaimed,[37] providing the answer to the mystery of the dress's seemingly subdued hue. From chocolates to a pearl necklace, Matthew continues to shower Anne with the choicest gifts for the modern girl, listed in the magazines contemporaneous with the writing of the novel. Suffused with sensuous detail, the dress and accessories were the fulfillment of Anne's desires and an important element in articulating the different dimensions of her identity. Nowhere is the pull between her distinct individualism and her desire to belong to a group better exemplified than in the realm of fashion—in her yearning for puffed sleeves.

Coming of Age

In Maud's era, fashion in dress and hair also presented important markers for growing up, and fashion-loving Maud indulged this interest by using fabrics and styles to show how they transform Anne into a young lady with new responsibilities and expectations. A threshold was crossed when the two school friends put up their hair in pompadour style. They were suddenly adults. During a "delicious" dressing ceremony in Diana's upstairs room,

> Diana did Anne's front hair in the new pompador [sic] style and Anne tied Diana's bows with the especial knack she possessed; and they experimented with at least half a dozen different ways of arranging their back hair. At last they were ready, cheeks scarlet and eyes glowing with excitement.[38]

This is a coming-of-age ritual, in which hair and dress are symbols of the girls' maturation. By putting up her hair and taming her tousled tresses, the girl suddenly appears as an adult and is treated thus. Even today people change their hair styles to mark important events such as career changes, marriage, or divorce; although today the boundaries of age are much more fluid and hair styles are no longer clear signposts of growing up. Maud's book supplies a nostalgic pleasure in such rituals. Anne and Diana's new identities are staged in public concerts and recitals, before the damsels regress into silly girls, racing and jumping onto Aunt Josephine Barry's bed in the Barrys' spare bedroom.

In her journal Maud fondly recalled how Frede, an eight-year-old freckled urchin, would sit on Maud's bed in her den, watching her doing her hair, combing and curling, preening and primping herself.

Frede was fascinated by the ritual and thought Maud very pretty. A continual source of happiness, these memories fueled the pleasurable bonding of the bosom friends in numerous intimate grooming scenes. Fashion was an inspiring subject during the era, and these fashion pleasures also reveal what was on Maud's mind at the time of writing *Anne*. Theodore Dreiser explored the forces of desire inherent in fashion in his 1900 novel *Sister Carrie*, Edith Wharton understood fashion as a finely calibrated class indicator in her 1905 *The House of Mirth* and in 1920's *The Age of Innocence*, but Maud understood that fashion is a powerful rite of female bonding. "You are not really friends if you haven't gone shopping together for clothes," says Alison Matthews David, who, in rereading *Anne*, could not help but be struck by the myriad of dress references and be moved by the nostalgia embedded in these fashion references.[39]

"'Put on your white organdy, by all means, Anne,' advised Diana decidedly." The dress, "soft and frilly and clinging," suits Anne better than the stiff muslin, and is just the thing for the concert at the White Sands Hotel.[40] The lightweight organdy is, according to pragmatic Marilla, "the most unserviceable stuff in the world."[41] It is also the very same fabric and style Maud herself wore as the bridesmaid at her friend Bertha MacKenzie's wedding on December 25, 1905, close to the time when she would have written the scene above. A rare wedding photo shows Maud clearly upstaging the bride in her fluffy organdy dress, decorated with little flowers and with puffed sleeves and frills. Meanwhile, pragmatic Marilla's words seem to apply more to Maud swathed in organdy in cold December than to Anne during the warm summer. Organdy is a fabric that was advertised for weddings as in the June 1905 "Weddings and Brides" column of *Modern Women*, and so also signals something about the expectations of adulthood.[42] The beautiful fabric softened the social pressure encoded in the symbol. Girls were expected to turn into responsible women, wives, and mothers, making the period of maidenhood all the more precious as a phase when the girls could still be girls.

Maidenhood

The Romantics and fin-de-siècle aesthetes celebrated youth as the ideal age. Maidenhood was the life stage that followed the onset of menstruation and preceded motherhood. Womanhood was the age of care, compromise, and adult responsibility. For Maud, on the verge of such responsibility, there was a deeply personal threshold that was being crossed. The "strange temperamental change" that came over her school chum Amanda Macneill "at the threshold of womanhood" was to Maud one of the mysteries of life, as she would later remember.[43] Her relationship with several girlfriends also mysteriously collapsed, as we shall see. The flow of time and change eroded what she had regarded as perfect "bosom" friendships. The anxiety and bewilderment Maud felt about these processes can be felt in the rapid, jolting way in which Anne develops into a young maiden.

In June 1901, there had appeared in *The Household*, a Boston family magazine to which Grandmother Macneill subscribed after *Godey's Lady's Book* folded, a full-page spread devoted to Henry Wadsworth Longfellow's poem "Maidenhood."

> Standing, with reluctant feet,
> Where the brook and river meet,
> Womanhood and childhood fleet![44]

The illustration depicted a girl holding a lily and wearing a flower wreath in her hair, surrounded by a frame in the shape of a cathedral window. "Bear a lily in thy hand," Longfellow commanded, as if it were the young girl's talisman against pitfalls that would inevitably entangle the adult woman: "Life hath quicksands,—Life has snares! / Care and age come unawares!" In November 1904, *The Ladies' Home Journal* devoted an entire page to W. L. Taylor's illustration of "Maidenhood," depicting an adolescent girl in a white dress and flower garland with caption: "Standing, with reluctant feet, / Where the brook and river meet."[45]

Given the poem's wide proliferation at the time, contemporary readers of *Anne of Green Gables* would immediately have understood the title of chapter thirty-one, "Where the Brook and River Meet." The chapter hints at physiological changes without ever naming them. A doctor's order sends Anne out-of-doors to prolong the time of dreaming, walking, and making merry before she must focus on studies, entrance exams, and leaving home. In Longfellow's poem, the maiden nostalgically mourns the passing of her childhood with a "shadow" in her eyes, just as Marilla is conscious of "a queer sorrowful sense of loss" in seeing fifteen-year-old Anne grow up and change.[46] Menstruation cannot be mentioned either in the poem or in the novel. Instead, natural, physiological change is encoded in images of liquid and fluidity. Longfellow's poem describes streamlets, swiftly advancing brooklets, gliding streams; the novel refers to brook, river—and a doctor's visit. Meandering through the novel, the brook links together the episodic chapters and connects the novel's conclusion to its commencement.

In later years Maud would always say that she did not want Anne to grow up. She wanted to leave Anne in carefree childhood, so she did not have to adjust to the realities of life. Anne should never have to compromise. And yet, in the last third of the novel we see Anne begin her process of transformation into adulthood. In the novel's first two thirds, time moves so slowly as if to come to a near standstill—suspended beyond time. The age of youth ends abruptly in chapter twenty-six, however, when Anne turns thirteen. Suddenly time speeds up. It moves through the years at a quick pace. "For Anne the days slipped by like golden beads on the necklace of the year," the narrator comments in November, the author's own birth month.[47] The final chapters rush Anne through her teens—in chapter thirty, she is almost fourteen; by chapter thirty-one, fifteen, and by the end, sixteen. By now Anne has changed from a gangly girl to an elegant miss. Readers similarly want Anne to stay true to her addled and unpredictable ways, a desire perhaps best expressed in *Anne of Green Gables—The Musical*. Its theme song is "Anne of Green Gables, never change."[48] And yet change has crept into her personality as it did her room, which is now decorated with a velvet carpet, a low white bed, and the fragrance of white lilies. The last third is the story of the transition from childhood to adulthood. Reliving her own pleasures, Maud was also releasing her own anxieties about growing up.

TWELVE

Farewells and Decisions

...nothing could rob her of her birthright of fancy or her ideal world of dreams. And there was always the bend in the road!
    "'God's in his heaven, all's right with the world,'" whispered Anne softly.
            — The final sentences of Anne of Green Gables[1]

A s Maud was writing the last third of *Anne of Green Gables* in the late fall of 1905, she suffered from depression. On November 8, 1905, a damp day of showers and mist and early snow, Maud was sitting in the kitchen looking at two chrysanthemums and a rose growing in her window boxes. "I look at my rose and I think—'God's in His Heaven, all's right with the world.' It is a song and hope and a prayer all in one."[2] For Maud, the little song was not a naïve affirmation of a perfect world, but a prayer for a better one. The line is drawn from Robert Browning's controversial 1841 verse drama *Pippa Passes*. Maud, however, may have culled the line when it was quoted earlier that June in an obituary tribute in *Zion's Herald*, followed by an inspirational poem by Margaret Sangster beginning with the line, "Live in the Sunshine, don't live in the gloom."[3] Browning was prominently featured in *Zion's Herald*, a Sunday school periodical in which Maud published extensively. Anxious and worried, she used such mantras during the difficult times of her life. "[T]his fall I really enjoy nothing. I hate to waken every morning," she concluded her entry. "But perhaps things will be better some day. That hope and my writing are all that keeps me alive."[4] Writing *Anne of Green Gables* was, in part, a kind of self-help therapy for Maud, but the ending ostensibly has a tone of adult compromise with the world. Growing up means assuming responsibilities and coping with the reality of change, such as aging and death. She drew on her sunshine mantras to keep the dark spirits at bay.

A Baptism of Pain

Maud pushed her novel to the finale with a series of visual tableaux that would both stir and haunt her readers. *Anne of Green Gables* may not share the architectural symmetry of Edith Wharton's *The House of Mirth*, but like Wharton's novel, Maud's prose made brilliant use of images and tableaux. In the second-to-last chapter, "The Reaper Whose Name Is Death," gentle Matthew dies in June, bringing the novel full circle to its June beginning. "In the parlor lay Matthew Cuthbert in his coffin, his long gray hair framing his placid face."[5] The fragrance of the white narcissus, the Prince Edward Island June lilies, continues to linger as a scent of both life and death. Matthew's death is a powerful *memento mori*. Real pathos has replaced the aesthetic make-believe of romantic deaths and comic funerals that thread through the earlier parts of the novel. The loss of a beloved person is the baptism of pain that marks the end of childhood. "Oh, Marilla, what will we do without him?" asks heartbroken Anne.[6] His death is as sudden and shocking for the reader as it is for the heroine.

Many readers have asked, "Why did Matthew have to die?" In later years, Maud said that she regretted his death, but that it was necessary so that there might arise the necessity of a sacrifice for Anne.[7] Some readers have praised the ending for its moral force, while others have condemned it as too traditional. But few readers may know the complexities that may have prompted this ending.

Earlier that year, on March 30, the Reverend Ewan Macdonald had presented a paper at the Cavendish Literary Society entitled "The Theories of Self-Culture and Self-Sacrifice and their Reconciliation in the Christian's life." Maud was not only present in the audience but also it was she who recorded the elaborate title in the minute book—though no further details are given.[8] During the era, "self-culture" referred to the Greek tradition of cultivating the self and the beautiful existence. It was the side of Anne that celebrates the pagan girl who indulges her contradictory impulses without resolving them. Yet such self-culture ought to be overcome, as R. L. Otley wrote in 1909 in his book *Christian Ideas and Ideals*: "The individual personality only shares in the larger life in so far as it does not isolate itself or claim independence, but loses itself in self-sacrifice and altruistic effort." Otley continues, "The isolated life is the barren and truncated life; the life that spends itself and is spent for others *beareth much fruit*."[9] The reader immediately senses the tension between the life Maud spent in the pagan solitude of Lover's Lane on one hand, and the Christian ideal devoted to service to community on the other. The majority of the novel indulged Anne's individualistic and pagan pleasures, but as Maud was bringing the novel to a close, she was trying to achieve a compromise. In fact, in closing her novels, Maud always chose a conventional structure, and in *Anne of Green Gables* she presented the solution that she had chosen in her own life—caring for Grandmother Macneill.

Maud was intimately familiar with the typical Victorian sacrifice tale, such as Ella Higginson's "One o' Them Still, Stubborn Kinds," which had appeared in June 1897 in *The Ladies' Home Journal*. Briefly consider the formula. Raised on a farm in the mountains of the pretty Puget Sound area near the ocean, budding writer Mindwell Ewens finds more inspiration in buttercups and dandelions than in dishes and cows. The ambitious and misunderstood daughter of a poor and widowed mother desires nothing more than to study in Boston and to make a career as a writer. But when the opportunity arises, Mindwell is faced with a moral dilemma. Suitcase in hand, she has a dramatic change of heart when she realizes that she is leaving her overworked mother to fend for herself. "Her eyes went to the silent, lonely mountains. A moment longer the struggle lasted. Then something that was beautiful shone in the girl's face." Her gaze upward to the mountains is the classic look of spiritual transfiguration. "Maybe the world won't think as much of me as if it would if I had a fine education," says Mindwell, "but I guess I'll think more of myself."[10]

Maud's September 1906 short story "Jane Lavinia" closely follows Higginson's plot, suggesting familiarity with both the story and the formula.[11] Yet in *Anne of Green Gables* she also modified, complicated, and queried the formula. "But I can't let you sacrifice yourself so for me.

It would be terrible," says Marilla, when her failing eyesight forces her to consider selling Green Gables. "There is no sacrifice," Anne replies as she comes to Marilla's rescue. "Nothing could be worse than giving up Green Gables—nothing could hurt me more."[12] Anne's response echoes the fierce determination Maud and her grandmother demonstrated when they felt they were being ousted from the old homestead by their own family. Maud was also drawing attention to her own heroic sacrifice, which had gone unrecognized—a sore point in her life. As her grandmother's companion since her grandfather's death in 1898, she lived in bondage, foregoing traveling, independence, and companionship, yet she had received little thanks or compensation, and her ending to *Anne* was a call for recognition. Anne's words, "I'm just as ambitious as ever," read like a reaffirmation of the author's own far-reaching goals launched from the remote Cavendish homestead.[13] In her characteristic and sometimes quixotic way of reconciling opposites, Maud's own example suggested that ambition must not sacrifice loyalty, nor must loyalty sacrifice high ambition.

The novel concludes with a mother-daughter tableau: the two women sitting together at the front door of Green Gables. "They liked to sit there when the twilight came down and the white moths flew about in the garden and the odor of mint filled the dewy air."[14] In fact, the halcyon image of Anne and Marilla sitting together is like a literary rendering of a photograph Maud had taken during the 1890s of her old school friend Alma Macneill, who had gone to live in Boston in 1893. In the center of the photograph, Alma and her mother are sitting in the open doorway of the entrance with the entire house surrounded by an old orchard, trees, and flowers. In the foreground, a lane leads the viewer's eye to the house. It is the ideal home. The two figures are distant, and their faces are blurred. We know who they are only because Maud identified them. This kind of blurring would have enabled Maud to project her fictional characters into the image. "I love you as dear as if you were my own flesh and blood," says the emotionally repressed Marilla in the end, a declaration of love Maud likely never heard from Grandmother Macneill, whom she called "the only mother I ever knew."[15] The novel's emotional core, it has been suggested by Margaret Atwood, is the relationship evolving between Marilla and Anne: "It may be the ludicrous escapades of Anne that render the book so attractive to children, but it is the struggles of Marilla that give it resonance for adults."[16] Maud's own quest for a mother's love and sympathy finds its artistic manifestation in fiction.

Haunt of Ancient Peace

"Reading to escape the present is neither a new behavior nor one peculiar to women who read romances," writes Janice Radway in *Reading the Romance: Women, Patriarchy, and Popular Literature*, emphasizing that romance novels perform an important "compensatory function for women."[17] Romance readers trust that everything will turn out happily. The unflagging optimism of the genre is appealing because, as Gaye Tuchman writes, romance novels "offer a vast reassurance that the world will come out right."[18] After all, these same conventions had sustained Maud herself during periods of stress and sadness. When anxious or depressed she slipped into the reading and writing of romance as one slips underneath a warm blanket. As an avid reader of Sir Walter Scott and the Brontës, Maud also knew how to manipulate the conventions of romance, achieving freshness and originality while satisfying the reader's desires. What is remarkable is how much Maud put herself into the ending and the final scene by sharing her own self-healing mantras. Consider the image of the final sunset, or rather post-sunset, just before the novel closes: ". . . it was past sunset and all Avonlea lay before her in a dreamlike afterlight—'a haunt of ancient peace.'"[19] The hour just past sunset with its warm afterglow was Maud's own favorite time of the day. The scene was a tribute to her own "Palace of Art," her own writing space in her den with the view she beheld while writing *Anne* in the twilight of the day. In fact, she made sure that her own life was tightly woven into the texture of the final pages by quoting in the novel's ending from her own July 3, 1904, journal entry, which discusses the view from her den just before darkness; years later, she added to this journal entry a photograph with the caption "Haunt of Ancient Peace."[20] The photo shows the familiar treed lane rounding in a gentle bend and disappearing from sight in the "green" and "dewy" fields beyond. And voilà, "A Bend in the Road" was also the title for the final chapter: "It has a fascination of its own, that bend, Marilla. I wonder how the road beyond it goes."[21] In Maud's scrapbook is a poem "The Bend of the Road" by Grace Denig Lichfield, celebrating the open-endedness that Maud cherished:

> Oh, that bend of the road, how it baffles, yet beckons!
> What lies there beyond—less or more than heart reckons!
> What ends, what begins, there where sight fails to follow?[22]

The idea of a limitless tomorrow, full of potential, must have called to Maud at the same time that it frightened her. Having been a virtual prisoner in Cavendish since her grandfather's death in 1898, Maud both enjoyed and feared the idea of freedom and independence. Attracted to a freedom from legal bonds and responsibilities, she also clung to the idea of stability and respectability that traditional marriage would afford. The seemingly inevitable chain of events that followed the writing of *Anne* would bring about a resolution, but at this point, the conflict was not yet resolved in her life.

This may explain why the love story between Anne and Gilbert is left open at the end of *Anne of Green Gables*. Maud could have presented Anne and Gilbert in the final visual depiction. She could have pictured the pair walking together in Lover's Lane—but she refused to provide this visual. Maud's ending is elusive—they are friends, not lovers. The reality of marriage seems indefinitely postponed. Her flirtation with Ewan Macdonald was not even a courtship at this point, as she asserted, even though he had been a faithful visitor for the duration of her novel writing. As if to make up for this gap, the publisher would later add a romantic illustration, supplying the missing pictorial evidence of romance. This allowed readers reading *for* the romance ending simply to make the leap, as the 1934 Hollywood movie did in turning the entire plot line into a "Boy Gets Girl—The End" type of romance between Anne and Gilbert. Maud's message was more radical than the movie adaptation, as Theodore Sheckels pointed out in "Anne in Hollywood: The Americanization of a Canadian Icon."[23]

In fact, the novel closes with the penultimate visual tableau of Anne sitting by the window of her little room. She is alone and dreaming, just as

Maud sat alone and dreaming up Anne's thoughts and words. Anne's last, softly whispered words, "God's in his heaven, all's right with the world," was Maud's own inspirational incantation during times of distress.

A Girl's Gift Book

Other sentiments would have attached themselves to this poetic line, which was also popular in girls' gift books and scrapbooks. *The Girl Graduate's Book*, a memento of a girl's last year in school or college, was often made and presented by a girlfriend as a gift. It typically featured pictures, names, and keepsakes of the graduate's last year in school or college as remembered through the lens of her girlfriend. In June 1903, *The Ladies' Home Journal* article "A Girl's Gift to a Girl's Graduate," for instance, explained how to make a scrapbook using dried flowers and poetry. The article recommended copying a stanza from Browning's "Pippa Passes," containing the same "God's in His Heaven..." lines.[24] Consequently, when Maud ended her novel with this quotation, readers would have recognized it from these contexts and the emotional charge would have carried over. Just like the Girl's Gift Book, so *Anne* was Maud's gift to the girl reader: a token of precious girlhood, focusing on the school years, that the recipient could return to nostalgically during her adult years, and later pass on to her own daughter as a shared emotional legacy. In just this way, *Anne* has been passed on from generation to generation as a gift from mother to daughter, grandmother to granddaughter, aunt to niece, girlfriend to girlfriend. *Anne* fans often recall that they have received the novel as a gift—and the stories of how they have received it are part of the novel's emotional power. The novel relied on a special bond with the reader. Maud saw the importance of this bond and faithfully answered her fan mail personally, cultivating the intimate triangle of Anne—Author—Reader.

Was *Anne* also Maud's parting gift to Penzie Macneill? On the first day of 1906, the very month in which she said she finished the novel, Maud visited her girlhood friend who was dying of consumption.[25] One last time, they resurrected the memories of their childhood and girlhood, and renewed the ties of friendship that had been severed after Penzie's marriage and move to New Glasgow. At a family reunion the summer before, Maud had been shocked to see how terribly thin Penzie had become. "Oh, Maud, my life is broken," she had said.[26] According to Maud, Penzie had worked herself to death in her eight-year-old marriage. Penzie makes an appearance in *Anne of the Island* as the dying Ruby Gillis, looking even handsomer than usual. Her eyes shine bright blue and her hands are transparent in their delicacy. Flighty Ruby, like Penzie, has no idea that she is dying, though everybody else does. Penzie died on February 28 at age thirty-three, leaving behind her husband and child. Nothing indicates that Maud was by her former girlfriend's side when she died, but in revising chapter sixteen, in which Diana visits bosom friend Anne, Maud added Anne's fantasy of nursing Diana while she is "desperately ill with smallpox."[27] In early March, Maud went to the funeral, but was emotionally detached. "I looked at that emaciated face in the casket and tried to believe it was the face of my old...merry school girl chum but I could not link the two together at all."[28] The chapter of Penzie, the wildwood rose of her love poem, had been closed some time ago. With her auburn hair and blue eyes, Penzie the girl was a distilled memory in the *Anne* books, somewhat like the waft of the beautiful summer rose Maud liked to preserve in her potpourri vase for winter.

We know from her April 16, 1907, journal entry that Maud finished the novel "sometime in January 1906," but we do not know if this time refers to penning the final line in the manuscript, or to writing her final revision.[29] The consistent upward slope of Maud's handwriting in the original manuscript speaks of energy and exuberance. Neither rising nor falling, the lines in the final chapter (and in many of the revision pages) are flatter, perhaps reflecting the darker mood, or perhaps just reflecting the different angle of light during writing. Yet even here, the dramatic t-strokes, hovering high above the words, suggest the willpower and ambition driving the author.[30] After years of apprenticeship, she had written her novel with the ease and confidence of the fully matured writer. "This is by far the tidiest, most clearly written, and most obviously inspired of all of the manuscripts," a literary scholar concluded after comparing *Anne of Green Gables* with Maud's other manuscripts housed in the Confederation Centre of the Arts Gallery. "The whole manuscript is a neat two and three quarter inch stack of 716 story pages and 137 pages of notes."[31]

Maud had her own system of doing revisions, using alphabetical letters and numbers to mark changes and additions, from A through S19. When I examined the manuscript I marked up my own text to understand where and how Maud had made changes in her manuscript during the revision stage. It is fascinating to note that she added many literary allusions. This suggests that Maud, fully realizing she had written an inspired text, was now determined to establish her role as a literary writer. In chapter two, for example, Anne says to Matthew, "You could imagine you were dwelling in marble halls, couldn't you?" Here Maud had added the allusion to the aria from Michael Balfe's 1843 comic operetta, *The Bohemian Girl*. The soprano sings "I dreamt I dwelt in marble halls," in act two, remembering her character's childhood; "But I also dreamt, which pleased me most, / That you loved me still the same."[32] Maud was ambitious to present her book in the category of a literary work, and yet she also positioned it as a juvenile story knowing that publishers would be interested in a lucrative sale.

Maud commented that she had worked hard on her style during the revision, altering words until she was almost bewildered.[33] But overall, the revisions consisted of tweaking, for no major rewriting or restructuring was required in this inspired novel. She heightened the color contrasts, adding references to the red soil of Prince Edward Island in particular in the first chapter.[34] She specified the season ("early" June) and Matthew's age ("he's sixty"); added the fact that Rachel and Marilla are friends; added the "born" to Marilla's desire to get "a born Canadian." In chapter three, she added to Anne's dramatic cry, "you don't want me," the explanation, "because I'm not a boy!"[35] Unfortunately, some of the revisions introduced racial slurs, for instance, the identification of the simple minded Mary Joe as "a buxom, broad-faced French girl from the Creek" in chapter eighteen and the reference to the "German Jew" in chapter twenty-seven.[36] Many additions relate to bosom friend Diana. She added Anne's verbose ramblings while Diana is busy consuming several tumblers of raspberry cordial (chapter sixteen),[37] added Anne's distressing fantasy of Diana marrying in a white dress (chapter twenty-five), and added a scene in which Anne, fearing she may be killed in the ridge-pole walk, bequeaths to Diana her pearl bead ring (chapter twenty-three). Once the revisions were completed, Maud typed out the novel on her second-hand typewriter.

Anne Goes Traveling

Anne was ready to spread her wings and fly into the world. Like a good mother, Maud was concerned for her daughter's success. For years Maud had slyly mailed her writings from the kitchen post office. If anyone else in Cavendish had known how many were rejected, she could not have mustered the courage to send the manuscripts out over and over again until they were finally accepted. Swathed in wrapping paper and chaperoned by stamps for her safe return, *Anne* first journeyed to Bobbs-Merrill of Indianapolis, a new firm and publisher of Riley's *Raggedy Man*.[38] Maud cried when the manuscript was returned—and boldly dropped *Anne* back into the mailbag, addressed to Macmillan, the New York publisher of Jack London's *The Sea-Wolf*, a novel she had loved.[39] Next Maud tried Lothrop, Lee and Shepard, the Boston Sunday-school-type publisher of the *Pansy* books and the *Wide Awake* magazine she had loved as a child.[40] Again, *Anne* came back.

Like the peddler selling the bad hair dye in Avonlea, Maud persisted, sending the novel to Henry Holt in New York. Back it came again—along with an ominous, typed note explaining that there was merit in the novel, but "not enough to warrant its acceptance."[41] Maud had not been discouraged by the previous, cold, pre-printed rejection letters. But this rejection, damning her manuscript with faint praise, was devastating.

Some readers know the legend of what follows. Maud said she took *Anne*, who by now would have shown some wear, dumped it in a hatbox, and deposited the package in the clothes room. Sometime in the future she was hoping to have the heart to cut her down to the original six or seven chapters. The clothes room was the rough-plastered, unfinished room where Maud and her grandmother kept cast-off items, generally one stage removed from being discarded.[42] This gabled northern room overlooked a wilderness of poplars and spruces. With the manuscript out of sight, Maud could try to forget her failure and overcome the hubris of thinking that this novel could be her breakthrough success. Mindful of waste, however, she did not burn *Anne*.

As with many other classics initially rejected for publication, one wonders how four publishers could pass on a work that would eventually become a stunning bestseller. Maud was a first-time author and thus a risk for any publisher. Her typescript—prepared on an old second-hand type-writer that could not print clean capitals and refused to print w's[43]—may have reinforced the impression that she was a raw amateur. Under these circumstances, it is unlikely that any of the publishers gave the book more than a cursory read. But then, even today, and contrary to advertisements, not every reader automatically loves *Anne*. Pulitzer Prize–winning author Carol Shields, for instance, found herself resisting Anne's romantic effu-sions. "She rhapsodized in a manner that felt false and silly," writes Shields. "I sensed, too, that she took a secret pride in her carrot-colored hair, and not the shame she flaunted."[44] It is possible that the Henry Holt reader stumbled over the missing romance at the end—the comradely handshake shared by Anne and Gilbert hardly qualifies for the big Boy-Gets-Girl finale that readers may have expected. The reader may have stumbled over a few rare though noticeable imperfections, like eleven-year-old Anne citing reams of literature when she had hardly had any education. And finally, although the genre of the orphan tale had pro-duced numerous bestsellers in the preceding forty years (*Ragged Dick*, *Little Men*, *Tom Sawyer*, *Huckleberry Finn*, *Little Lord Fauntleroy*, *Rebecca of Sunnybrook Farm*), by 1905, at the cusp of the modern era, editors may have thought that it had reached its peak (although *Pollyanna* and *Tarzan* would follow the success of *Anne of Green Gables*).[45]

What proud Maud never told her journal or her readers, what she buried deep inside herself (perhaps so deep that she later forgot about it) was the crisis that followed her second failure to publish a book. She was mum about how she felt, but her actions speak loudly, indicating that she was working to digest her disappointing failure with *Anne*. In fact, that winter she simply was unable to enjoy herself, even though the winter of 1906 was like a long and delicious spring, and the previous winter had been fiercely cold. But the unseasonably warm weather was lost on Maud. One bright light was the new garden on her kitchen windowsill, which she had relocated from outside into the kitchen. Her "glory of daffodils" was the talk of the community, making her almost forget her "constant, carking worry," as she noted in an unpublished February 25 journal entry.[46]

On April 8, she remembered Ephraim, whose December 17 letter had contained a gentle complaint that her previous letter had been "the first one that wasn't first rate."[47] She had been neglecting her Alberta pen pal, presumably because she was busy during the evening with writing *Anne*, but also because she did not need him quite as much, for she had a real-life distraction in Ewan Macdonald. Ewan had become a reliable romantic presence without, however, intruding too intimately into her space. When she finally wrote to Ephraim on April 8, she turned on her effervescent charm, providing a rare and intimate peak into her inner sanctum. In fact, she described herself lying on the couch of her den, indulging her dreams and escaping in fancy to "cloudless realms and starry skies," one of her favorite Lord Byron paraphrases.[48] It was a dramatic and personal way of engaging her bachelor friend. The author needed distraction after the lack of success in finding a home for *Anne of Green Gables*.

On April 18, thousands of miles away, over three thousand people lost their lives in a devastating earthquake in San Francisco, an event Maud would later refer to in her Anne sequels. Ephraim referred to it in his May 5 letter, but when Maud answered on June 21, her comment about the tragedy was perfunctory. Her most immediate thought concerned the stories that would be written about this event. More than the tragic devastation of life, she was captured by its potential as a dramatic topic for literature. Once again, we are struck by Maud's strange distance from other people's very real suffering and by the level of self-involvement in the writer whose literary forte was to reach people through emotion.

On Sunday evening, May 13, whiny and irritated Maud tried to cheer herself with the Mayflowers in her vases and the new gorgeous Bermuda lily that she had grown in her kitchen garden. Although she never once mentioned the novel, her existential crisis in the wake of her failure with her *Anne* book was evident, for her life consisted of "one unending series of pinpricks—petty annoyances and vexations from dawn to dusk." As she wrote in her unpublished journal entry, "I hate to wake up and come downstairs in the morning."[49] Grandmother was crying and lamenting about the spoilt family relations after the drawn-out quarrel with Uncle John. While Maud had been building her alternate family of dreams in the book, now sitting in a hatbox in the trunk room, her own family relations remained sadly in disrepair. At the same time that the homestead was deteriorating, so too were her old friendships. She had lost her patience with former bosom friend and school chum Amanda Macneill, with whom she had shared so many nature walks and fancies when they were young girls. The adult Amanda was sour and no help to Maud. "Our friendship died long ago," the author noted, adding, "every time I am in Amanda's company she robs this memory of its meed." A new level of cynicism concluded her musing: "But when things are dead there is no use wishing them alive again."[50] This dour entry of May 13 is followed by several months of silence.

Maud Decides

When Maud at last picked up the pen on October 12, 1906, she had made a life-changing decision. While there is absolute silence in the journal, her correspondence gives some clues about the sequence of events, which readers have never been privy to in a cohesive story before. On June 21, she had complained bitterly to Ephraim about the "wretched duties" eating up her time. "I feel tired down to my toes." She was referring to a Sunday school convention, presumably initiated by or with the help of Ewan Macdonald, at which she was exceedingly bored. In her letter to Ephraim she describes herself sitting up stiffly, "dressed in my best and looking attentive."[51] It was in fact the exact same pose that she would adopt as the minister's wife when she dutifully, albeit regretfully, went to teas and visited the community. As a busy church decorator, Sunday school teacher, choir director, and discussant of theology, she was being groomed for the duties of the minister's wife and was playing along, dazzling Ewan with her skills. Yet the more she involved herself in Ewan's church world, the more she could plainly see how very tedious and exhausting this sort of work would be on a permanent basis. In her heart of hearts she knew that she was better suited to communicating with people via her pen than sitting with them and listening to their woes. She loved her solitude and privacy. Meanwhile, Dame Gossip had been making her rounds in Cavendish and there seemed to be a tacit understanding in the community regarding Miss L. M. Montgomery and Mr. Macdonald. Their two names appeared to be curiously linked together in committees at the Literary, following each other on programs as if in a choreographed dance. Ewan also seemed to be engaging in some public wooing. On February 3, the Literary Society had debated the question "Which has been of the more benefit to humanity, Science or Literature." The Baptist minister Mr. Belyea and George Simpson took the side of Science. Mr. Ewan Macdonald "upheld the side of Literature," as "L. M. Montgomery, sec'y" noted, poker-faced, in the minute book.[52] Yet the Cavendish community waited for an announcement of an engagement in vain.

It was in the spring of 1906 that Maud, as she later admitted, first thought of Ewan seriously as a suitor. Her retrospective account of October 12, 1906, is so heavily self-censored, however, that it has not been easy to analyze (additionally it contains errors concerning Ewan's age and the spelling of his name, which she would consistently misspell as Ewan instead of Ewen, a spelling that has since become accepted by scholars).[53] It is true that her description of their courtship is missing the emotional drama that characterizes her other love affairs. But her journal suggests that Ewan's roguish smile, thick black hair, and old-time accent stirred something in her, albeit a pale shadow of the erotic passion aroused by Herman Leard. Sometimes when she talked with him she could sense that he desired her physically. He had a way of getting close to her, cautiously, without scaring her away. Perhaps he lingered and looked into her eyes a second or two longer than he should have, or perhaps he took her by the hand. He was never particularly subtle about these movements. And yet, never did he make any clear overtures or show any passion. His loyal and cheerful attention was pleasant, and she felt herself attracted to this man who had become a friend. But what would she do if he proposed? She said that she first asked herself this question in the spring of 1906, a full year after he had started his visits.

On the one hand, she felt attracted to Ewan precisely because he did not overpower her and provoke that horrible, shameful physical repugnance she had felt with Ed. On the other, she could not help but feel a little

cheated because she knew from her readings and from her deeply
anguished experience with Herman Leard that there could be more physical intensity. She knew that the chemistry of desire was more intoxicating.
No doubt she was confused by her own addiction to melodramatic love,
keenly aware of her habit of dramatizing feelings. When she said much
later that she had never loved Ewan, she may have been overstating the
case, her memory colored by years of unhappy marriage. But it is safe to
assume that her feelings for Ewan, lacking passion, were but a pale flame,
a shadow of the real thing called love. Moreover, Ewan was a good pastor,
with a respectable social station that would give her a good standing in the
community, but he did not have Ed's intellectual brilliance and he likely
would never be more than a country minister. Admittedly, he was easy to
get along with, but he was no match for her girlfriends, who had the gift
of tossing jokes and phrases back and forth like a ball. Sometimes their
conversations were a little awkward. As she mulled over these complexities
over the spring and summer, she was startled—in fact she was shocked and
shaken—when she suddenly learned from others that Mr. Macdonald was
leaving Cavendish and going to Glasgow.

The jolt seemed to bring about a decision. On Sunday, July 29, she
fired off a letter to George MacMillan in Scotland. After some preliminary
talk about the summer visitors, she offered a stunning kernel buried in its
center, misspelling Ewan's last name, just as she would consistently misspell his first. "By the way our minister here is leaving us—Mr. McDonald
[sic]—and is going to Scotland for the winter. He will be attending college
in Edinburgh I understand."[54] We are reminded of her 1899 short story
"The Way of the Winning of Anne,"[55] in which jealousy and fear of loss
motivate the heroine Anne Stockard's reluctant decision to marry and
bring to an end a drawn-out courtship.

Not long after Maud had learned of Ewan's plans, the pair drove
together to Will Houston's. On the way home, it was pitch dark and
rainy. It was then, in that darkness, over the sound of the rumbling
buggy, that she felt startled by Ewan's speech. "There is one thing that
would make me perfectly happy," she suddenly heard Ewan say. "It is that
you should share my life—be my wife."[56] She had thought about the possibility of his proposing many times and agonized over it. By nature loyal
and clinging, she could not let him go. As she disclosed in her journal

months later, she accepted his offer with the proviso that he must wait until she was free (after Grandmother's death), thus securing an important counterpromise and delay. She insisted that they keep the engagement a secret. There was a lot of complexity involved in this engagement contract and it was Maud who set the conditions. Truth be told, Maud did not cherish the idea of a husband and a corseted life. But the alternative—to live in a Charlottetown boarding house and write pot-boilers for a living, with no house and little status—was even grimmer. A lonely old age might be a terrible thing. "I wanted a home" and "I wanted children,"[57] she later noted in her journal. Coming on the heels of the multiple rejections of *Anne* the timing of her engagement to Ewan in the summer of 1906, after months of equivocation, speaks volumes. At this point, she considered herself a failure as a writer, and Ewan was the court of last resort who was planning to leave Cavendish.

Our knowledge concerning her sexual life with Ewan is as pitch dark as the night in which Ewan proposed. Hopelessly abstract, confused, and secretive, Maud's thicket of highly censored and edited language keeps her secrets intact. Yet it is safe to assume that she was sexually disappointed. Married to Ewan, she continued to celebrate Herman Leard as the ideal, the man she credits with her sexual awakening—though the relationship, overwrought with emotional melodrama, had remained safely unconsummated. A rare August 19, 1924, journal entry, in which Maud spoke about Ewan's sexuality in relation to his depression, is illuminating, however. "Last spring I decided that Ewan has always been a sub-thyroid and that any depressing event or situation, as well as epochal periods in his sex life, interfered with the functioning of the thyroid gland still further and produced his attacks of melancholia. I decided that when his next attack came on I would try the effect of some careful doses of thyroid."[58] What exactly did Maud imply with this tortured logic? While scholars have puzzled over Maud's sexuality, without being able to provide definite answers, few have asked questions about Ewan's.

"She may be referring to his low sex drive," says Maria Gurevich, a professor of psychology specializing in issues of sexuality and gender, whom I consulted trying to shed light into this murky area of Maud's life. Hypothyroidism (which Maud terms sub-thyroid) is "typically associated with depression and for many men low sex drive and functioning,"

Gurevich explains. In Ewan's case, it would appear the underactive thyroid led to depression and sexual problems. "And, of course, we know today that neurochemistry has a mutually reciprocal relationship to psychology and behavior, so that behavior and mood have an impact on how our minds and bodies function and the other way around."[59] Here may be a key to the mystery. Ewan was indeed a patient man, waiting for the sexual consummation of his relationship with Maud until 1911, the year they married and Maud became pregnant with Chester. The mores of the time, the geographic separation, and Maud's own habit of safeguarding herself from worry make it highly unlikely that there would have been premarital consummation of their sexual relationship. That Ewan's patience was, in part, due to hypothyroidism seems highly plausible. In her literature Maud made it her trademark to have the males wait patiently for years, and seemingly without making any sexual demands of the women they are waiting for. Think of Gilbert Blythe, but also of Dean Priest, who falls in love with Emily years before he can court her, who is also presented as a physically and emotionally wounded character ultimately not allowed to marry the heroine. The pattern would become a signature of her writing: "her ingenious manipulation of the series format...demonstrates the enormous expenditure of time and effort necessary to bring about 'The End' embodied by heterosexual union," writes Marah Gubar about the end of *Anne of Green Gables* and the other Anne books. "At the same time, she indicates that these lengthy delays make room for passionate relationships between women that prove far more romantic than traditional marriages."[60]

Maud had barely created clarity in her life, having made her decision to marry Ewan, when her restlessness and urge for emotional melodrama drove her once again to mischief. In August, her ex-fiancé Edwin Simpson visited Cavendish. For an hour Maud stood talking with him in the road, in full public view. She then took him home for tea. What better way to hide her new, secret engagement than by publicly flaunting her old flame? Engaged now to Ewan, she was flitting to the person Ewan had considered his most prominent rival in Maud's affections. No doubt she was also fanning the old desire in Ed, whom she had carefully avoided for the past eight years. The episode provided her with a sense of closure, ambivalent Maud asserted in her October 7 journal entry: "The past was—at last—dead."[61]

Yet the past she had proclaimed dead in October kept her awake the night of November 6, a few weeks after Ewan's departure for Scotland. Ed Simpson had written her a long letter, citing Dame Gossip and alluding to both her relationship with Ewan and to their own secret engagement eight years earlier. Readers will be intrigued to hear, for the first time, Ed's side of the story told in his own voice. "I hope these past eight years have been happy ones for you," he wrote in a fascinating letter she excerpted in an unpublished journal entry. "To me they have brought unexpected prizes; yet not all that I wished for has come, as I once believed it would. I sometimes wonder if it lives only in the past. If thus, better there than not at all."[62]

In reading these sentences, we are struck by Ed's frankness, which contrasts with Maud's editorial comments, which insinuate only the worst motives to his words. "Ed is merely *posing*—trying to protect his vanity," she writes.[63] Of course, she would know, for the two former foes were birds of a feather—both proud in their brilliance, both working their audiences most effectively, both posing for maximum attention. Yet whichever way Maud framed his words to herself, Ed comes across as the more honest and emotionally generous writer, who also shows a refreshing vulnerability that Maud rarely allowed others to see in herself. "I shall always consider it a privilege to serve you. Our meetings for me have been pleasant since then but exceedingly difficult—such a fearful self-consciousness will ever arise, I have wondered if it was so for you."[64] It was probably Ed's frankness and her instinctive tendency to hedge and cover the truth that made the answer to this letter so difficult. For here was a fundamental difference in communication. Ed was direct, whereas she worked behind the scenes, paltering, and yes, manipulating. Somehow she would never be capable of confessing her "physical repugnance," which she confessed in her journal and eventually to the world, but never to him. We see an almost thirty-two-year-old woman who is tragically caught up in the web of sex conventions of her time, but also in her own web of playacting and self-deception.

"Yes, it is very seldom indeed that a man and a woman can discuss *love* either pleasurably or profitably especially face to face," she would write to George MacMillan, a few months later, on April 1, 1907. "As you say, there is the danger of drifting into a flirtation or 'platonics.' Then again it is hard to separate self-consciousness from the subject."[65] To her pen friend, whom she had never seen face to face, she now revealed the secret of her fling with Herman, while she had been engaged with Ed. "Oh, it is a horribly perplexing subject and I grow dizzy thinking of it," she confessed to George.[66] In fact, the word that she used most persistently when talking about her love with men, including Ewan, is "perplexing," suggesting the entanglement, the complication, the bewildering mystery, and befuddlement she felt. Despite the genial friendship and good cheer, the emotional and physical awkwardness of her relationship with Ewan is palpable. She felt uncomfortable as soon as she moved beyond the rituals of flirtation into a realm that required more emotional honesty. Unable to silence the nagging doubts about her engagement, she relied on Ewan's "cheery" letters to reassure her.

Meanwhile, there was another secret she was keeping from Cavendish people. That fall, it had been raining steadily and the old house was leaking like a sieve. In earlier journal entries she had counted the water leaks, and by Monday, November 12, there were twenty leaks in total, through which the water was coming into the house. Uncle John refused to repair the leaks and Grandma prohibited Maud from bringing in an outsider to do the job. It was a battle of the wills. Maud placed buckets underneath the twenty dripping leaks. "Oh, and there are moments when I wish life was over, too. It seems so full of perplexing problems and harassing penalties," she wrote.[67] Alone in a badly leaking house, with Grandmother crying and sniffling, she counted on Ewan's cheer, which suddenly stopped in December. His letters became perfunctory; he said he suffered from headaches and insomnia.

Panic set in. Ewan's behavior remains a mystery. Was it a first emotional breakdown, as she would assert many years later? Or was he, perhaps, trying to gain some distance from Maud? Quiet and genial Ewan had diplomatically broken his first engagement, once he had put some geographical distance between himself and his fiancée. Had he perhaps developed doubts about the wisdom of his new engagement? A mistress of the manse was important to a minister, and he might have to wait a considerable time before she was free to assume her functions. Perhaps he sensed her ambivalence about being a minister's wife. It took until February 5, and a number of anxiously pressuring letters to Glasgow, for the routine of "cheery" letters to recommence. It was a huge relief, yet Maud never commented on the mystery of what had happened. We must assume that either she did not want to know, or what she found out was too embarrassing to confess even to her journal. We know that she had a way of simply ignoring what she did not like. But it is clear that there were troubles during their early engagement.

New Courage

By this time *Anne* had been hibernating in the hatbox in the frigid attic for a little less than a year. When the cold spell broke on Saturday, March 9, Maud took a walk in Lover's Lane with new energy in her step and new hope in her eyes. Years later, she would add a photograph of "Lover's Lane in Winter" to this entry. She blossomed underneath the lane's charismatic power: "Instantly new courage poured through every vein of me and I felt like something worthwhile again."[68] Passionate Maud suddenly felt what she would later describe in *Emily of New Moon* as "the flash"—a moment of felicity and intense pleasure that came rarely but struck her body and consciousness with a physical power, flooding her with a feeling of "immortal youth, where there was neither past, present, or future."[69] Perhaps it was this new courage that rekindled her belief in *Anne*. It was in late February or early March that Maud went upstairs to the trunk room and took the manuscript from the hatbox. According to her own retrospective *Anne* lore, amplified over the years and reported in its full bloom in *The Chatelaine* magazine in June 1928, Maud read the book from the first page to the last, as the sun sank behind the hills, its rays streaming through the gable window across the attic floor. "'If your own story could interest you after you have laid it away, until it made you forget all about your work like this—wouldn't it interest other people if it were printed,' whispered something."[70] She sent *Anne* off to L. C. Page in Boston.

Re-Enter Frede

The threads of the story of *Anne* and Maud's engagement also crossed with the story of Frede. Their intimacy had been steadily intensifying. They sought each other out whenever they could. Maud visited her in mid-February, when she was able to catch a ride up to Stanley. Sitting on the floor of Frede's little room, they had wrapped shawls around themselves and "talked ourselves out," as she had written in her journal. "I've been living on the memory and taste of it ever since."[71] Frede returned the visit on Thursday, March 22, when the two women spent the night in Maud's den. No doubt, Ewan Macdonald was a major point of conversation. The two women agreed on a pact. On March 24, they wrote letters to each other that were meant to be opened ten years later. This renewal of their friendship vows was presumably prompted by Frede's departure for Guelph, where she planned to study for a few months at the Ontario Agricultural College. The popular ritual of exchanging ten-year letters stemmed from Maud's childhood love for the *Pansy* books, where she had discovered the idea. In 1937, Maud copied these two letters into her journal, providing fascinating snippets of insight for this crucial time in the annals of *Anne*.

Maud's letter shows a woman who remained ambivalent about her future. Would she be Mrs. Macdonald with wrinkles and gray hair in ten years, she asked. "But I may be a literary old maid for all, living in my own castle cosy with a book or two for my children and a pen for a husband," although she hopes that both she and Frede would be happy wives and mothers.[72] Frede's letter adds pertinent details. Maud wore her engagement ring only at night, and had forbidden Ewan to visit her for two weeks after he was planning to return in April from his six-month stay in Glasgow.[73] It was Frede who pleaded on his behalf, playing the role of mediator and ameliorating Maud's secrecy and game playing.[74] The two friends referred to Ewan by the code-name "George Lorimer," and Frede now reassured Maud: if Ewan hadn't won Maud, she herself wouldn't have a place to spend her vacation, she said, clearly counting on continuing their intimate friendship. These two rare letters convey the sense of a romantic female friendship that was already being integrated into the future marriage.

"How I envied Ewan Macdonald for winning you," Frede in turn wrote in her ten-year letter to Maud on March 24, 1907. "I wanted you to be alone like myself but I'm sorry now for feeling so stingy, because you are just the same as you were when we last slept together on Friday night, Mar. 22, 1907." Ewan was in Glasgow, and the two friends were consolidating their bond, looking ahead into their future together, reassuring each other with an implicit promise, like Anne and Diana, that their friendship would be intensified and beautified in the coming decade. In the event of death, Maud sees herself with Frede, meeting in a world of laughter and jokes and happiness in the great Beyond; there is no mention of Ewan there.

Frede's letter, eerily prescient, sees herself with Maud and George Lorimer at the dinner table. "Dear old girlie, I hope all will turn out happily," Frede wrote, and with even more uncanny prescience added, just two weeks before L. C. Page of Boston would write his acceptance letter for the publication of *Anne of Green Gables*: "Oh, I wonder if you are still writing and if you have written a book that has made you famous."[75]

THIRTEEN

The Mystery of Anne Revealed

"... There's such a lot of different Annes in me. I sometimes think that is why I'm such a troublesome person. If I was just the one Anne it would be ever so much more comfortable, but then it wouldn't be half so interesting."
—*Anne to Diana in* Anne of Green Gables[1]

W hile Maud waits to hear about the fate of her package, the novel that would make her famous, the time has come to revisit the unsolved mystery of Anne. Ultimately, the key to this mystery allows us to understand how Maud was able to distill the formula genre and create an enduring classic. So far, we have explored the sources that went into the shaping of Green Gables, Avonlea, and the bosom friends and enemies that populate the novel. In Maud's palace of art, we have unlocked many doors, revealing how different influences blended together to give birth to the novel. Yet a crucial door remains to be opened. Maud had disclosed where Anne's face came from, but where did Anne come from? The secret that Maud never revealed to her readers concerns the discovery that Maud presumably did not want her readers to know.

I found the answer to the mystery of Anne serendipitously while searching for the elusive photograph of Evelyn Nesbit. In the old magazines that Maud read and published in, I stumbled over the fragments and influences that would have fueled the fire of her imagination and that may well have inhabited her notebook (the same in which she found the spark for her Anne story, "Elderly couple apply to an orphan asylum for a boy. By mistake a girl is sent them.")

To Anne

Maud's belated January 10, 1914, journal entry confirms that for several years, Grandmother Macneill had a subscription to *Godey's Lady's Book* during Maud's childhood and adolescence. For the voracious reader in a household of few books, "its monthly advents were 'epochs in my life.'"[2] In those days of bangs, bustles, and puffed sleeves, she opened the page of the Philadelphia periodical to gorgeous hand-tinted fashion plates with sewing instructions. The fashion pages were followed by the literary treats—short stories and serials, which Maud devoured. Useful too were the music sheets, as she was learning to play the organ. Although Maud made disparaging comments about its literary quality, the fashion and family magazine did boast original American writing by authors including Edgar Allen Poe, Longfellow, and Emerson, and actively encouraged its female readers' creative writing. Perhaps most fascinating in Maud's belated journal entry is her revealing sideways note about the reading influences of *Godey's Lady's Book*: "Do we ever really forget *anything* in our lives? I do not think we do. The record is always there in our subconscious minds, to be suddenly remembered when something brings it to our recollection—perhaps never to be remembered, but always there."[3] While she makes no mention of how *Godey's Lady's Book* might be related to the birth of Anne, the cluster of *Godey's* references from 1892 to 1894 suggests that they inspired incidents in *Anne*.

Consider a little poem, which Maud would have seen on *Godey's* jester's page in October 1893. The poem featured a silly mock rhyme poking fun at a woman's head of red hair and presciently titled "To Anne":

> They said
> Her hair was red.
> To me it was pure gold,
> A-blush, because it did enfold
> A face and neck so fair...

And yet they* said
Her hair was red.
　 * The Women.[4]

Although Maud's notebook no longer exists, there is evidence to suggest that Maud had clipped this ironic ode "To Anne" into her notebook, presumably in proximity to "The Boy with the Auburn Hair," also written in 1893. Eighteen-year-old Maud had written the little ditty about a boy, Austin Laird, she had nicknamed "Cavendish Carrots" for his flaming red hair, creating a feud in the school. Was it the poem's division between the flowery perspective of the male speaker and the ironic refrain, "Her hair was red" that caused Maud to conceive Anne, a romantic with a mundane head of hair? It seems too great a coincidence that there appeared, on the same jester's page, a joke concerning a wife who refuses to reconcile with her husband after a quarrel, insisting, "No; my feelings have been injured beyond repair." The remark, and the situation, recall Anne's melodramatic refusal to heal the breach after Gilbert pokes fun at her carroty hair, and her delight in indulging clichéd feeling: "Gilbert Blythe has hurt my feelings *excruciatingly*, Diana."[5] It was not a matter of copying the incident into her novel, but she was inspired by it, presumably chuckling as she was imagining the episode.

The secret Maud took to her grave, however, concerns my discovery in the New York Public Library of two Anns whose fictional lives Maud would presumably have recorded in her notebook, but never acknowledged. For in January 1892, the year a little orphan girl arrived in Cavendish in lieu of a boy, "Charity Ann" appeared in *Godey's Lady's Book*. And in July 1903, just two months before Evelyn Nesbit entered Maud's imagination, red-haired orphan "Lucy Ann" appeared in *Zion's Herald*, a Boston Methodist newspaper.

Charity Ann

The eight-year-old orphan runaway in Canadian writer Mary Ann Maitland's story "Charity Ann. Founded on Facts" arrives just before midnight, on a New Year's Eve in the early 1870s, at the home of an old

Scottish couple, Donald and Christy McKay. The McKays are simple farming folk, sitting by the kitchen fire when they hear a knock on the door.
The late-night visitor introduces herself as Ann, a little girl desperate to
escape the local poorhouse. Determined to find a home and earn her keep
as a servant with the McKays, she offers her services. "I can wash dishes,
and scrape pots, and peel tawties, and mind the babies, and everything,"[6]
she pleads. Scrawny Charity Ann "was not a pretty child. Her eyes were
gray, and in some other face might have been called beautiful, but they
were too large and lustrous to mate with that forlorn and hungry look.
Her tawny hair was dull and straggling....No, Ann was not a pretty
child."[7] Anne readers recall a similar description of Anne Shirley: "Mrs.
Thomas said I was the homeliest baby she ever saw, I was so scrawny and
tiny and nothing but eyes." The scrawny, big-eyed orphan was a formula
convention that also appeared in other literature. ("She ain't no beauty—
her face is all eyes," we read, for instance, in *Rebecca of Sunnybrook Farm*,
the 1903 novel that is often compared with *Anne of Green Gables* and was
based on the same formula literature.[8])

Like Anne Shirley, Charity Ann hates her name. Like Anne Shirley, she
has raised several sets of twins—"The babies? How many had she? Twins,
I suppose," Donald asks. Charity Ann retorts, "Yes, lots o' twins; nine o'
them." (Compare with Anne Shirley's predicament with Mrs. Hammond's
large family: "I like babies in moderation, but twins three times in succes-
sion is *too much*."[9]) Despite the humor of Maitland's dialect story, the
McKays are horrified to learn that Charity Ann has been physically
abused. She has purple marks on her arms and wrists. The graphic realism of these facts will be softened in *Anne of Green Gables*. Donald is
furious about the asylum matron, "that Peters woman." (She may well
have lent her name to Mrs. *Peter* Blewett in *Anne of Green Gables*, the
exploitative foster mother who is so keen on taking Anne Shirley home to
put her to work on her brood.) For Anne readers who have been wondering about Anne's reluctance to disclose what Marilla calls the "bald facts"
of her past, Anne's history lies embedded in these stories.

Soon Charity Ann is a treasured member of the family. She is a dili-
gent household helper for Christy McKay, who is plagued by rheumatism
and is grateful for the help. Meanwhile Donald McKay showers Charity
Ann with affection and gifts such as sweets and a little ribbon, just as

Matthew spoils Anne with chocolates and puffed sleeves. Eventually Charity Ann blossoms into a rosy, plump girl. In a seemingly contrived and happy ending, a long-lost McKay relative discovers that Charity Ann is—yes!—his daughter. The story's saccharine last line, "'Charity Ann' no more, but *Love Ann,* 'and the greatest of all is *Love!*'"[10], belies the social realism of the story's beginning. And although Maud would write similar endings for several of her orphan stories, it was not so for *Green Gables.*

Difficult to locate today, the ephemera of *Godey's Lady's Book* and other magazines are distilled and transformed into inspired and timeless scenes in *Anne of Green Gables.* As with other influences, such as the Cavendish orphan girl Ellen Macneill, Maud mentioned *Godey's Lady's Book* disparagingly in later years. While she makes no mention of Charity Ann, or the cluster of other *Godey's* references from 1892 to 1894, there can be no doubt that they inspired incidents in *Anne.*

Lucy Ann

The second Ann magazine story that helped shape *Anne of Green Gables* is the story of Lucy Ann. It arrived at the red kitchen door of the Macneill homestead in July 1903, in *Zion's Herald,* the Boston Methodist magazine to which Maud was a regular contributor of short stories. This particular issue of *Zion's Herald* contained Maud's own story "The Little Three-Cornered Lot"—and immediately following it was J. L. Harbour's "Lucy Ann."[11] Even if she were not in the habit of devouring her complimentary copies, which she was, the story would have caught her eye. Its title was also the name of her grandmother. Compared to "Charity Ann," Harbour's "Lucy Ann" was a more psychological story. The developing emotional bond between Lucy Ann and her adoptive mother, a middle-aged spinster, provided the seed for the mother-daughter bond that develops between Anne Shirley and Marilla Cuthbert.

Red-haired and freckled, Lucy Ann looks like Anne Shirley's twin sister. Twelve years old, "a-goin' on to thirteen," Lucy Ann lives in the workhouse in the city and arrives at the country railway station, sent to spend her holidays with Miss Calista May, who has reluctantly agreed to take her in. Like *Anne of Green Gables*, this orphan's story begins with a memorable buggy ride. Miss Calista May, prim and severe like Marilla, picks her up at the train station. On the way home, the city girl who has never been to the country cleverly sidesteps questions about her "folks" by rejoicing at the rural sights. "Oh, just see them lovely flowers in that fence corner! Ain't they *sweet?*" She delights at the sight of the birds, the corn, the flowers, and even ordinary apples. Her spirit is true to her last name—Joyce (the name Maud will also give Anne Shirley's first-born baby girl who dies in *Anne's House of Dreams*).

Lucy Ann is poor. Her straw hat is cheap, its blue ribbon faded, as is her dress, but she holds a Japanese fan as a proud talisman. "She's a humly little thing, with that red hair and all them freckles," Miss Calista muses to a neighbor, and yet she admits that there is "something kind o' likeable about her." Though she is a city girl, Lucy Ann has an innate love of nature and rejoices in life on the farm. She gathers wildflowers and enjoys wading in the brook at the foot of the orchard. She is messy in the house, but Miss Calista remarks that she cannot expect a child "to keep things just so, speshly a half-heather [sic] child like she is." Meanwhile, Miss Calista's "not very tender heart" is warming toward the forlorn little orphan. Her "unwonted gentleness" signals her growth as a person. When Lucy Ann saves the life of her benefactress, in a manner similar to the way in which Anne saves the life of Minnie May, the story ends with Miss Calista's happy decision to let her stay on the farm. "I think that we— we—we need each other," she says. In the final scene, Lucy Ann runs up to Miss Calista and they kiss. Here in this formula story was the birth of Marilla's warming toward Anne Shirley. Here was the seed of what would become one of the novel's central character developments.

In Maitland's "Charity Ann," the formula consisted in reconstituting a home for the orphan through a sudden and implausible reemergence of a long-lost relative. The lonely orphan recovers a place in the biological family, a popular fantasy that Maud used in several short stories prior to *Green Gables*.[12] In "Lucy Ann," however, the orphan finds an adoptive parent who is unrelated but benefits from the match, a resolution Maud also used in short stories as well as in *Green Gables*.[13] Post-Victorian orphan stories underwent a dramatic shift in emphasis. In stories of the Victorian period, the adopting family usually draws an economic or practical benefit from the adoption. For example, the orphan works as a hired hand or performs household tasks in exchange for food and board. While the social mood and social measures had begun to change at the turn of the century, with adoptive parents beginning to seek an emotional benefit from adopting a child, the backlash was powerful, and it was only during the 1910s and 1920s that adoption was cast more consistently in terms of emotional rather than pragmatic benefit.[14] The shift is perhaps most obvious in Harold Gray's comic strip *Little Orphan Annie*, which began in 1924. No longer marginal to the family, orphan Annie's new role is that of a cherished status symbol in the center of Daddy Warbucks' millionaire family. In both Maitland's and Harbour's stories the orphan girl has to earn the adoption by providing a service. *Anne of Green Gables* announces the dramatic shift in the genre. Clumsy at household tasks, Anne will actually talk her way into staying at Green Gables, bewitching Matthew (and Marilla) and awakening their emotions. "What good would she be to us?" asks Marilla. "We might be some good to her," is Matthew's sudden and unexpected retort.[15] By shifting the paradigm of the orphan narrative, *Anne of Green Gables* helped pave the way for the understanding of adoption that we share today.

Orphan stories were popular in the period for the sad reason that many mothers died during or following childbirth. The mortality rate in the early twentieth century was high, with six to nine women out of one thousand dying during or following childbirth due to poor obstetric or delivery practices (as compared to thirteen American women of one hundred thousand dying in 2004, according to the National Center for Health Statistics).[16] Orphan stories were as plentiful in the mass media magazines as whitewashed shells on the Cavendish beach. But, is there a text of origin, an *urtext*, for these Ann stories? One likely candidate is James Whitcomb Riley's *Little Orphant Annie* (1885), a popular nursery rhyme poem:

> Little Orphant Annie's come to our house to stay,
> An' wash the cups an' saucers up, an' brush the crumbs away,...
> An' make the fire, an' bake the bread, an' earn her board-an'-
> keep;...[17]

The Hoosier dialect poem was based on the life of Mary Alice (Allie) Smith, a girl orphaned at the age of ten during the American Civil War.[18] Smith found a home as a servant in the Riley household in Greenfield, Indiana, in the winter of 1862. She told the children tales of elves, witches, and goblins, using her oratory skills to keep the children in line and to build respect, for as an orphan she had no rights or powers. Somehow her name, Allie (from Alice) morphed to Annie during typesetting. Allie Smith had no idea she was the model for the famous poem. She was seventy years old before finding out that she was little orphan Annie. The popular poem spawned numerous spin-offs. It sparked the "Ann" orphan stories, "Charity Ann" and "Lucy Ann." (No doubt the poet Maitland would have been familiar with Riley's poem.) Of course, the name Ann, with or without an "e," was (and remains) popular: Maud's own grandmother and stepmother had "Ann" for a middle name.

The proliferation of these "Ann" stories, and the omnipresence of late Victorian adoption stories, undermines the arguments of those readers who see *Anne of Green Gables* as being too narrowly influenced by one novel, the bestselling *Rebecca of Sunnybrook Farm* (another work about which Maud was mum). Published in September 1903 by Philadelphia-born author Kate Douglas Wiggin, also known as Mrs. Riggs, this children's classic was made into a silent movie starring Mary Pickford in 1917. With her pink parasol in hand, her black hair and glowing eyes, Rebecca Rowena Randall is poised to win over her Aunt Miranda, a thin spare New England spinster living in Riverboro, Maine. Although the similarities are striking, a good many can, in fact, be traced to earlier sources and formula genres that both authors drew on. The book is not found in Maud's personal library, yet it is safe to assume that she was aware of the novel, which was discussed in the periodicals she read. "Rebecca with her quaint ways and vivid imagination, should find life almost unbearable when transplanted into a household of commonplace people," *The Delineator* book page noted in February 1904. "The story is told in Mrs. Riggs's happiest vein."[19] In reading *Rebecca*, one may be struck by her resemblance not so much to Anne but to Emily Byrd Starr, Maud's most autobiographical heroine who develops into a writer just like budding poet Rebecca. Yet Rebecca is also a model housekeeper whose story is laden with morals. Ironically, *Anne of Green Gables*, though written by a Sunday school teacher and future minister's wife, is a much more secular and subversive novel. "Montgomery has done more than imitate Wiggin's successful formula," as one scholar aptly puts it. "She has improved on her model."[20] Indeed, Maud transcended the formula character, for, like Maud herself, Anne Shirley's character pulls in many different directions.

Of course, Maud had also feasted on the orphan literature of the nineteenth century. The innocent, romantic children in Charles Dickens' fiction, David Copperfield and Oliver Twist, survive in a corrupt world while maintaining their moral integrity. Mark Twain used the characters of Huckleberry Finn and Tom Sawyer to develop his powerful satire of America's Gilded Age; Tom and Huck came to symbolize the unfettered freedom of the orphan. The early literature of orphan girls was steeped in moral correctness: *Goody Two-Shoes* (1765) is a lover of books and becomes a school teacher. By the mid-nineteenth century, many best-selling novels featured orphaned heroines who were notable for their strong religious sentiments. The orphan girl is unlikely to be convention-ally pretty, but invariably, she has strength of character. Charlotte Brontë's Jane Eyre is plain but passionate, and she defies abusive relatives and insti-tutional authorities. No matter that Maud may not have read all of these texts; she had imbibed the literary and popular orphan literature of the era and was able both to mimic and transform it.[21] With Anne Shirley, Maud was poised to make literary history, even though ironically her intent had been to write just a little formula story.

Anne's Prototype

In 1905, the silhouette of what would become Anne Shirley was emerging, when Maud was "giving birth" to a redhead who looked surprisingly sim-ilar to Anne. Her long-forgotten story "By the Grace of Sarah Maud" was published in June in the Boston magazine *Modern Women*.[22] The story's spirited and melodramatic heroine Sarah Maud Molloy is a freckled little witch with a ragged sailor hat topping her "carrotty" curls. Her clothing is faded, and the eight-year-old chatterbox luxuriates in grief when we first see her. The story provides a clue to Anne's temper.

"By the Grace of Sarah Maud" is about a young man coincidentally named Nesbitt, who is mad at himself because he has missed his train. Pretty Betty Stewart had given him an invitation to join her for a picnic at Maiden Lake, a golden opportunity to declare his love (Maiden Lake is also the name of the lake where Maud and Will picnicked and printed their names on the poplar). Nesbitt's sulking is interrupted by crying. Stretching his neck, he discovers a little redhead curled up on a bench. He tries to elicit the reason for her heartbreak. "I—can't—get to the picker-nic,"[23] the redhead sobs. She could not go with the mission children on a woodland picnic because she did not have the proper clothing. Here is also the kernel for Anne's dream of picnics and anguish about missing her own church picnic. Nesbitt spontaneously proposes a picnic to Sarah Maud: "You are what I really needed, Sarah Maud—a diversion." "'Ain't!' said Sarah Maud indignantly, 'I'm Irish.'"[24]

Anticipating Anne Shirley, the city urchin reveals an intuitive and poetic understanding of nature's beauty. Already she is a more sophisti-cated character than Harbour's Lucy Ann, whose appreciation of nature is much less spiritual and less sensuous. Nesbitt and Sarah Maud roam in the woodlands and pick flowers, wild roses, and daisies. With great green arches above her, Sarah Maud feels solemn and happy, as if she was "at Mass." Maud was working her own nature thrills into the story. With a rapacious appetite for information that anticipates Anne Shirley's, the lit-tle girl fires off a thousand questions at Nesbitt, who ends up revealing his love for Becky. At sunset, they leave the woods and take the train back home. In the train is Becky Stewart, returning from the picnic, cool because she thinks Nesbitt has neglected her. "Are *you* his girl?" asks Sarah Maud, and while Nesbitt gasps, Becky softens and admits that—yes, she is Nesbitt's "girl."[25]

Maud must have felt that this sparkling little redhead was a kindred spirit. She baptized the character with her own name: Sarah *Maud*, whose initials smm are close to her own lmm. "But maybe it's the Irish," she would note about herself in her journal many years later, trying to iden-tify the scintillating quality of her own face, a quality that transcended the puritanical Scottish Macneills and the dash of English Woolners and

LOOKING FOR ANNE • 217

Penmans.[26] In her Irish temper, Sarah Maud was a comic stock character, though more complex and intelligent than another of Maud's redheads. The handmaid Charlotta in her 1903 story "The Bride Roses" speaks in a thick brogue, makes silly errors such as weeding the flowers instead of the weeds. Looking like a messenger from pixieland, she insists on being called Charlotta with an "a" instead of the more common "Charlotte."[27]

Was our Anne Irish? Here in the little Irish redhead Sarah Maud was the tempestuous part of Anne Shirley's personality. The Irish stereotype is flaming red hair and temper to match, a love of fairies and leprechauns—which abound in *Anne of Green Gables*—and the green of the shamrock and St. Patrick. But Maud sidestepped the stereotype by shrewdly blending cultural references. Instead of Sarah Maud's Irish working-class parents, Maud endowed Anne Shirley's parents with a more noble poverty. Walter and Bertha Shirley teach at Bolingbroke High School and thus represent an educated class. Maud removed Sarah Maud's dialect, and instead gave Anne the language of books. Anne's melodramatic language is scripted and comic, and yet, she also speaks the language of visionaries and dreamers that crosses the boundaries of culture, class, and age. (Was Maud also thinking of Ephraim Weber, the German-Mennonite who had spoken his first English sentence at age twelve and yet was a brilliant reader of literature?) Anne's bookish language was foreign and yet familiar. There was nothing "rude or slangy" about her, as Marilla remarks when she begins to change her mind about Anne's staying at Green Gables: "She's ladylike. It's likely her people were nice folks."[28] The Irish redheaded little "mite of the slums" Sarah Maud had morphed into a personality that middle-class readers could identity with. In fact, both mainstream readers and new immigrants alike could identify with this character from away who cuts across social, cultural, and generational boundaries. Blending the cultural references was a brilliant stroke. It was like blending Tom Sawyer and Huckleberry Finn into one. The middle-class good-bad boy meets the true social rebel and outcast. In Anne's case, the tempestuous ugly duckling met the poetic dreamer. It was a happy marriage of opposites, a blending of seemingly contradictory qualities.

For the first time, we are able to understand Anne's complex and slowly evolving personality. For the first time, we are able to understand the depth of her character and her multifaceted personality, summarized in her own sentence, "There's such a lot of different Annes in me." Anne is made up of many Annes, and different readers can identify with different facets of her personality. Romantic Anne was a pagan wood nymph gazing up at the stars and dreaming (Evelyn Nesbit). Orphan Anne had a troubled history and was desperately hungry for a home (Charity Ann). She was a girl radiating sunshine and recruiting a mother (Lucy Ann Joyce). She was a girl who was supposed to have been a boy (Ellen Macneill), a rebellious and tempestuous little redhead, who appealed to Maud with her bold and fearless way of speaking to adults (Sarah Maud). Charismatic Anne was able to bind Maud to the chariot of her imagination. Maud adopted her and made her the heroine of her novel.[29]

For the first time these sources allow us to identify the two time periods that were particularly relevant for the birth of Anne: the period from 1892 to 1894, when Maud was a rebelling teenager aged seventeen to nineteen, living with her grandparents but planning to leave the homestead to teach; and the period from 1903 to 1905, when she was a mature but solitary writer caring for her grandmother and feeling ambivalent about her future. During these periods she squirreled away many pieces that would allow her imagination to build up Anne. The blending of these disparate time levels would result in a sense of timelessness, which also explains why fans and scholars who have tried to establish an historical chronology for Anne's life, tracing her birth year by using historical references, have found themselves in a maze of confusion and contradiction. Anne was the product of a long evolution. In fact, just as Maud would distill her winter potpourri from the blossoms of an entire summer, so she distilled Anne's character from a variety of "Anns" while also blending that distillation with her own nostalgic memories. That distillation is at the core of the novel's success.

For the first time, we recognize why "Charity Ann" and "Lucy Ann," the two formula Anns without the e, were merely ephemeral little stories, and why Maud's Anne with an e became the international success it is. As Anne herself notes in the novel in what must surely have been the author's tongue-in-cheek comment: "A-n-n looks dreadful, but A-n-n-e looks so much more distinguished."[30] Maud even mocked her own habit—Anne is a chatterbox who is constantly quoting, paraphrasing, and dramatizing clichés of the popular romantic literature she has read. That

Maud had effectively subsumed the magazine and newspaper Anns into her own Anne has been her secret for over a century. We must assume that she quietly discarded the evidence, for she destroyed her notebooks, as we know, and none of these stories are found in her personal papers, but are reborn after more than a century in this book. Maud was poking fun at herself for consuming the formula stories. She had, in effect, put them to excellent use, and had found her own literary voice by birthing a truly original character who paradoxically also represented a distilled version of a long tradition of orphan stories. Anne was the result of ten years of disquiet and turbulence, years of restlessness and loneliness. And Anne was now in Boston, where L. C. Page was contemplating whether or not to adopt this fiery orphan desperate to find a home.

PART 3

Anne Takes Off
Spring 1907–Fall 1938

FOURTEEN

The Most Popular Summer Girl

The critics and public are agreed that Anne is bound to be the most popular Summer girl—a delightful acquisition to any vacation party.
> —*Advertisement for* Anne of Green Gables, *July 1908*[1]

Advertisements would claim that everybody almost automatically loved Anne. And yet as Maud recounted the legend, Anne was battling a hostile world until she finally saw the light of day. Even her publisher was conflicted about Anne, Maud would say, drawing attention to the dangers surrounding her redheaded character. Yet Maud herself was conflicted in her feelings about Anne. To publish a book had been Maud's life-long dream, and yet she would often contradict herself when commenting on her novel.

Once again, Anne would be pulled in different directions. She would be shaped through the vision of a publisher with a marketing genius, but there was a tension between Anne's Canadian and American parents, as the two seemed to have different visions for the character's future. The tension in Maud's personality, and the fragmentary approach of her composition, were reflected in Anne's personality. These fragments, in turn, now seemed to mirror the tension felt by an entire era caught in the whirl of modernity and simultaneously searching for nostalgic peace.

How Anne Find∂ a Home in Bo∂ton

The New England Building at 200 Summer Street in Boston housed the publishing company of L. C. Page. Born in Switzerland, the son of an American consul, Louis Coues Page had grown up with all the privileges of wealth. Harvard-educated, he and his brother George worked in their stepfather's publishing firm Estes & Lauriat. After Louis had achieved the position of president and general manager in 1897 he renamed the company L. C. Page and Company, which in 1914 became simply The Page Company. In a photo taken in 1937, L. C. Page looks like the baron of the company.[2] With his head cocked up, mouth turned down, and shoulders squared, he could also pass for an army brigadier accustomed to giving orders. He had a penchant for philandering, gambling, and drinking. A conservative in politics and taste, he favored the romantic poetry of Bliss Carman and Charles G. D. Roberts, translations of the Italian poet Gabriele D'Annunzio, and classic novels by Charles Dickens, Sir Walter Scott, and Leo Tolstoy. Having also found a lucrative niche with juvenile fiction, he had a genius for marketing that set him apart.

At 200 Summer Street it was business as usual when *Anne* began making her rounds. After giving the novel the cursory read usually given to an unknown author, thirty-eight-year-old Louis said "No." This time, however, Anne was not so easily brushed aside. She had formed an alliance with staff member "Miss Arbuckle," one of the many expatriate Prince Edward Islanders in Boston, who was enchanted by the novel's nostalgic Prince Edward Island locale. Miss Arbuckle quietly but persistently championed Anne to other staff readers until several supported the novel. The effective lobbying campaign forced the mighty Louis to yield to Anne. On April 8, an acceptance letter was drafted. This, at least, is how Maud relayed the story in her journal on July 16, 1916, after her relations with the Page brothers had soured.[3] Unfortunately, Maud's early correspondence with her publisher has disappeared; it is not part of the L. C. Page papers at the New York Public Library.

Meanwhile on Prince Edward Island the weather was so cold that the Minto was stuck in ice and the passengers and mails were delayed. Just a week earlier Frede had penned in her ten-year letter to Maud, "Time will bring around events."[4] On April 15, Mr. Crewe's rumbling buggy finally arrived at the red kitchen door. In the kitchen with its low, whitewashed ceiling, its old-fashioned braided mats on the floor, and Daffy the cat drinking milk near the warm stove, Grandma handed Maud the letter from Boston. Her hands must have been shaking as her anxious eyes scanned the single typewritten sheet.

"We take pleasure in advising you that our readers report favorably with regard to your girls's [sic] story 'Anne of Green Gables', and if mutually satisfactory arrangements can be made, we shall be glad to add the book to our next season's list," the typed letter simply signed L. C. Page & Company read. Maud was given the option of selling the book for a set amount to be determined, or to have it published on a "moderate" royalty basis. The short letter ended by suggesting that if she was not otherwise at work, "it might be a good idea to write a second story dealing with the same character."[5] It was not unusual for publishers at the time to suggest a sequel long before a book had been tested by the market, as literary scholar Carole Gerson writes in her study on the Anne sequels. "In other words, the second Anne book, *Anne of Avonlea*, was generated not by the clamour of enchanted readers, but by the current practices of market publishing; the charismatic quality of *Anne of Green Gables* was not substantive to the production of its initial sequels, but rather an incidental surprise."[6]

Inebriated with joy, Maud may have kept her secret to relish by herself. Frede had just left to study at the Ontario Agricultural College in Guelph, but Ewan was scheduled to return to Prince Edward Island in April. She apparently made no record of this stunning news in her journal that night. But she must have responded to Page's letter without delay, for just a week later, on April 22, the L. C. Page Company issued the contract for L. M. Montgomery of "Cavendish, P. E. I." to sign over all the rights "including all serial rights, dramatic rights, translations, abridgements, selections" for the publication of "ANNE OF GREEN GABLES a juvenile story." She would receive a 10% royalty on the wholesale price for each copy "sold over and above the first thousand." In addition, the contract gave Page "the refusal of all her stories for book publication for a period of five years" on the same conditions that ruled this first contract.[7] The entire book deal was negotiated, contracted, and signed within a remarkable three weeks. She signed the contract on Thursday, May 2, 1907.

"Well, I must simply tell you my *great news* right off!" she wrote to Ephraim Weber on the night of her signing, bursting with the exuberance of the moment. Yet despite her bubbly effusiveness, her tone was modest and self-deprecating. Ephraim should not think that she had written "the great Canadian novel." It was "merely a juvenilish story, ostensibly for girls," but her hope was that "grown-ups may like it a little." She was pleased about having secured a reputable publisher, though not among the "top-notchers" like Harpers or MacMillan, as she admitted.[8]

There is shadow of nervousness. The novel was a labor of love, but would she be able to sustain the quality in a sequel? The lover of independence balked at the five-year binding clause in this publication marriage, although the insertion of such a clause, she told Ephraim, might be viewed by some as "rather complimentary." Nothing indicates, however, that she tried to negotiate this clause in any way or that she took the trouble to seek professional consult. While she generously dispensed publishing advice to her pen friends, no one was advising her. And after years of toiling and multiple rejections, she was relieved to have a contract. Her ingrained lack of negotiation skills, her solitary publishing habits, and her desperate desire to be published, however, would prove costly in later years. On August 16, she finally announced the news in her journal, and penned her now well known, indeed legendary, mini-biography of how *Anne* came about:

> I have always kept a notebook in which I jotted down, as they occurred to me, ideas for plots, incidents, characters and descriptions. Two years ago in the spring of 1905 I was looking over this notebook in search of some suitable idea for a short serial I wanted to write for a certain Sunday School paper and I found a faded entry, written ten years before:—'Elderly couple apply to orphan asylum for a boy. By mistake a girl is sent them.' I thought this would do. I began to block out chapters, devise incidents and 'brood up' my heroine. Somehow or other she seemed very real to me and took possession of me to an unusual extent. Her personality appealed to me and I thought it rather a shame to waste her on an ephemeral little serial. Then the thought came, "Write a book about her. You have the central idea and

character. All you have to do is to spread it out over enough chapters to amount to a book."

The result of this was "Anne of Green Gables".[9]

The notebook that contained the core spark for the novel has disappeared, but the story behind the notebook, and the complexity of Maud's Anne, has finally been unraveled. In this belated entry, her tone was restrained and retrospective, yet with an effusive capstone. The dream she dreamed in that old brown school desk had finally come true, she noted. "And the realization is sweet—almost as sweet as the dream!"

She closed the entry with what appears to be a secondary thread, an afterthought: "Ewan came home in April. He seemed very well and quite recovered from his headaches and insomnia."[10]

The Anne Sequel

Maud promptly began work on a sequel. She worked all summer, never pausing to write in her journal, but then again, summer was always a dearth for her journal. She collected fresh material, blocking out new characters, and devising incidents. She was brooding up her first Anne sequel. By fall, she burst into the rapture of writing—a feeling always strangely bodily, like a physical sensation. She marked the occasion by going to the shore. The day before she had written the first six pages of her new book, what would become *Anne of Avonlea*.

Even though the shore was close, Maud could go for months without taking a stroll along the beach because she was partial to the woods. But that Wednesday evening, October 9, with the air purified after a storm the day before, the clean-washed sand crunching underneath her step, and the salty smell of the water filling her lungs, her soul was filled with a nameless exhilaration. It was as if she was "borne on the wings of a raptured ecstasy into the seventh heaven," she enthused in an unpublished part of this journal entry. "Oh, you dear earth! Tonight I loved you so much that I could have flung myself face downward on you, my arms outstretched as if to clasp you."[11] Having mastered the most difficult hurdle—the opening, which was always excruciating for Maud—she was hoping that the rest would be fun. "*Anne* is as real to me as if I had given her birth—as real and as dear," she concluded this exuberant journal entry.[12] She was intoxicated with the joy of creation. Curiously, a full month later, on November 10, Maud described her ecstatic beach walk verbatim in her letter to Ephraim, but fibbed that it had happened three evenings earlier. It is a small but telling incident that indicates that dramatic immediacy was more important to our author than the literal truth. In the letter she referred to dryads and wood nymphs—presumably around the same time that she would have written chapter eight of the sequel, "A Golden Picnic," in which Anne and her girlfriends dance around the woodland pool like wood nymphs performing a pagan rite.

Despite the progress on the new novel, however, Maud's mood began to spiral downward. During the winter her writing world was out of joint because she had to work in the kitchen, where there were constant interruptions by post office visitors. Her misanthropy returned. "When I speak of *loving* Cavendish it is the *place* I love, not the people," she noted in her November 3 journal record.[13] In December, she dreaded the future, even a happy one, and with the night coming early, "dour gloom settles down on my soul."[14] In her dark mood, she was convinced that she was a creature whom no one could love. The only person she could share these feelings with was Frede, who had returned from Guelph after several months of studies. Maud missed her dear companion, and by February, 1908, she was tired of being cooped up at home and weary of asking others for rides. Her independence asserted itself and she simply walked the five miles on the frozen road. It took her one hour and fifty minutes to arrive at her destination in Stanley. "I was longing to see Frede."[15] The visit provided much-needed cheer. Always interested in psychic phenomena, Maud was trying to make her friends dream of her. She had commanded Frede to dream of her and it had worked.

On March 2, she offered to try the experiment on Ephraim: "I'll try to make you dream of me."[16] She also announced that *Anne of Green Gables* would be out on March 15. Preoccupied Ephraim was distracted by problems of his own, however. His life was unraveling, he reported on March 20. He stood to lose the land he had purchased. He was threatened by lawsuits and a sheriff's sale, and would eventually sell his land at a loss. On

April 5, Maud responded by saying that she was sorry to hear that his life was "on the rocks" but seeing that there was nothing she could do, she offered sympathy and hoped that he would find his way out of his difficulties. After this somewhat callous and cursory dismissal of a friend's problems, she returned to her topic. "I *did* dream of you one night," she wrote, insisting on sharing her own riveting dream narrative in which he starred as a man of adventure. Never once did she return to Ephraim's real-life problems.[17] Flattered to be the insistent object of fantasy for the romantic writer, the Alberta farmer "on the rocks" must have realized that there was a strange disconnect between reality and fantasy, for his Maritime writer friend was not interested in the prosaic reality of Ephraim's life—which may have painfully reminded her of her own father's failures.

On May 3, the eve of Anne's publication, Maud composed a 2,500 word mini-autobiography in her journal that has never been published. In a remarkably balanced tone, she described the effects of her father's departure and the Macneill grandparents' and uncles' nagging and fault finding of her as a child. "I received the impression of which to this day I have never been able quite to rid myself—that everybody disliked me and that I was a very hateful person." Miss Gordon, her school teacher and good friend, who had taken the reins of the Cavendish School when Maud was fourteen, allowed her to reinvent herself. "For the first time it dawned on me that I was not so unlovable as I had been made to believe. I found myself one of Miss Gordon's favorite pupils and this fact alone did more for me than all my previous years of 'schooling' put together."[18] It was a belated tribute to Hattie Gordon. With her golden hair and smart dresses, Hattie had been adored by her pupils, just like Miss Muriel Stacy in the first *Anne* book. These thoughts now shaped the writing of *Anne of Avonlea*, which explored Anne's two years as a teacher in Avonlea. She dedicated this new novel to Hattie Gordon—the friend with whom she had lost touch.[19]

After a prolonged phase of depression, she feared an impending breakdown: "But if I break down what will I do?" she asked. "There is no one to take care of me and I could not afford to go away for treatment or stop work and rest."[20] Remarkably, she did not appear to count on Ewan Macdonald's help. Her fiancé had accepted a call to the presbytery of

Bloomfield and O'Leary in western Prince Edward Island, a potato-farming community ninety kilometers from Cavendish and today home of the Prince Edward Island Potato Museum.[21] As a result, she saw Ewan seldom, but he had come for a visit in March. In her dark mood, on May 3, she also confessed to marriage jitters in her journal, wondering if she was fit to be anybody's wife. Her one wish, she said on May 24, was for Uncle John's family to disappear and for her to have "an independent home and existence here."[22] The thought of living by herself, independent in her own castle, again asserted itself as Maud's default ideal.

Sensitive and Imaginative Girlhood

In Boston, meanwhile, *Anne of Green Gables* was taking shape. Marketing wizard L. C. Page had put aside his reservations, if he had ever had any, to launch Anne like a fashionable debutante. There was some wrangling over the author's name. L. C. Page preferred the femininity and romance of 'Lucy Maud Montgomery.' Maud insisted on "L. M. Montgomery," the literary identity for which she had worked so hard.[23] The gender-bending name had a more serious, literary flavor than the more feminine pseudonyms such as Belinda Bluegrass or Maud Eglinton that she had cultivated in some short stories. Strike one would go to Maud. There was a delay in the book production because the illustrator L. C. Page had commissioned was overworked or sick. Page began marketing the novel in March 1908.

> Everyone, young or old, who reads the story of 'Anne of Green Gables' will fall in love with her.... Miss Montgomery will receive praise for her fine sympathy with and delicate appreciation of sensitive and imaginative girlhood.[24]

This announcement in the American book trade magazine *The Publishers' Weekly* set the stage for the birth of the little redhead. *Anne*, like most of Page's books, was advertised at a sales price of one dollar and fifty cents. Although announced as *"Ready in April,"* the novel was in fact delayed until June, the month featured so prominently in the novel.[25]

"PUBLISHED TO-DAY: Anne of Green Gables," *The Publishers' Weekly* proclaimed the launch on its cover page on Saturday, June 13, 1908. "In ANNE OF GREEN GABLES we believe that we have discovered another 'Rebecca,'" the blurb read. "Anne is one of the most original heroines in recent fiction." Indeed, *Anne* was proclaimed "the 'leading lady' of the book world of 1908."[26]

My First Book

The Island was exquisite that June. Just the right combination of rain and sunshine had graced the landscape. The grass was at its greenest. In Cavendish Mr. Crewe's rumbling wheels stopped at Grandmother Macneill's kitchen door to deliver the mailbag. It was Saturday, June 20, and there was a special packet for Maud. She unwrapped her parcel: "my first book!" she breathed to her journal. Excitement took her breath away. The thrill was intoxicating like a rich wine; "*mine, mine, mine,*" she repeated like a mantra in her journal. She had started writing the novel three years earlier, yet her book sounded depths that reached much further back. Her emotions and dreams lived in the novel. Opening the book to the dedication page, "To the Memory of my father and mother," she felt a pang of pleasure.[27]

Anne, she thought, was beautifully appareled with a cloth cover and a handsome portrait in the center. Bathed in a hue of Titian red, the model's hair was teased up into a Pompadour and gathered at the nape of the neck, clearly an adult style. Who was the Gibson Girl whose pointed chin and nude skin graced the cover of the first edition of *Anne of Green Gables*? Her identity is unknown but she was not Evelyn Nesbit, who by 1907 had become persona non grata. Evelyn's sordid story had sold millions of tabloids and tinted postcards, but had forever banished her image of innocence from the cover of a juvenile story. Missing, too, was the name of the *Anne* cover artist, for the simple reason that the cover was not original but recycled from the attractive January 1905 Gibson Girl cover of *The Delineator*. Nothing could better illustrate Page's marketing of the novel as a popular bestseller. Today a rare copy of *The Delineator* finally reveals the long-lost identity of the cover artist: "The January design is a marvelously beautiful type of the American Girl executed in pastel by George Gibbs."[28] Educated at the Corcoran School of Art in Washington, D. C. and the Art Student League in New York, magazine and book illustrator George Gibbs placed his work in the era's leading magazines such as *Scribner's*, *McClure's*, *Harper's*, *Cosmopolitan*, and *Colliers*. He would become the cover illustrator for Maud's subsequent books published by L. C. Page. By sending in ten cents in stamps for mailing, readers could acquire the Gibson Girl plate for home framing, so that by the time the novel came out, Anne was already a familiar face in the dens, parlors, or "Milady's boudoirs" of regular *Delineator* subscribers. L. C. Page purchased the original pastel painting from Gibbs, and had it framed and hung in the personal library of his Brookline mansion.[29] Unfortunately, like so much of the early history of *Anne*, it no longer exists.

The book's print and binding were also pretty, although the first edition, surprisingly, was published in cloth of three different colors—green, brown, and beige. "Most likely the multiple colors suggest that the publisher ran out of available cloth and simply used what was left over," explains Donna Campbell, an Ontario collector of L. M. Montgomery's first editions.

Opening the book, Maud would have seen the pretty frontispiece showing fifteen-year-old Diana fixing her friend's hair and dress and the caption "'There's something so stylish about you, Anne,' said Diana."[30] The packaging addressed the novel not to children, but to teenaged girls and young adults focused on fashion and dress.[31] Seven additional plates illustrated Anne's dramatic adventures: Arriving at Green Gables; Confronting Mrs. Lynde and stamping her foot on the floor; Going to Sunday school with wildflowers decorating her hat; Cracking the slate on Gilbert's head; Walking the roof pole; and so on. Maud thought the illustration of Anne arriving at Green Gables was the best: Matthew and Anne looked exactly as they did in her imagination.

The quality of the illustrations, however, was not in the same league as the work of renowned children's book illustrators Elizabeth Shippen Green or Jessie Willcox Smith (for whom Evelyn Nesbit had posed in Philadelphia). Illustrator William A. J. Claus, the Director of the Claus Art School in Boston, had honed his skills by copying religious paintings such as Raphael's Madonna for churches.[32] It is likely that most if not all of the illustrations for *Anne* were done by Claus's twenty-five-year-old wife May Austin Claus. Her initials M.A. came before his on the title page, and given his seniority, it is safe to assume that his name would have appeared first had he done the work. Maud quickly spotted some embarrassing errors. The book states that when Gilbert rescues Anne after the Lily Maid episode, her hair is short, having been just recently shingled after the hair-dyeing episode. In the illustration, long hair flows down her back.[33] When Anne confronts Mrs. Lynde, the lady is shown without a bonnet, suggesting a formal visit rather than a call. But these errors were less consequential than the final plate, which changed the ending. We see Gilbert and Anne walking down the lane as a romantic couple. Both are dressed for a courtship walk: Gilbert in a formal suit with tie, straw hat, and pleated trousers, Anne with an absurd open parasol when it is actually after sundown. Both look stiff and stilted as if they were drawn from "a 1908 fashion plate."[34] It is ironic that in the erroneous final plate, readers found conclusive evidence for Gilbert's romance with Anne. It seemed that while Maud was intentionally leaving the novel's ending ambiguous, as the decision was still open in her own life, the novel's packaging identified the direction of the sequel. This may help explain why Maud did not like the illustrations and would have preferred her novel to stand on its own without such interventions. "What happens to Gilbert and Anne?" was the question that journalists and fans would soon pester her about.

Coincidentally, in July, Ed Simpson passed through Cavendish on his buggy—his bride beside him. Maud had the presence of mind to flash him a quick smile, but he displayed an "unflattering indifference," she wrote on the night of July 16 in her journal.[35] It would take time for the wounds to heal. Her tone stung with vindictive poison when she wrote in her journal the local gossip—that Ed's bride was not beautiful but clever and in possession of a good fortune. One is struck at how the various plots concerning Maud's lovers seem to fall into Jane Austen categories.

A month later, *Anne* was leaping off Page's list of "Summer's Successes." The early critics tended to agree with Marilla: "No house will be ever dull that she's in."[36] The conservative *New York Times Saturday Review of Books* called her "one of the most extraordinary girls that ever came out of an ink pot" but also quibbled that Anne was altogether too queer: despite the fact that she has spent her life with illiterate folk and has had little schooling, she speaks with a vocabulary worthy of Bernard Shaw and has a reasoning power worthy of the Justice of the Supreme Court.[37] Nevertheless, the reactions were largely positive. "'Anne of Green Gables' is worth a thousand of the problem stories with which the bookshelves are crowded today," enthused the reviewer in the Toronto *Globe* on August 15.[38]

That same August, an incident at the homestead set new turbulences in motion. On a windy day, a spark from the cooking stove, which they kept outside during the summer, must have landed on the roof. The old kitchen roof caught fire. Maud dragged the ladder from the barn, and mounted it with pails of water, eventually putting out the fire. Her efforts were successful, and during better times the little adventure would have yielded a good story, but somehow it put her nerves on edge. What if the house, filled with two decades of pictures, journal pages, notebooks, letters, and recorded memories, had burnt down? What sort of fiction would Maud have written? We can only speculate about the effects on her style and content. The event left her feeling a sense of shock for weeks after, as she told George MacMillan on August 31. "I am glad you liked my book," she noted. She said she agreed with the critics who said that the ending was conventional, lacking the freshness of the earlier parts. If she had known there would be a sequel, she would simply have stopped, she added. In fact, when she made this statement (which she also repeated elsewhere and that has since been repeated by numerous scholars as evidence that the ending was no good) she was in a grim mood. She was feeling "soaked" with Anne, as she put it. "I'm sick of the sound of her name."[39] It was the beginning of an ambivalent love-hate relationship with her heroine.

In Cavendish, people immediately recognized some of the portraits, arousing Maud's defensiveness. "Yet there isn't a portrait in the book," she told Ephraim on September 10, adding, "They are all 'composites.'"[40] And yet she provided no information on how her vivid imagination had blended the characters, on how they were really a brilliant distillation of many different portraits that allowed many people to identify with the heroine. A clipping service provided her with reviews of her novel, and by September 10 she had collected an impressive list of about *sixty*, a number she proudly italicized.[41] Three were truly negative, two mixed, and the remaining highly flattering, she wrote to Ephraim. In fact, she laid it on thick, providing several pages of quotations. This was perhaps because Ephraim, besides recommending horseback riding to cure her headache and nerves, had commented on *Anne* in terms not as effusively laudatory as she may have hoped from her most ardent fan and admirer. Yet we can also sense her irritation. If she were "dragged at Anne's chariot wheels" the rest of her life, she would "bitterly repent having 'created' her," she explained three months after the novel's publication. "Every freak who has written to me about it, claims to be a 'kindred spirit.'"[42] A month later, by October, Maud recorded in her journal that her book was a "best seller," already in its fifth edition.[43]

Meanwhile in Toronto, the *Canadian Magazine* championed the novel's Canadian flavor in November. "Her environment, a picturesque section of Prince Edward Island, is thoroughly Canadian, and Miss Montgomery presents it in a piquant literary style, full of grace and whole-heartedness." The periodical was unstinting in its praise, calling *Anne* "a novel that easily places the author, Miss L. M. Montgomery, in the first rank of our native writers."[44] Ironically, it was not until 1942, the year of Maud's death, that the first Canadian edition of the novel was published by Toronto's Ryerson Press. "In 'Anne of Green Gables' you will find the dearest and most moving and delightful child since the immortal Alice," said Mark Twain in a letter to actor Francis Wilson, which Page promptly quoted in *The Publishers' Weekly* on December 5.[45] According to the December 26 advertisements in the same book trade magazine, her "most devoted admirers" now included "Bliss Carman, Mark Twain, Francis Wilson, Sir Louis H. Davies, of the Supreme Court of Canada, and Annie Fellows Johnston."[46] The kindred spirits clan was growing quickly.

Some of her relatives, such as cranky Uncle Leander, took her seriously for the first time. For the Reverend, who had studied theology at Princeton, she was no longer the poor insignificant country cousin but a published author worthy of a real conversation. Grandmother and Uncle John seemed more respectful after she had proven that her Waverly pen carried a heftier and more financially lucrative weight in the world than even the golden Island potato. Despite this new respect, however, Grandmother was still the same crabby person.

Cavendish was proud of Maud's achievements and yet, it appears, not unstintingly so. Curiously, the Literary Society never paid her the compliment she so yearned to hear. No notice of congratulation is found in the minute book, which soberly recorded that she resigned from the book committee in December 1908—the year of her success. Over the years she would hoard the compliments and attention, savoring her sweet success. But she also created a mental blacklist of all those who neglected to congratulate her. A sign of narcissistic self-involvement, it was also a mark of deep-seated insecurity and a lifelong desire for praise and acceptance. Nate Lockhart, with whom she had first shared her desire to write a book, never congratulated her on her novel, she complained. One wonders whether she congratulated him on the birth of two sons, both in the same year as *Anne*.[47] Her old resentment flared up when Aunt Emily said that she herself was not educated enough to appreciate the novel. One wonders if Grandmother Macneill or Uncle John read the novel and enjoyed it.

At Home in the Modern World

What accounts for the novel's success in the wide world? What made it so easy to connect with Anne? It is as if Maud had impregnated the story and characters with her own hunger for love. Or, as Maud's "fan" Isabel Anderson explained the attraction, "It is because of something for which you stand, which they long for and have not."[48] The novel has an uncanny way of entering into an intimate relationship with the reader. But the novel also resonated with the culture of the era including its fashions, fads, and fears. In the year *Anne* was launched, red hair seemed omnipresent. *The Metropolitan*, for instance, featured a series of red-headed cover girls including, in March, a Titian redhead in Gypsy-chic in the center of a Zodiac wheel; in August, a flower-wreathed redhead in an empire dress in a rural Garden of Eden with ripe red apples; and in September, an auburn beauty holding a crystal ball in a dark underworld forest. That same September, *The Delineator* published a beautifully illustrated poem, "The Redheaded Baby," by Reginald Wright Kauffman:

"Redheaded Baby, with laughing eyes,/ Dimple-cheeked, firm-limbed, brave little boy."[49]

A new culture of speed and leisure was emerging in advertisements for automobiles, motor boats, gramophones, phonographs, zonophones, and other "Talking Machines." *The Metropolitan* ran ads for Maja, the sister of Mercedes, the car "in reach of all lovers of good automobiles," and the Rambler, "The Car of Steady Service" by Thos. B. Jeffrey & Company. "Buy a Real Car," urged the American Motor Car Sales Company, advertising Roadsters and multi-passenger "Tourist" cars at up to 50–60 horsepower and ranging in price from $3,200 to $4,000.[50] The motorboat was no longer for the wealthy man alone, the ad proclaimed: "Probably one of the greatest joys of the clan is the cruise which corresponds to the touring trips of the automobilists."[51] There were also a multitude of advertisements for modern bathrooms, with plumbing fixtures that would provide absolute and perfect sanitation. How could this modern and urban world possibly be interested in the rural, backward world of Anne?

One might assume that such symbols of modernity would automatically render obsolete the old-fashioned buggy and the rural landscape of Green Gables, pushing both into the old and bygone Victorian era. However, the opposite appears to have been true. In June 1908, the very same time *Anne* was leaping off the presses, *The Metropolitan* featured "A Detail of Spring Motoring," a drawing by George Gibbs, the same—though at the time unacknowledged—artist who painted the *Anne* cover.[52] The drawing illustrates that the new automobile culture was in perfect harmony with nostalgia for rural nature: A car has come to a standstill in the midst of a pastoral scene; the man at the wheel looks on as the woman steps on the car seat to pluck white blossoms from the canopy of cherry trees. In the March issue, a Gibbs drawing entitled "Motor-Boating" depicts modern machinery against a backdrop of pastoral nature: a woman in a red sweater sits at the wheel of a speed boat, while a man with a green tie holds on to the railing. The boat cuts through the water at high speed, whirling up a huge splash of white foam. But visible in the background is a sailing boat and a placid, tree lined shore.[53] Modern consumer items appeared at their most exciting and desirable when packaged within the familiar, romantic nature ideal that was celebrated in *Anne*. The novel's old-fashioned world was perhaps the tonic that helped alleviate the anxieties whirled up by the speed of the new and unknown era.

Anne also captured something of the burgeoning social mood. By the time it was published, a national adoption campaign was in full swing. "The Delineator Child-Rescue Campaign" had been initiated by *The Delineator's* editor-in-chief, American author Theodore Dreiser, in September 1907. The goal of this widely publicized campaign was to find foster families or adoptive families for orphans. The ultimate goal was to dismantle the old-fashioned and deficient asylum system. Its motto, "For the Child that Needs a Home and the Home that Needs a Child,"[54] seemed to encapsulate the motto of *Anne of Green Gables.* Each month, *The Delineator* published portraits and profiles of orphan children in a concerted effort to recruit adoptive parents. Nine-year-old Bud and five-year-old Blossom, for instance, came from the Florida woods: "But as they belong to one family stem and are pretty as any flowers that grow, we have given them the nicknames." The October 1908 journalistic portrait of the pair echoes the language of orphan literature like *Anne of Green Gables.* "These are well-born children, free from any hereditary taint, and are affectionate and responsive," the column noted, just as Marilla reflects that Anne likely comes from a good family. "Their first ride on a train and street car was with the superintendent of the society. Their eyes fairly danced with the sight of the panoramic picture from country to town." And just like Anne, Bud and Blossom enjoy ice cream for the first time.[55]

Reaching all the way to the White House, with Theodore Dreiser meeting with President Theodore Roosevelt, this campaign helped contribute to the creation of the US Children's Bureau in 1912. It also echoed and reinforced the ideas of *Anne of Green Gables*—the new spirit of providing a loving home for children rather than viewing orphans for their use value. "[T]he orphans in tales aimed at female readers likewise 'stir up hearts,' bringing romance or reconciliation or other expressions of feelings in their wake."[56] Thus Anne brings to Green Gables the gift of the heart, triggering moments of emotional awakening for Matthew, for Marilla, for Aunt Josephine Barry, and numerous others in the sequels. By drawing on the language of orphan literature, *The Delineator's* child-rescue campaign also had the effect of promoting and popularizing "emotional" orphan literature. In particular, given its timing, the campaign helped to promote *Anne of Green Gables*. And vice versa: *Anne* helped promote the idea of adoption as we understand it today.

But the novel spoke to readers on a deep emotional and spiritual level as well. The book contained an implied promise of a fairy tale—the promise that things would come out all right, even if they looked dark. The heroine's irrepressible optimism made her a charismatic carrier of hope and perseverance. Readers were able to believe in the fairy tale because Maud had distilled a lifetime of dreams and hopes and passions and struggles into the novel. The simple but heartfelt message now inspired thousands of readers across boundaries of gender and class. They would reread the novel numerous times and pass it on as a gift to their best friends, children, and grandchildren. Maud marveled at the effect her book was having in the wider world. With Maud's genius for writing friendship, the novel spawned romantic communities of kindred spirits. With its irrepressible heroine, the forerunner for Pollyanna, the book became a classic in bibliotherapy. Jacqueline Stanley, the author of *Reading to Heal*, for instance, cites *Anne of Green Gables* as one of her favorite books growing up.[57] "I shall recommend it to all as a book to drive away the blues," the Page ad quoted Marguerite Linton Glentworth, Chairman of the New York Woman's Press Club, in November.[58] "Thousands of readers have been made happy by an acquaintance with the delightful ANNE OF GREEN GABLES," *The Publishers' Weekly* cover page claimed on December 26.[59] In a way, Anne turned Emersonian and Thoreauvian transcendentalism from the head to the heart. Maud wanted be "a messenger of optimism and sunshine."[60]

At the same time that *Anne* and Maud were being fêted, Evelyn Nesbit, the woman whose picture had been an inspiration for Anne's face, sat alone in her hotel room in New York on her twenty-fourth birthday. She was afraid to go out because of the notoriety that had followed her after her mentally unstable husband shot and killed her former lover, Stanford White. Although Evelyn had valiantly supported her husband with her testimony in court, her husband's relatives, the Thaw family, had cut off contact with her. At his second trial in 1908 the jury delivered a verdict of insanity and he was incarcerated in the Matteawan State Hospital for the Criminally Insane, where he occupied private quarters. A movie about the Thaw-Nesbit-White triangle had been scheduled to open in

New York, but the President of the New York Society for the Suppression of Vice, Anthony Comstock, rose up and protested the movie, as did the mayor of New York, George McClellan, who ordered the theaters in the city closed. According to one historian, "In the furor, the National Board of Review—the country's first movie watchdog group—was created."[61] Evelyn recalled in her memoir that on "Christmas Day, 1908, my birthday, dawned, desolate and cheerless." But there was one bright spot. She was thrilled to receive a most unusual pet as a gift, delivered to her in a basket: a six-foot Florida snake that she named Tara. "It really knew me and would curl up beside me while I read and sewed."[62] The avid reader and student of Theosophy (a belief in the unity of nature, body, and soul) would have been fascinated by the story of *Anne* and could have used the boost of knowing that she was the inspiration for Anne's face. Unfortunately, however, like two ships passing in the dark, the paths of Maud and Evelyn never crossed.

ABOVE: Front view, Alexander Macneill's old homestead with the windswept apple trees; the kitchen wing (left) in which Maud wrote the opening scene of *Anne of Green Gables*.

RIGHT: "My flower garden was beyond the open space." Maud loved the orchard her grandfather had planted.

University of Guelph Library Archival and Special Collections

LEFT: View of Cherry Tree Curve. Maud named this view from her little window "Haunt of Ancient Peace".

BELOW: The brook on Alex Macneill's farm. After the spring rains the old brooks would become wild and headlong.

University of Guelph Library Archival and Special Collections

"I feel like a caged creature." Winters were harsh and long, causing Maud to escape into dreams. TOP: Maud photographed the old homestead buried under snow dunes. BOTTOM: When the icebreaker *The Minto* was hemmed in by ice shards, the mail and passenger service stopped.

ABOVE: The old room in which *Anne of Green Gables* was written. Maud staged her den with a clock, a fern, books, and pictures, all facing the camera.

BELOW: "Twin Sentinels of the Trail" and "A Dim Forest Aisle." Some of Maud's beloved woodland images from *The Booklovers Magazine* (October 1904), the same issue that featured the Birch Path, are visible on the wall of her little room in Park Corner, where she stayed in 1911. *Kilmeny of the Orchard*, her 1910 novel, is displayed on the table.

ABOVE: The old parlor with the picture of Maud's mother hung above the mantelpiece. Maud would often sit and daydream in the rocking chair.

BELOW: The old Cavendish kitchen with Daffy lapping up the milk.

ABOVE: Cavendish Hall—the inspiration for Avonlea Hall and a rich source for literary satire.

BELOW: The home of the old brother and sister David and Margaret Macneill; the Cavendish model for Green Gables.

University of Guelph Library Archival and Special Collections

ABOVE: Maud said that this pond in the neighboring town of Park Corner inspired the *Lake of Shining Waters*.

BELOW: The old Presbyterian Church in Cavendish. On Sundays, Maud loved to decorate the church with ferns.

Scrapbook page with Clinton Scollard's poem "Winter in Lovers' Lane" clipped from the January 1905 issue of *The Delineator* with a red maple leaf from Maud's own Lover's Lane underneath.

Confederation Centre Art Gallery, Charlottetown, Prince Edward Island and The Lucy Maud Montgomery Birthplace Foundation

Scrapbook page with Grace Denig Lichfield's poem "The Bend of the Road."

Confederation Centre Art Gallery, Charlottetown, Prince Edward Island and The Lucy Maud Montgomery Birthplace Foundation

TOP: The first page of the original *Anne of Green Gables* manuscript shows the ease and rapid flow of Maud's writing.

BOTTOM: Crossing out two names Maud changed her mind in naming Diana: "Her name is ~~Laura~~ ~~Gertrude~~ Diana."

TOP: "... <u>mine, mine, mine</u>." On Saturday, June 20, 1908, Maud exuberantly announced the publication of *Anne of Green Gables* in her journal.

University of Guelph Library Archival and Special Collections

BOTTOM: Her contract with L. C. Page of Boston dated April 22, 1907, shows earned royalties in Maud's own handwriting.

Library and Archives Canada

"... physically, she was the original." On November 29, 1934, three decades after writing the novel, Maud put this clipping of Evelyn Nesbit in her journal.

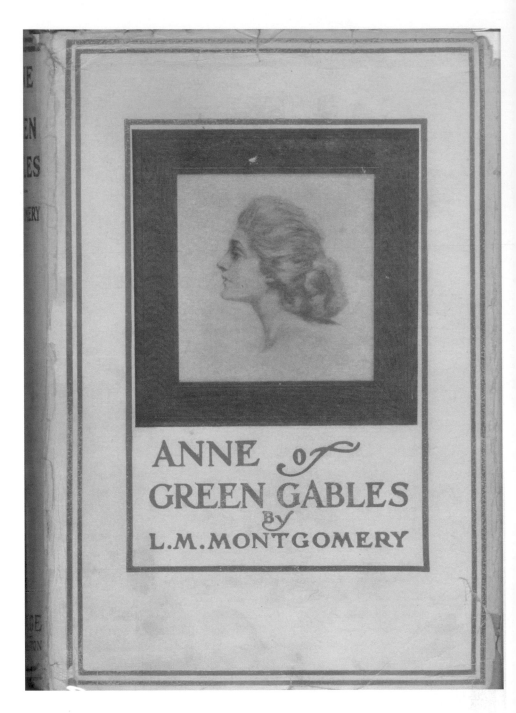

The cover of the first edition of *Anne of Green Gables* with the Gibson Girl drawn by George Gibbs from the January 1905 issue of *The Delineator*.

Library and Archives Canada, Amicus No. 9802890

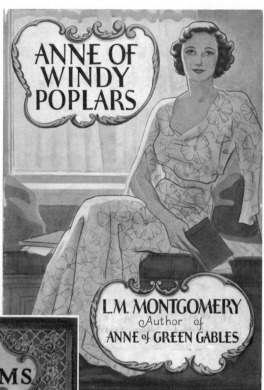

ABOVE: The sequels continued to be popular and the covers reflected the changing fashions of the times. *Anne of Windy Poplars* in 1936.

Library and Archives Canada, Amicus No. 6263926

LEFT: *Anne's House of Dreams* with cover image by M. L. Kirk, the first sequel published in Canada, severing her ties with the Boston L. C. Page Company.

Library and Archives Canada, Amicus No. 3159046

ANNE
of GREEN GABLES

L. M. Montgomery

ABOVE: Ryerson Press was the first Canadian publisher of *Anne of Green Gables*. This popular 1964 edition featured cover art by Hilton Hassell.

Estate of Hilton Hassell, Toronto, Ontario

LEFT: This lithograph poster of the 1919 Hollywood *Anne of Green Gables* starring Mary Miles Minter is one of the few surviving remnants of the popular silent movie.

Library and Archives Canada

The desk of Japanese translator Muraoka with a copy of *Anne of Green Gables* and her own translated manuscript.

Danièle Allard, Halifax, Nova Scotia

Anne of Green Gables, illustrated by Kan Kazama. Tokyo: Shinchosha, 1989.

Library and Archives Canada

Anne of Green Gables: Junior Edition, illustrated by Nippon Animation Co. Tokyo: Shinchosha, 1992.

Library and Archives Canada

FIFTEEN
The Vows Kept for Life

...My arm is getting so wobbly now I must stop. Sorry I had to tell you Anne isn't real. But if she is real to you that is all that matters. She looks very real in the picture "Anne of Windy Willows" and very like what I pictured her.

With all good wishes I am

Yours sincerely

L. M. Montgomery Macdonald

—Letter to Gertrude Ramsey, July 26, 1940[1]

Maud's bond with her fans was emotional and lasted a lifetime and beyond, yet it also had a surprisingly pragmatic side. In the letter cited above, Maud was purposefully enlisting the help of twelve-year-old fan Gertrude Ramsey. Would Gertrude write a letter to Hollywood's R.K.O. Motion Pictures to tell them that she would like to see *Anne's House of Dreams* and *Anne of Ingleside* on the screen, Maud asked. In her letter to Gertrude, Maud included the California address, explaining the lobbying plan to produce movies of these two *Anne* novels: "My agent is trying to get them to produce them and I think letters from my readers might help. Only don't tell them I asked you to do this. (One girl did.)"[2] This correspondence reveals just how deft Maud was in putting her fans to work. Illuminating too is the fact that the author of *Anne of Green Gables* cultivated a bond of secrecy and complicity with her young *Anne* fan.

A key point of Maud's legend was that after the publication of *Anne of Green Gables*, her struggle was over; the seismic change from obscure writer to celebrity and mistress with a maid in her own home was part of her mythology. But the fragmented selves and the labor of reconciling them, as well as the many secrets of her life were also catching up with her in her professional and private lives. In her home life, more than ever, she was in need of daydreams and fantasy. In her relationships and friendships, she was laboring to keep broken things together. Loyal and self-protective Maud was still putting together the scraps and fragments of her own life with effects that would be occasionally tragic.

New Sequels and Secrets

Maud finished her new and still unchristened *Anne* book in the late fall of 1908, but on December 26, L.C. Page & Company announced that since *Anne of Green Gables* "is bound to continue one of the best sellers of the Winter and Spring," "ANNE AT AVONLEA" would not appear before the fall of 1909.[3] And that's when it did appear, with a new redheaded Gibson Girl portrait by George Gibbs on the cover. Grown-up Anne, as Maud had told Ephraim Weber on September 10, the year before, "couldn't be made as quaint and unexpected as the child Anne."[4] Yet there is plenty in the novel to appeal to the reader, including new romantic haunts, such as Hester Gray's garden and the Crystal Lake, a cast of familiar and new characters such as Marilla's adopted twins Davy and Dora Keith, and the adventures of the Avonlea Village Improvement Society. Conscious of her wide American readership, the precocious student poet Paul Irving is a born "Yankee" who comes to live on Prince Edward Island.

Ironically, while Maud was giving her readers the dream of fairy-tale liberation and transformation, nothing had changed to loosen the chains of her own imprisonment. She was angry because she had to decline an invitation to speak in Toronto, for she could not leave her grandmother. She was angry because Grandmother Macneill's own children left all the care for their aging parent to Maud: Aunt Emily, for example, had visited only once in three years. Her feeling toward her own family was "intense, unforgiving, *bitter* resentment."[5] How much she confided in Ewan, who was in Bloomfield, is not clear, but he must have had an inkling. In

February 1909, he sent her Bliss Carman's *The Making of Personality*, the book that had been promoted alongside hers on the Page publishing list. It was a kind of self-help book based on Theosophy, emphasizing harmony of the mental, spiritual, and physical. (Maud would later fictionalize its healing power in the spiritual nature writings of John Foster in her 1926 novel *The Blue Castle*.)[6] Her February 20, 1909, journal entry indicates that she was also feeling guilty about past friendships with girls, confessing to her journal that in her childhood she had formed girl intimacies that did her "no good," in fact did "positive harm." She was determined to form intimacies only with those who were kindred spirits like Frede.[7]

Along with a new book, the golden September of 1909 brought romantic excitement. Enter cousin Oliver Macneill, the wealthy, good-looking, mustached divorcé who had made his fortune in North Dakota. The infatuation that followed reinforces the sense that Maud's feelings for Ewan were comradely rather than passionate during the three years of their engagement. Walking with Oliver among the maples of Lover's Lane, she responded to his caressing tones and physical nearness. Their secret courtship flared up like an intense bright light. On September 21, she recorded in her journal that he kindled in her "a devastating flame of the senses."[8] True to her pattern of compartmentalizing sex, she was warmly responsive when there were safe boundaries that prevented sex from being acted out. On the rebound and in search for a new wife, Oliver proposed marriage. Perhaps sensing her innate desire for freedom, he even proposed all sorts of "absurd" arrangements. Yet the Presbyterian side won the battle and she chastised herself for the "evil demon." She said she knew that she could not marry Oliver. He was too contradictory, she said—a little like herself. He was too unpredictable—too impulsive. She crushed her sexual passion. His departure was followed by months of longing and loneliness. She makes no mention of the web of evasion, lies, and subterfuge she must have used to hide the infatuation from Ewan. Meanwhile, her pen pal Ephraim Weber married schoolteacher Annie Campbell Melrose at Christmas 1909, and wrote to Maud about it in January.[9]

The success of her novel brought financial independence. The royalty income is recorded, in her hand, on the title page of the contract: "Feb. 22. 1909. $1000 / Mar 22. 1909 $729 / Feb 19. 1910. Regular sales etc. $3634.48."[10] The contract for *Anne of Avonlea*, similarly notes the February

1910 royalties: $3698.49. Page had begun selling the serial rights almost immediately, and as a result, *Anne of Green Gables* was published in Canada, from 1909 to 1910, in Montreal, as a serial in *The Family Herald and Weekly Star*.[11] Already Anne had begun to conquer the world. The Swedish translation in 1909 was followed by the Dutch in 1910 and the Polish in 1912, and it was only the beginning.[12]

In 1905 Beatrix Potter, aged thirty-nine and unmarried, used her royalties from her lucrative *Peter Rabbit* tales to purchase Hill Top Farm in the Lake District, which later became a literary site.[13] In her fiction, Maud occasionally dreamed of idealized houses occupied by single women. Yet despite the financial power, like a child she was prohibited from traveling, keeping a maid, or entertaining friends. Readers and visitors who wanted to see how the author of *Anne* lived were carefully kept away from the house, for showing them the destitute homestead was too embarrassing. For now, there was one thing she was able to do with the royalties from *Anne*. She persuaded Frede Campbell, who had returned to teaching after her brief 1907 stint at the Ontario Agricultural College, to give up teaching and get a university degree. At first reluctant, Frede eventually yielded to Maud's plan and studied Household Science at Macdonald College of McGill University in Montreal. The financial gift intensified their friendship, and the Campbells later came to rely on Maud for loans. Clan bonds were strong, and Maud was a generous woman with her new wealth, but one also senses that clinging Maud was buying loyalties, cementing them into the future.

The Making of a Celebrity Author

Meanwhile, Maud was also inventing herself as a public persona. It was a quiet revolution. Her deeply rooted insecurity about not being loved for her own self had left a cavernous emptiness waiting to be filled by the mirage of accolade and fame. Although fundamentally shy, she had all the ingredients for a celebrity.[14] An accomplished elocutionist, she could address groups of people. She loved fashion and photo opportunities. She was a bit of an actress who knew how to mask her feelings. Her already entrenched pattern of evasiveness and obfuscation was also a useful tool. When by

1910, the author of *Anne* leapt from the obscurity of Cavendish onto the world stage, two events were crucial in the birth of the celebrity author.

First she met Earl Grey, the Governor General of Canada during Prime Minister Wilfrid Laurier and Prime Minister Robert Borden's era. A man with ideas for social reform, who also gave his name to the Grey Cup of the Canadian Football League, he was an avid promoter of Canadian culture. Grey was also "an ardent admirer," and when he visited Prince Edward Island in September 1910, he asked to visit with L.M. Montgomery.[15] Although not exactly attractive—balding and with "squirrel teeth," as she described him—he was a good conversationalist who made the shy author feel at home. He invited Maud for a private walk down a winding path at the Andrew Macphail homestead in Orwell. Grey stopped at a little white-painted secluded building and sat down on the step with Maud, oblivious that it was the Macphail outhouse. While they were holding court, a number of ladies from the viceregal party, looking for the W.C., slunk hurriedly away after seeing them sitting there.

Being with people was exhausting to Maud, but being singled out by the statesman "warm[ed] the cockles" of the Macneills, in particular Aunt Mary Lawson, who seemed more excited even than Maud herself.[16] She was gaining the attention of the clan, finally restoring the old glory of the Macneill name.

Even more important in her transformation was a November 1910 visit to L.C. Page in Boston. Grandmother had given permission for her to go on the "business" trip. Accompanied by jolly Stella Campbell, the almost-thirty-six-year-old writer loved the journey, arriving in Boston on a beautiful Sunday morning. For the first time in her life she rode in a car, which had been sent by Mr. L.C. Page. Maud stayed in Page's mansion at 67 Powell Street in Brookline, a wealthy and picturesque town that was also home to modernist poet Amy Lowell.

Boston and the surrounding towns had perhaps more literary shrines per square foot than any other American city. The spirits of Louisa May Alcott, Margaret Fuller, and Harriet Beecher Stowe lived on in their literary homes, which had become tourist sites. Nearby Concord was home to Ralph Waldo Emerson and Nathaniel Hawthorne. South of Concord was Walden Pond with the world's most famous wood cabin home built by nature philosopher Henry David Thoreau. Brooke Farm was the site of

246 • IRENE GAMMEL

another utopian living experiment. Boston was also a city of living writers, among them Jefferson Lee Harbour, the editor of *Youth's Companion* and author of "Lucy Ann" who lived in nearby Dorchester.[17]

When Maud finally met her publisher Louis Page in person, she thought he was "one of the most fascinating men I have ever met."[18] She was captivated by his charisma, wealth, and breeding, although she also claimed to have had suspicions about his character. In his personal library she saw the original Gibbs pastel of Anne. The Pages were aggressively smart, as she noted, but she was a quick study. Throwing her economical instincts overboard, she purchased expensive clothing. Looking into a full-length mirror door in her room, she enjoyed the sight of herself head to toe in full fashionable regalia. Presumably adding to her ebullience was a love note from Frede, signed with her initials FEC on a postcard: "I dwell in Macdonald Halls but the sweetest thing is that you love me still the same."[19] Curiously, this postcard, which adapted the lyrics Maud had used in *Anne of Green Gables*, is found in Maud's journal of 1935. It had been sent from Macdonald Hall in Montreal where Frede was studying courtesy of the *Anne* royalties.

A celebrity in Boston, Maud was fêted as "The Canadian Jane Austen." *The Republic* likened her visit to "Charlotte Bront[ë] coming up to London."[20] In her journal she proudly quoted the journalist who had written that she was "petite, with the fine, delicate features of an imaginative woman."[21] Maud gave interviews. When the *Boston Herald* asked what she thought on the subject of suffrage—an important question considering the activism of, for instance, the College Equal Suffrage League—she answered in her typical exasperating casuistry. She said she did not think very much about it at all, but thought that yes, women should be allowed to vote. She did not think it would effect as great a change as both the champions and adversaries seemed to think, and therefore she confessed that "it does not seem to me worth while to worry about it."[22] This opportunistic answer, that tried to appease both positions at once, was disingenuous considering that she came from a family of politicians, and had listened to the fierce debates regarding suffrage in the Cavendish Literary Society. The pose of the philosophically dreamy gentlewoman was self-serving and yet also characteristic of her hallmark equivocation, trying to accommodate two contradictory positions at once. The newspapers described her as a quiet little woman, childlike, with aquiline features and with little interest in suffrage.

The Boston authors' club hosted a reception in her honor at the Kensington Hotel. Maud's gown "shimmered and dazzled," as she later quoted the newspapers saying in her November 29 journal entry. Here she met, for the first time, many of the authors she had read, including Nathan Haskell Dole, Charles Follen Adams, Helen Winslow—and J. L. Harbour.[23] When she was introduced to Jefferson Lee Harbour, and when she shook his hand, would she not have remembered that his 1903 tale "Lucy Ann" was one of the formula orphan stories that helped inspire her novel's heroine? Would he have dropped a hint or ignored the matter like a gentleman? Poker-faced Maud was mum on this issue in her journal. Given her genius for self-deception, it is entirely possible that she had forgotten about "Lucy Ann." However, exactly two months later, on the evening of Friday, January 27, she wrote, for the first time, a lengthy entry in her journal detailing all the personal and local references for *Anne of Green Gables*. It seems that the author who had reacted so defensively to the Cavendish folk who suggested that she had copied from "real life" now seemed to agree with them. She carefully identified the Cavendish models for Green Gables, Lover's Lane, the Haunted Wood, Lynde's Hollow, the Lake of Shining Waters, and so on in a lengthy entry that would later allow Parks Canada to establish many of the these landmarks as part of the Green Gables tourist site.[24] She also identified Ellen Macneill as her inspiration and talked about "another odd co-incidence," such as the adult Ellen looking the same as the *Anne* cover girl.[25] Conscious of her literary legacy, Maud was now keen on referencing the homegrown roots of *Anne of Green Gables* because they allowed her to prove the originality of her book.

On her last day in Boston she attended a reception at the home of Prince Edward Island–born writer Basil King. By now Maud had upgraded her wardrobe and style. She had her hair done up in town and decorated with tiny pink satin roses, and for the first time she wore a low-necked chiffon evening dress that made her feel almost naked. Never mind that the new velvet slippers she wore were hurting her feet excruciatingly. The next day she had her picture taken for the Press bureau. The pose was decidedly feminine, foregrounding her bosom, while her eyes looked dreamy with hooded lids, her gaze slightly turned away from the camera as if involved

in some imaginative thought. The *Anne* celebrity author was complete—
not exactly beautiful, but feminine, stylish, smart, and imaginative.

Ending her trip on a high note, she had also become caught in Page's
web. Against her better judgment, having received information regarding
Page's dubious business ethics, she signed a new contract binding herself
for five more years to Page. Why? Reluctant to break the spell of his personal charm, she also felt obliged to sign, having stayed in Page's lavish
home as a guest. Moreover, she had never learned the art of friendly sparring with an adversary, an art Ed Simpson might have taught her. A
lifelong habit of evading unpleasant truths caught up with her, as she
chose to ignore warning signs, committing herself to another long contract with a publisher she knew to be exploitative. On the day of her
departure, with the new contract signed and sealed, Louis Page took
Maud to the train, where a delegation of the Canadian and
Intercontinental clubs said goodbye with yellow chrysanthemums. She
bathed in the feeling of recognition and achievement.

When she arrived at the train station on Prince Edward Island,
George Campbell picked her up on the cold and rattling buggy. Sleet blew
into her face the whole way home.

A Funeral and a Wedding

Four months later, in March 1911, Grandmother Macneill died of pneumonia at the age of almost eighty-seven. Maud cared for her in her final days,
with Grandmother sleeping in the warm kitchen and Maud keeping vigil.
For the first time since their quarrel in the fall 1905, Uncle John came to
visit. Until this moment, he had not spoken with his mother. The Macneill
pride had stood in the way of reconciliation. Aunt Annie Campbell of
Park Corner and Aunt Emily Montgomery of Malpeque arrived. Once
again the parlor was the host for a casket. The loyal woman, who had
been the only mother she had known, lay surrounded by flowers. The
scene uncannily mirrored Clara in her coffin thirty-five years earlier. After
the funeral, Aunt Annie and Aunt Emily helped disperse their mother's
possessions. Maud had only a few days to vacate the premises. For the first

time since the old homestead was built it stood empty—no light shining from the kitchen window. The home fire had finally gone out. It would remain a ghost house until Uncle John tore it down in April 1920. Taking the belongings that could be fitted into a little room, she found a temporary home in Park Corner, which had always been a second home to her. Grieving the loss of Grandmother Macneill and her beloved home, she was now a lonely vagrant.

By this time Ewan Macdonald had lived away from Cavendish for five years. A year earlier he had assumed a presbytery in Leaskdale and Zephyr in Ontario and their relationship had assumed the form of a correspondence, like the ones she cultivated with Ephraim and several others. Maud rushed to fill the vacuum in her life, never experiencing the opportunities of freedom, travel, and purchasing a home. A date was set; she and Ewan would marry on July 5. Frede rushed back from Montreal to help her with the preparations. The excitement of being a bride gripped her. Frede and Stella took pictures of Maud's wedding trousseau purchased in Montreal and Toronto, pictures she would later put in her journal in lieu of a wedding photo. Her wedding dress of white silk crêpe de soie with pearl beading can be seen today at her birthplace in New London. The local newspapers announced the event—interestingly with the same misspelling of Ewan's name that Maud favored. Evidently she took pride in publicizing her wedding to a respectable member of the community.

At noon on July 5, Maud stood ready in her little room. On her neck she wore a necklace of amethysts and pearls, a gift from Ewan. In her arms lay a bouquet of roses and lilies-of-the-valley. Stella and the Howatts provided the chorus as thirty-six-year-old Maud descended the stairs on the arm of Uncle John Campbell, Frede's father. Ewan Macdonald, just two weeks shy of his forty-first birthday, waited for her in the parlor, along with friends, neighbors, and the Reverend John Stirling of Cavendish. In *Anne's House of Dreams*, Maud interestingly shifts the focus to Gilbert's feelings at the very moment he first spies Anne in her bridal gown. "She was his at last, this evasive, long-sought Anne, won after years of patient waiting.... Was he worthy of her? Could he make her as happy as he hoped? If he failed her—if he could not measure up to her standard of manhood—then, as she held out her hand, their eyes met and all doubt was swept away in a glad certainty."[26] If Maud had the same expectations for Ewan, it was a great deal of pressure, given her volatile mood swings and exceedingly high ideal of manhood. Several men had already failed the test.

Frede's wedding dinner was sumptuous, showing off the latest Household Science skills. Yet when Maud sat down by her husband's side, something in her revolted and doubt asserted itself. "I felt a sudden horrible inrush of *rebellion* and *despair*. I *wanted* to *be free!*" Having lived in bondage for several years, she now felt again "a hopeless prisoner."²⁷ She felt like tearing off her wedding ring and freeing herself—but of course, the Presbyterian in her asserted control. How hard rebellious Maud had to work to make these feelings subside, we do not know. It is fascinating, though, that there is no wedding photograph. The photograph taken of them during their honeymoon anticipates many other photographs taken of the middle-aged couple. The body language is stiff and awkward. Each faces the camera with a smile, each proudly and distinctly connecting with the camera but not with each other. There is a safe distance between the two.

Maud's royalties would augment Ewan's minister's salary for the next three decades, and allow the couple some luxuries including cars and trips. Ewan typically served as the chauffeur, the role of escort that Maud had always found useful with men. Her royalties also paid for the three-month wedding trip from early July to late September, which took them to the literary shrines of Scotland and England—Scott's Abbotsford, J. M. Barrie's Kirriemuir, Charlotte Brontë's Haworth, Wordsworth's Lake Windermere. She was pleasing herself with this journey and she was in her element. The journey became a major part of her legend as a writer, as readers of *The Alpine Path* know well.²⁸ In her journal she even confessed to the romantic pleasure of "a little bit of 'honeymooning'" sitting alone with Ewan above the water in the green seclusion of Buttermere Lake.²⁹ But she never said a word about the physical side of their relationship, signaling disappointment in her characteristic way: first through silence and in later years through unfavorable comparisons with Herman Leard. In Scotland, they met George MacMillan, "a slight, fair, nice-looking man."³⁰ Maud was relieved to have found a good conversationalist. Walking ahead with George, Maud left Ewan to entertain George's fiancée Miss Allan, who later complained that Maud monopolized George with discussions about literature. In Edinburgh, she suffered from cystitis. In London, for the first time, Maud saw "a flying machine soaring across the sunset sky like a huge bird."[31] In Dunwich, on the crumbling Suffolk coast, she saw her Grandmother's old Woolner House, a building of red brick surrounded by trees and with a garden in the front. It was like coming home. Suddenly she could visualize the childhood of Grandmother Macneill, when twelve-year-old Lucy was growing up and leaving this home behind to go to Canada. As she was hoping to become a mother herself, she was connecting with the woman who had been her reserved yet loyal mother.

The House of Dreams

Another snapshot followed a year later. Frede was in the Leaskdale Manse, helping Maud with the birth of her first son. Frede took to Chester as if he was her own. Happy Maud noted in her journal on September 22, 1912: "Frede and I work together in beautiful concord and at last I have the home I had dreamed of having."[32] A photo of the Macdonald dinner table pictures the marriage idyll in a staged photograph: Maud in the lead role in foreground but looking wan and tired; Frede, glowing and smiling, as if she were the proud mother sitting beside Ewan, and Ewan holding the baby yet slightly out of focus. Perhaps the perfect marriage included Frede, just as it included motherhood. "Motherhood is *heaven*," claimed Maud who was remarkably uninhibited in detailing the bodily changes and processes of pregnancy and childbirth.[33] As for married life, it was not the rosy dream she had dreamed as a teenager. As she wrote to her friend Fannie Wise, seven months after the wedding, she had "learned to find happiness in the small sweet things of 'the trivial round and the common task.'"[34]

In the following years, the most contented ones of her marriage, we see a woman addicted to activity, running a home, caring for two sons, fulfilling her duties as the minister's wife, while also maintaining an impressive creative productivity and public presence. Up to 1911, she had authored four books—*Anne of Green Gables*, *Anne of Avonlea*, *Kilmeny of the Orchard*, and *The Story Girl*. Between 1911 and 1939, she would write *Chronicles of Avonlea*, *The Golden Road*, *Anne of the Island*, *Anne's House of Dreams*, *Rainbow Valley*, *Further Chronicles of Avonlea*, *Rilla of Ingleside*, *Emily of New Moon*, *Emily Climbs*, *The Blue Castle*, *Emily's Quest*, *Magic for*

Marigold, A Tangled Web, Pat of Silver Bush, Mistress Pat, Anne of Windy Poplars, Jane of Lantern Hill, and *Anne of Ingleside*—in addition to thousands of pages of journal, memoir, personal correspondence, verse, and hundreds of short stories.

Maud never had the daughter she desired, and the life of her fictional daughter Anne was determined by her publishing marriage with L. C. Page. While their correspondence no longer exists, snippets of it survive in court documents in the Library and Archives of Canada and they show how aggressively L. C. Page was assuming paternity of Anne. The documents reveal how strongly and persistently L. C. Page urged Maud to write a third Anne book, what would become *Anne of the Island,* and how strongly she resisted. In fact, when she worked on putting together the 1912 collection of early stories *Chronicles of Avonlea,* his urgent pressuring to "bring in our dear Anne as much as possible" shows her publisher to have been an active partner in the production of Anne for selling purposes:

> Please do your very best to have Anne appear in as many of the stories as possible, even if she only speaks 'My lord, the carriage waits.' But, of course, the idea will be to have her a real character in all of the stories, and she should certainly be at least mentioned in all of them. It will make a tremendous difference in the success of the book.[35]

In 1915, *Anne of the Island* delved into Anne Shirley's college years, again a topic suggested by Louis Page as early as 1910, but resisted by Maud. She wrote "Anne III," as the Great War was raging in Europe, finishing it just before she turned forty. She dedicated the novel

> TO
> ALL THE GIRLS ALL OVER THE WORLD
> WHO HAVE 'WANTED MORE' ABOUT
> ANNE.[36]

As a student at Redmond College in Kingsport, Anne shares a house with Priscilla (Prissy) Grant, Philippa (Phil) Gordon, and Stella Maynard. The ideal of the independent bachelor girls living together in one household with a housekeeper had been laid out in "The Bachelor Girl" in *Godey's Lady's Book* in November 1893.[37] In the novel, Diana marries Fred Wright in a June wedding, while Anne Shirley graduates with a B.A. with honors in English Literature—the dream Maud had for herself and realized in part by giving Frede a university education (Frede completed a vocational program at college, but did not study toward a B.A. at university). The novel ends with Anne's engagement to Gilbert Blythe. No sooner were they engaged than Page pressured Maud to write about Anne's married life. By the time Maud wrote *Anne's House of Dreams*, with its focus on marriage and motherhood, she was contemplating her divorce from L. C. Page.

She finished the inspired *Anne's House of Dreams* in a record writing time of six months, despite the clouds of the war and Page's threats of legal action, should she choose to leave L. C. Page and take *Anne* to a new publisher. Maud was asserting her rights with the help of her new agent, John McClelland. She had joined the Author's League of America and was planning to achieve better royalty conditions for *Anne's House of Dreams*. Carole Gerson, who has studied L. C. Page's business practices and the complex legal wrangles involving his authors, concludes that L. M. Montgomery's complaints about the Page Company's exploitative business practices were more than justified and consistent with the problems encountered by other authors.[38] In 1913, for instance, Louis Page had begun cultivating a competing juvenile series, Eleanor H. Porter's *Pollyanna*, whose central character was, like Anne Shirley, an irrepressibly optimistic orphan and a force of exuberant happiness. Not only was the novel and its sequel *Pollyanna Grows Up* (1915) a direct competitor to *Anne*, but Page turned the character into a franchise. At least eleven more sequels were written not by Eleanor Porter, but by other authors. "Glad Clubs" sprang up, followed by numerous adaptations including a silent Hollywood movie in 1920 starring Mary Pickford and, eventually, a Disney movie in 1960 starring Hayley Mills. The L. C. Page Papers at the New York Public Library reveal that in 1960 Disney turned down a proposed film version of *Anne* with the rationale that it was too similar to the *Pollyanna* story. Page treated Anne as a cheap popular book, a franchise like *Pollyanna*. Meanwhile, Maud was concerned with her literary legacy.

In January 1918, after publishing *Anne's House of Dreams* with McClelland and Stewart in Canada and Stokes in the US, Maud squared off with her former publisher in a Boston court. She had sued Page for unpaid royalties.[39] They each took the box and not surprisingly, Maud was a superb witness. She settled with Page for $18,000, signing over all the rights to *Anne of Green Gables* and earlier sequels to Page. But in early 1919, immediately after settling, Page sold the film rights to RKO for $40,000. It was a devastating blow, but a minor event compared to another life tragedy unfolding in Montreal.

From Boston, Maud rushed by train to Montreal where, in the early morning hours of January 25, 1919, Frede Campbell lay dying of the Spanish flu. When she passed, Maud was by her side. She was devastated. Maud's beloved companion had been a fixture of the household, accepted by Ewan as she had been by Grandmother Macneill, spending her vacation there and writing regularly when she was not. Maud mourned her as more than a friend and a cousin. She mourned the loss of a life partner, wishing that Frede had left a child for her to raise.[40] Intensely loyal Maud would grieve for the rest of her life, her love and loss fueling the idealization of Frede, whose memory filled the growing emotional void of Maud's life. As if the event had unhinged their lives, just a few months later, Ewan suffered a mental breakdown.

Keeping Vows

In 1919, a dark cloud began to settle over Maud's domestic happiness, as the delicate balance of romantic, family, and professional life began to crumble. Writing in her journal on September 1, 1919, Maud charged that Ewan had intentionally hidden his psychological condition before they were married. (Divorce should be allowed in cases of incurable insanity, she said on October 18, 1923.[41]) Yet in truth, her own consistent pattern of refusing to see what she did not like to see was probably equally responsible, a truth she failed to accept. Nor had she herself been entirely truthful regarding her own emotional stability or the complex motivations that prompted her to marry him. Even though she liked to cast herself in the role of martyr, she had never been too sympathetic with a friend's suffering. And there was no Frede to provide emotional sustenance, although the boyishly handsome and charming Reverend Edwin Smith and other friends occasionally took on the role of mediators. For the rest of his life, as we know well from Maud's journal, Ewan would suffer from attacks of severe depression and phobia, accompanied by headaches and insomnia; during these attacks he believed he was destined for hell and damnation.

In February 1920, Maud fumed when she saw Hollywood's silent movie version of *Anne of Green Gables* at the Regent Theatre in Toronto.[42] Sugary-sweet seventeen-year-old Mary Miles Minter starred as Anne and said it was her favorite role. Library and Archives Canada holds two lithograph posters that show Minter wearing a shawl and holding a parasol (evocative of *Rebecca of Sunnybrook Farm*), looking a little like Mary Pickford. Maud was furious about the changes. At Anne's graduation, the Stars and Stripes were prominently displayed. In one scene Anne appears at the door of her school, "a shotgun in hand, standing off a crowd of infuriated villagers who were bent on mobbing her because she had whipped one of her pupils!"[43] Coincidentally, as Maud learned years later, Mary Minter's career ended in scandal and notoriety when director William Desmond Taylor was found murdered in his Hollywood home in 1922, a crime that still remains unsolved. In the course of the investigation it was discovered that Mary Miles Minter, who was drawn to older film directors as father figures, had loved the married director "not wisely but too well," as Maud would write.[44] Ironically, like Evelyn Nesbit, Mary Miles could no longer be cast as the innocent child waif. Her career was over and the movie itself has disappeared.

There was more to make Maud's temper flare up. Without her permission, L. C. Page had published *Further Chronicles of Avonlea* using earlier, discarded stories. He had boldly put a red haired girl on the cover, insinuating that the loosely connected stories were centrally about Anne. He was now tampering with her literary reputation. The writer who had her heroine crack a slate over a boy's head would prove a formidable foe in open combat. In June 1920, the color of Anne's tresses was central to the Boston court case Maud brought against her publisher L. C. Page. During a full day of testimony, Maud and the lawyers wrestled over the meaning of "Titian red." Maud insisted that she had had in mind "a sort of flame-red," whereas the other side argued that Anne's hair was "dark red."[45] These legal battles would go on until March 1925, when the Supreme Court of Massachusetts decided in her favor. Page knew that most women would submit rather than go to the law, she wrote to George MacMillan in February 1929. "But I come of a different breed of cats."[46]

On November 29, 1934, just one day before her sixtieth birthday, Maud saw the Hollywood *Anne of Green Gables* in sound in Toronto. She liked the movie and the actress Dawn O'Day. She was pleased that Prince Edward Island and Canada were represented. That same evening, as relayed in detail in chapter one of this volume, Maud disclosed in her journal that Anne's face was based on Evelyn Nesbit's, who coincidentally had published her memoir *Prodigal Days: The Untold Story* that year. As to how much Maud actually knew concerning the model's identity, she took that secret—like the story of the hair dye—to her grave.

By this time Maud, a grandmother, had reached the zenith of her remarkable but fluctuating career. L. M. Montgomery's work continued to be popular, but during an era of buoyant Canadian nationalism, the gods of the literary establishment were suspicious of success achieved south of the border. Over the next decades, they also successfully purged the canon of anything they regarded as feminine or sentimental. Meanwhile, Maud fought back by raging against the "common rut of modern fiction with its reeking atmospheres of brothel and latrine."[47] While new generations of readers embraced *Anne* in Canada, the United States, Britain, Australia, Poland, and other countries, it would take until the mid-1980s for her fiction to find academic appreciation in the author's own country.

In 1935 Maud settled in Toronto in her own home on 210 Riverside Drive at the Humber River. Sadly, it was not an inspired or happy home. Increasingly dependent on heavy medication, Maud and Ewan seemed to reinforce rather than alleviate each other's depressions. "Takes fractious spells occasionally, but mostly he's just vacant and good humoured and harmless," Maud had written in *Anne's House of Dreams* about Dick Moore, where Leslie Moore is living in a nightmarish marriage. "That's the burden Leslie has had to carry for eleven years—and all alone."[48] Her spiritual home and refuge, even after almost three decades in Ontario, was still Prince Edward Island. During her frequent visits, she appeared to the Islanders as a famous, bejeweled woman, touring in a car. "She seemed as if she thought she was a little better than the rest of us," said Keith Webb, recalling her visits to Cavendish.[49] She always carried a little notebook, still jotting down impressions, phrases, jokes, and characters for future use in her books. As if she was crawling back into the safety of her own fiction, she would often stay at "Green Gables," the home of Myrtle Macneill Webb (Keith's mother)—the very house on which she had modeled the home of Matthew and Marilla Cuthbert years earlier. Maud would sleep in the upstairs room, what Ernest Webb (Myrtle's husband) called "Anne's room"—a bizarre blending of fact and fiction. In 1936, to mark one of her visits, she placed a postcard of "'Green Gables' Cavendish P.E. Island" in her journal. The house onto which she had projected her feelings of home would be maintained by the Canadian Government as a centerpiece of the new national park, with Ernest Webb as the first park warden.[50] Published in 1936, *Anne of Windy Poplars* offered a glimpse of Green Gables that merged with the postcard view of Webb's Green Gables, now part of the national park. The fairies had disappeared from the noisy world, she said, but they were still alive on Prince Edward Island. It was a world filled with "home-y ghosts—my ain folk." It was still home. She walked through Lover's Lane, which had never lost its magic. "I am always young back there," she noted in her journal.[51]

In 1938, Maud, along with the rest of the world, felt a new wave of worry after Hitler annexed Austria. On September 12, a hot and muggy day in Toronto, she began to write *Anne of Ingleside*. (Maud had written *Rilla of Ingleside* in 1921, focusing on the Great War, when Anne was in her fifties, and in *Anne of Ingleside* she returned to a chronological time prior to *Rilla*, when Anne is in her thirties.) *Anne of Ingleside* was Maud's final Anne novel published during her lifetime and she chose to focus on Anne as a young mother.[52] Once more, one last time, she was roaming in the world of Lover's Lane, the Haunted Wood, Idlewild, the Birch Path. She was living in all the spots she loved. It had been a year and a half since she had last written a line of fiction. "But I can *still* write," she noted in her journal that night; "And I was suddenly *back in my own world* with all my dear Avonlea and Glen folks again."[53]

One last time, she conjured up the world of Anne and Diana meeting in the old haunts as adult women and young mothers. "Anne...but we *have* kept our old 'solemn vow and promise,' haven't we?" says Diana. "Always...and always will," answers Anne, now the mother of five children. "Anne's hand found its way into Diana's." Quietly and silently they walk home, "their old unforgotten love burning in their hearts."[54]

Dramatis Personae

Readers may wonder about what happened to some of the dramatis personae in Maud's life:

The Page brothers' conservative taste in literature made readers turn elsewhere. Their company's revenues decreased. Following the drawn-out court battle against L. M. Montgomery, George died in 1927. Louis sent a telegram to Maud strongly insinuating that she was responsible. Meanwhile Louis's propensity for philandering and drinking caught up with him. His third wife, Mildred, whom Maud had met during her visit to Boston, divorced him. And yet he outlived L. M. Montgomery by a decade and a half, dying in 1956. A year later Farrar, Straus, and Giroux purchased the L. C. Page Company but discontinued its imprint in 1980.

Evelyn Nesbit became notorious when on the night of June 25, 1906, her husband Harry K. Thaw shot and killed her former lover Stanford White. Dubbed the Murder of the Century, the story was front-page news around the world—sparking a tabloid frenzy of unprecedented proportions. The trial began in New York on January 23, 1907, but it was Evelyn's testimony in February that brought the frenzy to its climax. It was front-page news even in Cavendish, with regular updates that stretched to early March when the local newspapers reported about the intimate details of Evelyn's seamy life with Stanford White: "Seated in the big witness chair and looking like a sweet little school girl, Evelyn Nesbitt [sic] Thaw today denounced Stanford White as her betrayer,"

The Charlottetown Daily Patriot reported on February 11. "Her thrilling story of how pitfalls are arranged by great and rich men to trap young and pretty girls caused the flesh of every man and woman in court to creep."[1] On February 23, an illustration of Evelyn Nesbit in the witness box graced the cover of the *Charlottetown Guardian*.[2] Garbed in a demure dress with high collar, the twenty-two-year-old looked very different from the sensuous portrait that Maud had clipped from *The Metropolitan* fewer than four years earlier. Whether or not Maud made the connection between the picture in her room that had provided the face for Anne and the woman in the center of the scandal, we have no conclusive evidence one way or the other.

Evelyn survived neurasthenia, morphine addiction, a suicide attempt, and a second marriage ending in divorce in 1933. Against all odds, the model did achieve a semblance of a "normal" life. During the mid-twenties she opened a tearoom on West Fifty-Second Street near Broadway. A photograph shows her in her mid-thirties, wearing a housewife's gingham dress, ready to serve her customers in her homey little tearoom. In the concluding lines of her 1934 memoir *Prodigal Days: The Untold Story*, the single mother sounded a note of maternal happiness: "And having successfully raised Russell, I no longer feel that I have lived in vain."[3] The notorious woman had found more happiness in her quiet family life than Maud had. Sculpting and teaching ceramics, Evelyn also served as the adviser for the 1955 movie, *The Girl in the Red Velvet Swing* (with Joan Collins playing Evelyn). Outliving her notoriety, Evelyn died at the age of eighty-two in Santa Monica, California.

Ellen Macneill, the Nova Scotia orphan who provided the spark for *Anne of Green Gables*, married Garfield Stewart and lived first in Dundas, in the eastern part of Prince Edward Island, and then in Brackley Point. She raised a large family of twelve children, whom she introduced to the *Anne* books. According to her daughter Ruth, Ellen "always wondered" if *Anne of Green Gables* was based on her, but it was not until four years before her death in 1974 that she was gratified to receive the long-awaited confirmation. Francis Bolger's *The Years Before Anne* cited Maud's unpublished journal and identified Pierce Macneill's little orphan girl as an important inspiration for the novel.[4] The journals also indicate that

Rachel Lynde had been named after Ellen's mother Rachael. In fact, in the table of contents of the original edition of *Anne* book, Rachel Lynde's name is spelled Rachael, like Ellen's mother, a mistake that was repeated in several printings. Ellen died in 1978.

Ephraim Weber attended Queen's University in Kingston, and pursued graduate studies toward a Ph.D. at the University of Chicago. His subject, German Literature, turned out to be a wild-goose chase because of the impending World War I and anti-German sentiment. In the summer of 1928, after three decades of corresponding, Maud and Ephraim first met face to face in Norval. The meeting was awkward. "We almost called for pen and ink," recalls Ephraim: "The face-to-face way wasn't the same thing."[5] They stayed pen pals for the rest of her life. Ephraim died in 1956. The high school teacher and pacifist quietly penned a satiric novel entitled "Aunt Rachel's Nieces," which has been discovered only recently.

Ed Simpson was a successful minister in Wisconsin and retired in the mid 1930s after being diagnosed with diabetes. In November 1937, he visited Toronto and rang up sixty-three-year-old Maud to introduce his young second wife Mary Fiske. They met for tea in his hotel. Although old and wrinkled and sick, he talked as incessantly as ever. Maud was offended that he monopolized the conversation, never mentioning her family or literary success. It was the last time they saw each other and, sadly, the dynamics between these two proud opponents were unchanged. Anne's words to Gilbert, "we've been good enemies," seemed prophetic.[6] In real life, Maud was unable to overcome her resentment. Maud's comment in her journal that night contained vicious poison: she liked Ed's wife, she noted, but could not imagine "why she ever wanted to marry a broken-down invalid like Ed."[7]

Oliver Macneill: The summer after their frantic courtship, Oliver returned, but Maud's feelings had cooled. She tried to pass him on to some eligible Cavendish women, Campsie Clark and Lucy MacLure, but her efforts at matchmaking produced only ill will in many corners. Oliver married Mabel Lea of Summerside, one of Maud's former Belmont pupils. He told Maud diplomatically that his bride reminded him a little of her.[8] Twenty years later, in 1923, Maud met him again during a visit to Prince Edward Island and found him very changed, but did not provide any details. He was living with his wife in Summerside, and Maud found his wife to be the best-dressed woman there.[9]

Uncle John Franklin Macneill died in 1936, three years after his wife Annie. Their house, the old homestead site, and the surrounding fields were passed on to his son. Today his grandson John and his wife Jennie still live in Uncle John's old house. After reading Maud's journals, they lovingly restored the ruins of the homestead, planted flower beds, and nurtured the old apple trees. A bookstore displays the old post office scales. Jennie and John retell the stories of Lucy Maud Montgomery and her love for the old homestead, as she told them in her journal. In 2005, the homestead property was designated a Canadian National Historic Site. A replica of it is exhibited in Robertson Library at the University of Prince Edward Island. Also held at the university is a painting of the homestead by James Lumbers, entitled *Twilight Sorceries*.

Ewan Macdonald retired from the ministry in Norval in 1935. He died one year after Maud in 1943 and was buried beside her in the Cavendish cemetery, overlooking the sea. Today, however, the simple grave also overlooks a gas station and a motel. Curiously, on the gravestone Ewan's name is spelled in two ways, the correct way "REV. EWEN MACDONALD," and the way Maud misspelled his name: "LUCY MAUD MONTGOMERY / MACDONALD / WIFE OF / EWAN MACDONALD." The latter erroneous way has since been adopted by biographers, editors, and scholars for consistency's sake, underscoring the power of Maud's pen in transforming the "real." Maud's sons **Chester** became a lawyer and **Stuart** a medical doctor.

Frede Campbell made good use of the university education provided by Maud. She spent two years at Macdonald College studying Household Science before accepting a one-year position at Red Deer Ladies College in Alberta in the winter of 1913. In the fall she returned to Macdonald College as a demonstrator to the Homemakers Clubs of Quebec. Maud was happy to have her relatively near Leaskdale. After several unhappy love affairs, Frede became a war bride in May 1917, marrying Cameron

MacFarlane in a ceremony that did not include Maud. Maud was at her bedside when she died in January 1919 and also organized the funeral and cremation. Frede's sister Stella married in 1919 and settled in Los Angeles, California. At age 41, she gave birth to a son and named him Ewan after Ewan Macdonald.[10]

Abbreviations

Archives

AOT — Archives of Ontario, Toronto

CTA — City of Toronto Archives

CCAG — Confederation Centre Art Gallery, Charlottetown, Prince Edward Island (*Anne of Green Gables* manuscript, scrapbooks)

HRM — Hudson River Museum, Yonkers, NY (Eickemeyer Letters)

LAC — Library and Archives of Canada, Ottawa, Ontario (L.C. Page contracts; Ephraim Weber and G.B. MacMillan letters)

MLC — Modern Literature and Culture Research Centre, Ryerson University, Toronto

NYPL — New York Public Library (magazines)

PEIPA — Prince Edward Island Public Archives and Records Office, Charlottetown (the minute book: Cavendish Literary Society)

PHC/SNMAH — Photographic History Collection, Smithsonian National Museum of American History, Washington, D.C. (Eickemeyer Papers)

UGA — University of Guelph Archives, Guelph, Ontario (L.M. Montgomery Collection)

UPEI — University of Prince Edward Island (Penzie Macneill letters)

TRL — Toronto Reference Library (magazines)

Names

EM — Ewan Macdonald

EN — Evelyn Nesbit

EW — Ephraim Weber

FEC — Fredericka (Frede) Elmanstine Campbell

GBM — George Boyd MacMillan

LMM — L.M. Montgomery

PM — Penzie Macneill

Titles of Books, Manuscripts, and Journals

AA — L.M. Montgomery. *Anne of Avonlea*. New York: Bantam-Seal, 1984.

AGG — L.M. Montgomery. *Anne of Green Gables*. New York: Bantam Books, 1992.

AAGG — L.M. Montgomery. *The Annotated Anne of Green Gables*. Ed. Wendy E. Barry, Margaret Anne Doody, and Mary E. Doody Jones. New York: Oxford UP, 1997.

AHD   L. M. Montgomery. *Anne's House of Dreams*. New York: Bantam Books, 1998.

AP   L. M. Montgomery. *The Alpine Path: The Story of My Career*. Markham, ON: Fitzhenry & Whiteside, 1917.

CCL   *Canadian Children's Literature / Littérature canadienne pour la jeunesse*

EC   L. M. Montgomery. *Emily Climbs*. Toronto: McClelland and Stewart, 1989.

ENM   L. M. Montgomery. *Emily of New Moon*. Toronto: McClelland and Stewart, 1989.

GGL   *The Green Gables Letters from L. M. Montgomery to Ephraim Weber, 1905–1909*. Ed. Wilfrid Eggleston. Ottawa: Borealis, 2001.

HT   *Harvesting Thistles: The Textual Garden of L. M. Montgomery, Essays on her Novels and Journals*. Ed. Mary Henley Rubio. Guelph, ON: Canadian Children's Press, 1994.

ILLMM   *The Intimate Life of L. M. Montgomery*. Ed. Irene Gammel. Toronto: University of Toronto Press, 2005.

LMMCC   *L. M. Montgomery and Canadian Culture*. Ed. Irene Gammel and Elizabeth Epperly. Toronto: University of Toronto Press, 1999.

MA   *Making Avonlea: L. M. Montgomery and Popular Culture*. Ed. Irene Gammel. Toronto: University of Toronto Press, 2002.

MDMM   *My Dear Mr. M: Letters to G. B. MacMillan from L. M. Montgomery*. Ed. Francis W. P. Bolger and Elizabeth R. Epperly. Toronto: Oxford University Press, 1992.

PD   Evelyn Nesbit. *Prodigal Days: The Untold Story of Evelyn Nesbit*. New York: Julian Messner, Inc., 1934. Reprinted by Deborah Dorian Paul, 2004.

SJ   *The Selected Journals of L. M. Montgomery, v. 1: 1889–1910, v. 2: 1910–1921, v. 3: 1921–1929, v. 4: 1929–1935, v. 5: 1935–1942*. Ed. and intro. Mary Rubio and Elizabeth Waterston. Toronto: Oxford University Press, 1985, 1987, 1992, 1998, 2004.

SSLT   *Such a Simple Little Tale: Critical Responses to L. M. Montgomery's Anne of Green Gables*. Ed. Mavis Reimer. Metuchen, NJ: The Children's Literature Association and The Scarecrow Press, 1992.

UJ   L. M. Montgomery. Unpublished Journals in 10 Legal Size Ledgers, 1889–1942. Archival and Special Collections, University of Guelph Archives.

YBA   Francis W. P. Bolger, *The Years Before 'Anne.'* Halifax: Nimbus, 1991.

A Note on the Sources

Unpublished material by L. M. Montgomery is drawn from the University of Guelph Archives, unless otherwise indicated in endnotes.

Endnotes

Prologue

1 AGG, ch. 5, pp. 38–39.

2 See the essays in my edited volume *The Intimate Life of L. M. Montgomery* theorizing Maud's strategies of life writing including journals, photography, letters, and scrapbooks. Selections of the journals were published under the meticulous editorship of Mary Rubio and Elizabeth Waterston as *The Selected Journals of L. M. Montgomery, Volumes 1–5*, covering the years from 1889 to 1942; selections of the scrapbooks were published digitally in *Picturing a Canadian Life: L. M. Montgomery's Personal Scrapbooks and Book Covers.* http://lmm.confederationcentre.com/

3 LMM, Feb. 8, 1932, SJ 4, p. 165.

4 AP, p. 72.

Chapter 1

1 LMM, May 3, 1908, UJ 2, pp. 448–49.

2 LMM, May 3, 1908, UJ 2, p. 450.

3 LMM, May 3, 1908, UJ 2, p. 457.

4 LMM, May 3, 1908, UJ 2, pp. 449–50.

5 LMM, May 3, 1908, UJ 2, p. 450–51

6 LMM, Aug. 1, 1892, UJ 1, p. 186.

7 LMM, Aug. 1, 1892, UJ 1, p. 187.

8 LMM, Aug. 1, 1892, UJ 1, p. 178.

9 LMM, Aug. 1, 1892, UJ 1, p. 178; AGG, ch. 20, p. 166, p. 165.

10 LMM, May 3, 1908, UJ 2, p. 450.

11 LMM, May 3, 1908, UJ, 2 p. 451.

12 Ella Rodman Church and Augusta De Bubna, "Tam! The Story of a Woman," *Godey's Lady's Book* (March 1884), p. 238.

13 LMM, Mar. 21, 1901, SJ 1, pp. 258–59.

14 [Chelifer], "Gilbert Parker's Canadian Fiction," *Godey's Lady's Book* 130 (1895/1896), p. 656.

15 See Nick Mount, *When Canadian Literature Moved to New York* (Toronto: University of Toronto Press, 2005), for an illuminating study on the topic; see also Clarence Karr, *Authors and Audiences: Popular Canadian Fiction in the Early Twentieth Century* (Montreal & Kingston: McGill-Queen's University Press, 2000).

16 LMM, EC, p. 304.

17 LMM, EC, pp. 314–15.

[18] LMM to GBM, Dec. 29, 1903, MDMM, p. 2.

[19] LMM, Dec. 3, 1903, SJ 1, p. 290.

[20] LMM to GBM, Dec. 29, 1903, MDMM, p. 3.

[21] LMM, July 16, 1925, SJ 3, p. 240; this entry gives a full account of *A Golden Carol*. See also Cecily Devereux's scholarly edition of *Anne of Green Gables* (Peterborough: Broadview Press, 2004), pp. 18–19, pp. 385–90, for a discussion of the Pansy book influences in AGG.

[22] LMM, Nov. 29, 1934, SJ 4, p. 326.

[23] LMM, Nov. 29, 1934, SJ 4, pp. 325–26.

[24] LMM, Nov. 29, 1934, SJ 4, p. 325.

Chapter 2

[1] AGG, ch. 2, pp. 11–12.

[2] Rudolf Eickemeyer Jr.'s Campbell studio's address for the period is found in an advertisement in the Photographers' column of *The Theatre Magazine* 2 (1902), Advertisement section, TRL. The ad reads: "The Campbell Studio, under the management of Rudolf Eickemeyer Jr, at 564–568 Fifth Avenue, New York."

[3] Rudolf Eickemeyer Papers, HRM, contain a number of articles about the photographer including Sadakichi Hartman, "The Work of Rudolf Eickemeyer, Jr." *The Photo-American* (July 1904), pp. 195–99 (Item No. 576); and Sidney Allen, "Rudolf Eickemeyer, Jr.: An Appreciation," *Photo Era: The American Journal of Photography* 15.3 (Sept. 1905), pp. 79–83.

[4] Mary Panzer, *In My Studio: Rudolf Eickemeyer, Jr. and the Art of the Camera*, Exhibition Catalogue (Yonkers: Hudson River Museum, 1986), p. 63.

[5] EN, PD, p. 7. *Prodigal Days* is a rewritten version of the earlier memoir, which Evelyn had written under her married name Thaw, *The Story of My Life* (London: John Long, [1914]), NYPL Performance Library, Lincoln Centre.

[6] *Portrait of Rudolf Eickemeyer, Jr.*, Photo by Campbell Art Co, ca 1900, Eickemeyer Scrapbooks (PHA05–1231. 2005–30238), PHC/SNMAH.

[7] EN, PD, p. 7.

[8] Postcard featuring EN, Rudolf Eickemeyer scrapbooks, PHC/SNMAH.

[9] EN, PD, p. 23.

[10] "Miss Evelyn Florence," Photo by Rudolf Eickemeyer, Jr., *The Theatre Magazine* 2 (July 1902). TRL.

[11] LMM, Nov. 18, 1901, SJ 1, p. 270.

[12] "Read the Metropolitan Magazine for *September*," *What to Eat* (Sept. 1903), Advertisement section; in the same issue of this periodical, pp. 75–79, appeared LMM's short story "The Minister's Daughter"; The Ryrie-Campbell Collection, L. M. Montgomery Institute, UPEI.

[13] LMM, Apr. 9, 1904, SJ 1, p. 295.

[14] LMM, Aug. 12, 1903, UJ 2, p. 281.

[15] Advertisement from *The College Record* (April 1894), LMM Scrapbook CM 67.5.12, p. 33, CCAG.

[16] "A Portfolio of Portraits [Evelyn Nesbit]," Photo by Rudolf Eickemeyer, Jr., 1901, *Metropolitan Magazine* (Sept. 1903), p. 849, NYPL; pose, tint and size (12 × 15 cm) of the *Metropolitan* Nesbit photo are a perfect match with the original clipping LMM pasted in her manuscript journal on Nov. 29, 1934 (see above).

[17] "Miss Evelyn Nesbitt [sic]," Photo by Rudolf Eickemeyer, Jr. *Metropolitan Magazine* (Sept. 1903), p. 851, NYPL.

[18] Elizabeth Rollins Epperly, *Through Lover's Lane: L. M. Montgomery's Photography and Visual Imagination* (Toronto: University of Toronto Press, 2007), p. 8.

[19] "The Dog at His Master's Grave": Devereux identifies this poem in her Broadview edition of AGG as "A poem by American poet Lydia Howard Huntley Sigourney (1791–1865)."

[20] Milton H. Horowitz, "Adolescent Daydreams and Creative Impulse," *Adolescent Psychiatry: Developmental and Clinical Studies* 22 (1998), p. 10.

Chapter 3

[1] AGG, ch. 30, p. 239.

[2] LMM, Feb. 20, 1904, UJ 2, p. 299.

[3] Sigmund Freud, *Standard Edition of the Complete Psychological Works of Sigmund Freud: Creative Writers and Day-Dreaming*, vol. 9, ed. James Strachey (London: Hogarth Press, 1959), pp. 149–50.

[4] LMM, Feb. 6, 1904, UJ 2, p. 299.

[5] Olivia E. Phillips, "Advice from Everywhere, II. Care of Children," *Godey's Lady's Book* 124 (Feb. 1892), pp. 177–78.

[6] LMM, May 5, 1904, UJ 2, p. 314.

[7] Photo of Hugh John Montgomery (1841–1900), UGA. For biographical details, see Francis W. P. Bolger, YBA, pp. 7–24, and Mary Beth Cavert, "Anne of Green Gables—1908: To the Memory of My Father and Mother. Hugh John Montgomery," *Kindred Spirits* (Spring 1999), pp. 8–10; and (Summer 1999), pp. 10–13.

[8] LMM to Penzie Macneill, Bolger, YBA, p. 92; and LMM to GBM, Dec. 29, 1903, MDMM, p. 2.

[9] LMM, Feb. 1, 1891, SJ 1, p. 45.

[10] Bolger, YBA, p. 119.

[11] AGG ch. 5, p. 41; ch. 6, p. 45, p. 46.

[12] LMM, Feb. 9, 1911, SJ 2, p. 47.

[13] See Bolger, YBA, p. 70, p. 77.

[14] LMM, May 5, 1904, UJ 2, p. 315.

[15] LMM, July 5, 1891, SJ 1, p. 57.

[16] LMM, July 31, 1891, SJ 1, p. 59.

[17] John Keats, *The Examiner* (May 5, 1816), http://www.bl.uk/onlinegallery/features/keats/keatsexaminer.html. See also Sarah S. Uthoff, "Our Kindred Spirits Share," *Kindred Spirits* (Spring 1994), p. 6, and Virginia Careless, "L. M. Montgomery and Everybody Else: A Look at the Books," *Windows and Words: A Look at Canadian Children's Literature in English*, ed. Aïda Hudson and Susan-Ann Cooper (Ottawa: University of Ottawa Press, 2003), pp. 161–65.

[18] LMM, July 5, 1904, UJ 2, pp. 322–24.

[19] LMM, Sept. 29, 1894, SJ 1, p. 121.

[20] See Devereux's 2004 edition of AGG, p. 314, n. 1.

[21] LMM, "A Correspondence and a Climax," *Sunday Magazine* (Aug. 20, 1905), pp. 13–14; reprinted in *Across the Miles: Tales of Correspondence*, ed. Rea Wilmshurst (Toronto: McClelland & Stewart, 1996), p. 6, p. 14.

[22] LMM to EW, GGL, Mar. 7, 1905, p. 25, p. 26, p. 32.

[23] LMM to EW, GGL, Mar. 7, 1905, p. 27.

[24] LMM, *The Blue Castle* (Toronto: McClelland and Stewart, 1926), dedication page.

[25] LMM to EW, Mar. 7, 1905, GGL, pp. 24–25.

[26] AGG ch. 20, p. 163.

[27] LMM, Dec. 20, 1904, UJ 2, p. 336.

[28] George du Maurier, *Trilby: A Novel* (New York: Harper and Brothers, 1894), p. 15.

[29] LMM, Apr. 20, 1904, UJ 2, p. 313.

[30] LMM, Apr. 12, 1903, SJ 1, p. 286.

[31] LMM to GBM, Aug. 2, 1915, MDMM, p. 75. See also Edwin L. Sabin's poem "The Castle in Spain," *Days of Youth*, n.d. p. 6, found among LMM's Magazine Clippings CM 67.5.24, CCAG.

[32] Washington Irving, *Tales of the Alhambra* (Leon: Editorial Everest, 2006), p. 42. See also Epperly, *Through Lover's Lane*, pp. 145–51.

[33] LMM, Feb. 15, 1902, UJ 2, p. 232.

[34] LMM, Oct. 31, 1904, UJ 2, p. 329.

[35] AGG, ch. 1, p. 1.

[36] Tennyson, [Alfred, Lord]. "Song of the Brook." *Pansy Sunday Book* (Boston: Lothrop Publishing Company, 1898), n.p.

[37] The Russell, Russell, and Wilmshurst bibliography (1986) lists 37 stories published in 1903 and 43 in 1904. LMM to EW, Mar. 7, 1905, GGL, p. 27.

Chapter 4

[1] AGG, ch. 5, pp. 39–40.

[2] Margaret Atwood, "Revisiting Anne," LMMCC, pp. 225–26.

[3] See Mary Beth Cavert, "Clara Macneill," *Kindred Spirits* (Winter 1998/1999), p. 9; this short article (pp. 8–10) provides a biographical portrait.

[4] LMM, Jan. 2, 1902, SJ 1, p. 300–3; two photos of Clara Woolner Macneill (1853–1876), portrait and full-body, UGA; portrait reproduced in SJ 1, p. 232, Nr. 64.

[5] LMM, Jan. 2, 1902, SJ 1, p. 300.

[6] Mrs. Theodore W. Birney, "Growing up with One's Children," *The Delineator* (Apr. 1904), p. 681.

[7] LMM, Jan. 2, 1902, SJ 1, p. 300, p. 301.

[8] LMM, Jan. 2, 1902, SJ 1, p. 303.

[9] Alexander Macneill's will, dated January 23, 1897, is displayed in the Bookstore of the Homestead Site, Cavendish, PEI, courtesy of John and Jennie Macneill.

[10] LMM, Dec. 31, 1898, SJ 1, p. 230.

[11] AGG, ch. 5, p. 39.

[12] Boyde Beck and Edward MacDonald, *Everyday and Extraordinary: Almanac of the History of Prince Edward Island* (Charlottetown: PEI Museum and Heritage Foundation, 1999), p. 80.

[13] LMM, Feb. 7, 1905, UJ 2, p. 346.

[14] AGG, ch. 12, p. 86.

[15] LMM, Apr. 14, 1905, UJ 2, p. 358.

[16] The phrase "peg away" is used in letter dated Mar. 7, 1905, in GGL, p. 26.

[17] LMM, "The Understanding of Sister Sara," *The Pilgrim* (Aug. 1905), pp. 11–12; reprinted in LMM, *Across the Miles*, ed. Wilmshurst, p. 45; AGG, ch. 5, p. 39.

[18] LMM, "The Running Away of Chester," *Boys' World* (Nov.–Dec. 1903), reprinted in LMM *Akin to Anne*, ed. Wilmshurst, p. 133; AGG, ch. 6, p. 48.

[19] Louise R. Baker, "An Adopted Daughter," *The Major's Sunshine, The Sunday School Advocate for Boys and Girls* (Jan. 7, 1905), pp. 1–3.

[20] Bessie R. Hoover, "The Sunshine Girl," *The Sunday School Advocate for Boys and Girls* (Mar. 25, 1905), p. 91.

21 Confederation Life Building listed in *City of Toronto Directory, 1905*, pp. 225–26 (Reel 51), CTA. This building housed numerous church organizations and missionary societies including the Presbyterian Home Mission and Widow and Orphan Fund, and the Women's Foreign Missionary Society.

22 Letter no longer extant; LMM summarized it for EW, GGL, p. 26.

23 LMM, "Lavender's Room," *East and West: A Paper for Young Canadians* 3.6 [Toronto] (Feb. 11, 1905), p. 41. LMM Magazine Clippings CM 67.5.24, CCAG.

24 LMM to EW, Mar. 7, 1905, GGL, p. 26.

25 Quoted in Charlotte Gray, *Flint and Feather: The Life and Times of E. Pauline Johnson, Tekahionwake* (Toronto: HarperCollins, 2002), p. 304.

26 Most of her previous and later stories are set in simply generic locations, and some have explicitly U.S. locales, while others have Canadian references. Even some of her later stories from the 1930s have generic locations, which may be surprising to readers given that her work is often assumed to be totally about PEI.

27 LMM, Aug. 16, 1907, SJ 1, p. 330.

28 LMM, Jan. 27, 1911, SJ 2, p. 40.

29 Ruth Gallant interviewed by telephone by Irene Gammel, Oct. 25, 2007. My thanks to Ruth Gallant for making accessible original photography and a copy of the 1900 Census document (see below).

30 Ellen Macneill (1889–1978). Ruth Gallant's information is based on two sources: her mother's own statement that she was not a Barnardo child and on documentation found in Pierce Macneill's home, in particular, a Prince Edward Island Census Record of 1900, in which Ellen Macneill is recorded as having been born in Nova Scotia. John H. Willoughby, *Ellen* (Charlottetown: n.p., 1995), suggests that Ellen was a Barnardo child from England, because adoptions from one province to another were unusual, but provides no source evidence for the claim. In fact, Willoughby admits in the epilogue that "attempts to locate Ellen's roots were unsuccessful" (p. 211); moreover, the facsimile reproduction of the application for a Home Child featured on p. 35 belongs to a different child who is clearly not Ellen.

31 AGG, ch. 1, p. 6.

32 See Willoughby, *Ellen*, pp. 45–47. For more on the Barnardo child, see also Gail Corbett, *Nation Builders: Barnardo Children in Canada* (Toronto: Dundurn Press, 1997, 2003), and Kenneth Bagnell, *The Little Immigrants: The Orphans Who Came to Canada* (Toronto: Dundurn Press, 2001).

33 Willoughby, *Ellen*, p. 38.

34 LMM, Jan. 27, 1911, SJ 2, p. 40.

35 LMM, Jan. 27, 1911, SJ 2, p. 40.

36 Richard Le Gallienne, "Hans Christian Andersen: The Friend of the Children," *The Delineator* (April 1905). TRL.

37 See Lesley Willis's article, "The Bogus Ugly Duckling: Anne Shirley Unmasked," *Dalhousie Review* 56.2 (1976), pp. 246–51.

38 LMM, May 21, 1905, UJ 2, p. 361.

39 LMM, Aug. 16, 1907, SJ 1, p. 330.

Chapter 5

1 AGG, ch. 2, p. 14.

2 LMM describes the scene in her journal on Apr. 18, 1914, SJ 2, p. 147; see also Oct. 18, 1935, SJ 5, p. 41; and LMM, "Is This My Anne?," *The Chatelaine* (Jan. 1935), reprinted in

Deborah Quaile, *L.M. Montgomery: The Norval Years, 1926–1935* (n.p.: Wordbird P, 2006), pp. 171–74.

3   *Anne of Green Gables*, Manuscript, p. 1, CM 67.5.1, CCAG. The quotation transcribes the first draft without the revisions. The manuscript page reveals several additions and amendments that are reflected in the published novel.

4   LMM to GBM, Nov. 9, 1904, MDMM, p. 7. See also LMM's journal entry of Oct. 31, 1904, UJ 2, p. 329, for an almost identical description of the brook.

5   LMM, Dec. 4, 1892, UJ 1, p. 198.

6   Obituary reprinted in *Kindred Spirits* (Dec. 2003); LMM, Oct. 12, 1906, SJ 1, pp. 320–22.

7   LMM, June 21, 1903, ILLMM, p. 81.

8   LMM, Oct. 12, 1906, SJ 1, pp. 320–22.

9   LMM, May 18, 1905, SJ 1, p. 307, and UJ 2, p. 358.

10 LMM, "The Old South Orchard," *The Outing Magazine* 51.4 (Jan. 1908), p. 413. For a discussion of publication delays, see LMM to EW, Apr. 8, 1906, GGL, p. 41.

11 AGG, ch. 2, p. 14.

12 AGG, ch. 2, p. 18.

13 Elizabeth von Arnim, *Elizabeth and her German Garden* (London: Virago Press, 2006), p. 42.

14 LMM, Jan. 27, 1911, SJ 2, p. 40. See also LMM, Sept. 22, 1929, SJ 4, p. 9.

15 AGG, Manuscript, p. 46, CCAG.

16 LMM, May 21, 1905, UJ, p. 361.

17 LMM, "Diana's Wedding Dress," *Farm and Fireside* (Mar. 1902); *Holland's Magazine* reprinted the story in 1912; The Ryrie-Campbell Collection, L.M. Montgomery Institute, UPEI.

18 AGG, ch. 6, p. 49.

19 In AP, pp. 75–76, LMM indicates that the original serial was seven chapters long, but chapter six has, in fact, a perfect tone of conclusion, while chapter seven, "Anne Says Her Prayers," rounds out the Sunday school theme.

20 LMM, "Is this My Anne?" p. 172.

21 AGG, ch. 8, p. 56.

22 On Aug. 16, 1907, SJ 1, p. 331, LMM first noted that she had begun writing the novel "one evening in May" 1905, finishing in January 1906; in her 1917 memoir (AP, p. 72), however, she indicated that she had begun writing in "the spring of 1904" finishing it "in the October of 1905." On LMM's secrecy, see also Cecily Devereux, "'See my Journal for the full story': Fictions of Truth in *Anne of Green Gables* and L.M. Montgomery's Journals," ILLMM, pp. 249–55.

23 LMM to EW, June 28, 1905, GGL, p. 34.

24 LMM to EW, June 28, 1905, GGL, p. 33.

25 Ward MacLeod, "Cut Flowers for Decorative Use in the Home," *The Delineator* (Jan. 1904), p. 155.

26 LMM, Aug. 2, 1931, SJ 4, p. 145.

27 LMM, Feb. 28, 1904, UJ 2, p. 301.

28 LMM, Nov. 22, 1926, SJ 3, p. 317.

Chapter 6

1   AGG, ch. 8, p. 58.

2   M.J. Shepperson, "Envelopes, Friends and Books," *The Ladies' World* [New York] (Oct. 1902), p. 22. In 1893, LMM had published her first poem, "The Violet's Spell" in *The Ladies' World*; see LMM, Sept. 28, 1893, SJ 1, p. 94.

3 Carroll Smith-Rosenberg, "The Female World of Love and Ritual: Relations between Women in Nineteenth Century America," *Signs: Journal of Women in Culture and Society* 1.1 (1975), pp. 1–29.

4 Lillian Faderman, *Surpassing the Love of Men: Romantic Friendship and Love between Women from the Renaissance to the Present* (1981; New York: Perennial, 2001), p. 125.

5 Lisa Moore, "'Something More Tender Still than Friendship': Romantic Friendship in Early-Nineteenth-Century England," *Feminist Studies* 18.3 (1992), pp. 499–520.

6 T. H. Farnham, "To Lesbia. The Greek Poet's Tribute to his Love," *Godey's Lady's Book* 124 (March 1892), 254. Julian Hawthorne's story "Brabazon Waring: A Romance," *Godey's Lady's Book* 125 (Dec. 1892), stars an opera singer named "Lesbia," dubbed by her maid "Miss Lesby," p. 576, p. 583. *Godey's* does not mention Sappho's sexual relationships with women.

7 S. Millington Miller, M.D., "Sappho—The Woman and the Time," *Godey's Lady's Book* 130 (Feb. 1895), p. 115, p. 116.

8 Anonymous, *Sappho in Boston*, advertised by Moffat, Yard & Company, *The Publishers' Weekly* (Sept. 26, 1908), p. 668. The novel was advertised as possessing "unusual charm and piquancy."

9 Mary Beth Cavert has provided a few brief summary biographies in "Nora, Maud, and Isabel," ILLMM, pp. 106–25; and "Kilmeny of the Orchard—1910: To my Cousin Beatrice A. McIntyre," *Kindred Spirits* (Summer 1998), pp. 16–19.

10 AGG, ch. 8, p. 59.

11 LMM, May 8, 1891, SJ 1, p. 50.

12 LMM, Dec. 28, 1893, UJ 1, p. 247.

13 LMM, Jan. 27, 1911, SJ 2, p. 42.

14 LMM, Jan. 7, 1910, SJ 1, p. 384; see also LMM, Jan. 27, 1911, SJ 2, p. 42. Maud visited Aunt Emily in March of the year Miss Izzy Robinson was the Cavendish teacher (Summer 1887 to Dec. 1888).

15 AGG, ch. 4, p. 36.

16 LMM, July 1, 1894, UJ 1, p. 302.

17 LMM, July 1, 1894, UJ 1, p. 303.

18 LMM, July 1, 1894, UJ 1, p. 305.

19 The old school was being torn down a day later, on Monday, July 2, 1894, UJ, p. 306.

20 LMM visited Penzie's son, Chester Bulman, in New Glasgow, PEI, on Oct. 20, 1936, SJ 5, p. 106.

21 LMM, Dec. 2, 1890, in Bolger, YBA, p. 101. The originals are held in Robertson Library UPEI.

22 LMM to PM, Dec. 16, 1890, in Bolger, YBA, p. 103.

23 LMM to PM, Feb. 25, 1891, in Bolger, YBA, p. 121.

24 LMM to PM, Nov. 3, 1890, in Bolger, YBA, p. 96. The poem was titled "My Friend's Home."

25 LMM to PM, Sept. 20, 1890, in Bolger, YBA, p. 88.

26 LMM, Mar. 13, 1928, SJ 3, p. 365.

27 LMM to PM, Oct. 6, 1890, in Bolger, YBA, p. 91.

28 LMM to PM, Dec. 2, 1890, in Bolger, YBA, p. 101.

29 LMM, Oct. 20, 1936, SJ 5, p. 106; also she regrets her statement in which she claimed she hated Nate Lockhart.

30 LMM, "The 'Teen-Age Girl," *The Chatelaine* (Mar. 1931), reprinted in Quaile, *L. M. Montgomery*, p. 162.

[31] Quoted in Cavert, "Nora, Maud, and Isabel," ILLMM, p. 109.

[32] LMM, "In Lovers Lane," *The Delineator* (July 1903), pp. 16. The spelling of Lovers' Lane is inconsistent with a shift from plural to singular and back. Anne specifies that her Lover's (singular) Lane is not for pairs of lovers, but even within the novel the spelling is inconsistent.

[33] LMM, Aug. 2, 1931, SJ 4, p. 145–46. For more details, see Irene Gammel, "Mirror Looks: The Visual and Performative Diaries of L. M. Montgomery, Baroness Elsa and Elvira Bach," *Interfaces: Women, Autobiography, Image, Performance*, ed. Sidonie Smith and Julia Watson (Ann Arbor: Michigan UP, 2003), pp. 293–98.

[34] LMM, Oct. 24, 1904, UJ 2, pp. 326–27; both photos on p. 327.

[35] Emma E. Walker, M. D., "Pretty Girl Papers: iv: Crushes Among Girls," *The Ladies' Home Journal* (Jan. 1904).

[36] LMM to FEC, Mar. 24, 1907, SJ 5, p. 154.

[37] AGG, ch. 15, p. 107.

Chapter 7

[1] AGG, ch. 12, p. 87.

[2] AGG, ch. 12, p. 87.

[3] LMM, Apr. 8, 1902, UJ, p. 239.

[4] "What Month Were You Born?" *Modern Women* (June 1905), p. 23; AGG, ch. 12, p. 88.

[5] Temma F. Berg, "Sisterhood is Fearful: Female Friendship in L. M. Montgomery," HT, p. 39. For mythological readings, see Elizabeth Waterston, *Kindling Spirit: Lucy Maud Montgomery's 'Anne of Green Gables'* (Toronto: ECW Press, 1993), p. 43, and Margaret Anne Doody, "Introduction," AAGG, pp. 25–27.

[6] Marah Gubar, "'Where Is the Boy?': The Pleasures of Postponement in the *Anne of Green Gables* Series," *The Lion and the Unicorn* 25.1 (2001), pp. 47–69; Cecily Devereux, "Anatomy of a 'National Icon': *Anne of Green Gables* and the 'Bosom Friends' Affair," MA, pp. 32–42; and Laura Robinson, "Bosom Friends: Lesbian Desire in L. M. Montgomery's Anne Books," *Canadian Literature* 180 (Spring 2004), pp. 12–28.

[7] J. Adams, "The Full Lucy," *The Globe and Mail* (Jan. 17, 2004), p. R1.

[8] LMM, Feb. 11, 1932, SJ 4, p. 166.

[9] AGG, ch. 15, p. 108.

[10] D. Davidson, "Forest Trails in the White Mountains," *The Booklovers Magazine* 4.4 (Oct. 1904), pp. 479–82. LMM mistakenly identifies the photo as coming from the *Outing* magazine, Jan. 27, 1911, SJ 2, p. 42.

[11] AGG, ch. 15, p. 106.

[12] LMM to EW, Oct. 8, 1906, GGL, p. 46.

[13] LMM, Aug. 1, 1892, UJ 1, p. 184. A truncated summary of her adventures with the Nelson boys appears in AP, pp. 28–33.

[14] LMM, Aug. 1, 1892, UJ 1, pp. 176–77.

[15] Gertrude Bartlett, "A Pagan's Prayer," *Ainslee's Magazine* (Nov. 1902), p. 87; LMM's poem "Harbor Sunset," *Ainslee's Magazine* (Jan. 1902), p. 490, had appeared a few months earlier. See also Bartlett's "Song of Diana," *The Metropolitan* (Feb. 1903), p. 174; and Marie Frances Upton, "Diana," *Godey's Lady's Book* (Aug. 1893), p. 222.

[16] AGG, ch. 2, p. 21.

[17] Review of Margaret Oliphant's *Diana*, *Godey's Lady's Book* (July–Dec. 1892), p. 521. See Faderman, *Surpassing the Love of Men*, pp. 162-63, pp. 166–67, for further details on the Diana figure in literature.

[18] LMM, Feb. 7, 1919, SJ 2, p. 303. Once again, LMM's dates are unreliable. Born on February 22, 1883, Frede was in fact closer to eight years younger, not nine as indicated in LMM's account. Also, LMM recalled that Frede arrived in Stanley in 1905, but FEC writes that it was 1904; it was "two and a half years ago," she writes in her March 24, 1907, letter, transcribed by LMM on Apr. 5, 1937, SJ 5, p. 154.

[19] LMM, Feb. 7, 1919, SJ 2, p. 303.

[20] LMM, Feb. 7, 1919, SJ 2, pp. 303–4.

[21] FEC to LMM, Mar. 25, 1917, copied into LMM's journal Apr. 5, 1937, SJ 5, p. 158.

[22] LMM, Feb. 7, 1919, SJ 2, p. 304; AGG, ch. 30, p. 244. See Margaret Atwood's discussion of the phrase as an example of Maritime women's self-reliance, in "Revisiting Anne," LMMCC, p. 224; see also Carole Gerson, "'Fitted to Earn Her Own Living': Figures of the New Woman in the Writing of L. M. Montgomery," *Children's Voices in Atlantic Literature and Culture* (Guelph, ON: Canadian Children's Press, 1995), pp. 24–34.

[23] LMM, Apr. 11, 1915, SJ 2, p. 163.

[24] Franklin B. Wiley, "The Court of Last Resort," *The Ladies Home Journal* (May 1905), p. 19.

[25] LMM, "The Promise of Lucy Ellen," *The Delineator* (Feb. 1904), reprinted in *The Doctor's Sweetheart and Other Stories*, ed. Catherine McLay (1979; Toronto: Bantam-Seal, 1993), p. 58.

[26] LMM, "The Promise of Lucy Ellen," pp. 61–62.

[27] LMM, "The Promise of Lucy Ellen," p. 62.

[28] LMM, "The Promise of Lucy Ellen," p. 64, p. 66.

[29] AGG, ch. 15, p. 119.

[30] AGG, ch. 30, p. 240.

[31] LMM, Jan. 7, 1910, SJ 1, p. 385.

[32] LMM, July 10, 1898, SJ 1, p. 224.

[33] LMM, May 24, 1917, SJ 2, p. 217.

[34] LMM, Feb. 7, 1919, SJ 2, p. 294.

[35] LMM, Feb. 7, 1919, SJ 2, p. 301.

[36] LMM, Mar. 23, 1919, SJ 2, p. 311; Feb. 7, 1919, SJ 2, p. 306.

Chapter 8

[1] AGG, ch. 15, p. 111.

[2] See also Elizabeth Waterston, "Marigold and the Magic of Memory," in HT, pp. 155–66.

[3] LMM, "To My Enemy," *The Smart Set* (Jan. 1902), p. 92. The poem is reprinted in SJ 5, p. 234, although LMM misidentifies the periodical in which it was published as *The Delineator*.

[4] LMM to GBM, Dec. 3, 1905, MDMM, p. 18. See also Harold H. Simpson, *Cavendish: Its History, Its People* (1973), typescript, PEIPA.

[5] See LMM, Feb. 2, 1897, SJ 1, p. 179.

[6] Allison Johnson interviewed by Maria O'Brien (on behalf of the author), Belmont, Oct. 2003. Allison Johnson is the nephew of Ed Simpson, Maud's one-time fiancé. See also W. I. Belmont, *The History of Belmont*, typescript, PEIPA.

[7] Ruth Johnson (1909–), Interviewed by Maria O'Brien (on behalf of the author), Summerside, PEI, Oct. 2003.

[8] LMM, Feb. 11, 1932, SJ 4, p. 168.

[9] "Minute Book: Cavendish Literary Society" (Feb. 1886–Jan. 7, 1924), PEIPA. The Cavendish Literary Society was organized with its own constitution and bylaws.

[10] My emphasis; Minute book, Dec. 18, 1908, p. 135.

[11] Minute book, Mar. 27, 1890, p. 33; Arthur Simpson was President of the Literary in 1901, 1904, 1905, 1906.

[12] Minute book, Feb. 5, 1891, p. 41.

[13] Minute book, Jan. 20, 1893, p. 54.

[14] LMM, Dec. 4, 1891, SJ 1, p. 70.

[15] George Woodside Simpson (1858–1906). Minute book, Nov. 2, 1906, p. 121. For his photo and the funeral notice, see LMM Scrapbook CM 67.5.12, p. 52, CCAG.

[16] Minute book, Nov. 27, 1889, p. 27; LMM, Nov. 23, 1889, SJ 1, pp. 4–5, p. 395; Clemmie Macneill was Maud's foe and inspiration for Josie Pye; see SJ 1, p. 2.

[17] AGG, ch. 33, p. 273.

[18] LMM Scrapbook CM 67.5.12, p. 54, CCAG; see also LMM, Dec. 24, 1890, SJ 1, p. 37 about her recitation and tableau "The Five Foolish Virgins" in Prince Albert. As a minister's wife in Ontario, LMM was involved in numerous community performance projects.

[19] Minute book, Feb. 3, 1899, p. 81.

[20] LMM, May 21, 1892, UJ 1, p. 165.

[21] LMM, "Aunt Susanna's Birthday Celebration," *New Idea Woman's Magazine* (Feb. 1905), 30; reprinted in *Across the Miles*, ed. Wilmshurst, p. 157.

[22] AGG, ch. 15, p. 110.

[23] AGG, ch. 15, p. 108.

[24] LMM, Aug. 6, 1905, p. 369.

[25] LMM, SJ 1, p. 17, p. 20. See also Mary Beth Cavert, "Whatever Happened to Nate Lockhart?" *Kindred Spirits* (Dec. 2005) for his biography.

[26] Nathan Lockhart (1875–1954) is first listed with a recitation on Apr. 6, 1888, p. 19, that is, a full 20 months before Maud's first recital in Nov. 1889; in fact, Nate appears to have had a hand in introducing Maud to the Literary Society; Minute book, Nov. 1, 1889, p. 27.

[27] AGG, ch. 30, p. 246.

[28] LMM, Feb. 17, 1890, SJ 1, p. 15.

[29] In Oct. 1889, Mr. Nathan Lockhart was elected "Librarian" of the Literary Society, but it wasn't until Dec. 1903, long after Nate left, that Maud was appointed to the Society's Book Committee, giving her influence over which books were purchased.

[30] LMM, Feb. 18, SJ 1, p. 16.

[31] Nate Lockhart photo, Vaughan Memorial Library, Acadia University. Nate married school teacher and Dalhousie University graduate Mabel Celeste in North Sydney, Nova Scotia, on Feb. 6, 1906; LMM scrapbooks, Red Album, CM 675.12, p. 45, CCAG.

[32] LMM, Aug. 6, 1905, UJ 2, p. 369, p. 370, p. 371.

[33] LMM, Mar. 26, 1892, SJ 1, p. 78. Edwin (Ed) Simpson (1872–1955).

[34] Arnold Barrett (Edwin Simpson's grandnephew), interviewed by Maria O'Brien (on behalf of the author), Belmont, Sept. 2003.

[35] LMM, June 30, 1897, SJ 1, p. 189; for a more detailed discussion, see also Irene Gammel, "'I loved Herman Leard Madly': L.M. Montgomery's Confession of Desire," ILLMM, pp. 129–53.

[36] Alice Munro, "Afterword," ENM, p. 358.

[37] For studies of the feminist dimensions of AGG, see Gabriella Åhmansson, *A Life and Its Mirrors: A Feminist Reading of L.M. Montgomery's Fiction* (Stockholm: Almqvist & Wiksell, 1991); and K.L. Poe, "The Whole of the Moon: L.M. Montgomery's *Anne of Green Gables* Series," *Nancy Drew and Company: Culture, Gender, and Girls' Series*, ed.

Sherrie A. Inness (Bowling Green, OH: Bowling Green State University Popular Press, 1997).

[38] Mollie Gillen, *The Wheel of Things: A Biography of L. M. Montgomery, Author of Anne of Green Gables* (Toronto: Fitzhenry and Whiteside, 1975), p. 88.

Chapter 9

[1] AGG, ch. 18, p. 140.

[2] Jennie Rubio, "'Strewn with Dead Bodies': Women and Gossip in *Anne of Ingleside*," HT, p. 174.

[3] Mary Rubio, Introduction, HT, p. 6; see also Rubio, "*Anne of Green Gables*: The Architect of Adolescence," SSLT, pp. 65–82.

[4] AGG, ch. 9, pp. 64–65.

[5] Compare this scene with Sophie Gates Kerr's "A Daughter of Maryland," *The Ladies World* (Oct. 1902), pp. 4–5; *The Ladies World* is a New York magazine in which LMM published her poem "The Violet's Spell" in Sept./Oct. 1893. The wording is remarkably close to AGG, although we have no evidence that LMM owned this particular issue. The story of Anne Winter is set in Annapolis in 1774. Anne Winter, "a slender maid with flashing eyes," defends her father, an empire loyalist, against the patriots.

> "Hush!" cried Anne, "don't you dare say another word against father! I'll never forgive you, Jack Fairfax, never. Don't you ever speak to me again as long as you live, never. I despise you!" Emphasizing her anger with her stamp of her foot, Anne turned and fairly ran into her own door.... Anne rushed blindly up-stairs and into her own room, there to fling herself upon the spotless canopied bed and sob heavily for the evil times that had befallen.... by five o'clock Anne was herself again.... With head held very high, she came downstairs...(p. 4).

> By means of a clever trick—putting pepper in the steaming tea kettle—she is able to disperse the mob of patriots who have come to the house to confiscate the tea. Although Anne Winter is a young woman confronting a political mob, while Anne Shirley confronts Mrs. Rachel Lynde, the scene is similar in wording and impact. Both girls tackle a formidable foe and emerge victorious, taking wicked delight in their actions. Maud would have been interested in the story because of the Empire Loyalist connection; some of her own relatives were Empire Loyalists and their stories are told in her novel *The Story Girl*.

[6] Genevieve Wiggins, *L. M. Montgomery* (New York: Twayne, 1992), p. 26. See also Frank Davey, "The Hard-Won Power of Canadian Womanhood: Reading *Anne of Green Gables* Today," LMMCC, pp. 163–82.

[7] Yoshiko Akamatsu, "Japanese Readings of *Anne of Green Gables*," LMMCC, pp. 201–12.

[8] Mrs. Theodore W. Birney, "Childhood: A Chapter on Manners," *The Delineator* (Jan. 1904), p. 129, p. 130, NYPL. LMM owed this issue from which she clipped Clinton Scollard's "Winter in Lovers' Lane" for her scrapbook.

[9] See Cecily Devereux, "'not one of those dreadful new women': Anne Shirley and the Culture of Imperial Motherhood," *Windows and Words: A Look at Canadian Children's Literature in English*, ed. Aïda Hudson and Susan-Ann Cooper (Ottawa: University of Ottawa Press, 2003), pp. 119–30; and Erika Rothwell, "Knitting Up the World: L. M. Montgomery and Maternal Feminism," LMMCC, pp. 133–44.

[10] Mrs. Theodore W. Birney, "Childhood," *The Delineator* (June 1904), p. 1076, NYPL. Mrs.

Birney's column counseled parents on proper discipline for children: Children exhibiting excitable or nervous sensibility "are those most frequently in need of discipline; that is, according to a superficial view of the matter." These children are full of nervous energy and mothers should be "cognizant of the danger signals which in most cases precede an outburst of temper, and the wise and just mother is she who will, through exercise and patience, prevent such outbursts" (p. 1074).

[11] AGG, ch. 10, p. 73.

[12] LMM, Dec. 24, 1895, SJ 1, p. 151.

[13] LMM, Mar. 7, 1892, UJ 1, p. 156; and Apr. 8, 1898, SJ 1, p. 209.

[14] LMM, Jan. 7, 1910, SJ 1, pp. 383–84. See also AP, pp. 13–16.

[15] LMM, May 3, 1908, UJ 2, p. 453.

[16] LMM, July 1, 1894, UJ 1, p. 301.

[17] LMM, Feb. 17, 1893, UJ 1, p. 202. Lucy (Lu) Macneill was her cousin and friend and neighbor, the daughter of Uncle John Macneill.

[18] LMM, May 18, 1892, UJ 1, p. 165.

[19] LMM and Nora Lefurgey, ILLMM, p. 35; for more details, see Jennifer Litster, "The 'Secret' Diary of Maud Montgomery, Aged 28¼," ILLMM, pp. 88–105.

[20] AGG, ch. 2, p. 15.

[21] Like George W. Simpson, LMM was often listed as the Secretary, as well as being a member of the entertainment, newsletter and book committees. When Maud did speak up she depended upon a carefully prepared text. In Mar. 1905, she gave a paper on Elizabeth Barrett Browning—Arthur Simpson being one of the respondents (Minute book, Mar. 3, 1905, p. 112), but complained in her journal that it was a waste of time and "gray matter." By this time the Literary had perhaps outlived its function as a training ground for the writer (Mar. 11, 1905, SJ 1, p. 305).

[22] Minute book, Dec. 14, 1894, p. 63. While Maud (being in Bideford) would have missed this particular discussion, she was present for others. Minute book, Apr. 1, and Apr. 15, 1892, pp. 49–50.

[23] Minute book, Mar. 19, 1886, p. 5.

[24] Minute book, Nov. 17, 1899, p. 87.

[25] Minute book, Mar. 1, 1901, p. 95.

[26] Minute book, Nov. 15, 1901, p. 97.

[27] Minute book, Nov. 15, 1907, p. 128.

[28] Italian, AGG, ch. 27, p. 217; German Jew, AGG, ch. 27, p. 217; Irish, AGG, ch. 1, pp. 3–4 (the joke refers to the stereotype of the crime-prone Irishman).

[29] AGG, ch. 1, p. 6.

[30] Rev. R. Murray, "Prince Edward Island," The Easternmost Ridge of the Continent, ed. George Munro Grant (Chicago: Alexander Belford, 1899), p. 131. See Gavin White, "L.M. Montgomery and the French," CCL 78 (1995), pp. 65–68.

[31] LMM, Jan. 7, 1910, SJ 1, p. 386.

[32] Ram's Horn (Mar. 14, 1903), p. 9; this issue also featured an ad for A Book of Fact warning against the "subtle perils of modern dance" (p. 16), and ads for sex education books by Puritan Publishing (p. 17). Maud read these issues (NL, ILLMM, p. 60), and published poems and short stories in Ram's Horn in March and May.

[33] Minute book, Nov. 21, 1890, p. 37, p. 42.

[34] Minute book, Feb. 20, 1891, p. 42.

35 Gerald Hallowell, "Prohibition," *The Canadian Encyclopedia*, http://www.thecanadianencyclopedia.com; see also AAGG, p. 186, n. 9. Quebec was overwhelmingly anti-prohibition, resulting in the failure of federal Prohibition legislation.

36 On wine making, see LMM, Dec. 16, 1922; SJ 3, pp. 105–6; Ewan's mood apparently improved after a glass of wine. On enjoying wine during Boston visit, see LMM, Nov. 29, 1910, SJ 2, p. 30.

37 Cecily Devereux, "Introduction," *Anne of Green Gables* (Peterborough: Broadview, 2004), p. 19.

38 Helen M. Winslow, "Women as After-Dinner Speakers," *The Delineator* (Mar. 1905), p. 514. See also Mary Henley Rubio, "L. M. Montgomery: Scottish-Presbyterian Agency in Canadian Culture," LMMCC, pp. 89–105. Oral speech was cultivated in Presbyterian culture and poor oration considered a serious shortcoming. LMM puts the most partisan remarks in the mouths of those already flagged as comical characters, allowing LMM to make irreverent comments (p. 94).

39 LMM, Mar. 25, 1894, UJ 1, p. 264.

40 LMM, Aug. 13, 1894, UJ 1, p. 316.

41 LMM, May 1, 1893, UJ 1, p. 208.

42 Walter King, "When Night Comes," *The Sunday School Advocate* (Jan. 7, 1905), p. 3; Walter King, "Childhood as Portrayed in Art," *The Sunday School Advocate* (Jan. 14, 1905), p. 11; and "Now I Lay Me," *The Sunday School Advocate* (June 10, 1905), p. 181, NYPL. The child's bedtime prayer is also listed in the 1784 edition of *The New England Primer*; AAGG, p. 99, n. 3.

43 "Now I lay me down to sleep," illustration, *Ram's Horn* (Jan. 10, 1903), p. 3, NYPL.

44 LMM, Oct. 12, 1906, SJ 1, p. 321.

45 LMM, Aug. 6, 1905, UJ 2, p. 368.

46 Minute book, Jan. 29, 1904, p. 106; Mar. 17, 1905, p. 13.

47 LMM to EW, Apr. 8, 1906, GGL, p. 38.

48 AGG, ch. 21, p. 171.

49 LMM, ILLMM, p. 81.

50 AGG, ch. 21, p. 171. LMM, ILLMM, p. 77.

51 AAG, ch. 21, p. 176.

52 See AGG, ed. Cecily Devereux, p. 345. LMM had used the episode in earlier stories including "A New Fashioned Flavoring," *Golden Days for Boys and Girls* (Aug. 27, 1898), pp. 641–42, reprinted in AGG, ed. Devereux, pp. 344–64; other variants are also reprinted here.

53 AGG, ch. 21, p. 171.

54 LMM, Sept. 27, 1913, SJ 2, p. 133.

Chapter 10

1 AP, p. 72.

2 LMM to GBM, Aug. 23, 1905, MDMM, pp. 11–12.

3 Diana Fuss, *The Sense of an Interior: Four Writers and the Rooms that Shaped Them* (New York: Routledge, 2004), pp. 17–18.

4 AGG, ch. 1, p. 3. For research on the history of the Macneill homestead, see James de Jonge, "Through the Eyes of Memory: L. M. Montgomery's Cavendish," MA, pp. 252–67. See A. Edward Powell's 2003 scaled model of the homestead, Robertson Library, UPEI.

5 FEC to LMM, Mar. 25, 1917, SJ 5, p. 158; see also LMM, Sept. 27, 1913, SJ 2, p. 127.

[6] AGG, ch. 1, p. 4.

[7] LMM, Photo of Grandma Lucy Macneill holding Edith Macneill (Box 1: XZ1 MS A097012 # 72), ca. 1900, UGA.

[8] Donna J. Campbell has researched the dimensions of the different rooms in the home-stead and indicates that the kitchen measures 18 feet and 6 inches by 16 feet. Donna J. Campbell, interviewed by Irene Gammel, Ryerson University, Toronto, 2006.

[9] LMM, Apr. 30, 1904, UJ 2, p. 314.

[10] See LMM, July 16, 1925, SJ 3, p. 239.

[11] LMM, Apr. 30, 1904, UJ 2, p. 313, p. 314. See also Laura Higgins, "Snapshot Portraits: Finding Montgomery in her 'Dear Den,'" HT, pp. 101–12. When LMM recopied her journals and added the many snapshots of her den in 1919, she had lost all privacy in her life as a famous writer, a wife, and a mother of two.

[12] LMM, June 7, 1900, SJ 1, p. 251.

[13] LMM, Photo of LMM's old room with bookcase view (# 12), ca. 1895, UGA.

[14] LMM, July 3, 1904, UJ 2, p. 321.

[15] LMM, July 3, 1904, UJ 2, p. 321. "Haunt of Ancient Peace," a quotation from Tennyson's poem "The Palace of Art" (1832), is also the caption for her photograph of the old lane viewed from her den, which accompanies this passage; LMM uses the very same phrase to describe the dreamlike past-sunset atmosphere in Avonlea, AGG, ch. 38, p. 308.

[16] LMM, July 8, 1894, UJ 1, p. 307.

[17] LMM, "The Gable Window," Ladies' Journal (May 1897); reprinted in Higgins, "Snapshot Portraits," HT, p. 110–11. For a variation of this motif, see LMM's poems "The Little Gable Window," The Designer (May 1907), p. 58; and "Down Home," East and West (May 12, 1917), p. 1; The Ryrie-Campbell Collection, L. M. Montgomery Institute, UPEI.

[18] LMM, May 10, 1893, UJ 1, p. 211.

[19] AGG, ch. 1, p. 4.

[20] Susan Glickman, The Picturesque and the Sublime: A Poetics of the Canadian Landscape (Montreal and Kingston: McGill-Queen's University Press, 1998), p. ix.

[21] Elizabeth Rollins Epperly, The Fragrance of Sweet-Grass: L. M. Montgomery's Heroines and the Pursuit of Romance (Toronto: University of Toronto Press, 1992), pp. 17–38.

[22] See Janice Fiamengo, "Towards a Theory of the Popular Landscape in Anne of Green Gables," MA, pp. 225–37.

[23] AGG, ch. 2, p. 18.

[24] ENM, ch. 1, p. 15.

[25] LMM, Jan. 27, 1911, SJ 2, p. 40.

[26] Epperly, Fragrance, p. 32, p. 28.

[27] Quoted in Zona Gale, "The Things That Are Real," The Delineator (Mar. 1905), p. 415. NYPL.

[28] Marian C. L. Reeves, "On her Sixth Birthday: A Leap-Year Story," Godey's Lady's Book (Feb. 1892), p. 170. NYPL.

[29] LMM to EW, Apr. 5, 1908, GGL, p. 67; see also LMM to EW, Mar. 2, 1908, GGL, p. 61.

[30] LMM, Aug. 16, 1907, SJ 1, p. 331.

[31] LMM, Aug. 4, 1905, UJ 2, pp. 367–68.

[32] Bolger, YBA, pp. 84–85.

[33] LMM, Apr. 18, 1906, SJ 1, p. 319.

[34] LMM, SJ 1, p. 310.

[35] AGG, ch. 38, p. 304.

[36] LMM, SJ 1, p. 310.

[37] LMM, Jan. 22, 1911, SJ 2, p. 36.

[38] AGG, ch. 4, p. 32; LMM, Jan. 22, 1911, SJ 2, p. 37.

[39] AGG ch. 27, p. 214.

[40] LMM, Jan. 27, 1911, SJ 2, p. 38. For a discussion of the Webb farm, see also De Jonge, "Through the Eyes of Memory," pp. 254–57.

[41] See Alexandra Heilbron's interview with Keith Webb, who was born in "Green Gables" in 1909, in *Remembering Lucy Maud Montgomery* (Toronto: Dundurn Press, 2001), p. 42.

[42] AHD, ch. 4, p. 20.

[43] LMM to GBM, Aug. 23, 1905, MDMM, p. 13.

[44] LMM, Apr. 12, 1903, SJ 1, p. 286. See Dorothy MacKay, "Two Old Houses: A Comparative Study of L. M. Montgomery's *Anne of Green Gables* and Nathaniel Hawthorne's *The House of Seven Gables*," *Abegweit Review* 7.1 (1992), pp. 33–37.

[45] AGG, ch. 2, 19.

[46] Mattie Sheridan, "The Next Lady of the White House," *Godey's Lady's Book* 125 (Sept. 1892), p. 369; illustration with caption "Mrs. Grover Cleveland at 'Gray Gables,'" p. 371.

[47] Thelma Loring, Bourne Historical Society, Bourne, MA, interviewed by telephone by Irene Gammel, Oct. 26, 2005.

[48] AGG, ch. 4, p. 31.

[49] Sheridan, "The Next Lady of the White House," p. 369.

[50] Alice M. Kellogg, "Modern House Building: No. 3—'High Gables,'" *The Delineator* (Mar. 1905), pp. 448–49. The High Gables design is by Everitt K. Taylor.

[51] AHD, ch. 4, p. 21.

[52] AWP, pp. 7–8, all four ellipses in the original text; see also Clarence Karr, *Authors and Audiences*, pp. 126–27.

[53] LMM, Jan. 7, 1910, SJ 1, p. 381.

[54] LMM, "In Lovers [sic] Lane," *The Delineator* (July 1903), p. 16, NYPL.

[55] Clinton Scollard, "Winter in Lovers' Lane," *The Delineator* (Jan. 1904), p. 60, NYPL. A clipping of the poem (without magazine reference) and a red maple leaf underneath are found in LMM Scrapbook, CM 67.5.12, p. 40, CCAG.

[56] AGG, ch. 20, p. 161.

[57] AGG, ch. 15, p. 105.

[58] LMM, Jan. 27, 1911, SJ 2, p. 42.

[59] AGG, ch. 15, p. 105. The title *Lover's Lane* had been circulating widely in popular culture, as seen, for instance, in the popular Broadway musical *Lovers Lane—A Pastoral Comedy* (February to May 1901), a light romantic comedy written by dramatist Clyde Fitch performed in the Manhattan Theater (and turned into a silent movie in 1924).

[60] LMM, Dec. 11, 1910, SJ 2, p. 34.

[61] LMM to GBM, Aug. 23, 1905, MDMM, p. 13.

[62] Rev. Robert Murray, "Prince Edward Island," *The Easternmost Ridge of the Continent*, ed. George Munro Grant with wood-engravings from original drawings by others. (Chicago: Alexander Belford & Co., 1899), p. 128.

[63] LMM quoted in Maude Petitt Hill, "The Best Known Woman in Prince Edward Island. Part II: L. M. Montgomery, After Her First Success," *The Chatelaine* (June 1928) reprinted in Alexandra Heilbron, *Remembering Lucy Maud Montgomery*, p. 222.

[64] Marian C. L. Reeves, "On her Sixth Birthday. A Leap Year Story," *Godey's Lady's Book* (Feb. 1892), p. 189.

[65] "Old Home Carnival Program," *The Daily Examiner* (May 16, 1905), front page. See also "The Celebration of Old Home Week Begins," *Charlottetown Guardian* (July 25, 1905); "Old Home Week Celebration," *Charlottetown Guardian* (July 26, 1905); and Boyde Beck and Edward Macdonald, *Everyday & Extraordinary: Almanac of the History of Prince Edward Island* (Charlottetown: PEI Museum and Heritage Foundation, 1999), p. 80.

[66] AGG, ch. 29, p. 232, p. 234, p. 235. According to the article "What is an Exhibition for?" *Charlottetown Guardian* (Sept. 6, 1905), the purpose of the Exhibition was to showcase the improvements made in farm stock and produce, to allow local farmers to sell at better prices than they could obtain elsewhere, and to provide amusement for the men and women tired of monotonous farm work. Farmers could attend "the races, acrobatics, trapeze, herizonital [sic] bar and gymnastic amusements."

[67] AGG, ch. 29, p. 238.

[68] AGG, ch. 33, p. 276. Similar to Anne's rootedness, so "Maud Cavendish" was the proud moniker Maud had used to sign her early stories, and "Cavendish, PEI" graced the top of almost every entry in her journal following the date, locating identity in landscape.

[69] Shauna McCabe, "Representing Islandness: Myth, Memory, and Modernisation in Prince Edward Island," PhD Dissertation, University of British Columbia, 2001, p. 135. McCabe also notes, "It is through memory that continuity and change may converge, for memory is at once a mark of transience and a trace of inherited worlds" (p. 109).

[70] Beck and McDonald, *Everyday and Extraordinary*, p. 74.

[71] AGG, ch. 29, p. 231.

[72] AGG, ch. 33, p. 274.

[73] AGG, ch, 18, p. 145.

[74] LMM, Aug. 11, 1890, SJI p. 25, p. 26.

[75] The speech is paraphrased in "The day Sir John A. came to Summerside," *The Journal-Pioneer* (Aug. 14, 1890), reprinted in a special heritage edition on Aug. 14, 1992. For LMM's impressions of the events, see Aug. 11, 1890, SJ I, pp. 25–26.

[76] AGG, ch. 1, p. 6. Owen Dudley Edwards and Jennifer Litster, "The End of Canadian Innocence: L. M. Montgomery and the First World War," LMMCC, p. 31, express their surprise at Marilla's insistence for "a born Canadian," given that the novel is set in the general period soon after PEI reluctantly became part of the Confederation in 1873.

[77] AGG, ch. 18, p. 140 (chapter 18, embedded in the center of the novel, contains numerous references to Canada); see also ch. 15, p. 107 and ch. 30, p. 241 for references to studying Canadian history.

[78] Janice Fiamengo, "Towards a Theory of the Popular Landscape in *Anne of Green Gables*," MA, p. 234, p. 235.

[79] LMM, Oct. 15, 1905, UJ 2, p. 375.

[80] LMM, Oct. 15, 1905, UJ 2, p. 374, p. 375.

[81] LMM, Oct. 15, 1905, UJ 2, p. 375.

Chapter 11

[1] AGG, ch. 2, p. 17.

[2] Carole Gerson, "L. M. Montgomery and the Conflictedness of a Woman Writer," *Storm and Dissonance: L. M. Montgomery and Conflict*, ed. Jean Mitchell (Newcastle, UK: Cambridge Scholars Press, 2008, 67–80).

[3] Frank Davey, *Reading "Kim" Right* (Vancouver: Talonbooks, 1993), p. 17; and Davey, "The Hard-Won Power of Canadian Womanhood," LMMCC, pp. 163–82.

[4] Eliza Haweis, *The Art of Beauty and the Art of Dress* (1878; New York: Garland, 1978), p. 17.

[5] Haweis, *Art of Beauty*, p. 274.

[6] Haweis, *Art of Beauty*, pp. 190–91.

[7] *Daily Examiner*, October 13, 1882. On Nov. 30, 2000, the centennial anniversary of Wilde's death, Catherine Hennessey of Charlottetown commemorated Oscar Wilde's visit to Charlottetown with an article; http://www.catherinehennessey.com/onestory.php3?number=83.

[8] LMM, "Is this My Anne?," *The Chatelaine* (Jan. 1935), reprinted in Quaile, *L. M. Montgomery*, p. 172.

[9] LMM, Jan. 7, 1910, SJ 1, p. 372.

[10] LMM, May 6, 1903, ILLMM, p. 72.

[11] LMM, June 24, 1895, SJ 1, p. 140.

[12] Emilie Ferguson, "The History and Hygiene of the Hair," *Modern Women* (October 1905), p. 139; AGG, ch. 33, p. 275.

[13] AGG, ch. 9, p. 66.

[14] "Red Hair and Genius," *The World* [New York] (Mar. 17, 1901).

[15] AGG, ch. 27, p. 217.

[16] LMM, Jan. 27, 1911, SJ 2, p. 44.

[17] AGG, ch. 1, p. 5.

[18] Advertisement for Hall's Vegetable Sicilian Hair Renewer, *Modern Women* (June 1905), p. 22. An advertisement for the same product, in another issue (*Modern Women* [August 1905], p. 84) described the dye: "It is the guardian of youth, the key to beauty. It is safe, sure, reliable."

[19] LMM, Oct. 14, 1927, SJ 3, p. 355. See also SJ 2, p. 44: A Cavendish girl dyed her red hair black after the novel was written but before it was published, so everybody assumed LMM had copied the incident for her book.

[20] Eleanor Rogers, M.D., "Freckles 'And Such,'" *The Delineator* (Jan. 1905), p. 138.

[21] AGG, ch. 2, p. 17.

[22] AGG, ch. 26, p. 210.

[23] AGG, ch. 22, p. 181.

[24] Ann F. Howey, "'She look'd down to Camelot': Anne Shirley, Sullivan, and the Lady of Shalott," MA, p. 160.

[25] Gustav Kobbé, "The Stage and the Second Self," *The Delineator* (Apr. 1905), p. 611.

[26] Gustav Kobbé, "The Stage and the Second Self," p. 610.

[27] Gustav Kobbé, "The Stage and the Second Self," p. 608.

[28] Gustav Kobbé, "The Stage and the Second Self," p. 612.

[29] Corinne Parker, "The Tribulations of a Stage Debutante," *The Metropolitan* (Sept. 1903), pp. 785–92. Parker writes that she is recounting the typical story of hundreds of young girls who arrive in New York, seeking a foothold on the metropolitan stage. Interestingly, the full-page photograph of Corinne Parker is by Rudolf Eickemeyer, Jr. (p. 787).

[30] LMM, July 30, 1905, SJ 1, p. 309.

[31] AA, ch. 5, p. 35.

[32] "Ladies' Jackets; Sleeves, etc." *The Delineator* (Feb. 1905), p. 203.

[33] Priscilla Wakefield, "A Girl's Personal Appearance and Dress," *The Delineator* (Jan. 1905), p. 164. Coincidentally, on the opposite page is an advertisement for the cover girl poster that would eventually become the cover for *Anne of Green Gables*.

[34] AGG ch. 15, p. 196.

[35] Charles Battell Loomis, "Man's Humiliation," *Modern Women* (Aug. 1905), p. 71.

[36] Alison Matthews David, interviewed by Irene Gammel, June 6, 2007, Ryerson University, Toronto.

[37] Mrs. Osborn, "Fashions in New York," *The Delineator* (Jan. 1904), pp. 12–13.

[38] AGG, ch. 19, p. 153.

[39] Alison Matthews David, interviewed by Irene Gammel, June 6, 2007, Ryerson University, Toronto.

[40] AGG, ch. 33, p. 266, p. 268.

[41] AGG, ch. 33, p. 269.

[42] "Weddings and Brides," *Modern Women* (June 1905), p. 22; this issue also featured LMM's own story "By the Grace of Sarah Maud."

[43] LMM, Jan. 27, 1911, SJ 2, p. 42.

[44] Henry Wadsworth Longfellow, "Maidenhood," *The Household* (June 1901), p. 9. The following quotations from "Maidenhood" are all from p. 9.

[45] W. L. Taylor, "Maidenhood," *The Ladies Home Journal* (Nov. 1904), p. 3. Interestingly, the 1892 edition of Susan Warner's 1852 classic *The Wide Wide World* (Philadelphia: J. B. Lippincott Company, 1892) also features a snippet of the "Maidenhood" poem, "Bear a lily in thy hand" on the frontispiece.

[46] AGG, ch. 31, p. 255.

[47] AGG, ch. 30, p. 247.

[48] Quoted in Carrie MacLellan, "Listening to the Music in *Anne of Green Gables: The Musical*," MA, p. 220.

Chapter 12

[1] AGG, ch. 38, p. 310.

[2] LMM, Nov. 8, 1905, UJ 2, p. 376.

[3] "Translation of Dr. William R. Clark" (Obituary Tribute), *Zion's Herald* (June 21, 1905), p. 775; Margaret E. Sangster, "Live in the Sunshine," *Zion's Herald* (June 21, 1905), p. 781.

[4] LMM, Nov. 8, 1905, UJ 2, p. 377.

[5] AGG, ch. 37, p. 296.

[6] AGG, ch. 37, p. 297.

[7] LMM, Jan. 27, 1911, SJ 2, p. 44.

[8] Minute Book, Mar. 30, 1905, p. 120, Cavendish Literary Society, PEIPA.

[9] R. L. Otley, *Christian Ideas and Ideals: An Outline of Christian Ethical Theory* (London: Longmans, Green, and Co., 1909), pp. 9–10.

[10] Ella Higginson, "One o' Them Still, Stubborn Kinds," *The Ladies' Home Journal* (June 1897), p. 4; all quotations are from this page. LMM notes on Feb. 13, 1922 (SJ 3, p. 39) that "for twenty-five years" she had been trying to get into *The Ladies' Home Journal*, confirming that her interest began around 1897 when Higginson's story was published. Compare the wording of Mrs. Ewens' line after having upset her daughter, "I wish I hadn't twitted her about her stories" with Marilla's line to Mrs. Lynde, "You shouldn't have twitted her about her looks" (AGG, ch. 9, p. 66)—in each case describing the heroine's sensitivity and temper aroused by adults' insensitive comments. Mrs. Ewens refers to Mindwell as "one o' them still, stubborn kinds," while Mrs. Lynde describes

Anne as "obstinate as a mule" (AGG, ch. 38, p. 305). Mindwell "saw the long, lonely year stretching drearily before her mother" just as Anne is touched to the quick by Marilla's dejected attitude.

11 LMM replayed Higginson's story "One o' Them Still, Stubborn Kinds" as a template in "Jane Lavinia" (*Zion's Herald*, Boston [Sept. 26, 1906], pp. 1230–32, NYPL), the story of the aspiring visual artist who has the opportunity to work and study in New York; Jane Lavinia gratefully accepts the offer of an education and then changes her mind when she overhears her Aunt Rebecca's lament and discovers she is loved and needed at home. The internal conflict is immediately resolved in favor of home, necessitating a "sacrifice" on the part of the heroine.

12 AGG, ch. 38, pp. 304–5.

13 AGG, ch. 38, p. 305.

14 AGG ch. 38, p. 306.

15 AGG, ch. 37, pp. 297–98; LMM to GBM, May 4, 1911, MDMM, p. 55.

16 Margaret Atwood, "Revisiting Anne," LMMCC, p. 226; see also Margaret Anne Doody, Introduction, AAGG, p. 21, who writes that "the real 'love story' of the novel" is the difficult one between Anne and Marilla.

17 Janice A. Radway, *Reading the Romance: Women, Patriarchy, and Popular Literature* (Chapel Hill: University of North Carolina Press, 1984), p. 89.

18 Quoted in Kristin Ramsdell, *Romance Fiction: A Guide to the Genre* (Englewood, CO: Libraries Unlimited, Inc., 1999), p. 17.

19 AGG, ch. 38, p. 308.

20 LMM, July 3, 1904, UJ 2, p. 321.

21 This sentence was added during the revision stage; AGG, ch. 38, p. 305; AGG Manuscript, p. 135, Note N19, CCAG.

22 Scrapbook 67.5.12, page 26, CCAG. Grace Denig Lichfield (1849–1944). Above the poem is the clipping of a vividly colored illustration of a bend in a dirt road with a fence, and trees in reddish foliage, and yellow and blue flowers in the foreground.

23 Theodore F. Sheckels, "Anne in Hollywood: The Americanization of a Canadian Icon," LMMCC, pp. 183–91. See also Benjamin Lefebvre, "Stand by Your Man: Adapting L.M. Montgomery's *Anne of Green Gables*," *Essays on Canadian Writing* 76 (Spring 2002), pp. 149–69.

24 Carolyn Wells, "A Girl's Gift to a Girl Graduate," *The Ladies' Home Journal* (June 1903), p. 30. It is interesting to note that the proposed title for this gift book is "A Day in June." Besides the Browning stanza, Shakespeare verses are also popular. See also "THE GIRL GRADUATE: HER OWN BOOK. In which to keep the happy record of her last year in school or college. A book she will always value," Timely Gift Books Advertisement column, *The Publishers' Weekly* (May 2, 1908), p. 1480.

25 LMM, Jan. 1, 1906, SJ 1, p. 317; and Mar. 12, 1920, SJ 2, p. 375.

26 LMM, Mar. 12, 1920, SJ 2, p. 374; Maud misspells her name Pensie. For dates and spelling, see Bolger, YBA, p. 84.

27 AGG, ch. 16, p. 125. In the manuscript, Maud inserted the note Z8 for the addition.

28 LMM, Mar. 2, 1906, UJ 2, p. 390.

29 LMM, Aug. 16, 1907, SJ 1, p. 331. The usual confusion reigns, for in her memoir (AP, p. 72), she notes that she finished the book in October 1905 (presumably meaning that she finished writing the manuscript).

30 See also Marian Gimby Brannan, "Lucy Maud Montgomery," *Twenty Remarkable*

Women Seen Through Their Handwriting (Little River, CA: Little River Press, 2004), pp. 98–106, for a graphological analysis of one of Maud's letters.

31 Elizabeth Epperly, "Approaching the Montgomery Manuscripts," HT, p. 75. See also Epperly, "L.M. Montgomery's Manuscript Revisions," *Atlantis* 20.1 (1995), pp. 149–55.

32 AGG, ch. 2, p. 12. Alfred Bunn (lyrics) and M. W. Balfe (music), *The Bohemian Girl: Opera, In Three Acts* (London: Boosey & Co, 1872), p. 14. In her revisions, LMM added, for instance, the allusion to Hepzibah in Hawthorne's *The House of the Seven Gables* (ch. 2). Anne's own voracious reading is emphasized with literary additions, allowing her show off her book knowledge, as when she muses on the naming of a rose (ch. 5), her naming of herself Lady Cordelia Fitzgerald (a lengthy addition in ch. 8), the explanation for the naming of Willowmere, which is taken from a book Diana lent Anne (ch. 13). LMM also added references to popular literature, citing Josiah Allen's wife (aka author Marietta Holley); and the *Pansy* book (ch. 15), from the popular series by Isabella Macdonald Alden (aka Pansy), which LMM had read in childhood. Another addition is Anne's pseudonym, "Rosamond Montmorency," under which she writes bad fiction; note that the last name of the pseudonym echoes LMM's last name, as well as recalling "Mrs. Montmorency Welles," a member of the "Sappho Society" who is ridiculed as a hopelessly bad writer with pretensions at writing high tragedy in Cornelia Reamond's story "Dora Merideth's Engagement," *Godey's Lady's Book* 721 (July 1890), pp. 17–21.

33 LMM to EW, Sept. 10, 1908, GGL, p. 73.

34 In chapter 1, the steep hill observed by Mrs. Lynde becomes "the steep red [added] hill" (p. 2); "Matthew should have been sowing his [turnip seed] on the big red [added] brook field" (p. 2). See also the list of sample revisions in Mary Henley Rubio and Elizabeth Waterston's edition of AGG (New York: Norton, 2007), pp. 262–67.

35 AGG, ch. 3, p. 24.

36 AGG, ch. 18, p. 143; ch. 27, p. 217.

37 Another interesting longer addition is Mrs. Lynde's critical reflections that Marilla dresses Anne in old-fashioned dresses (ch. 25). As if admitting the novel's debt to the popular magazines, Maud added a sentence describing Anne and Diana studying the rules of the Etiquette Department of the *Family Herald* (ch. 22).

38 LMM, Aug. 16, 1907, SJ 1, p. 331.

39 "He can write, that fellow [Jack London]," LMM to EW, May 8, 1905, GGL, p. 31.

40 For LMM's childhood reading of *Pansy*, see her journal entries of Dec. 14, 1890, SJ 1, p. 37 and Oct. 18, 1900, SJ 1, p. 253; for *Wide Awake*, and the naming of the cats, Jan 7, 1910, SJ 1, p. 379. Lothrop had also published the novel *Five Little Peppers* by Margaret Sidney (aka Harriett Lothrop, the publisher's wife). By July 1900, the company had moved into adult reading; by 1904, it was purchased by Lee and Shepard, the American publisher of *Alice in Wonderland*.

41 LMM, Aug. 16, 1907, SJ 1, p. 331. She did not submit her novel to Houghton Mifflin, the 1903 publisher of *Rebecca of Sunnybrook Farm*, or to Little Brown, or any of the many other publishers who featured juvenile stories.

42 LMM, Apr. 25, 1910, SJ 2, p. 6.

43 LMM, Aug. 16, 1907, SJ 1, p. 331.

44 Carol Shields, Review, *The Globe and Mail*, Oct. 3, 1998; reprinted in *The Lucy Maud Montgomery Album*, compiled by Kevin McCabe, ed. Alexandra Heilbron (Toronto: Fitzhenry and Whiteside, 1999), p. 407.

[45] Jerry Griswold, *The Classic American Children's Story: Novels of the Golden Age* (New York: Penguin, 1996), viii; and Claudia Nelson, *Little Strangers: Portrayals of Adoption and Foster Care in America, 1850–1929* (Bloomington: Indiana University Press, 2003), p. 185, n. 1.

[46] LMM, Feb. 25, 1906, UJ 2, p. 389.

[47] EW, Dec. 17, 1905, quoted in GGL, p. 37.

[48] LMM to EW, Apr. 8, 1906, p. 38.

[49] LMM, May 13, 1906, UJ 2, p. 393.

[50] LMM, May 13, 1906, UJ 2, p. 394, p. 395.

[51] LMM, June 21, 1906, GGL, p. 42.

[52] Minute book of the Cavendish Literary Society, Feb. 3, 1906, p. 117, PEIPA.

[53] LMM, Oct. 12, 1906, SJ 1, pp. 320–23. LMM's entry indicates that EM was thirty-four instead of thirty-six years old, suggesting that she retrospectively revised her earlier journal entries. Her biographers Mollie Gillen, *The Wheel of Things* (Toronto: Fitzhenry and Whiteside, 1975) and Mary Rubio and Elizabeth Waterston, *Writing a Life: L. M. Montgomery* (Toronto: EWC, 1995) have adopted LMM's way of misspelling her husband's name. Rubio and Waterston also note that the page describing Ewan Macdonald was carefully removed from her original journal and a new page carefully inserted (SJ 1, p. xxiv).

[54] LMM to GBM, July 29, 1906, MDMM, p. 24.

[55] LMM, "The Way of the Winning of Anne," *Springfield Republican* (Dec. 10, 1899), p. 18, reprinted in *At the Altar: Matrimonial Tales by L. M. Montgomery*, ed. Rea Wilmshurst (Toronto: McClelland & Stewart, 1994), pp. 161–72.

[56] LMM, Oct. 12, 1906, SJ 1, p. 323.

[57] LMM, Oct. 12, 1906, SJ 1, p. 322.

[58] LMM, Aug. 19, 1924, SJ 3, p. 200.

[59] Maria Gurevich, Psychology Department, Ryerson University, interviewed by Irene Gammel, May 14, 2007.

[60] Gubar, "'Where is the Boy,'" p. 47.

[61] LMM, Oct. 7, 1906, SJ 1, p. 319.

[62] Ed Simpson, quoted in LMM, Nov. 6, 1906, UJ 2, p. 410.

[63] Ed Simpson, quoted in LMM, Nov. 6, 1906, UJ 2, p. 410.

[64] Ed Simpson, quoted in LMM, Nov. 6, 1906, UJ 2, p. 410–11.

[65] LMM to GBM, Apr. 1, 1907, MDMM, p. 28.

[66] LMM to GBM, Apr. 1, 1907, MDMM, p. 30.

[67] LMM, Nov. 12, 1906, UJ 2, p. 413.

[68] LMM, Mar. 10, 1907, UJ 2, p. 425. LMM's unpublished journal indicates that the cold spell was in full swing from Feb. 25 to Mar. 9, with storms and delayed mails.

[69] LMM, Mar. 10, 1907, UJ 2, p. 426. During the very same time period, the Charlottetown newspapers were reporting on the trial of Harry Thaw, Evelyn Nesbit's husband, who had killed Stanford White a year earlier; Evelyn Nesbit's name appeared on the front pages. In sifting through the Charlottetown papers, the reader cannot help be struck by the extent of LMM's romanticizing of PEI realities. For example, side by side with the Thaw trial account on Apr. 12, 1907, was also the gruesome account of Tennyson Smith aka "King Alcohol" who had been tried in an "exciting trial" the night before in Charlottetown, found guilty "whereupon the judge sentenced the prisoner to death by having his neck broken immediately. A plea for private execution by the prisoner's counsel was overruled... Then the execution was proceeded with, the executioner

breaking the prisoner's neck." The assembled multitude applauded the execution ("King Alcohol Found Guilty," *The Guardian*, April 12, 1907, front page).

70 Maude Petitt Hill, "The Best Known Woman in Prince Edward Island. Part II: L.M. Montgomery, After Her First Success," *The Chatelaine* (June 1928), reprinted in Heilbron, *Remembering Lucy Maud Montgomery*, p. 222.

71 LMM, Feb. 25, 1907, SJ 1, p. 330.

72 LMM to FEC, Mar. 24, 1907, quoted in full in LMM, Apr. 5, 1937, SJ 5, p. 153.

73 FEC to LMM, Mar. 24, 1907, quoted in full in LMM, Apr. 5, 1937, SJ 5, p. 155.

74 LMM's behavior is consistent here, as she exhibited the same pattern in her courtship with others. When she was courted by Jack Sutherland during her college year, for instance, LMM and her close friend Mary Campbell built up an elaborate and hugely enjoyable deception scheme, pretending that Jack was courting Mary until the hoax was uncovered; see LMM, Apr. 6, 1894, UJ 1, pp. 268–69.

75 FEC to LMM, Mar. 24, 1907, quoted on Apr. 5, 1937, SJ 5, p. 155.

Chapter 13

1 AGG, ch. 20, p. 163.

2 LMM, Jan. 10, 1914, SJ 2, p. 141. *Godey's Lady's Book* (1830–1898): Founded by Louis A. Godey (1804–1878) of Philadelphia; edited by Sarah J. Hale, who boosted its literary contributions; see Albert H. Hardy, "Godey's, Past and Present," *Godey's Lady's Book* 125 (1892), pp. 363–68.

3 LMM, Jan. 10, 1914, SJ 2, p. 142.

4 W. J. Lampton, "To Anne," *Godey's Lady's Book* 127 (Oct. 1893), p. 450.

5 W. J. Lampton, "No Time for a Joke," *Godey's Lady's Book* 127 (Oct. 1893), p. 450. AGG, ch. 15, p. 113.

6 M[ary] A[ann] Maitland, "Charity Ann. Founded on Facts," *Godey's Lady's Book* 124 (Jan. 1892), p. 71. Maitland (1839–1919) was an immigrant from Elgin, Scotland, and lived in the Niagara, Ontario, region, where her husband George, a photographer, owned studios specializing in tinted photographs and cameo pictures. The couple had four girls and a son (George Junior would later join the *Toronto Star* editorial staff). A devout Baptist, Maitland published secular and religious poetry and stories in Canadian and American magazines, as well as two books of poetry, *Autumn Leaves* (1907) and *God Speed the Truth* (1919); see "A Talented Lady," *The St. Mary's Journal* (Ontario) (Mar. 6, 1919) and "Mrs. Maitland Dead at Age 80," *The Stratford Daily Herald* (Feb. 25, 1919), AOT.

7 Maitland, "Charity Ann," p. 71.

8 AGG, ch. 5, p. 39; Kate Douglas Wiggin, *Rebecca of Sunnybrook Farm* (1903; New York: Penguin, 1994), p. 33.

9 Maitland, "Charity Ann," p. 71; AGG, ch. 5, p. 41. Cf. Wiggin, *Rebecca*, p. 8: "Hannah and I haven't done anything but put babies to bed at night"; twins and triplets are discussed on p. 10. It is also interesting to note that fans expected LMM to be the mother of twins, as twins were evidently a convention of this type of literature.

10 Maitland, "Charity Ann," p. 73.

11 LMM, "The Little Three-Cornered Lot," *Zion's Herald* (July 29, 1903), pp. 954–55; J. L. Harbour, "Lucy Ann," *Zion's Herald* (July 29, 1903), pp. 956–57; the following quotations are all from this source.

12 Several of LMM's stories collected by Rea Wilmshurst in *Akin to Anne: Tales of Other Orphans* (Toronto: McClelland and Stewart, 1987) end with the reunion of separated

family members including "Why Not Ask Miss Price" (1904), "Millicent's Double" (1905), "The Fraser Scholarship" (1905), "Her Own People" (1905), "Penelope's Party Waist" (1904).

[13] See LMM, "Charlotte's Ladies" (1911), reprinted in *Akin to Anne*, 237–50; like Anne Shirley, Charlotte has difficulties being adopted because of her freckles and mouse-colored hair.

[14] For details, see Claudia Nelson, *Little Strangers: Portrayals of Adoption and Foster Care in America, 1850–1929* (Bloomington: Indiana UP, 2003), p. 5.

[15] AGG, ch. 3, pp. 29–30.

[16] Division of Reproductive Health, National Center for Chronic Disease Prevention and Health Promotion, CDC, "Achievements in Public Health, 1900–1999: Healthier Mothers and Babies," *Morbidity and Mortality Weekly Report* 48.38 (Oct. 1, 1999), pp. 849–58.

[17] James Whitcomb Riley, "Little Orphant Annie," *The Complete Work of James Whitcomb Riley* (Indianapolis: Bobbs-Merrill, 1916), p. 1169. "Little Orphant Annie" inspired Harold Gray's 1924 comic strip *Little Orphan Annie*, the 1918 Raggedy Ann Doll (a combination of *Little Orphant Annie* and Riley's *Raggedy Man*); Gray's *Little Orphan Annie* became the Broadway musical *Annie* in 1977.

[18] Mary Alice (Allie) Smith (1850–1924).

[19] "Among the Newest Books," *The Delineator* (Feb. 1904), p. 307; Maud owned a copy of this issue, which also contained her story, "The Promise of Lucy Ellen"; see ch. 2.

[20] T. D. MacLulich, "L. M. Montgomery and the Literary Heroine: Jo, Rebecca, Anne, and Emily," CCL 37 (1985), p. 11. The *Outlook* magazine (Aug. 22, 1908; reprinted in AAGG, p. 487), reviewed the novel by saying that Anne is a "sort of Canadian 'Rebecca of Sunnybrook Farms,'" but the book is "by no means an imitation; it has plenty of originality and character."

[21] On May 20, 1905 (SJ 1, p. 306), LMM notes rereading Dickens's *Pickwick Papers* and *David Copperfield*.

[22] LMM, "By the Grace of Sarah Maud," with drawings by Maud Tousey, *Modern Women* (June 1905), pp. 4–5, reprinted in August 1916 in *Maclean's* (then a Canadian monthly offering a digest of stories, articles and features). This was story # 213 (Rea Wilmshurst, "L. M. Montgomery's Short Stories: A Preliminary Bibliography," CCL 29 [1983], p. 30). LMM indicated to EW (June 28, 1905, GGL, p. 36) that she received $15 for it.

[23] LMM, "Sarah Maud," p. 4.

[24] LMM, "Sarah Maud," p. 5.

[25] LMM, "Sarah Maud," p. 5.

[26] LMM, June 27, 1929, SJ 3, p. 398.

[27] LMM, "The Bride Roses," *Christian Endeavor World* (Oct. 1903); reprinted in LMM, *After Many Days*, ed. Rea Wilmshurst (Toronto: Bantam, 1992), pp. 13–25.

[28] AGG, ch. 5, p. 42.

[29] LMM, Aug. 16, 1907, SJ 1, p. 330.

[30] AGG, ch. 3, p. 25.

Chapter 14

[1] L. C. Page's advertisement for *Anne of Green Gables* in the New York book trade journal *The Publishers' Weekly* (July 18, 1908), p. 68.

[2] My thanks to Donna J. Campbell for a photocopy of this photograph. L. C. Page's first name is often Americanized as Lewis, but *Who's Who in America* spells it consistently as Louis, as does LMM (see editors' note, LMM, SJ 2, p. 408).

[3] LMM, July 30, 1916, SJ 2, p. 187. L.C. Page & Company to LMM, Apr, 8, 1907, UGA.

[4] FEC to LMM ("ten-year letter"), Mar. 24, 1907, SJ 5, p. 155.

[5] L. C. Page & Company to LMM, Apr. 8, 1907, UGA.

[6] Carole Gerson, "Dragged at Anne's Chariot Wheels," LMMCC, p. 54.

[7] Agreement between L. M. Montgomery and L. C. Page & Company (Inc), Apr. 22, 1907, LAC. The contract further specifies that annual statements are prepared on the first day of each February and payable in March of each year; that she receives 6 complimentary copies of the book and can purchase books at the wholesale price of 40% off.

[8] LMM to EW, May 2, 1907, GGL, p. 51, p. 52.

[9] LMM, Aug. 16, 1907, SJ 1, p. 330–31.

[10] LMM, Aug. 16, 1907, SJ 1, p. 331.

[11] LMM, Oct. 9, 1907, UJ 2, p. 432.

[12] LMM, Oct. 9, 1907, SJ 1, p. 332.

[13] LMM, Nov. 3, 1907, UJ 2, p. 434.

[14] LMM, Dec. 17, 1907, UJ 2, p. 440.

[15] LMM, May 3, 1908, UJ 2, p. 447.

[16] LMM to EW, Mar. 2, 1908, GGL, p. 64.

[17] LMM to EW, Apr. 5, 1908, GGL, p. 66.

[18] LMM, May 3, 1908, UJ 2, pp. 450–51, p. 454.

[19] Mary Beth Cavert, "Back to School: Lucy Maud Montgomery's Dedicated Teacher," Kindred Spirits (Fall 1994), pp. 13–15.

[20] LMM, May 3, 1908, UJ 2, p. 446.

[21] "In Memoriam of Rev. Ewan Macdonald" (Obituary), The Presbyterian Record (Feb. 1944), reprinted in Kindred Spirits (Dec. 2003), p. 13. EM served in Bloomfield and O'Leary until 1910, when he was called to Leaskdale and Zephyr near Toronto.

[22] LMM, May 24, 1908, SJ 1, p. 335.

[23] LMM to GBM, Jan. 8, 1908, MDMM, p. 37.

[24] Advertisement for AGG, The Publishers' Weekly (Mar. 21, 1908), p. 1157. Following the ad was an ad for Helen M. Winslow's Peggy at Spinster Farm, character sketches and bits of biography of farm animals; the two books would appear side by side in several ads, although Winslow's title was generally truncated to Spinster Farm.

[25] Advertisement for AGG, The Publishers' Weekly (Mar. 21, 1908), p. 1157.

[26] Advertisement for AGG, The Publishers' Weekly (June 13, 1908), cover page.

[27] LMM, June 20, 1908, SJ 1, p. 335.

[28] George Gibbs (1870–1942). Advertisement for cover art poster, The Delineator (Jan. 1905), p. 165; a single The Delineator issue cost 15 cents (p. 165). Donna J. Campbell discovered that the September 1908 issue of The Delineator featured the mirror image of the January 1905 cover; personal conversation.

[29] See LMM, Nov. 29, 1910, SJ 2, p. 27.

[30] Frontispiece, Anne of Green Gables (Boston: L. C. Page & Company, 1908), LAC.

[31] On the marketing of the novel for adults, see also Mary Rubio, "Introduction," HT, p. 2.

[32] "W. A. J. Claus," Wisdom Monthly (May 1902), 121. My thanks to Donna J. Campbell for a copy of this article. The German-American William Anton Joseph Claus (1962–1926) was born in Mainz, Germany; May Austin Claus (1882–?) in Berlin, NY.

[33] LMM to EW, Sept. 10, 1908, GGL, p. 73.

[34] LMM, Aug. 26, 1932, SJ 4, p. 195.

[35] LMM, July 16, 1908, SJ 1, p. 337.

[36] Rev. in *The Chicago Record-Herald* cited in *The Publishers' Weekly* (July 18, 1908), p. 68. AGG, ch. 14, p. 104.

[37] "A Heroine from an Asylum," *The New York Times Saturday Review of Books* (July 18, 1908); reprinted in Appendix, AGG, ed. Cecily Devereux (Peterborough: Broadview, 2004), p. 391. See also, LMM to EW, Sept. 10, 1908, GGL, pp. 71–72, with snippets of the reviews and LMM's comments.

[38] *The Globe* (Toronto) (Aug. 15, 1908), reprinted in Appendix, AGG, ed. Devereux, p. 393.

[39] LMM to GBM, Aug. 31, 1908, MDMM, p. 38, p. 41.

[40] LMM to EW, Sept. 10, 1908, GGL, p. 73.

[41] LMM to EW, Sept. 10, 1908, GGL, p. 71.

[42] LMM to EW, Sept. 10, 1908, GGL, p. 74, p. 76.

[43] LMM, Oct. 15, 1908, SJ 1, p. 339.

[44] *The Canadian Magazine* (Toronto) 32.1 (Nov. 1908), p. 87. The Ryrie-Campbell Collection, L.M. Montgomery Institute, UPEI.

[45] S. L. Clemens (Mark Twain) quoted in a letter written by his secretary to LMM, Oct. 3, 1908, UGA; quoted in L.C. Page's ad for AGG in *The Publishers' Weekly* (Dec. 5, 1908), cover page. It appears that LMM had sent Mark Twain the book because the secretary's letter begins with a thank-you for the book.

[46] L. C. Page & Company ad for AGG, *The Publishers' Weekly* (Dec. 26, 1908), cover page.

[47] Nate Lockhart's first son was born in Jan. 1908, his second son in Nov. of the same year; see Mary Beth Cavert, "Whatever Happened to Nate Lockhart," *Kindred Spirits* (Dec. 2005), p. 12.

[48] Isabel Anderson, quoted in LMM, Feb. 8, 1932, SJ 4, p. 165.

[49] Reginald Wright Kauffman, "The Redheaded Baby," *The Delineator* 72 (Sept. 1908), p. 410.

[50] *The Metropolitan Magazine* 27 (Oct. 1907–Mar. 1908), Ad section (no page numbers).

[51] "The Growth and Uses of the Motor-Boat," *The Metropolitan Magazine* 29 (Mar. 1909), p. 641.

[52] George Gibbs, "A Detail of Spring Motoring," *The Metropolitan Magazine* 28 (June 1908).

[53] George Gibbs, "Motor-Boating," *The Metropolitan Magazine* (Mar. 1908).

[54] See, for example, "The Delineator Child-Rescue Campaign," *The Delineator* (Sept. 1908), p. 405. On Theodore Dreiser's expansion of the magazine's social reform campaign and social critique, see also Christopher Weinmann, "The Delineator," *A Theodore Dreiser Encyclopedia*, ed. Keith Newlin (Westport, Connecticut: Greenwood Press, 2003), pp. 86–87. Claudia Nelson, *Little Strangers: Portrayals of Adoption and Foster Care in America, 1850–1929* (Bloomington: Indiana University Press, 2003), p. 117, illustrates that these child campaign efforts ironically also boosted discourses regarding "race suicide," advocating against those "who refused parenthood."

[55] "The Children We Offer This Month," *The Delineator* (Oct. 1908), p. 576.

[56] Nelson, *Little Strangers*, p. 130.

[57] Jacqueline Stanley, *Reading to Heal* (Boston: Element Books, 1999), p. x.

[58] L.C. Page ad, *The Publishers' Weekly* (Nov. 28, 1908), p. 71.

[59] L.C. Page ad, *The Publishers' Weekly* (Dec. 26, 1908), cover page.

[60] LMM, Oct. 15, 1908, SJ 1, p. 339.

61 James R. Petersen, "Playboy's History of the Sexual Revolution, Part I (1900–1910): The City Electric," *Playboy Magazine* (Dec. 1996), p. 171

62 EN, PD, p. 118, p. 119.

Chapter 15

1 LMM to Gertrude (Trudy) Ramsey, July 26, 1940; *The Lucy Maud Montgomery Album*, ed. Heilbron comp., p. 311.

2 LMM to Trudy Ramsay, July 26, 1940, *The Lucy Maud Montgomery Album*, comp. McCabe, ed. Heilbron, p. 311.

3 L.C. Page ad, *The Publishers' Weekly* (Dec. 26, 1908), cover page.

4 LMM to EW, Sept. 10, 1908, GGL, p. 74.

5 LMM, Oct. 31, 1908, SJ 1, p. 341.

6 Bliss Carman's *The Making of Personality* (Boston: L.C. Page & Company, 1908) was advertised on L.C. Page's list alongside AGG, *The Publishers' Weekly* (July 4, 1908), cover page. See also Sylvia DuVernet, *Minding the Spirit: Theosophic Thoughts Concerning L.M. Montgomery* (Toronto: n.p., 1993).

7 LMM, Feb. 20, 1909, SJ 1, p. 347.

8 LMM, Sept. 21, 1909, SJ 1, p. 359.

9 See the mini-biography provided by Hildi Froese Tiessen and Paul Gerard Tiessen, *After Green Gables: L.M. Montgomery's Letters to Ephraim Weber, 1916–1941* (Toronto: University of Toronto Press, 2006), p. 12.

10 LMM's handwritten comments on her contract with L.C. Page & Company (Inc), Apr. 22, 1907, LAC.

11 "Anne of Green Gables," *Family Herald and Weekly Star* 1 in between Dec. 1909 and Mar. 1910. My thanks to Benjamin Lefebvre. In December 1909, *The Housewife* (New York) launched *Anne of Green Gables* as a serial on its front page, illustrated with attractive drawings by Mabel L. Humphrey, and reprinted the entire book except for four chapters in a serial ending in June 1910; My thanks to Donna J. Campbell.

12 See Cecily Devereux, "'Canadian Classic' and 'Commodity Export': The Nationalism of 'our' *Anne of Green Gables*," *Journal of Canadian Studies* (Spring 2001), pp. 1–28.

13 See Linda Lear, *Beatrix Potter: A Life in Nature* (New York: St. Martin's Press, 2007), p. 4.

14 See also E. Holly Pike, "Mass Marketing, Popular Culture, and the Canadian Celebrity Author," MA, pp. 238–51; and Lorraine York, "'I Knew I Would "Arrive" Some Day': L.M. Montgomery and the Strategies of Literary Celebrity," CCL 113–114 (Spring–Summer 2004), pp. 98–116.

15 LMM, Sept. 7, 1910, SJ 2, p. 12.

16 LMM, Sept. 11, 1910, SJ 2, p. 12.

17 Lindsay Swift, *Literary Landmarks of Boston* (Boston: Houghton Mifflin Company, 1922).

18 LMM, Nov. 29, 1910, SJ 2, p. 25.

19 FEC to LMM, Postcard, 1910, UGA; reproduced in SJ 5, p. 52.

20 LMM, Nov. 29, 1910, SJ 2, p. 30.

21 LMM, Nov. 29, 1910, SJ 2, p. 30.

22 LMM, "Topics Worth While," *Boston Herald* [Nov. 1910], Scrapbook, UGA.

23 LMM, Nov. 29, 1910, SJ 2, p. 29.

24 See also De Jonge, "Through the Eyes of Memory," pp. 252–67.

25 LMM, Jan. 27, 1911, SJ 2, p. 40.

26 AHD, ch. 4, pp. 20–21.

27 LMM, May 23, 1911, SJ 2, p. 68.

[28] AP, pp. 80–95. The memoir ends with the journey to Europe, a literary pilgrimage, with two full chapters out of ten devoted to its description as a culmination of her development into a writer.

[29] LMM, Aug. 27, 1911, SJ 2, p. 75.

[30] LMM, July 19, 1911, SJ 2, p. 70.

[31] LMM, Sept. 18, 1911, SJ 2, p. 77.

[32] LMM, Sept. 22, 1912, SJ 2, p. 108.

[33] LMM, Sept. 22, 1912, SJ 2, p. 99–100.

[34] LMM to Fannie Wise, Jan. 30, 1912, in *The Lucy Maud Montgomery Album*, comp. McCabe, ed. Heilbron, p. 216.

[35] L. C. Page quoted in the Memorandum written by Judge F. T. Hammond, Commonwealth of Massachusetts, Superior Court, *Lucy M. Montgomery Macdonald v. The Page Company et al*, n.y., p. 3, LAC.

[36] LMM, *Anne of the Island* (1915) (Toronto: The Ryerson Press, 1942), p. v.

[37] Oliver Bell Bunce, "The Bachelor Girl," *Godey's Lady's Book* (Nov. 1893), pp. 586–88.

[38] Carole Gerson, "'Dragged at Anne's Chariot Wheels': The Triangle of Author, Publisher, and Fictional Character," LMMCC, pp. 49–63. Another reason LMM wanted to break up with Page was because he had no interest in publishing a book of her poems. McClelland offered to publish the poems, probably knowing the book would not sell, as a way of luring her to their company; my thanks to Benjamin Lefebvre for this point.

[39] For an update of the legal issues, while they were still ongoing, see LMM, Jan. 12, 1919, SJ 2, p. 284.

[40] LMM, Mar. 23, 1919, SJ 2, p. 311.

[41] LMM, Oct. 18, 1923, SJ 3, p. 150.

[42] LMM, Feb. 22, 1920, SJ 2, p. 373.

[43] LMM, "Is This My Anne?" *The Chatelaine* (Jan. 1935), reprinted in Quaile, *L. M. Montgomery*, p. 172. See also Faye Hammill, "'A New and Exceedingly Brilliant Star': L.M. Montgomery, *Anne of Green Gables*, and Mary Miles Minter," *Modern Language Review* 101.3 (2006), pp. 652–70; and Robert Klepper, "Mary Miles Minter: Beauty Wronged," http://www.classicimages.com/1997/july97/minter.html.

[44] LMM, Oct. 13, 1929, SJ 4, p. 20.

[45] LMM, June 18, 1920; SJ 2, p. 382.

[46] LMM to GBM, Feb. 10, 1929, MDMM, p. 142; this letter provides a detailed and retrospective chronology of her legal troubles with L. C. Page. LMM was not the first to suffer roughshod treatment and violation of contract with L. C. Page and Company. The L. C. Page papers at the NYPL contain a 1900 letter handwritten by Gabriele d'Annunzio and addressed to "Monsieur Page editeur" with a complaint about unauthorized translations of his novel *Le Feu*.

[47] LMM to GBM, Feb. 10, 1929, MDMM, p. 138.

[48] AHD, ch. 11, p. 76.

[49] Interviewed by Alexandra Heilbron, *Remembering Lucy Maud Montgomery* (Toronto: The Dundurn Group, 2001), p. 38.

[50] LMM, Oct. 10, 1936, SJ 5, p. 97.

[51] LMM, Oct. 10 and 11, 1936, SJ 5, p. 98.

[52] LMM's final novel, *The Blythes Are Quoted*, has remained unpublished.

[53] LMM, Sept. 12, 1938, SJ 5, p. 278.

[54] AI, ch. 2, 12–13.

Epilogue

[1] "Judge and Jury Moved to Tears," *The Charlottetown Daily Patriot* (Feb. 11, 1907).

[2] Courtroom illustration accompanying article "Strenuous Day for Mrs. Thaw," *The Charlottetown Guardian* (Feb. 23. 1907), front page.

[3] EN, PD, p. 170.

[4] Bolger, YBA, p. 189.

[5] EW, "L.M. Montgomery as a Letter-Writer," *Dalhousie Review* 22 (Oct. 1942), p. 304; see also Paul Gerard Tiessen and Hildi Froese Tiessen, "Epistolary Performance: Writing Mr. Weber," ILLMM, pp. 222–38.

[6] AGG, ch. 38, p. 309.

[7] LMM, Nov. 9, 1937, SJ 5, p. 217.

[8] LMM, Jan. 30, 1921, SJ 2, p. 401.

[9] LMM, Aug. 16, 1923, SJ 3, p. 145–46.

[10] LMM, Dec. 27, 1920, SJ 2, p. 394.

Selected Bibliography

I. SELECTED UNPUBLISHED SOURCES

Manuscripts of LMM's novels including *Anne of Green Gables*, CCAG.

Eickemeyer papers, HRM.

Eickemeyer scrapbooks, PHC/SNMAH.

L. C. Page papers, NYPL.

LMM papers including photographs and 10 legal-size ledger books with LMM's unpublished journals and other records, UGA.

LMM's scrapbooks, CCAG and UGA.

LMM's contracts with L. C. Page, LAC.

LMM's correspondence with Ephraim Weber and G. B. MacMillan, LAC.

Minute book: Cavendish Literary Society (Feb. 1886–Jan. 7, 1924), PEIPA.

II. SELECTED PUBLISHED SOURCES

1. Selected Works by L. M. Montgomery

Across the Miles: Tales of Correspondence. Ed. Rea Wilmshurst. Toronto: McClelland and Stewart, 1995.

After Green Gables: L. M. Montgomery's Letters to Ephraim Weber, 1916–1941. Ed. Hildi Froese Tiessen and Paul Gerard Tiessen. Toronto: University of Toronto Press, 2006.

After Many Days: Tales of Time Passed. Ed. Rea Wilmshurst. Toronto: McClelland-Bantam, 1992.

Akin to Anne: Tales of Other Orphans. Ed. Rea Wilmshurst. Toronto: McClelland and Stewart, 1987.

Along the Shore: Tales by the Sea. Ed. Rea Wilmshurst. Toronto: McClelland and Stewart, 1989.

The Alpine Path: The Story of My Career. 1917. Toronto: Fitzhenry and Whiteside, 1997.

Among the Shadows: Tales from the Darker Side. Ed. Rea Wilmshurst. Toronto: McClelland and Stewart, 1990.

Anne of Avonlea. 1909. New York: Bantam Books, 1992.

Anne of Green Gables. 1908. Ed. Mary Henley Rubio and Elizabeth Waterston. New York: Norton, 2007.

Anne of Green Gables. 1908. Ed. Cecily Devereux. Peterborough: Broadview Press, 2004.

Anne of Green Gables. 1908. London: The Folio Society, 2004.

Anne of Green Gables. 1908. New York: Bantam Books, 1992.

Anne of Green Gables. 1908. Adapted edition. Toronto: Key Porter, 1992.

Anne of Green Gables. 1908. Toronto: The Ryerson Press, 1942.

Anne's House of Dreams. 1917. New York: Bantam Books, 1998.

Anne of Ingleside. 1939. New York: Bantam Books, 1992.

Anne of the Island. 1915. New York: Bantam Books, 1992.

Anne of Windy Poplars. 1936. New York: Bantam Books, 1998.

The Annotated Anne of Green Gables. Ed. Wendy E. Barry, Margaret Anne Doody, and Mary E. Doody Jones. New York: Oxford UP, 1997.

At the Altar: Matrimonial Tales. Ed. Rea Wilmshurst. Toronto: McClelland and Stewart, 1995.

The Blue Castle. 1926. Toronto: McClelland-Bantam, 1988.

"Aunt Susanna's Birthday Celebration." *New Idea Woman's Magazine* (Feb. 1905). Reprinted in Montgomery. *Across the Miles* 155–62.

"By the Grace of Sarah Maud." Drawings by Maud Tousey. *Modern Women* (June 1905): 4–5. NYPL.

"The Cake that Prissy Made." *The Congregationalist and Christian World* (July 11, 1903): 59. Reprinted in Montgomery. *Anne of Green Gables.* Ed. Devereux 360–64.

"Charlotte's Ladies." *Epworth Herald* (Feb. 1911). Reprinted in Montgomery. *Akin to Anne* 237–50.

Chronicles of Avonlea. 1912. New York: Bantam Books, 1993.

"Diana's Wedding Dress." *Farm and Fireside* (Mar. 1902). The Ryrie-Campbell Collection, L. M. Montgomery Institute, UPEI.

The Doctor's Sweetheart and Other Stories. Ed. Catherine McLay. Toronto: McGraw-Hill Ryerson Press, 1979. Bantam, 1993.

Emily Climbs. Toronto: McClelland and Stewart, 1925. NCL edition 1989.

Emily of New Moon. Toronto: McClelland and Stewart, 1923. NCL edition 1989.

Emily's Quest. Toronto: McClelland and Stewart, 1927. NCL edition 1989.

"The Fraser Scholarship." *Boys' World* (Apr. 1905). Reprinted in Montgomery. *Akin to Anne* 177–85.

Further Chronicles of Avonlea. 1920. Toronto: McGraw-Hill Ryerson, 1972.

"The Gable Window." *Ladies' Journal* (May 1897). Reprinted in Laura Higgins. "Snapshot Portraits: Finding L. M. Montgomery in Her 'Dear Den.'" In Rubio. *Harvesting Thistles* 110–11.

The Golden Road. 1913. Toronto: Ryerson, 1944.

The Green Gables Letters from L. M. Montgomery to Ephraim Weber, 1905–1909. Ed. Wilfrid Eggleston. Ottawa: Borealis, 2001.

"Harbor Sunset." Poem. *Ainslee's Magazine* (Jan. 1902): 490.

"Her Own People." *American Messenger* (Aug. 1905). Reprinted in Montgomery. *Akin to Anne* 187–97.

"In Lovers [sic] Lane." *The Delineator* (July 1903): 16. NYPL.

"Is this My Anne?." *The Chatelaine* (Jan. 1935). Reprinted in Deborah Quaile, *L. M. Montgomery* 171–74.

Jane of Lantern Hill. Toronto: McClelland and Stewart, 1937.

"Jane Lavinia." *Zion's Herald* (Sept. 26, 1906): 1230–32. NYPL.

Kilmeny of the Orchard. 1910. Toronto: Ryerson, 1944.

"Lavender's Room." *East and West: A Paper for Young Canadians* (Feb. 11, 1905): 41–42. LMM Magazine Clippings CM 67.5.24, CCAG.

"The Little Gable Window." *The Designer* (May 1907): 58. The Ryrie-Campbell Collection, L. M. Montgomery Institute, UPEI.

"The Little Three-Cornered Lot." *Zion's Herald* (July 20, 1903): 854–55. NYPL.

"The Minister's Daughter." *What to Eat* (Sept. 1903). The Ryrie-Campbell Collection, L. M. Montgomery Institute, UPEI.

"Millicent's Double." *East and West* (Dec. 1905). Reprinted in Montgomery. *Akin to Anne* 143–53.

Magic for Marigold. 1929. Toronto: McClelland-Bantam, 1988.

Mistress Pat. Toronto: McClelland and Stewart, 1935.

My Dear Mr. M: Letters to G. B. MacMillan from L. M. Montgomery. Ed. Francis W. P. Bolger and Elizabeth R. Epperly. Toronto: Oxford University Press, 1992.

"A New Fashioned Flavoring." *Golden Days for Boys and Girls* (Aug. 27, 1898): 641–42. Reprinted in Montgomery. *Anne of Green Gables.* Ed. Devereux 344–64.

"The Old South Orchard." *The Outing Magazine* (Jan. 1908): 413–16. TRL.

"The Osbornes' Christmas." *Zion's Herald* (Dec. 16, 1903): 1604–5. NYPL.

"Our Uncle Wheeler." *Golden Days for Boys and Girls* (Jan. 22, 1898), pp. 145–46. Reprinted in Montgomery, *Anne of Green Gables.* Ed. Devereux 335–44.

Pat of Silver Bush. Toronto: McClelland and Stewart, 1933.

"Patty's Mistake." *Zion's Herald* (Apr. 16, 1902): 494. Reprinted in Montgomery. *Anne of Green Gables.* Ed. Devereux 356–60.

"Penelope's Party Waist." *The Designer* (Mar. 1904). Reprinted in Montgomery. *Akin to Anne* 155–64.

The Poetry of Lucy Maud Montgomery. Ed. John Ferns and Kevin McCabe. Don Mills, ON: Fitzhenry and Whiteside, 1987.

"The Promise of Lucy Ellen." *The Delineator* (Feb. 1904). Reprinted in Montgomery. *The Doctor's Sweetheart* 58–66.

Rainbow Valley. 1919. New York: Bantam Books, 1992.

Rilla of Ingleside. Toronto: McClelland and Stewart, 1921.

The Road to Yesterday. Toronto: McGraw-Hill Ryerson Press, 1974.

"The Running Away of Chester." *Boys' World* (Nov. Dec. 1903). Reprinted in Montgomery. *Akin to Anne* 104–42.

The Selected Journals of L.M. Montgomery, v. 1: *1889–1910,* v. 2: *1910–1921,* v. 3: *1921–1929,* v. 4: *1929–1935,* v. 5: *1935–1942.* Ed. and intro. Mary Henley Rubio and Elizabeth Waterston. Toronto: Oxford University Press, 1985, 1987, 1992, 1998, 2004.

The Story Girl. 1911. Toronto: McGraw-Hill Ryerson Press, 1944.

A Tangled Web. 1931. Toronto: McClelland and Stewart, 1972.

"The Understanding of Sister Sara." *The Pilgrim* (August 1905): 11–12. Reprinted in Montgomery. *Across the Miles* 39–50.

"To My Enemy." *The Smart Set* (Jan. 1902): 92. NYPL.

The Watchman and Other Poems. Toronto: McClelland, Goodchild, and Stewart, 1916.

"The Way of the Winning of Anne." *Springfield Republican* (Dec. 10, 1899): 18. Reprinted Anon. "The Winning of Anne." *Family Herald* (May 1900): 22. Reprinted in Montgomery. *At the Altar* 161–72.

"'. . . where has my yellow garter gone?' The Diary of L. M. Montgomery and Nora Lefurgey." Ed. Irene Gammel. In *The Intimate Life of L. M. Montgomery.* Ed. Gammel 19–87.

"Why Not Ask Miss Price." *Girls' Companion* (Nov. 1904). Reprinted in Montgomery. *Akin to Anne* 83–91.

2. Selected Source Influences and Context for Anne of Green Gables
For studies concerning the specific literary allusions to the Bible, Robert Browning, Lord Byron, Walter Scott, William Shakespeare, and others in *Anne of Green Gables*, see Devereux's "A Note on Montgomery's Literary Allusions"; Epperly's *Fragrance*; Doody and Barry's "Literary Allusion and Quotation in *Anne of Green Gables*"; and Wilmshurst's "L.M. Montgomery's Use of Quotations and Allusions in the 'Anne' Books" (all cited below in Section **4. Selected Secondary Sources**).

A'hmuty Nash, Louisa. "Homeless Children Homed." *The Ladies' World* (Oct. 1902): 6.

Alcott, Louisa May. *Little Women*. Boston: Roberts Brothers, 1868.

Andersen, Hans Christian. *Fairy Tales*. London: Sampson Low, Marston, Low and Searle, 1872.

Arnim, Elizabeth von. *Elizabeth and her German Garden*. New York: The Macmillan Company, 1901. London: Virago, 2006.

Baker, Louise R. "An Adopted Daughter," *The Major's Sunshine*, *The Sunday School Advocate for Boys and Girls* (Jan. 7, 1905): 1–3.

Barrie, James M. *Sentimental Tommy: The Story of His Boyhood*. New York: Scribner, 1896.

———. *Tommy and Grizel*. 1902. n.p.: Press of the Readers Club, 1943.

Bartlett, Gertrude. "A Pagan's Prayer." Poem. *Ainslee's Magazine* (Nov. 1902): 87.

Battell Loomis, Charles. "Man's Humiliation." *Modern Women* (Aug. 1905): 71.

Birney, Mrs. Theodore W. "Childhood: A Chapter on Manners." *The Delineator* (Jan. 1904): 129–30. NYPL.

———. "Childhood: Growing Up With One's Children." *The Delineator* (April 1904): 680–83. NYPL.

———. "Childhood: Temperament and Discipline." *The Delineator* (June 1904): 1074–77. NYPL.

Bell Bunce, Oliver. "The Bachelor Girl." *Godey's Lady's Book* (Nov. 1893): 586–88.

Bunn, Alfred (lyrics) and M. W. Balfe (music). *The Bohemian Girl: Opera, In Three Acts*. London: Boosey & Co, 1872.

Denig Lichfield, Grace. "The Bend in the Road." Scrapbook 67.5.12, p. 26. CCAG.

Dickens, Charles. *The Personal History of David Copperfield*. London: Bradbury & Evans, 1850.

———. *The Posthumous Papers of the Pickwick Club*. London: Chapman & Hall, 1837.

Du Maurier, George. *Trilby*. New York: Harper and Brothers, 1894.

Farnham, T. H. "'To Lesbia. The Greek Poet's Tribute to His Love." *Godey's Lady's Book* (Mar. 1892): 254.

Gale, Zona. "The Things That Are Real." *The Delineator* (Mar. 1905): 414–21. NYPL.

Gates Kerr, Sophie. "A Daughter of Maryland." *The Ladies World* (Oct. 1902): 4–5. MLC.

Harbour, J. L. "Lucy Ann." *Zion's Herald* (July 29, 1903): 954–55. NYPL.

Haweis, Eliza. *The Art of Beauty and the Art of Dress*. London: Chatto & Windus, Piccadilly, 1878. MLC. Reprinted New York: Garland, 1978.

Hawthorne, Nathaniel. *The House of the Seven Gables*. 1851. New York: Norton, 2005.

Higginson, Ella. "One o' Them Still, Stubborn Kinds." Illustrations by Elizabeth Shippen Green. *The Ladies' Home Journal* (June 1897): 4. MLC.

Hoover, Bessie R. "The Sunshine Girl." *The Sunday School Advocate for Boys and Girls* (Mar. 25, 1905): 91. NYPL.

Hull, Florence. "Apple Blossoms." *Godey's Lady's Book* (Dec. 1893): 736–39. NYPL.

Irving, Washington. *Tales of the Alhambra*. Leon: Editorial Everest, S.A., 2006.

Kellogg, Alice M. "Modern House Building: No. 3—'High Gables,'" *The Delineator* (Mar. 1905): 448–49. NYPL.

Kobbé, Gustav. "The Stage and the Second Self." *The Delineator* (Apr. 1905): 608–12. NYPL.

Lampton, W. J. "No Time for a Joke." *Godey's Lady's Book* (Oct. 1893): 450. NYPL.

———. "To Anne." *Godey's Lady's Book* (Oct. 1893): 450. NYPL.

Le Gallienne, Richard. "Hans Christian Andersen: The Friend of the Children," *The Delineator* (Apr. 1905). TRL.

Longfellow, Henry Wadsworth. "Maidenhood." *The Household* (June 1901): 9. MLC.

Maitland, Mary Ann. "Charity Ann: Founded on Facts." *Godey's Lady's Book* (Jan. 1892): 70–73. NYPL.

MacLeod, Ward. "Cut Flowers for Decorative Use in the Home." *The Delineator* (Jan. 1904): 155–57. NYPL.

Miller, S. Millington. "Sappho—The Woman and the Time." *Godey's Lady's Book* (Feb. 1895): 114–22. NYPL.

"Now I lay me down to sleep." Illustration with caption. *Ram's Horn* (Jan. 10, 1903): 3. NYPL.

Pansy Sunday Book. Boston: Lothrop Publishing Company, 1898. (Contains Lord Alfred Tennyson's "Song of the Brook," "Keep a Scrap Book," etc.). MLC.

Phillips, Olivia E. "Advice from Everywhere. II. Care of Children." *Godey's Lady's Book* (Feb. 1892): 177–78. NYPL.

Reamond, Cornelia. "Dora Merideth's Engagement." *Godey's Lady's Book* (July 1890): 17–21. NYPL.

Reeves, Marian C. L. "Eve of St. John: A Midsummer Day's Dream." *Godey's Lady's Book* (June 1892): 503–5. NYPL.

———. "On her Sixth Birthday: A Leap-Year Story." *Godey's Lady's Book* (Feb. 1892): 168–71. NYPL.

Rodman Church, Ella and Augusta de Bubna. "Tam! The Story of a Woman." Novel in 26 chapters serialized in 6 installments in *Godey's Lady's Book* (Jan. 1884–June 1894). NYPL.

Rogers, Eleanor. "Freckles 'And Such.'" *The Delineator* (Jan. 1905): 138. NYPL.

Sabin, Edwin L. "The Castle in Spain," *Days of Youth* (n.d.): 6. LMM Magazine Clippings CM 67.5.24. CCAG.

Sangster, Margaret E. "Live in the Sunshine." *Zion's Herald* (June 21, 1905): 781. NYPL.

Scollard, Clinton. "Winter in Lovers' Lane." *The Delineator* (Jan. 1904): 60, NYPL. A clipping of the poem (without magazine reference) is found in LMM's Scrapbook, CM 67.5.12. 40. CCAG.

Shepperson, M. J. "Envelopes, Friends and Books." *The Ladies' World* (Oct. 1902): 22.

Sheridan, Mattie. "The Next Lady of the White House." *Godey's Lady's Book* (Sept. 1892): 369–73. NYPL.

Tennyson, Alfred, Lord. "Lancelot and Elaine." *Idylls of the King*. Ed. J. M. Gray. London: Penguin, 1983. 168–205.

———. "The Palace of Art." *Poems*. Ed. Christopher Ricks. London: Longman, 1969.

Upton, Marie Frances. "Diana." *Godey's Lady's Book* (Aug. 1893): 222. NYPL.

Wakefield, Priscilla. "A Girl's Conscience." *The Delineator* (Mar. 1905): 522–23. NYPL.

———. "A Girl's Personal Appearance and Dress." *The Delineator* (Jan. 1905): 164–65. MLC.

————. "A Talk about Pictures." *The Delineator* (Feb. 1904): 334–35. NYPL.

Wells, Carolyn. "A Girl's Gift to a Girl Graduate." *The Ladies' Home Journal* (June 1903): 30. NYPL.

Wiggin, Kate Douglas. *Rebecca of Sunnybrook Farm* 1903. New York: Penguin, 1994.

Wiley, Franklin B. "The Court of Last Resort," *The Ladies Home Journal* (May 1905): 19.

Winslow, Helen M. *Peggy at Spinster Farm.* Boston: L.C. Page & Company, 1908; New York: Grosset & Dunlap, 1908. The work was first serialized in 1905 in *The Delineator,* with The Butterick Publishing Company holding the 1905 and 1906 copyright.

3. Selected Magazine Sources

Ainslee's (New York)

The Booklovers Magazine (Philadelphia)

The Charlottetown Daily Patriot (Charlottetown, PEI)

The Charlottetown Examiner (Charlottetown, PEI)

The Charlottetown Guardian (Charlottetown, PEI)

The Delineator (New York)

East and West: A Paper for Young Canadians (Toronto)

The Epworth Herald (Chicago and New York)

Godey's Lady's Book (Philadelphia)

The Household Magazine (Boston)

The Journal-Pioneer (Summerside, PEI)

The Ladies' Home Journal (Philadelphia)

The Metropolitan (New York)

Modern Women (Boston)

The Publishers' Weekly (New York)

Pure Words (Cincinnati)

Ram's Horn (Chicago)

Sunday School Advocate for Boys and Girls (New York)

What to Eat (A National Food Magazine, Chicago)

Zion's Herald (Boston)

4. Selected Secondary Sources

Åhmansson, Gabriella. *A Life and Its Mirrors: A Feminist Reading of L.M. Montgomery's Fiction.* Stockholm: Almqvist & Wiksell, 1991.

Akamatsu, Yoshiko. "Japanese Readings of *Anne of Green Gables.*" In *L.M. Montgomery and Canadian Culture.* Ed. Gammel and Epperly 201–12.

Allard, Danièle. "*Taishu Bunka* and Anne Clubs in Japan." In *Making Avonlea.* Ed. Gammel 238–51.

Allen, Sidney. "Rudolf Eickemeyer, Jr.: An Appreciation." *Photo Era: The American Journal of Photography* 15.3 (Sept. 1905): 79–83.

Atwood, Margaret. "Revisiting Anne." In *L.M. Montgomery and Canadian Culture.* Ed. Gammel and Epperly 222–26.

Baldwin, Douglas. "L.M. Montgomery's *Anne of Green Gables*: The Japanese Connection." *Journal of Canadian Studies* 28.3 (Fall 1993): 123–33.

Baldwin, Douglas and Thomas Spira. *Gaslight Epidemics and Vagabond Cows: Charlottetown in the Victorian Era.* Charlottetown: Ragweed Press, 1988.

Barry, Wendy E. "The Geography of *Anne of Green Gables.*" In Montgomery. *The Annotated Anne of Green Gables.* Ed. Barry, Doody, and Doody Jones 415–18.

———. "The Settlers of P.E.I.: The Celtic Influence in *Anne*." In Montgomery. *The Annotated Anne of Green Gables*. Ed. Barry, Doody, and Doody Jones 418–21.

Beck, Boyde and Edward MacDonald. *Everyday and Extraordinary: Almanac of the History of Prince Edward Island*. Charlottetown: PEI Museum and Heritage Foundation, 1999.

Berg, Temma F. "*Anne of Green Gables*: A Girl's Reading." *Children's Literature Association Quarterly* 13.3 (1988): 124–28.

———. "Sisterhood is Fearful: Female Friendship in Montgomery." In *Harvesting Thistles*. Ed. Rubio 36–49.

Berman, Marshall. *All That Is Sold Melts Into Air: The Experience of Modernity*. New York: Penguin, 1988.

Blackford, Holly. *Out of this World: Why Literature Matters to Girls*. New York: Columbia University Teachers College Press, 2004.

Bolger, Francis W. P. *The Years Before "Anne."* 1974. Halifax: Nimbus, 1991.

Boym, Svetlana. *The Future of Nostalgia*. New York: Basic Books, 2001.

Brannan, Marian Gimby. "Lucy Maud Montgomery." *Twenty Remarkable Women Seen Through Their Handwriting*. Little River, CA: Little River Press, 2004. 98–106.

Brennan, Joseph Gerard. "The Story of a Classic: Anne and After." *The American Scholar* 64 (1995): 247–56.

Bruce, Harry. *Maud: The Life of L. M. Montgomery*. New York: Bantam, 1994.

Carman, Bliss. *The Making of Personality*. Boston: L.C. Page & Company, 1908.

Clarkson, Adrienne. "Foreword." In *L. M. Montgomery and Canadian Culture*. Ed. Gammel and Epperly ix–xii.

Classen, Constance. "Is 'Anne of Green Gables' An American Import?" *Canadian Children's Literature / Littérature canadienne pour la jeunesse* 55 (1989): 42–50.

Careless, Virginia. "L. M. Montgomery and Everybody Else: A Look at the Books." In *Windows and Words*. Ed. Hudson and Cooper 161–65.

Carter, Alice. *The Red Rose Girls: An Uncommon Story of Art and Love*. New York: Harry N. Abrams, Inc., 2000.

Cawelti, John G. *Adventure, Mystery, and Romance: Formula Stories as Art and Popular Culture*. Chicago: University of Chicago Press, 1976.

Cavert, Mary Beth. "Anne of Green Gables—1908. To the Memory of My Father and Mother. Part 1: Clara Macneill." *Kindred Spirits* (Winter 1998–1999): 8–10.

———. "Part 2: Hugh John Montgomery." *Kindred Spirits* (Spring 1999): 8–10; and (Summer 1999): 10–13.

———. "Back to School: Lucy Maud Montgomery's Dedicated Teacher." *Kindred Spirits* (Fall 1994): 13–15.

———. "Whatever Happened to Nate Lockhart." *Kindred Spirits* (Dec. 2005): 12–13.

Crocket, Beverly. "Outlaws, Outcasts, and Orphans: The Historical Imagination and *Anne of Green Gables*." In *Imagining Adoption: Essays on Literature and Culture*. Ed. Marianne Novy. Ann Arbor: The University of Michigan Press, 2001. 57–81.

Currie, Dawn H. *Girl Talk: Adolescent Magazines and Their Readers*. Toronto: University of Toronto Press, 1999.

Davey, Frank. "The Hard-Won Power of Canadian Womanhood: Reading Anne of Green Gables Today." In *L. M. Montgomery and Canadian Culture*. Ed. Gammel and Epperly 163–82.

———. *Reading "Kim" Right*. Vancouver: Talonbooks, 1993.

Dawson, Janis. "Literary Relations: Anne Shirley and her American Cousins." *Children's Literature in Education* 33.1 (Mar. 2002): 29–51.

DeJean, Joan. "Portrait of the Artist as Sappho." *Germaine de Staël: Crossing the Borders.* Ed. Madelyn Gutwirth. New Brunswick: Rutgers University Press, 1991. 122–37.

De Jonge, James. "Through the Eyes of Memory: L.M. Montgomery's Cavendish." In *Making Avonlea.* Ed. Gammel 252–67.

Devereux, Cecily. "Anatomy of a 'National Icon': *Anne of Green Gables* and the 'Bosom Friends' Affair." In *Making Avonlea.* Ed. Gammel 32–42.

———. "A Note on Montgomery's Literary Allusions." In Montgomery. *Anne of Green Gables.* Ed. Devereux 33–38.

———. "'See my Journal for the full story': Fictions of Truth in *Anne of Green Gables* and L.M. Montgomery's Journals." In *The Intimate Life of L.M. Montgomery.* Ed. Gammel 241–27.

———. "'Canadian Classic' and 'Commodity Export': The Nationalism of 'Our' *Anne of Green Gables.*" *Journal of Canadian Studies* 36.1 (Spring 2001): 11–28.

Doody, Margaret Anne. "Gardens and Plants." In Montgomery. *The Annotated Anne of Green Gables.* Ed. Barry, Doody, and Doody Jones 434–38.

Doody, Margaret Anne and Wendy E. Barry. "Literary Allusion and Quotation in *Anne of Green Gables.*" In Montgomery. *The Annotated Anne of Green Gables.* Ed. Barry, Doody, and Doody Jones 457–62.

Doody Jones, Mary E. "The Exceptional Orphan Anne: Child Care, Orphan Asylums, Farming Out, Indenturing, and Adoption." In Montgomery. *The Annotated Anne of Green Gables.* Ed. Barry, Doody, and Doody Jones 422–29.

DuVernet, Sylvia. *Minding the Spirit: Theosophic Thoughts Concerning L.M. Montgomery.* Toronto: n.p., 1993.

Edwards, Owen Dudley and Jennifer H. Litster. "The End of Canadian Innocence: L.M. Montgomery and the First World War." In *L.M. Montgomery and Canadian Culture.* Ed. Gammel and Epperly 31–48.

Epperly, Elizabeth Rollins. "Approaching the Montgomery Manuscripts." In *Harvesting Thistles.* Ed. Rubio 74–83.

———. *The Fragrance of Sweet-Grass: L.M. Montgomery's Heroines and the Pursuit of Romance.* Toronto: University of Toronto Press, 1992.

———. *Through Lover's Lane: L.M. Montgomery's Photography and Visual Imagination.* Toronto: University of Toronto Press, 2007.

Faderman, Lillian. *Surpassing the Love of Men: Romantic Friendship and Love between Women from the Renaissance to the Present.* New York: Perennial, 2001.

Fenwick, Julie. "The Silence of the Mermaid: *Lady Oracle* and *Anne of Green Gables.*" *Essays on Canadian Writing* 47 (1992): 51–64.

Fiamengo, Janice. "Towards a Theory of the Popular Landscape in *Anne of Green Gables.*" In *Making Avonlea.* Ed. Gammel 225–37.

Frever, Trinna. "Vaguely Familiar: Cinematic Intertextuality in Kevin Sullivan's *Anne of Avonlea.*" *Canadian Children's Literature / Littérature canadienne pour la jeunesse* 91–92 (1998): 36–52.

Fuss, Diana. *The Sense of an Interior: Four Writers and the Rooms that Shaped Them.* New York: Routledge, 2004.

Gammel, Irene. *Baroness Elsa: Gender, Dada, and Everyday Modernity—A Cultural Biography.* Cambridge, MA: The MIT Press, 2002. German translation, Berlin: Ebersbach Verlag, 2003.

———, ed. *The Intimate Life of L.M. Montgomery.* Toronto: University of Toronto Press, 2005.

————, ed. *Making Avonlea: L. M. Montgomery and Popular Culture*. Toronto: University of Toronto Press, 2002.

————. "Mirror Looks: The Visual and Performative Diaries of L. M. Montgomery, Baroness Elsa von Freytag-Loringhoven, and Elvira Bach." *Interfaces: Women, Autobiography, Image, Performance*. Ed. Sidonie Smith and Julia Watson. Ann Arbor: The University of Michigan Press. 2003. 289–313.

————. "Safe Pleasures for Girls: L. M. Montgomery's Erotic Landscapes." In *Making Avonlea*. Ed. Gammel 114–27.

Gammel, Irene and Ann Dutton. "Disciplining Development: L. M. Montgomery and Early Schooling." In *L. M. Montgomery and Canadian Culture*. Ed. Gammel and Epperly 106–19.

Gammel, Irene and Elizabeth Epperly, ed. *L. M. Montgomery and Canadian Culture*. Toronto: University of Toronto Press, 1999.

Gay, Carol. "'Kindred Spirits' All: Green Gables Revisited." *Children's Literature Association Quarterly* 11 (1986): 9–12.

Gerson, Carole. "'Dragged at Anne's Chariot Wheels': The Triangle of Author, Publisher, and Fictional Character." In *L. M. Montgomery and Canadian Culture*. Ed. Gammel and Epperly 49–63.

————. "'Fitted to Earn Her Own Living': Figures of the New Woman in the Writing of L. M. Montgomery." *Children's Voices in Atlantic Literature and Culture*. Guelph, ON: Canadian Children's Press, 1995. 24–34.

Gillen, Mollie. *The Wheel of Things: A Biography of L. M. Montgomery, Author of Anne of Green Gables*. Toronto: Fitzhenry and Whiteside, 1975.

Glickman, Susan. *The Picturesque and the Sublime: A Poetics of Canadian Landscape*. Montreal and Kingston: McGill-Queen's University Press, 1998.

Griswold, Jerry. *The Classic American Children's Story: Novels of the Golden Age*. New York: Penguin, 1996.

Gubar, Marah. "'Where is the Boy?': The Pleasures of Postponement in the *Anne of Green Gables* Series." *The Lion and the Unicorn* 25.1 (2001): 47–69.

Hammill, Faye. "'A new and exceedingly brilliant star': L.M. Montgomery, *Anne of Green Gables*, and Mary Miles Minter." *Modern Language Review* 101.3 (2006): 652–70.

Hartman, Sadakichi. "The Work of Rudolf Eickemeyer, Jr." *The Photo-American* (July 1904): 195–99.

Heilbron, Alexandra. *Remembering Lucy Maud Montgomery*. Toronto: The Dundurn Group, 2001.

Hilder, Monika B. "'That Unholy Tendency to Laughter': L. M. Montgomery's Iconoclastic Affirmation of Faith in *Anne of Green Gables*." *Canadian Children's Literature / Littérature canadienne pour la jeunesse* 113–114 (2004): 34–55.

Hoff, Eva. "A Friend Living Inside Me—The Forms and Functions of Imaginary Companions." *Imagination, Cognition and Personality* 24.2 (2004–2005): 151–89.

Horowitz, Milton M. "Adolescent Daydreams and Creative Impulse." *Adolescent Psychiatry: Development and Clinical Studies*. Hillsdale, NJ: The Analytic Press, 1998. 3–23.

Howey, Ann F. "'She look'd down to Camelot': Anne Shirley, Sullivan, and the Lady of Shalott." In *Making Avonlea*. Ed. Gammel 160–73.

Hudson, Aïda and Susan-Ann Cooper. *Windows and Words: A Look at Canadian Children's Literature in English*. Ottawa: University of Ottawa Press, 2003.

Inness, Sherrie A., ed. *Nancy Drew and Company: Culture, Gender, and Girls' Series*, ed. Bowling Green, OH: Bowling Green State University Popular Press, 1997.

Jamison, Kay Redfield. *Exuberance: The Passion for Life*. New York: Alfred A. Knopf, 2006.

Johnston, Rosemary Ross. "'Reaching beyond the Word': Religious Themes as 'Deep Structure' in the 'Anne' Books of L. M. Montgomery." *Canadian Children's Literature / Littérature canadienne pour la jeunesse* 88 (1997): 7–18.

Katsura, Yuko. "Red-Haired Anne in Japan." *Canadian Children's Literature / Littérature canadienne pour la jeunesse* 34 (1984): 57–70.

Kornfeld, Eve and Susan Jackson. "The Female Bildungsroman in Nineteenth-Century America: Parameters of a Vision." *Journal of American Culture* 10.4 (1987): 69–75.

Kotsopoulos, Aspasia. "Our Avonlea: Imagining Community in an Imaginary Past." In *Pop Can: Popular Culture in Canada*. Ed. Lynne Van Luven and Priscilla Walton. Scarborough, ON: Prentice Hall Allyn and Bacon Canada, 1999. 98–105.

Lefebvre, Benjamin. "Pigsties and Sunsets: L. M. Montgomery, *A Tangled Web*, and a Modernism of Her Own." *English Studies in Canada* 31.4 (Dec. 2005): 123–46.

———. "Stand by Your Man: Adapting L.M. Montgomery's *Anne of Green Gables*." *Essays on Canadian Writing* 76 (Spring 2002): 149–69.

Lessard, Suzannah. *The Architect of Desire: Beauty and Danger in the Stanford White Family*. London: Phoenix, 1997.

Lunn, Janet. *Maud's House of Dreams: The Life of Lucy Maud Montgomery*. Toronto: Doubleday, 2002.

Lynes, Jeanette. "Consumable Avonlea: The Commodification of the Green Gables Mythology." In *Making Avonlea*. Ed. Gammel 268–279.

McCabe, Kevin, comp., and Alexandra Heilbron, ed. *The Lucy Maud Montgomery Album*. Toronto: Fitzhenry and Whiteside, 1999.

McCabe, Shauna. "Representing Islandness: Myth, Memory, and Modernisation in Prince Edward Island." Dissertation. University of British Columbia, 2001.

MacDonald Mooney, Michael. *Evelyn Nesbit and Stanford White: Love and Death in the Gilded Age*. New York: William Morrow and Company, 1976.

MacKay, Dorothy. "Two Old Houses: A Comparative Study of L. M. Montgomery's *Anne of Green Gables* and Nathaniel Hawthorne's *The House of Seven Gables*." *Abegweit Review* 7.1 (1992): 33–37.

MacLeod, Elizabeth. *Lucy Maud Montgomery: A Writer's Life*. Toronto: Kids Can Press, 2001.

MacLulich, T. D. "L.M. Montgomery and the Literary Heroine: Jo, Rebecca, Anne and Emily." *Canadian Children's Literature / Littérature canadienne pour la jeunesse* 37 (1985): 5–17.

Mills, Claudia. "Children in Search of a Family: Orphan Novels Through the Century." *Children's Literature in Education* 18.4 (1987): 227–39.

Moore, Lisa. "'Something More Tender Still than Friendship': Romantic Friendship in Early-Nineteenth-Century England." *Feminist Studies* 18.3 (1992): 499–520.

Mount, Nick. *When Canadian Literature Moved to New York*. Toronto: University of Toronto Press, 2005.

Munro, Alice. "Afterword." Montgomery. *Emily of New Moon*. Toronto: McClelland and Stewart, 1989. 357–61.

Murray, Robert. "Prince Edward Island." *The Easternmost Ridge of the Continent*. Ed. George Munro Grant. Chicago: Alexander Belford & Co., 1899. 127–40.

Nell, Victor. *Lost in a Book: The Psychology of Reading for Pleasure*. New Haven and

London: Yale University Press, 1988.

Nelson, Claudia. *Little Strangers: Portrayals of Adoption and Foster Care in America, 1850–1929*. Bloomington: Indiana University Press, 2003.

Nesbit, Evelyn. *The Story of My Life*. London: John Long, 1914. NYPL Performance Library.

———. *Prodigal Days: The Untold Story of Evelyn Nesbit*. New York: Julian Messner, Inc., 1934. Reprinted by Deborah Dorian Paul, 2004.

———. *Souvenir Album of Evelyn Nesbit Thaw*. New York: Lipshitz Press, n.d. TRL.

Nodelman, Perry. "Progressive Utopia: Or, How to Grow Up Without Growing Up." In *Such a Simple Little Tale*. Ed. Reimer 29–38.

Nolan, Jason, Jeff Lawrence, and Yuka Kajihara. "Montgomery's Island in the Net: Metaphor and Community on the Kindred Spirits E-mail List." *Canadian Children's Literature / Littérature canadienne pour la jeunesse* 91–92 (1998): 64–77.

Panzer, Mary. *In My Studio: Rudolf Eickemeyer, Jr. and the Art of the Camera 1885–1930*. Yonkers, NY: The Hudson River Museum, 1986.

Patterson, Martha H. *Beyond the Gibson Girl: Reimagining the American New Woman, 1895–1915*. Urbana and Chicago: University of Illinois Press, 2005.

Petitt Hill, Maude. "The Best Known Woman in Prince Edward Island. Part II: L.M. Montgomery, Author of Anne of Green Gables." *The Chatelaine* (May 1928); Part II: "L.M. Montgomery, After Her First Success." *The Chatelaine* (June 1928). Reprinted in Alexandra Heilbron. *Remembering Lucy Maud Montgomery*. Toronto: Dundurn Press, 2001. 210–30.

Pike, Holly. "Mass Marketing, Popular Culture, and the Canadian Celebrity Author." In *Making Avonlea*. Ed. Gammel 238–51.

Poe, K. L. "The Whole of the Moon: L.M Montgomery's *Anne of Green Gables* Series." In *Nancy Drew and Company*. Ed. Inness 15–35.

Quaile, Deborah. *L.M. Montgomery: The Norval Years, 1926–1935*. n.p.: Wordbird Press, 2006.

Radway, Janice A. *Reading the Romance: Women, Patriarchy, and Popular Literature*. Chapel Hill: University of North Carolina Press, 1984.

Ramsdell, Kristin. *Romance Fiction: A Guide to the Genre*. Englewood, CO: Libraries Unlimited, Inc., 1999.

Reimer, Mavis, ed. *Such a Simple Little Tale: Critical Responses to L.M. Montgomery's Anne of Green Gables*. Metuchen, NJ: The Children's Literature Association and The Scarecrow Press, 1992.

Robinson, Laura M. "Bosom Friends: Lesbian Desire in L.M. Montgomery's Anne Books." *Canadian Literature* 180 (Spring 2004): 12–28.

———. "'Pruned down and branched out': Embracing Contradiction in *Anne of Green Gables*." In *Children's Voices in Atlantic Literature and Culture: Essays on Childhood*. Ed. Hilary Thompson. Guelph, ON: Canadian Children's Press, 1995. 35–43.

Rothwell. Erika. "Knitting Up the World: L.M. Montgomery and Maternal Feminism." *L.M. Montgomery and Canadian Culture*. Ed. Gammel and Epperly 133–44.

Rubio, Jennie. "'Strewn with Dead Bodies': Women and Gossip in *Anne of Ingleside*." In *Harvesting Thistles*. Ed. Rubio 167–77.

Rubio, Mary Henley. "*Anne of Green Gables:* The Architect of Adolescence." In *Such a Simple Little Tale*. Ed. Reimer 65–82.

———. "'A Dusting Off': An Anecdotal Account of Editing the L.M. Montgomery Journals." *Working in Women's Archives: Researching Women's Private Literature and*

Archival Documents. Ed. Helen M. Buss and Marlene Kadar. Waterloo, ON: Wilfrid Laurier University Press, 2001. 51–78.

———, ed. *Harvesting Thistles: The Textual Garden of L. M. Montgomery, Essays on her Novels and Journals*. Guelph, ON: Canadian Children's Press, 1994.

———. "Subverting the Trite: L. M. Montgomery's 'Room of Her Own.'." *Canadian Children's Literature / Littérature canadienne pour la jeunesse* 65 (1992): 6–39.

Rubio, Mary and Elizabeth Waterston, *Writing a Life: L. M. Montgomery*. Toronto: ECW Press, 1995.

Russell, Ruth Weber, D. W. Russell, and Rea Wilmshurst, *Lucy Maud Montgomery: A Preliminary Bibliography*. Waterloo, ON: University of Waterloo Library, 1986.

Santelmann, Patricia Kelly. "Written as Women Write: *Anne of Green Gables* within the Female Literary Tradition." In *Harvesting Thistles*. Ed. Rubio 64–73.

Sheckels, Theodore F., Jr. "Anne in Hollywood: The Americanization of a Canadian Icon." *L. M. Montgomery and Canadian Culture*. Ed. Gammel and Epperly 183–91.

———. "In Search of Structures for the Stories of Girls and Women: L. M. Montgomery's Life-Long Struggle." *American Review of Canadian Studies* 23.4 (1993): 523–38.

Shields, Carol. "Loving Lucy." *The Globe and Mail* (Oct. 3, 1998): D18.

Smith-Rosenberg, Carroll. "The Female World of Love and Ritual: Relations between Women in Nineteenth Century America." *Signs: Journal of Women in Culture and Society* 1.1 (1975): 1–29.

Sorfleet, John R., ed. *L. M. Montgomery: An Assessment*. Guelph, ON: Canadian Children's Press, 1976.

Spears, Tom. "'Outrageously Sexual' Anne Was a Lesbian, Scholar Insists." *Ottawa Citizen* (May 25, 2000): A3.

Squire, Shelagh J. "Literary Tourism and Sustainable Tourism: Promoting 'Anne of Green Gables' in Prince Edward Island." *Journal of Sustainable Tourism* 4.3 (1996): 119–34.

Steffler, Margaret. "The Canadian Romantic Child: Travelling in the Border Country, Exploring the 'Edge.'" *Canadian Children's Literature / Littérature canadienne pour la jeunesse* 89 (1998): 5–17.

Stoffman, Judy. "Anne in Japanese Popular Culture." *Canadian Children's Literature / Littérature canadienne pour la jeuncsse* 91–92 (1998): 53–63.

Thaw, Harry K. *The Traitor*. Philadelphia: Dorrance and Company, 1925.

Thomas, Clara. "Anne Shirley's American Cousin: *The Girl of the Limberlost*." In *Harvesting Thistles*. Ed. Rubio 58–63.

Van der Klei, Alice. "Avonlea in Cyberspace, Or an Invitation to a Hyperreal Tea Party." In *Making Avonlea*. Ed. Gammel 310–16.

Waterston, Elizabeth. *Kindling Spirit: Lucy Maud Montgomery's 'Anne of Green Gables.'* Toronto: ECW Press, 1993.

———. "Orphans, Twins, and L. M. Montgomery." In *Family Fictions in Canadian Literature*. Ed. Peter Hinchcliffe. Waterloo, ON: University of Waterloo Press, 1987. 68–76.

Wiggins, Genevieve. *L. M. Montgomery*. New York: Twayne Publishers, 1992.

Willoughby, John H. *Ellen*. Charlottetown, PE: n. p., 1995.

Wilmshurst, Rea. "L. M. Montgomery's Short Stories: A Preliminary Bibliography." *Canadian Children's Literature / Littérature canadienne pour la jeunesse* 29 (1983): 25–34.

————. "L.M. Montgomery's Use of Quotations and Allusions in the 'Anne' Books."
   Canadian Children's Literature / Littérature canadienne pour la jeunesse 56 (1989): 15–45.
Wood, Kate. "In the News: *Anne of Green Gables* and PEI's Turn-of-the-Century Press."
   Canadian Children's Literature / Littérature canadienne pour la jeunesse 99 (2000): 23–42.
York, Lorraine. "'I Knew I Would 'Arrive' Some Day': L.M. Montgomery and the
   Strategies of Literary Celebrity." *Canadian Children's Literature / Littérature canadienne
   pour la jeunesse* 113–114 (2004): 98–116.
————. *Literary Celebrity in Canada*. Toronto: University of Toronto Press, 2007.

Acknowledgments

L
ooking for Anne has taken me on many surprising roads—to Manhattan, Yonkers, Washington D. C., Ottawa, Toronto, Guelph, Charlottetown, Hunter River, Prince Edward Island's North Shore Road, Cavendish, New London, and Park Corner. Funding for the archival research has been provided by the Social Sciences and Humanities Research Council of Canada and the Canada Research Chairs program.

As there are legions of fans and readers who have helped make Anne the international icon she is, so it was legions of collectors, archivists, researchers and assistants who helped me tell the story. I would like to thank the Heirs of L. M. Montgomery, in particular Kate Macdonald Butler and literary consultant Sally Cohen who first met with me and were as enthusiastic about my discoveries as I was. I want to thank the many incredibly generous scholars who have answered questions that found their way into the book: Ruth Allan, Wendy E. Barry, Francis W. P. Bolger, Donna J. Campbell, Ronald I. Cohen, Mary Beth Cavert, Cecily Devereux, Elizabeth R. Epperly, Maria Gurevich, Jennifer H. Litster, Simon Lloyd, Shauna McCabe, Ed MacDonald, Alison Matthews David, Elizabeth MacLeod, Eri Muraoka, Mary H. Rubio, René Steinke, Don Snyder, David Slater, and Elizabeth Waterston. Each authoritative study also relies on what has preceded it and this debt is acknowledged in the references.

Many archivists have gone out of their way to help excavate the story of Anne: Linda Amichand and Lorne Bruce at the University of Guelph Archives; Kevin Rice at the Confederation Center Art Gallery; Michelle Anne Delaney at the Smithsonian; Laura L. Vookles at the Hudson River Museum; as well as the staff at the New York Public Library, the Toronto Reference Library, the PEI Public Archives and Records Office, and the

Library and Archives of Canada. I am grateful to Martin Tétreault at the Library and Archives of Canada for boldly taking on Anne in a national exhibition; and to Sharon Larter and James De Jonge of Parks Canada. Thanks, also, to those who preserve the memory of L. M. Montgomery—in particular John and Jennie Macneill at the Site of Lucy Maud Montgomery's Cavendish Home, the L. M. Montgomery Institute at the University of Prince Edward Island, and the L. M. Montgomery Society of Ontario.

For careful readings and insights into the various incarnations of this book, I wish to thank Holly Blackford, Carole Gerson, Benjamin Lefebvre, and Patricia Srebrnik. I am extremely grateful to an energetic team of research assistants, in particular Alla Gadassik, Beth Knazook, Tsukasa Nishibori, Cheryl Ramage, Maria O'Brien, Nicola Spunt, and Kate Zieman, who provided assistance with research, copyright, image cataloguing, as well as feedback on different stages of the text. Ryerson Press was the first Canadian publisher of *Anne of Green Gables* in 1942, and Ryerson University, the English Department, and Arts Faculty, in particular Dr. Carla Cassidy, have provided a fertile ground for researching this Canadian national icon in the Modern Literature and Culture Research Center.

I am grateful to Jordan Fenn for acquiring this book for Key Porter and to the entire Key Porter team, in particular Marijke Friesen for a wonderful design. My deepest thanks go to Linda Pruessen at Key Porter for being a fantastic editor with the perfect balance of encouragement and critique needed to shape the wealth of ten years of research; to my agent extraordinary Hilary McMahon of Westwood Creative Artists for believing in this project and embracing it so enthusiastically; to Michael Flamini, my editor at St. Martin's Press for enthusiastic support and input; and to Jean-Paul Boudreau who is not exactly an Anne fan, but who went out of his way to help find her anyway.

Index